Catholic Churches of London

Catholic Churches of London

Denis Evinson

Sheffield
Academic Press

Copyright © 1998 Sheffield Academic Press

Published by Sheffield Academic Press Ltd
Mansion House
19 Kingfield Road
Sheffield S11 9AS
England

Printed on acid-free paper in Great Britain
by The Cromwell Press
Trowbridge, Wiltshire

British Library Cataloguing in Publication Data

A catalogue record for this book is available
from the British Library

ISBN 1-85075-819-0

Contents

Foreword		7
Preface		9
Illustrations		11
Illustrations: Sources and Acknowledgments		17
Abbreviations		19
Introduction		21
I	City of London	29
II	City of Westminster	32
III	Camden	67
IV	Greenwich	92
V	Hackney	109
VI	Hammersmith and Fulham	119
VII	Islington	132
VIII	Kensington and Chelsea	147
IX	Lambeth	170
X	Lewisham	187
XI	Southwark	198
XII	Tower Hamlets	221
XIII	Wandsworth	243
Glossary		261
Select Bibliography		264
Index of Persons		265
Index of Churches by Borough		275
Index of Churches by Name		278

Foreword

DENIS Evinson's latest book, *Catholic Churches of London*, is the product of painstaking research, lovingly undertaken and expertly written.

Moving through the inner London boroughs of the Greater London Council, we are given a comprehensive guide to each Catholic church. The historical foundation of the mission or parish; the succeeding buildings that accommodated the growing Catholic population; the architects and the many other influences on those historic buildings, as well as the current churches that now serve established communities: each receives comprehensive coverage.

Not only are we given architectural descriptions of these buildings, but also fascinating insights into their decoration, their furnishings and the artefacts that adorn them. In some cases there is an evaluation of the reordering that has taken place as a consequence of the liturgical decrees of the Second Vatican Council.

Here, at last, is a comprehensive study of the Catholic churches of London and the influences that caused them to be established. *Catholic Churches of London* is already a standard work of reference in chronicling the development of the Catholic Church in London since the early part of the nineteenth century. In congratulating and thanking Dr Evinson on this masterly work, I have no doubt that it will find a place in the library of every parish, school and college. It is part of our history.

Monsignor George Stack
Administrator of Westminster Cathedral

Preface

IN recent years the Liturgy Commission of the Bishops' Conference of England and Wales initiated a series of reports on the fabric and contents of diocesan churches. The author's contributions on London churches have now been expanded to form this book.

It has seemed advisable to limit the area treated here to the Cities of London and Westminster, plus the surrounding boroughs that once comprised the London County Council. Even so, this area contains 140 Catholic churches open to the public, many of them distinguished historically and architecturally. I have noted every church within the above confines, but have excluded private chapels and cemetery chapels.

The entries treat the foundation of each mission, the acquisition of the land, the role of the clergy and of lay patrons, building history, architectural character and permanent furnishings. The sources of information follow each entry. A general introduction places architecture and furnishings within their historical perspective.

I am grateful to all those who have assisted in any way, especially those numerous parish priests who have answered my questions, corrected my errors and volunteered additional information. Particularly helpful also were the archivists of the Westminster and Southwark dioceses, of the English Province SJ, of St Dominic's Priory and of the Redemptorist church at Clapham.

In addition I am grateful to the following for specific information: Mr Myles Dove, Mr C.P. Fanning, Mr P. Howell, Miss J.O. Maynard, Mr L.P. Seglias, and the late Professor Stephen Welsh. The drawings made by William Wardell for his London churches constitute the most outstanding new material used here. I am happy to acknowledge the approval of the Mitchell Library, State Library of New South Wales, for their publication. I am indebted also to the Librarians and their staffs for their assistance at the following institutions:

> Allen Hall (Westminster Diocesan Seminary)
> Birkbeck College
> The British Library
> The Catholic Central Library
> Fulham Library
> Hammersmith Library
> Royal Institute of British Architects
> University of London Library

To all of these I am indeed grateful.

The book is as free from errors as all

interested parties could make it, but for any errors that remain I must undertake sole responsibility.

Would readers kindly note that all the churches in the gazeteer are described as having the sanctuary to the east, whether they are correctly oriented or not.

Denis Evinson
Feast of St Benedict 1997

Illustrations

I
The City of London

1	Moorfields, St Mary	29
2	Moorfields, St Mary, plan	30
3	Moorfields, St Mary, the church of 1820	31

II
The City of Westminster

1	Westminster Cathedral, exterior	33
2	Westminster Cathedral, Bentley's final plan	34
3	Westminster Cathedral, the sanctuary	37
4	Westminster Cathedral, the nave	40
5	Farm Street, The Immaculate Conception, 1844	42
6	Farm Street, The Immaculate Conception, 1844	43
7	French Church, Notre Dame de France	46
8	Maiden Lane, Corpus Christi	49
9	Marylebone, Our Lady of the Rosary	51
10	Ogle Street, St Charles Borromeo	53
11	Pimlico, Holy Apostles	55
12	St John's Wood, Our Lady, the original plan	57
13	St John's Wood, Our Lady	57
14	Soho Square, St Patrick, plan	59
15	Soho Square, St Patrick, St John Bosco by Anton Dapre	60
16	Spanish Place, St James, plan	62
17	Spanish Place, St James, St Joseph's altar	63
18	Warwick Street, Our Lady of the Assumption, Lady altar	65
19	Warwick Street, Our Lady of the Assumption, plan	66

III
Camden

1	Camden Town, Our Lady of Hal	67
2	Copenhagen Street, The Blessed Sacrament	68
3	Ely Place, St Etheldreda, the upper church	69
4	Hampstead, St Mary	72
5	Haverstock Hill, St Dominic, west elevation	73
6	Italian Church, St Peter	78
7	Kentish Town, Our Lady Help of Christians	81
8	Kilburn, Sacred Heart of Jesus	82
9	Kilburn West, Immaculate Heart of Mary	84
10	Laxton Place, St Anne, west elevation	85
11	Lincoln's Inn Fields, Ss Anselm and Cecilia	86
12	Lincoln's Inn Fields, Ss Anselm and Cecilia	88
13	Somers Town, St Aloysius	89
14	Swiss Cottage, St Thomas More	91

IV
Greenwich

1	Abbey Wood, St Benet	92
2	Abbey Wood, St David	93
3	Blackheath Village, Our Lady Help of Christians	94
4	Charlton, Our Lady of Grace	96
5	Eltham, Christ Church	97
6	Greenwich, Our Lady, Wardell's elevation	99
7	Greenwich, Our Lady, Wardell's plan	100
8	Greenwich, St Joseph	101
9	Kidbrooke, St John Fisher	103
10	Plumstead, St Patrick, Church of 1893	104
11	Plumstead Common, Holy Cross	105
12	Woolwich 1, St Peter	107
13	Woolwich 2, St Catherine Laboure	108

V
Hackney

1	Clapton, St Scholastica	109
2	Hackney, St John the Baptist, 1848	111
3	Hackney, St John the Baptist, 1956	112
4	Homerton, Immaculate Heart of Mary and St Dominic	114
5	Hoxton, St Monica	115
6	Kingsland, Our Lady and St Joseph	116
7	Stoke Newington, Our Lady of Good Counsel	118

VI
Hammersmith and Fulham

1	Brook Green, Holy Trinity, Wardell's tower design	119
2	Brook Green, Holy Trinity, Wardell's plan	120
3	Brook Green, Holy Trinity, Wardell's interior design	121
4	Fulham, St Thomas	122
5	Fulham, St Thomas	123
6	Hammersmith, St Augustine	124
7	Parsons Green, Holy Cross	126
8	Shepherds Bush, Holy Ghost and St Stephen	128
9	Stephendale Road, Our Lady	129
10	White City, Our Lady of Fatima	130

VII
Islington

1	Clerkenwell, Ss Peter and Paul	133
2	Highbury, St Joan of Arc	135
3	Highgate, St Joseph	133
4	Highgate, St Joseph, plan	137
5	Highgate, St Joseph, section	138
6	Holloway, Sacred Heart	139
7	Islington, St John the Evangelist	140
8	Islington, St John the Evangelist, plan	141
9	Tollington Park, St Mellitus	144

VIII
Kensington and Chelsea

1	Bayswater, St Mary of the Angels	147
2	Chelsea 1, St Mary, plan	149
3	Chelsea 1, St Mary, exterior	150
4	Chelsea 1, St Mary, Pulpit	151
5	Chelsea 2, Holy Redeemer, plan	152
6	Chelsea 2, Holy Redeemer, interior	153
7	Fulham Road, Our Lady of Dolours	154
8	Kensal New Town, Our Lady of the Holy Souls, plan	156
9	Kensal New Town, Our Lady of the Holy Souls, exterior	157
10	Kensington 1, Our Lady of Victories	158
11	Kensington 2, Our Lady of Mount Carmel	160
12	Notting Hill, St Francis of Assisi, Baptistery	161
13	Oratory, Immaculate Heart of Mary, Selected Design	164
14	Oratory, Immaculate Heart of Mary, exterior design	165
15	Oratory, Immaculate Heart of Mary, interior	167

IX
Lambeth

1	Brixton Hill, Corpus Christi	171
2	Brixton Hill, Corpus Christi, plan	172
3	Clapham, Our Lady of Victories	173
4	Clapham, Our Lady of Victories, Wardell's plan	174
5	Clapham, Our Lady of Victories, section by Wardell	175
6	Clapham Park, St Bede	176
7	Norbury, St Bartholomew	177
8	Norwood West, St Matthew	178
9	Stockwell, St Francis of Sales and St Gertrude	179
10	Streatham, English Martyrs	180
11	Streatham Hill, Ss Simon and Jude	183
12	Vauxhall, St Anne	184

X
Lewisham

1	Brockley, St Mary Magdalen	188
2	Catford, Holy Cross	189
3	Deptford, The Assumption, detail of sculpture	191
4	Forest Hill, St William of York	192
5	Lee, Our Lady of Lourdes	193
6	Lewisham, St Saviour	194
7	Sydenham, Our Lady and St Philip Neri	196

XI
Southwark

1	Southwark Cathedral, Pugin's second design	198
2	Southwark Cathedral, interior	200
3	Bermondsey, Holy Trinity, 11th Station by A.C. Brown	202
4	Borough, Precious Blood	205
5	Camberwell, Sacred Heart	207
6	Dulwich East, St Thomas More	208
7	Dulwich Wood Park, St Margaret Clitherow	210
8	Herne Hill, Ss Philip and James	211
9	Kennington Park, St Wilfred, detail of sculpture	212
10	Peckham, Our Lady of Sorrows	214
11	Peckham Rye, St James	216
12	Rotherhithe, St Peter and the Guardian Angels	217
13	Surrey Docks, Our Lady of the Immaculate Conception	218
14	Walworth, English Martyrs	220

XII Tower Hamlets

1	Bethnal Green, Our Lady of the Assumption	221
2	Bethnal Green, Our Lady of the Assumption, plan	222
3	Bethnal Green, Our Lady of the Assumption	222
4	Bow, Our Lady and St Catherine	223
5	Commercial Road, Ss Mary and Michael, Wardell's design	227
6	Commercial Road, Ss Mary and Michael, Wardell's plan	228
7	German Church, St Boniface	229
8	Limehouse, Our Lady Immaculate	231
9	Lithuanian Church, St Casimir	232
10	Mile End, Guardian Angels	233
11	Millwall, St Edmund, 1877	234
12	Poplar, Ss Mary and Joseph	236
13	Tower Hill, English Martyrs	237
14	Underwood Road, St Anne	239
15	Wapping, St Patrick	241

XIII Wandsworth

1	Balham, Holy Ghost	243
2	Battersea (West), Sacred Heart	245
3	Battersea Park, Our Lady of Mount Carmel and St Joseph	246
4	Clapham Common, St Vincent de Paul	247
5	Earlsfield, St Gregory	249
6	Putney, Our Lady of Pity and St Simon Stock	250
7	Putney, Polish Church	251
8	Roehampton, St Joseph	252
9	Roehampton, St Joseph, interior	252
10	Tooting, St Boniface	253
11	Tooting Bec, St Anselm	256
12	Wandsworth, St Thomas a Becket	257
13	Wimbledon Common, Our Lady and St Peter	260

Illustrations: Sources and Acknowledgments

Academy Architecture
VIII 6; X 6; XIII 12; XIII 12

The Architect
III 8; XII 11; XII 15; XIII 8; XIII 9

The Architectural Review
VI 4

Archives of the Archbishop of Westminster
II 1, II 3, II 4

British Architect
XI 4

John Britton, *Illustrations, II*
I 3

The Builder
I 1, I 2; II 6, II 16; III 6; VII 7, VII 8; VIII 5, VIII 7; XII 2

Builder's Journal
II 2

Building News
II 8, III 2, III 5; VII 3, VII 4, VII 5, VII 6; VIII 13, VIII 14, VIII 15; IX 1; XII 13

Catholic Building Review
III 10, III 13, IV 5; V 6; VII 2; XI 2

Civil Engineer and Architects' Journal
VIII 1

W. de l'Hopital
VIII 2, VIII 8, IX 2

J. Arthur Dixon
VI 6

C. Eastlake
VIII 12

Farm Street Archives
II 5, II 6

Marylebone Public Library
II 12

Bruno Medici
II 10

Mitchell Library, Sydney, NSW
IV 6, IV 7; VI 1, VI 2, VI 3; IX 4, IX 5; XII 5, XII 6

R. Murphy
VIII 11

M. O'Brien
V 7

W.J. Pinks, *The History of Clerkenwell*
VII 2

H. Pragnell
X 5

A.W. Pugin, *Present State*
XI 1

F. Rabson
VI 5

RCHME © Crown Copyright
II 14, II 19; IX 12

The Tablet
V 2

Abbreviations

AAS	Archives of the Archbishop of Southwark
AAW	Archives of the Archbishop of Westminster
Anson	P.F. Anson, *Fashions in Church Furnishings* (London: Studio Vista, 1965)
AR	*Architectural Review*
BN	*Building News*
Baker	L.A.J. Baker, *Churches in the Hundred of Blackheath* (Greenwich: Greenwich and Lewisham Antiquarion Society, 1961)
Bogan	B. Bogan, *The Great Link* (London: Burns and Oates, 1958)
Br	*The Builder*
CAR	*Catholic Annual Register*
CB	*Church Building*
CBR.N	*Catholic Building Review* (Northern)
CBR.S	*Catholic Building Review* (Southern)
CD	*Catholic Directory of England and Wales*
Colvin	H.M. Colvin, *Biographical Dictionary of British Architects* (London: John Murray, 2nd edn, 1978)
CRS	*Catholic Record Society publications*, 1904–
de l'Hopital	W. de l'Hopital, *Westminster Cathedral and its Architect* (2 vols.; London: Hutchinson, 1919)
Eastlake	C. Eastlake, *A History of the Gothic Revival* (London: Longmans/Green, 1872)
Evinson	D. Evinson, *Pope's Corner* (Hammersmith: Fulham and Hammersmith Historical Society, 1980)
Gillow	J. Gillow, *Bibliographical Dictionary of the English Catholics* (5 vols.; London: Burns and Oates, 1885–98)
GR	H.S. Goodhart-Rendel, manuscript index of churches, National Monuments Record
Guide	H. Willows (ed.), *A Guide to Worship in Central London* (London: Central YMCA, 1988)
Is. Chapels	Philip Temple, *Islington Chapels* (Savile Row: RCHM, 1992)
Harting	J. Harting, *London Catholic Missions* (London: Sands, 1903)
Kelly	B.W. Kelly, *Historical Notes on English Catholic Missions* (London: Kegan Paul/Trench/Trubner, 1907)
Kirk	F.J. Kirk, *Reminiscences of an Oblate* (London: Burns and Oates, 1905)
Little	B. Little, *Catholic Churches since 1623* (London: Robert Hale, 1966)
Rottmann	A. Rottmann, *London Catholic Churches* (London: Sands, 1926)
SOL	*Survey of London*
Ward	B. Ward, *Catholic London a Century Ago* (London: Catholic Truth Society, 1905)

Introduction

THE first official post-Reformation place of Catholic worship was the Queen's Chapel, begun in 1623 by Inigo Jones. Another for Henrietta Maria, also by Jones, was built in 1635–36 at Somerset House. A new chapel at Whitehall for Mary of Modena was begun in 1685. Its architect was Christopher Wren in his capacity of Surveyor General. Only the first of these royal chapels survives. All three were conceived in Classical terms, firmly rejecting mediaeval Gothic. By means of sumptuous decoration, both Jones and Wren linked exported Italian decoration with the royal chapels of the Stuarts. Apart from these, there was little Catholic work of note in the seventeenth century. George Con, the Papal Agent, set up a chapel in his London house in 1636, and there erected an Altar of Repose whose classical derivation followed Jones's contemporary altars in the royal chapels.

Following the flight of James II, Catholic chapels were chiefly remarkable for their paucity. Prior to 1791 only the illegal domestic chapels of provincial squires, and in London the embassy chapels of foreign powers, were attempted. Most of the embassy chapels were plain rooms containing a minimum of ecclesiastical furnishings. The Sardinian and Portuguese chapels alone had pretensions to artistic merit.

The Portuguese chapel erected in South Street in 1736 was rectangular in plan, with galleries and double rows of windows. It was distinguished by a tribune for the ambassador and a large altar-piece of the Crucifixion. Very similar was the Sardinian chapel in Lincoln's Inn Fields, dating from 1759 and repaired in 1781 after being wrecked in the Gordon Riots. Its Georgian interior consisted of nave and aisles, non-projecting transepts and an apsidal chancel. The altar-piece of the Deposition focussed attention on the sanctuary, which was also distinguished by its Ionic pilasters and the ambassador's tribune. A rail across the nave separated subscribers in the 'enclosure' from the poor further west, while double galleries accommodated numerous patrons of the middle class.

When the Toleration Act of 1791 rendered Catholic chapels no longer unlawful, native English foundations were made (with some assistance from French exiles). As a result, the embassy chapels simply dwindled and disappeared. The

Bavarian, Sardinian and Spanish chapels developed eventually into parish churches, and the remainder (Portuguese, Venetian, Neapolitan, Imperial, French and Florentine) were closed. Meanwhile, Bishop James Talbot anticipated the Toleration Act by rebuilding the chapel in Warwick Street, still happily extant. Opened in 1790, it was under his own control, but nominally under the aegis of the Bavarian envoy.

From 1791 the provision of new chapels was steady but not spectacular. In this decade there appeared Spanish Place, Westminster (Horseferry Road), Greenwich and Southwark chapels, all architect-designed, and Soho Square, an adapted assembly room.

In the first decade of the new century came the German chapel in the City, and St Aloysius at Somers Town. There followed in the next decade chapels at Chelsea, Hammersmith and Hampstead (which still stands). All of the foregoing were of sober Georgian cast, with plain exteriors and crowded interiors, and were chiefly distinguished by their elaborate altar-pieces. Pre-eminent, however, was St Mary Moorfields, opened in 1820, with its facade classically detailed, and sumptuous interior decoration. From this time, London Catholics built public churches rather than private chapels, but the pace remained sluggish for twenty years. Two churches by J.J. Scoles—Holy Trinity at Bermondsey and Our Lady at St John's Wood—meanwhile illustrated the growing popularity of Gothic. The classically trained Scoles then designed St John's Islington in Norman terms to Pugin's horror, but reverted to Gothic with his confident design for Farm Street church of the 1840s. An archaeologically correct approach to the Gothic Revival appeared with Pugin's St Peter at Woolwich, followed by St Thomas at Fulham. His major contribution, St George's Cathedral at Southwark, was gutted in 1941 and modified in its subsequent restoration. Surviving, however, to hint at its original character are the plan, the Blessed Sacrament chapel, the Petre Chantry and the aisle windows.

Pugin's early death in 1852 released forthcoming church work for other hands. Waiting in the wings was his highly competent admirer William Wardell, already experienced with schemes at Hackney, Millwall, Kentish Town and Hampstead. In addition to lesser works at Kingsland, Lincoln's Inn Fields and Palace Street, Wardell produced churches at Clapham Common, Greenwich, Brook Green, Commercial Road and Poplar, in a correct Gothic manner almost indistinguishable from Pugin's own. Wardell's wayward spacing of clerestory windows, however, and his pragmatic approach to planning heralded widespread departures from Pugin's Decorated Gothic ideal.

Meanwhile, those functional compromises known as school chapels were raised at Marylebone by Gilbert Blount and at Bunhill Row by Edmund Kelly. One at Bayswater by Thomas Meyer was quickly superseded by the fine church later finished by Henry Clutton and J.F. Bentley. The evolution of dual-purpose buildings demonstrates the delicate financial position of the Catholics—coupled, however, with a simultaneous drive in missionary fervour.

INTRODUCTION 23

Following the emigration of Wardell in 1858, other designers came into prominence. Comparable to the best of Wardell is Underwood Road, St Anne, 1855 by the little-known Gilbert Blount, who also designed St Catherine's at Bow. His church for the Dominicans at Haverstock Hill was begun, but superseded after his death by C.A. Buckler's design. By this time the innovatory built-in confessional had been taken up and developed by Wardell. Early examples had appeared at Scoles's Islington and Farm Street churches, and in Pugin's St George's, Southwark. Wardell, however, developed the concept from the simplest rectangular space to a penitent's compartment on either side of the priest, who had his own desk and fire in a species of small study.

Following Pugin's death, an interest in continental Gothic slowly burgeoned among English architects. William Burges and Henry Clutton won the competition for Lille Cathedral in 1856, and this sparked off the fashion for French Gothic. Clutton designed St Francis, Notting Hill, in an uncompromising thirteenth-century French idiom. Clutton's assistant, J.F. Bentley, added a baptistery here, and an outer north aisle to the Bayswater church also in Early French Gothic. Churches based upon French models followed—St Charles, Ogle Street by S.J. Nicholl, and George Goldie's Kensington church. Edward Pugin's early churches at Kentish Town, Peckham and Kensington were in a staid Early English mode, but French detail accompanied his improvisatory planning at Tower Hill. This and another late church at Kilburn were finished by Edward Pugin's brothers following his early death. At Hoxton, Edward Pugin's innovatory plan appears to be the earliest Catholic example of Gothic aisles narrowed to the role of access passages. Passage aisles in a Gothic setting subsequently appeared in F.A. Walters's churches at Bow Common and Vauxhall. The concept further developed by narrow aisles formed from pierced internal buttreses is exemplified in F.W. Tasker's English Martyrs at Walworth. From 1900 narrow aisles appeared regularly in the round-arched style of Benedict Williamson and others. Straight-ended English chancels persisted, but French apses fitfully reappeared at Millwall (1874), Fulham Road, Greenwich St Joseph, Haverstock Hill, Spanish Place, Eltham Christ Church and Bethnal Green (1912).

A revival of the Perpendicular phase of Gothic initiated by George Gilbert Scott at St Agnes, Kennington, in 1875 had a Catholic following. J.F. Bentley's seminary chapel at Hammersmith is of a late-Perpendicular stamp, and so was Edward Goldie's scheme of 1886 for rebuilding St Mary's, Hampstead. Fleeting examples of Perpendicular appear at Christ Church, Eltham, by Canon Scoles, Guardian Angels, Mile End, and St Wilfrid, Newington, both by F.A. Walters.

Alongside the various trends that practice brought into fashion, a deep sense of responsible archaeology persisted among patrons and architects. The magic name of Pugin, evoking a mythical golden age of Catholic achievement was never forgotten. The acquisition of the mediaeval St Etheldreda's, Ely Place, in the 1870s confirmed the Catholics' sense of architectural as well as spiritual heritage. Thus there emerged in the 1890s Our Lady's at Blackheath and English Martyrs at Streatham, splendidly detailed Decorated Gothic essays by A.E. Purdie, after the manner of 40 years earlier.

Correct historicism apart, Anglican architects such as G.E. Street and James Brooks made design a matter of sculptural form. In their wake the outstanding Romanist figure was J.F. Bentley, whose churches at Chelsea, Kensal New Town and Brixton Hill rank him well above his contemporaries. Bentley's personal vision of Gothic may be observed in the subtle interplay of his nave arcades against the internal walls; the rising tiers of arcades on his east walls; and his wish to leave his nave arcades uninterrupted by evident transepts long before he planned Westminster Cathedral.

Approximating Bentley's vision of mature Gothic was that of Leonard Stokes, whose Gothic details are so distilled, however, as to be more personal than historic. At Holy Ghost, Balham, Stokes rejected buttresses, mouldings and capitals, introducing a stylistic functionalism that was soon to flourish in Romanesque rather than in Gothic-derived terms.

By 1900 the long rule of Gothic was virtually ended in Catholic building. The classicizing element that stemmed from the royal chapels had long persisted in embassy chapels and in eighteenth-century missionary chapels. The *Rundbogenstil* imported from Germany in the 1840s flourished before the serious onset of Gothic. Catholic churches in non-Gothic modes surfaced continually in every decade. The trend produced St John's, Islington, in 1843 and the Classical front of St Mary's, Hampstead, in 1850. Early Christian were the two designs (1853 and 1863) for the Italian Church at Clerkenwell and the church of 1877 at Homerton. Classical details characterize F.W. Tasker's church of 1879 at Wapping. The Renaissance style of the Oratory has been admired ever since its opening in 1884. Also bearing Italianate details were Highgate St Joseph's and Brockley St Mary Magdalen, both of 1889, Soho St Patrick's and Battersea The Sacred Heart 1893, and Chelsea The Holy Redeemer, 1895.

The turning point in stylistic preference was Westminster Cathedral. Nominally Byzantine, planned from the inside out and capable of immediate use though lacking its decorations, its innovative character clearly generated a revised philosophy of church design even prior to the cathedral's opening in 1903. The advantages, financial and aesthetic, of sheer walls brick-built, circular or rectangular piers and round unmoulded arches were manifest.

Thus in its wake there emerged a type of parish church akin to Romanesque in style, simply planned and sparsely detailed, costing a mere fraction of Gothic or Renaissance work. Between 1902 and 1908 about 20 such 'Ellis churches' were built in south London, so called after their benefactress, the wealthy Miss Frances Ellis. Participating architects included Claude Kelly at Clapham Common; Lawrence Butler at

Wandsworth East Hill; Clement Jackson at Streatham Hill; Benedict Williamson at Earlsfield, Tooting, Norbury and Abbey Wood; and F.W. Tasker at Bermondsey South, Stockwell, Catford and Camberwell. Following Tasker's death in 1904, subsequent builders of 'Ellis churches' seem frequently to have copied his standard models of a Greek cross plan, or nave, (aisles) and chancel. Among such lacking a firmly identified architect are the churches at Kennington Park, Norwood West, Peckham Rye, Nunhead, Clapham Park, Forest Hill and Herne Hill. Some of the foregoing have been added to or superseded altogether by later buildings. Meanwhile, in the wake of Westminster Cathedral, there arose between 1902 and 1916 a crop of churches in various national and historical round-arched styles. In Southwark diocese are those at Rotherhithe, Lewisham, Charlton and Putney. In Westminster diocese there are Moorfields, Kingsway, the Lithuanian church, Copenhagen Street and Hammersmith.

This commentary would be incomplete without reference to school chapels and acquired buildings. Adaptation of secular buildings was a regular expedient of the impoverished Catholics. At Soho, the Assembly Rooms were adapted in 1792 as the first St Patrick's Church; in Bermondsey, a coach-house and later a dissecting room from Guy's Hospital; in King William Street the Lowther Rooms, a former dance hall; at Kingsland, a former factory; near Leicester Square, the Rotunda showplace. Occasionally redundant Nonconformist chapels were converted: for example, at Clerkenwell and Stockwell.

The best-known acquisition is St Etheldreda's, the pre-Reformation domestic chapel of the Bishops of Ely. More numerous were the school chapels that never quite overcame the problem of dual planning. B.W. Kelly's Dictionary notes 90 school chapels in England by 1906. Ten of these were in London: at Brockley, Bunhill Row, Drury Lane, Kensal New Town, Millwall, Paddington, Parsons Green, Rotherhithe, Vauxhall and Waterloo. Together they highlight the acute Catholic problem of financing both schools and churches.

Following the cessation of building occasioned by the First World War, nine churches were erected in inner London in the 1920s and 30s. As a group they illustrate the English reserve towards stylistic innovation, all of them being firmly rooted in historic forms. Only three, however, were designed in Gothic terms: that at Dulwich being Decorated, and those at Eltham Well Hall and Limehouse being Early English-derived. Two designs bear continental influences: the church at Camden Town resembling Belgian Renaissance and that at Tooting Bec combining Spanish Romanesque with early Gothic details. At Lee there is a lone Early Christian example. In neo-Romanesque terms are Parsons Green, Stephendale Road and Stoke Newington. Their plans tend towards the traditional, with nave, (aisles) and sanctuary. Clearly under the influence of Westminster Cathedral, however, may be noted the incidence of stout piers of simple profile plus the inclusion of baldacchinos at Borough and Poplar. The extended use of marble as a wall-facing to sanctuaries and chapels also occurs: for example, at

Lewisham, Bermondsey Melior Street and Poplar.

Following the Second World War, several churches of other sects were acquired and adapted to Catholic use at Kilburn, Tollington Park, Shepherds Bush Polish Church, Clapton Park, Plumstead and Kentish Town. There were extensions at Nunhead and restoration at Bow Common. At Tooting (Links Road), a parish hall serves as the church, and at Plumstead Common a prefab has served since 1950.

Numerous post-war replacements generally followed traditional planning forms of nave, (aisles) and sanctuary: for example, at Camberwell, Hackney, Pimlico, Kensington (Carmelites), Kensington (Our Lady of Victories), the German Church, Bermondsey Dockhead, Woolwich (St Catherine), Highbury, Clapton, Kingsland, Marylebone, Abbey Wood (St David), Kidbrooke and White City. Windows too tended towards the traditional, as early Gothic lancets, neo-Perpendicular or round-headed Romanesque. The innovative T-plan of nave, sanctuary and transepts at Earlsfield and Dulwich Wood Park seems not to have generated a following. The most inspired design is that of Adrian Gilbert Scott at Poplar, where a Greek cross plan, elliptical arches and tasteful furnishings throughout point towards the shape of custom-designed things to come. Contemporary with this is the French Church rebuilt by Hector Corfiato. Its circular plan, dictated by the previous building, hugs both sanctuary and worshippers within its columned ambulatory, but was taken up only at Beckenham Hill. In the wake of the Second Vatican Council (1962–65), congregational-oriented planning came into its own during the sixties and seventies. The oval nucleus placed within a larger rectangle at Somers Town, and the nearly elliptical plan at Swiss Cottage were followed by the uncluttered simple ellipse of Laxton Place. Meanwhile, the rectangular plan of Upper Holloway reappeared at Wimbledon Common, where the altar and entrance stand in opposite corners. Variations on these geometrical themes appeared with the irregular hexagon of Sydenham Kirkdale, and the fan-shape of Surrey Docks. The notion of screened rectangles, capable of enlarging the major spaces at will, appeared at Manor House and notably at Harrow Road.

These diverse experiments indicate that policy and practice are not yet finalised. Moreover, the swing of conservative taste may yet conceivably revive plans embracing nave, aisles, crossing, transepts, sanctuary and side chapels. The last church listed above dates from 1988. Two churches are in prospect in the 1990s, and their contributions may add another footnote to the ongoing story.

Furnishings

Since furnishings loom large in Catholic churches, a brief survey may be helpful. If the architecture of the seventeenth-century royal chapels was grand, the furnishings were even grander. Paramount were the elaborate Baroque altarpieces sculpted by Grinling Gibbons and François Dieussart. These set the ideal at least until modern times. Few altars

Introduction

could have matched the marble sculpture of that at Wardour Castle. Even eighteenth-century survivals are few and far between, however, and in London fonts are found only at Warwick Street and Bunhill Row, together with sarcophagus altars at Moorfields and Lincoln's Inn Fields. Of later Georgian churches there are altar-pieces of uncertain provenance at Lincoln's Inn Fields and Hampstead.

With the advent of the Gothic Revival, however, Pugin-designed furnishings issued from the Lambeth workshops of George Myers. There are examples at Southwark Cathedral, Farm Street and Fulham, where an early example in London of the ubiquitous octagonal font appears. Theodore Phyffers, brought from Belgium by Pugin, produced sculpted works at Commercial Road, Farm Street, Notting Hill, Ogle Street, Soho Square and Chelsea St Mary. Contemporary with this group is the relief of The Assumption by J.E. Carew at Warwick Street. Rising firms supplied sculpted furnishings—Thomas Earp at Maiden Lane, Greenwich, Farm Street, Islington and Notting Hill; R.L. Boulton at Haverstock Hill, Kilburn, Soho Square, Hammersmith and Tower Hill; Farmer & Brindley at Bow, Underwood Road, Farm Street, Spanish Place, Westminster Cathedral and the Oratory; and A.B. Wall at Streatham, Ogle Street and Shepherds Bush. Mayer of Munich supplied more items than all the foregoing together. From the Lady statue of 1861 at Farm Street to a pietà of 1909 at Chelsea Holy Redeemer, carved, cast and sculpted works poured forth. Outstanding are the carved altar at Hoxton; two angels in the nave of Soho Square; and the bronze St Peter and the Holy Redeemer at Fulham Road. With a branch in London, the firm diversified into painting: for example, the Stations at Spanish Place, and stained glass exemplified at Kilburn, Underwood Road and seven windows at Brook Green. Meanwhile, other bronze copies of St Peter's statue in Rome, originating from the house of Froc-Robert in Paris, appeared around 1904 at the Oratory, Holloway and Walworth churches.

The most patronised supplier of stained glass was the Catholic firm of John Hardman at Birmingham. By Hardman are numerous windows at Streatham, Fulham, Brook Green, Haverstock Hill and Commercial Road. There are examples also at Bethnal Green, Kilburn, Farm Street, Holloway, Norbury and Roehampton. Outstanding twentieth-century glass by H. Clark of Dublin is exemplified at Southwark Cathedral and Eltham. Since 1945, Goddard & Gibbs have installed extensive works in glass at Hackney, Homerton and Highbury, plus single examples at Forest Hill, Sydenham, Southwark Cathedral and Underwood Road. Charles Blakeman designed much glass for the restored St Etheldreda, Ely Place, and for the new churches of Pimlico and Our Lady of Victories at Kensington. A final mention must be made of the windows of the Polish Church, Islington, made by Lowndes & Drury from designs of Adam Bunsch.

Twentieth-century artists in wood and stone were not lacking. Fr Gregory Chedal produced carved work for Charlton, Brockley and Bethnal Green churches, but outstanding was Anton Dapre, sometime chief carver at Burns Oates, represented by complete sets of Stations at Dulwich, Nunhead, Holloway and Streatham, as well as statues at Walworth, Bow Common and Fulham. Sculpted works by Philip Lindsey Clark appear at Westminster Cathedral, Pimlico and Streatham Hill; and by his son Michael at St Johns Wood, Kingsland, Kensington Our Lady of Victories, Streatham and Harrow Road.

The rise of mosaic decoration should be noted, from its initial use by J.F. Bentley in the Lady chapel of Warwick Street in 1875. The extensive use of mosaic at Westminster Cathedral has included works by George Bridge, Gilbert Pownall and Boris Anrep. The subsequent widespread use of mosaic decoration in altars and shrines continues to the present day. Throughout the twentieth century, the influence of Westminster Cathedral, both architectural and artistic, has been paramount on the Catholic churches of London. As we approach the millennium, it seems impossible to predict what trends may henceforth dominate the scene.

I
City of London

Moorfields St Mary, Eldon Street, EC2

THE only Catholic church in the City of London, this was formerly in the London Borough of Hackney. Owing to boundary changes, it was brought into the City on 1 April 1994. The foundation has a long and proud history. A chapel was opened in 1686, but had to be suspended in 1689. From 1736 there was a chapel in Ropemakers' Alley, whose fabric and furniture were destroyed in the Gordon Riots, and it was succeeded by a chapel in White Street. Its replacement in 1820 by a large Classical church in Finsbury Square, sponsored by laymen, marked a turning point in the size and stylistic aspirations of Catholic churches. Its architect, John Newman, entertained the notion of concealing the source of light for the altar-piece, and journeyed on the Continent in search of examples. He found the example he required in Paris in the church of St Sulpice, which confirmed his intention of using the idea. The plan consisted of nave, aisles and apsidal sanctuary. The glory of the church, however, was the altar-piece with six columns framing the sarcophagus altar, its surrounding fenestration concealed from view. On the terminal wall was a fresco of Mount Calvary executed by Angelo Aglio, 55 feet high and 33 feet wide, containing over 50 principal figures. Its scale may be envisaged from the dimensions of the

1. *Moorfields, St Mary*

cross alone, which was 18 feet high. This final church of the first wave of building that succeeded the 1791 Catholic Relief Act was probably the finest in structure and decoration. As the permanent seat of the Vicar Apostolic, it served as the pro-cathedral from 1850 to 1869.

That part of the City having become less of a residential centre, this illustrious church was pulled down in 1899 and replaced by the present church in Eldon Street, which was opened on 25 March 1903. The builders were Holliday & Greenwood, and Cardinal Vaughan's chosen architect was George Sherrin, already known for the completion of the London Oratory dome and such works as colleges, houses and underground stations.

Sherrin clearly did the best he could to provide a church that need not be compared unfavourably with its predecessor, while battling against the difficulties of a restricted site. The front to Eldon Street is flanked by shops, and allowed no display of a conventional church façade. The most that Sherrin could provide here was an arched entrance of Portland stone with quattrocento detailing, surmounted by a group of sculptures by J. Daymond representing the Virgin and Child. The entrance is tactfully blended with the adjacent shops and the domestic windows of the presbytery above.

Inside, a narrow vestibule leads to the nave, necessarily lowering the floor level some three feet owing to difficulties here with ancient lights. In plan, the interior consists of four nave bays, the north aisle with its chapel, and the chancel. In the west gallery is the organ, by Corps &

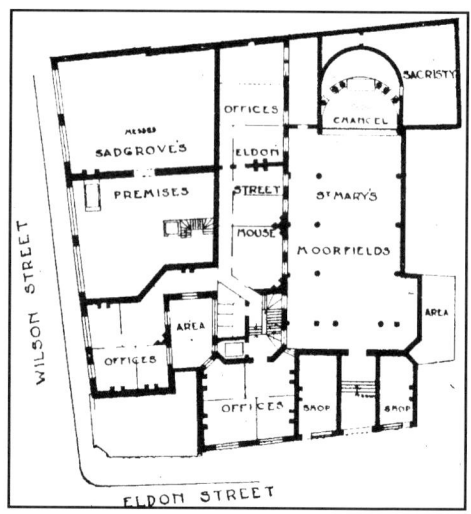

2. *Moorfields, St Mary, plan*

Son of Finsbury Park. The walls are panelled in oak, and above a cornice in the nave is an elliptical ceiling, with rectangular windows along its length. At the west end are a small baptistery with a marble font, surviving from the old church; a screen of marble and bronze; and two confessionals with oak doors carved by J. Daymond.

Between nave and aisle is an arcade of four Devonshire marble columns with Doric capitals. Across the fourth bay lie the altar rails of pavonazzo, with panels of various other inlaid marbles. At the end of the aisle is the Blessed Sacrament altar, its mensa resting on squared legs with incised panels and foliage capitals. The frontal is recessed, and bears geometrical decoration. Behind is a window (a memorial to Mary Burton) depicting the Assumption, and on the surrounding walls there are canvas paintings by G. Pownall of Regina Apostolorum, St Thomas of Canterbury, St Thomas More, St Edmund and angels.

I. CITY OF LONDON

3. *Moorfields, St Mary, the church of 1820*

Within the sanctuary is the original sarcophagus altar framed by the six columns reused by Sherrin, and there is an echo here of the spectacular theatrical effect observed in pictures of the old church. The columns are of Como marble, monoliths 18 feet high and two feet in diameter, designed by Giovanni Battista Comolli after those of the Choragic monument of Lysicrates at Athens. Positioned some distance from the rear of the apse, they form a dignified frame for the altar. The apse itself is now faced with tall vertical panels of marble revetments, of light blue colour flecked generously with white.

Bibliography
Kelly, pp. 281-22; Rottmann, pp. 158-62; Harting, pp. 80-99; Ward, pp. 104-106, 191-94; Little, pp. 58-59, 158; *J. Britton, Illustrations of the Public Buildings of London* (London: J.Taylor, J Britton and A. Pugin, 1828), II, pp. 5-11; AAW, R 79 (building accounts and correspondence of Bishop Poynter and John Newman); *The Tablet*, 5 September 1857, p. 564; 11 July 1874, p. 51; 16 October 1875, p. 499; *British Architect*, 4 September 1903, pp. 168-70; BN, 3 April 1903, p. 474; Br, 31 August 1907, p. 248; 5 October 1907, pp. 361-62; *Westminster Record*, June 1992, p. 6.

II
City of Westminster

Cathedral of the Most Precious Blood, Victoria Street, SW1

FOLLOWING the restoration of the hierarchy in 1850, St Mary Moorfields—and from 1869 Our Lady of Victories in Kensington—served Cardinals Wiseman and Manning as pro-cathedrals. The question of raising a worthy cathedral at Westminster haunted Manning, whose financial priority, however, was the provision of diocesan schools for some 20,000 poor children. Thus, as a long-term plan, Manning contented himself with finding a site. Initially he acquired land in Carlisle Place in 1867–68 which he later relinquished in favour of the adjacent site of the Tothill Fields Bridewell, on which the present cathedral was eventually built.

In the meantime, Manning obtained plans for a Gothic cathedral from Henry Clutton in 1873, but wisely dropped this expensive scheme almost immediately. Another scheme surfaced in 1882 when Sir Tatton Sykes, a wealthy Protestant patron of churches, offered to mark his proposed conversion to Catholicism by paying for a major church that would be modelled on the *Votivkirche* in Vienna. This rendered the vision of Westminster Cathedral realistic initially. However, Sir Tatton Sykes apparently decided to remain a Protestant and his building proposal was lost sight of, so that Manning's permanent achievement remained the acquisition of the site.

Following Manning's death in 1892, Cardinal Vaughan arrived at Westminster aged 60, and conscious of the need to erect a cathedral quickly in the limited time he was likely to have. Initially Vaughan obtained yet another Gothic scheme, this time from A.M. Dunn. But the estimate of £230,000, and the prospect of a long gestation caused Vaughan to think again. The cardinal then flirted with the idea of a competition; but J.F. Bentley, perhaps the best-known Catholic architect refused point blank to take part in one. Since he wanted Bentley, Vaughan therefore appointed him directly as the architect of the cathedral. Cardinal Vaughan's conditions required the cathedral to have a wide nave with an unimpeded view of the chancel; the shell to be completed quickly, leaving the decoration to future generations; and, to avoid detrimental comparison with Westminster Abbey, the style should not be Gothic. Bentley would have preferred Gothic, but

1. *Westminster Cathedral, exterior*

dissuaded the cardinal from an Italian basilican design, in favour of the Christian Byzantine style. From November 1894 to March 1895, Bentley travelled in Italy, visiting Milan, Pisa, Florence, Rome, Naples, Assisi, Perugia, Ravenna, Venice, Verona and Turin. He was unable to visit Constantinople owing to an outbreak of cholera, and yet the roots of the design that he made on his return lie closer to St Sophia than to any of the churches that he saw in Italy.

Bentley made three plans altogether for the cathedral, before arriving at the ideal answer to Cardinal Vaughan's requirements. The cardinal's recorded statement implies a generous faith in Bentley's ability to give of his best when free from interference. He wrote:

> Having laid down certain conditions as to size, space, chapels and style, I left the rest to him. He offered me the choice between a vaulted roof and one of saucer-shaped domes; I chose the latter. He wished to build two campaniles; I said one would be enough for me. For the rest he had a free hand (J.G. Snead-Cox, *Life of Cardinal Vaughan* [London: Burns and Oates, 1912], II, pp. 344-45).

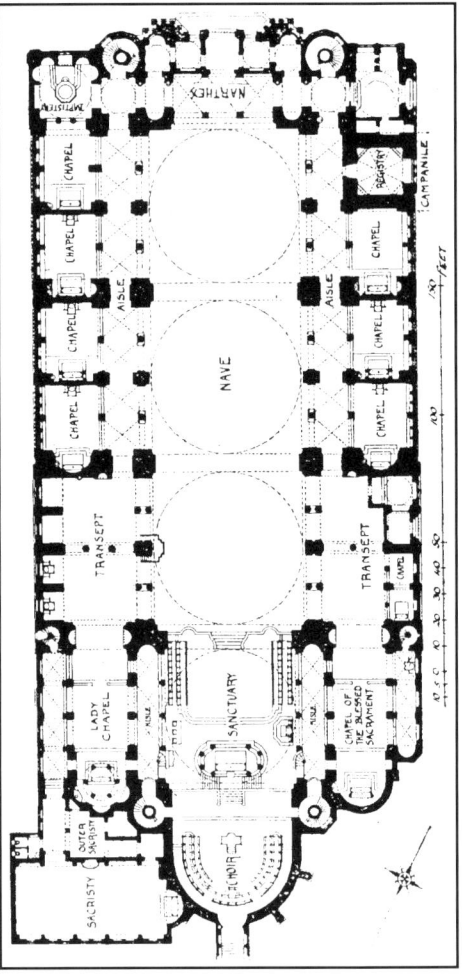

2. *Westminster Cathedral, Bentley's final plan*

Bentley's final plan has the campanile to the north-west. The narthex with the organ gallery above it is now screened from the nave by a triple arch. There are three shallow domes above the nave, and a fourth with windows in it above the sanctuary. Flanking the nave are processional aisles and beyond them chapels on each side; the buttressing is within the building, and the outer walls are sheer. The nave arcade is carried across the transepts (a device cherished by Bentley who discovered a mediaeval precedent for it at Pisa). On either side of the sanctuary are two long, apsed chapels, and beyond it is the retro-choir with crypt beneath. Thus, as Pevsner has observed, the cathedral as a longitudinal domed building is really the Gesu scheme translated into Byzantine.

Bentley oriented the cathedral north to south, with the chancel at the latter point, siting it entirely to the east side of the four-acre site. The row of houses between the cathedral and Victoria Street having rights to light and air, the west front had to be stepped back. In consequence, behind and above the portico, the narthex is recessed some 20 feet; and the terminal wall of the nave a further 20 feet.

The foundation stone was laid on 29 June 1895. The builders were Messrs Shillitoe & Sons of Bury St Edmunds. The materials used were brick mostly (over 12 million, including broken bricks mixed into the concrete for the domes); Cornish granite plinths; and dressings of Portland stone. The structure was complete and some of the decoration was begun when Bentley died, aged 63, on 1 March 1902. Although he had prepared detailed designs, Bentley had made no provision for the continuation of the work in the event of his death. Therefore, the firm of John F. Bentley, Son & Marshall was hastily constituted. Bentley's assistant John Marshall provided continuity of ideas and tradition, following Bentley's drawings whenever possible. Provision was made for the architect's son Osmond to join Marshall as soon as he had sufficient professional experience.

One year later, before the completed cathedral was consecrated to the uses of religion, the first London performance was given therein of Elgar's *The Dream of Gerontius*. In the event, no formal opening took place, the cathedral being used for the first time for the Requiem of Cardinal Vaughan in June 1903.

Approached from Victoria Street, the (ritual) west front presents to the eye a complex mass of shapes fashioned in red brick with generous bands of Portland stone. The north-west campanile towers over all, while respecting the symmetry of the ground-level arrangements. Here, the broad main entrance flanked by polygonal turrets exhibits its own artwork. The mosaic in the tympanum of Our Lord, Our Lady, St Joseph, St Peter and St Edward was designed by R. Anning Bell following Bentley, and executed in 1916 by Powell & Co. Between the columns below are medallions displaying 12 distinguished Archbishops of Canterbury, sculpted by Farmer & Brindley. Above the northwest doorway is a mosaic of 1982 by Nicolette Gray. On the south side (to Morpeth Terrace), the overall brick and stone exterior is varied by the fenestration of the nave, the transept and the chancel-cum-Lady Chapel. The effect is further enhanced by their varied roof lines, the canted buttresses of the nave, the double gable of the transept and the elliptical curve of the chancel window. All these features are punctuated by minor towers and turrets which tend to go unnoticed in the shadow of the campanile.

For the interior, Bentley drew up a scheme of decoration which to date has only partially been carried out. In it, marble predominated, monoliths on moulded bases of Labradorite to support the galleries, and fine slabs for the revetments of the piers. For the marble revetments, appropriate shades frequently appear, to confirm a chapel's dedication: black and white for the Holy Souls' chapel; blue Hymettian and white Pentellic for St Andrew; Connemara green and Cork red for St Patrick. Two columns of red Norwegian granite in the narthex assert the cathedral's dedication to the Precious Blood. The eight columns in the nave of verde antico are from the same Thessalian quarries as those of Santa Sophia, rediscovered by W. Brindley. Elsewhere, superb columns of red Languedoc marble divide the south transept into east and west halves; and the crypt ambulatory is formed of monolithic Norwegian granite columns with Ionic capitals. These and capitals elsewhere of unpolished white statuary marble were designed by Bentley in a variety of foliage and linear shapes as a faithful development of Early Christian forms.

The artwork of the chapels and chancel is detailed below, clockwise from the north-west entrance. Passing two bronze panels in the north aisle, which list the pastors of the church in England with their papal contemporaries, one arrives at the **Chapel of the Holy Souls**. This best of all represents Bentley's intentions, since all was designed or approved by him. The opus-sectile altar-piece of Christ the Redeemer was by W.C. Symons. The marble panelled walls and floor appear in black and white tones, the mosaic ground of silver rather than gold executed by George Bridge and his lady mosaicists in 1902–1903. A column of Labradorite divides the bronze gilt grille; and opposite is a column of white pavonazzo.

The artwork of the **Chapel of St George and the English Martyrs** is characterised by marbles of red and white, the colours of St George. Its altar-piece, a relief in Hopton Wood stone of Our Lord as Priest and King, flanked by Saints John Fisher and Thomas More, was executed by Eric Gill in 1946. The reredos is diapered with the white rose, and St George's cross. The altar steps are of Greek Pentellic marble, and in the floor is a rose inlaid with lapis lazuli and mother-of-pearl. Against the left wall is a figure of St George by Philip Lindsey Clark, flanked by memorial panels to service personnel. Beside the grille, in a bronze casket, lies the body of St John Southworth, executed for his priesthood in 1654, and placed here in 1930. The column to the aisle is of Swiss cipollino.

Within the **Chapel of St Joseph**, the rectangular plan is enhanced by an apse hollowed out of the buttress. Here the altar-piece is a gilt bronze triptych of St Joseph and the Child Jesus, by H.C. Fehr. The altar designed by the Bentley firm is of pavonazzo, its frontal of Siena marble bordered with lapis lazuli and gold, in its centre a lozenge of Irish green marble bordered with lapis lazuli and pearl. For the rest, Bentley left designs for the details of the marbling, which was completed by Fennings of Fulham around 1950. The chapel's floor is of Hopton Wood stone, patterned with red and green porphyry. The west wall bears large panels of Greek cipollino. Between the windows a large column of Italian fleur de pêche stands within an arcade of Iberian agate and Canadian onyx. The column to the aisle is of Greek cipollino.

In the north transept is the **Chapel of St Thomas of Canterbury** or Vaughan Chantry. Framed by two black and white breccia columns, its gilt bronze screen with scrolls and frieze wrought by hand was designed by J. Marshall and made by Singer & Co. of Frome. Inside, the walls are panelled in pavonazzo, the altar in thick slabs of verde antico. Facing the altar is the effigy of Cardinal Vaughan, of white Pentellic marble, designed by J. Marshall and sculpted by Henry McCarthy. Also in the transept is a mosaic of St Joan, 1909, by W.C. Symons and executed by George Bridge. A single central column of verde antico supports the gallery, whilst between transept and nave are columns of Greek cipollino (two), breccia and verde antico.

Flanking the chancel is the **Blessed Sacrament Chapel**, long, aisled and apsed. The openings to the aisles are faced with pavonazzo, verde antico and other marbles, muted in tone in contrast with the mosaics and metalwork. The screens of bronze gilt designed by Marshall were complete by 1907. Noteworthy are the communion rails adorned with enamel plaques and the pelican above the gates. The altar is of cipollino, Siena and Carrara marbles; its steel tabernacle faced with silver repoussé. This and the hexagonal timber canopy were designed by Marshall. The mosaics of 1960–62 by Boris Anrep display themes of the Old Testament in the nave, and of the New Testament in the sanctuary.

In the chapel's left aisle is the **Shrine of the Sacred Heart**, executed in 1910–11 by Farmer & Brindley. The general effect of the marble wall-linings is of green and white; but red and gold dominate the mosaic upper reaches, patterned with repeated symbols. Red also is the altar of Cork marble, its frontal bearing a bas-relief of St Michael and the Dragon. The alabaster statue of the Sacred Heart was the work of Farmer &

3. *Westminster Cathedral, the sanctuary*

Brindley; the silver lamp designed by Osmund Bentley & Marshall; and the Holy Face mosaic opposite the altar done by W.C. Symons in 1911.

Slightly less broad than the nave is the raised **sanctuary**, and higher still within the apse is the choir space. The altar is a solid block of Cornish marble, undecorated and said to weigh 12 tons. Above it is the magnificent baldacchino designed by Bentley and erected in 1905–1906. Eight monoliths of Verona marble support the canopy vaulted with lapis lazuli, mother-of-pearl and gold mosaic. Within the tympanum high above the altar is a mosaic of Our Lord in Glory by Gilbert Pownall. Behind it, a bas-relief by Philip Lindsey Clark in Hopton Wood stone conceals the conductor. Within the apse is the small organ of 1915 by T.C. Lewis. The grand organ in the west gallery, of 1922 by Henry Willis III, can also be played from the apse. The arcades flanking the sanctuary rise in two storeys, with upper columns of pavonazzo, and lower columns of French jasper and pink Norwegian. The archbishop's throne is copied from the papal chair in St John Lateran; its canopy, however, was designed by the Bentley firm, of oak and walnut inlaid with holly and ebony. The chancel stalls by L.H. Shattock are of oak, inlaid with contrasting wood. The great crucifix between chancel and nave was designed by Bentley and painted by W.C. Symons. On its obverse is the figure of Christ with symbols of the evangelists at the extremities; and on the reverse is Our Lady of Sorrows.

Flanking the chancel on the south side is the **Lady Chapel**, the earliest part of the cathedral to be opened for regular use, on 25 March 1903. Its plan consists of nave of three bays plus a triply apsed sanctuary. There is an extended cornice of white statuary marble with various darker marbles below. In the nave, vertical bands of white alternate with such deeper colours as rosso antico and pink pavonazzo. The altar mosaic of the Virgin and Child and the four alcove heads of prophets were designed by R. Anning Bell and executed by Miss Martin in 1908. The higher mosaics of 1931–32 by Gilbert Pownall comprise an extensive iconographical scheme relating to the Virgin Mary. Within the apse is Christ and the Tree of Life flanked by Our Lady and St Peter. Scenes from the life of Our Lady interspersed with Ave medallions surround the upper walls. On the left is a plaque to Our Lady of Vilma, 1944. The marble floor was completed in 1956.

The semicircular **crypt** may be reached from the Lady Chapel. Six massive columns of Norwegian granite support the vault; the walls and altar are of green cipollino. To the east and north are the tombs of Cardinal Griffin and Cardinal Godfrey. Above the altar is a mosaic of St Peter by G. Pownall. Behind it is the crypt chapel of St Edmund, directly beneath the cathedral's high altar. Here are the tombs of two cardinals brought from Kensal Green in 1907: Wiseman's Gothic monument is by E.W. Pugin; Manning's effigy sculpted by John Adams-Acton was cast in bronze by Singer & Sons; the mosaic heads of cherubim above it by Boris Anrep. Above the Derbyshire marble altar is a mosaic of St Edmund blessing

II. City of Westminster

the City of London by C. Symons.

The south transept forms in plan an extension of the Lady Chapel. Separating the transept from the nave are columns of Greek cipollino, Italian breccia and verde antico. In the centre are two superb columns of warm red Languedoc marble supporting a bridge between the triforium gallery and the south wall. Within the transept is the Canadian Air Force memorial of silvered nails by David Partridge with lettering by Edward Wright; and a bronze plaque of St Teresa of Lisieux by Manzu.

Adjacent to the south transept is the **Chapel of St Paul**, given by the Anstey family whose arms appear opposite the altar. Like the corresponding chapel on the north side, this has an apse that contains the altar of pavonazzo and statuary marble designed by J. Marshall. Above is a bas-relief of St Paul, of gilt bronze set in a niche with folding doors. The pavement inlaid with coloured stones was designed by Edward Hutton. The mosaics of 1964 were done by Justin Vulliamy in consultation with Boris Anrep. Beneath a tent-like roof appear Christ handing the scroll of law to Ss Peter and Paul; the shipwreck at Malta; the road to Damascus; and the three churches of Rome's *Tre Fontane*. The chapel's stalls were executed by J. Plucknett of Warwick.

Blue and white marbles dominate **St Andrew's Chapel**, decorated in 1910–15 at the expense of the Fourth Marquess of Bute, on condition that it was designed by Robert Weir Schultz. The altar is of Scottish stone, the mensa of Alloa on columns of red Peterhead and a base of Aberdeen granite. The bronze crucifix is flanked by relief sculptures of Ss Ninian, Margaret, Bride and Columba by Stirling Lee. The marble work was executed by Farmer & Brindley, including the floor inset with fish after Bentley's unexecuted scheme for the nave. The mosaics, designed by George Jackson and executed by Gaetano Meo, include representations of six cities associated with St Andrew. On the walls are inscribed the names of Scottish saints. The ebony stalls inlaid with ivory are by Ernest Gimson. The screen to the aisle is of tin, by W. Bainbridge Reynolds, punctuated by a column of Swiss cippolino. In the aisle between this and the next chapel is a beautiful panel of golden breccia.

Marbles of green hue, and the symbols of shamrock and snake dominate the decoration of **St Patrick's Chapel**. The altar frontal is of Connemara green, its centre of red Victorian marble from Cork. The mensa is of black Irish marble, decorated with intertwined snakes and inlaid mother-of-pearl shamrock. The altar was designed by J. Marshall, and constructed in 1910 by Farmer & Brindley. The gilt bronze statue of St Patrick is by Arthur Pollen. On the south wall a blank arcade of intersecting arches contains the badges of Irish regiments that fought in the war of 1914–18. The shamrock and the oak leaves of St Brigid reappear in the white marble screen to the aisle. The marble column here is of Greek cipollino. In the aisle is a mosaic of St Oliver Plunket by Boris Anrep.

The marble work of the **Chapel of Ss Gregory and Augustine** was designed by Bentley, and was the only marble

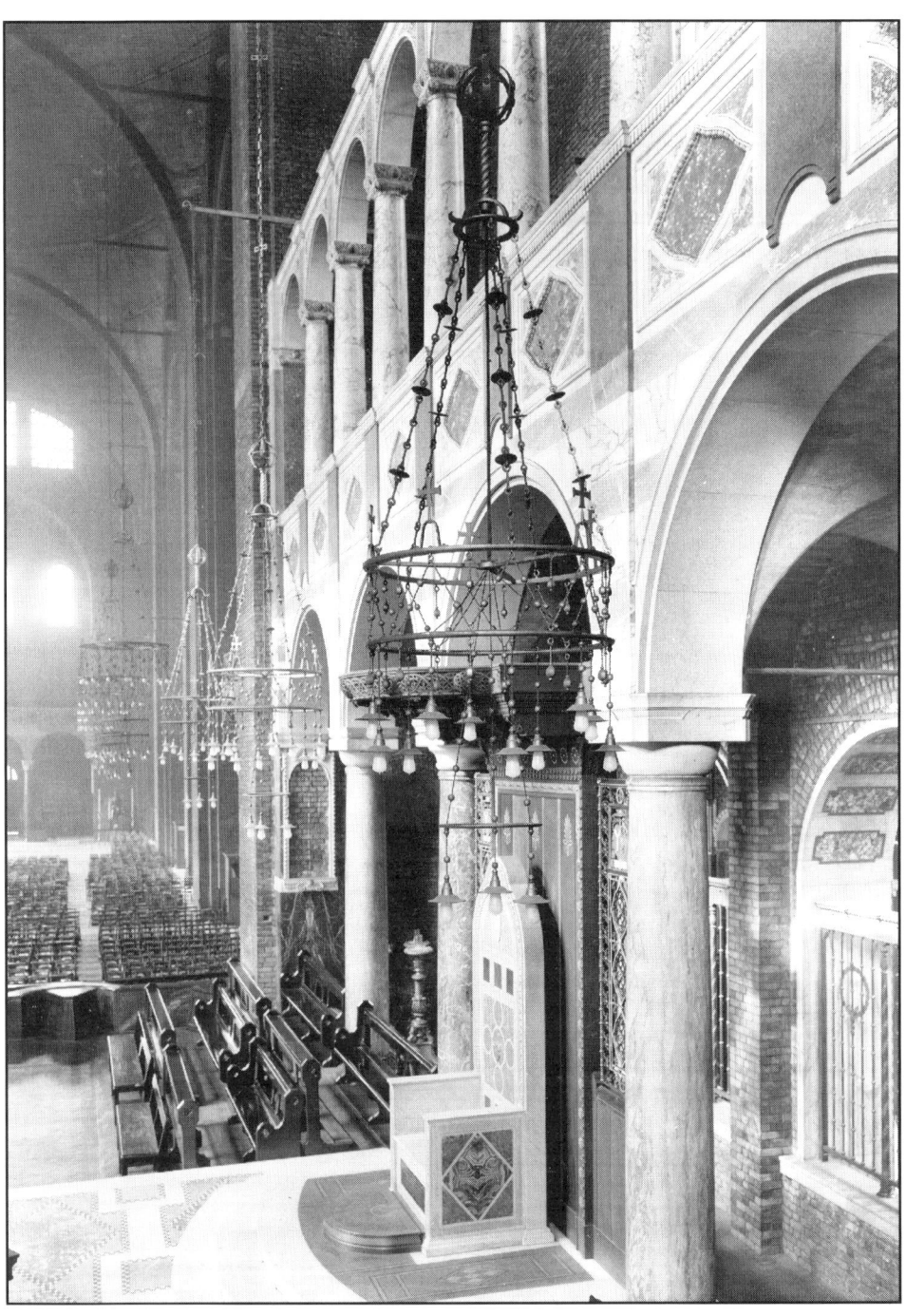

4. *Westminster Cathedral, the nave*

revetment that he saw. It was installed by Messrs Whitehead in 1901–1902. The extensive iconography depicts the early saints of England: in the tympanum St Gregory's charge to St Augustine; in the lunette St Augustine received by King Ethelbert. These works in mosaic and opus sectile were designed by J.R. Clayton of Clayton & Bell. The mosaics were executed by George Bridge. Two columns of Swiss cipollino separate the chapel from the aisle.

A marble and bronze screen with columns of pavonazzo, executed by Messrs Whitehead, leads into the **baptistery**. The font was made in Rome from Bentley's design in 1901; its plinth and coping are of pavonazzo, the angle pilasters and lower panels of verde antico. The floor, of white marble inlaid with squares of Siena and Connemara, was constructed by Farmer & Brindley.

Finally, the nave, the widest in England, with its eight superb columns of verde antico. The marble revetments of the galleries were completed in the 1950s. In the nave is the statue of St Peter, a copy of that in St Peter's in Rome. The light fittings were designed by J. Marshall, possibly following a design of Bentley. The original pulpit, made in Rome in 1902 by Cavalier Aristide Leonori, was thought to be too small, and its solid base was modified with columns in the present design by L.H. Shattock executed in 1934. Its opus sectile panel of Our Lady of Walsingham was made by John Trinick. Near the pulpit is an early fifteenth-century alabaster statue of Our Lady of Walsingham, acquired in 1955. On the faces of the piers are Eric Gill's Stations of the Cross of 1913–18: 14 subjects sculpted in low relief with a firm intensity of line, and a distinct absence of sentimentality. Here Gill matched perfectly Bentley's concept of plastic planning, uniting liturgy and architecture in accordance with his brief.

Perhaps without realising it, Bentley had already laid the foundations of twentieth-century thinking on simplicity and design. Following the influence of the Malines Conference (1909), Gill linked Westminster with Continental thinking when he matched his Stations of the Cross to Bentley's timeless interior. In the long term, the simply adorned forms of Westminster were to exert their own influence upon the Modern Movement.

Bibliography
Kelly, pp. 426-27; de l'Hopital; Rottmann, pp. 1-14; *Westminster Cathedral Record*, 1896–1902; W.R. Lethaby, 'Westminster Cathedral', AR 11 (January 1902), pp. 3-7; C.F. Hadfield, 'Westminster Cathedral', *RIBA Journal*, 3rd series, 10 (21 March 1903); 249-72; Peter Howell, 'Westminster Cathedral' (unpublished).

The Immaculate Conception, Farm Street, W1

The Society of Jesus had a house in York Place by the 1840s, and were anxious to extend their London foothold by obtaining the charge of a mission. Several attempts to do so were unsuccessful owing to the inflexibility of Bishop Griffiths, who feared that neighbouring secular missions might suffer financially from the proximity of Jesuits or other regulars. The Jesuits' request to build a church in Farm Street was carried to Rome in 1843. The papal decision was in their favour and building began soon afterwards. The foundation stone was laid by Fr Randall Lythgoe on 31 July 1844, and the church was opened for use in 1846, the formal opening taking place on 31 July 1849. The chosen architect was J.J. Scoles, whom the Jesuits had employed at Stonyhurst and elsewhere. The builder was Thomas Jackson, and interior decorations were by Henry Taylor Bulmer. The materials used were Kentish rag with Box Hill stone dressings.

5. *Farm Street, The Immaculate Conception, 1844*

The difficulties of the site clearly rendered transepts and a tower impossible. Nevertheless, Scoles furnished a practical plan, which has been perfected by subsequent additions. When opened, the plan was T-shaped with sanctuary, side chapels and nave, and only three bays of aisles owing to the difficulty of obtaining adjacent land. Following a fire, the (ritual) south-east chapel was rebuilt in 1860. The south aisle with chapels was built in 1878, the north aisle with its chapels in 1899–1903.

Only the east and west fronts may be viewed from Mount Street and Farm Street. The west front is a modified version of Beauvais Cathedral's south transept. Its arched and gabled central door is supported by gabled niches, above it a low parapet and traceried main window; a strong emphasis is provided by its matching angle turrets. The gable and flanking pinnacles were simplified in 1951 by Adrian Gilbert Scott.

From Mount Street one sees the sanctuary window, its tracery copied from Carlisle Cathedral, flanked by the Sacred Heart Chapel gable and the flat-roofed St Ignatius Chapel. The porch here received its sculpture in 1914, a consummate piece of late Gothic Revival work with four orders of columns, above them bands of foliage with animals, and angels playing musical instruments beneath an ogee arch. In the tympanum is the Assumption of the Virgin with angels.

Inside, the plan reads as west entrance with organ gallery over, nave and aisles with their numerous chapels, and chancel with flanking chapels. This bald outline scarcely does justice to the graceful interior with its wealth of marble facings and the carved work bestowed on the structure and its furnishings over many years—for this interior is as richly

II. CITY OF WESTMINSTER

6. *Farm Street, The Immaculate Conception, 1844*

detailed as any in the land. The effect on the Catholic visitor must be one of visual fulfilment achieved by heart-warming familiarity. The nave is of eight bays, with clustered piers of red Peterhead granite, 16 clerestory windows (with varied tracery) above a pierced parapet. The original stencilled ceiling decorations by

Bulmer are long since obliterated, the scheme of 1987 by Austin Winkley presenting sacred monograms within wreaths, and a foliate pattern alternating with a star motif.

The high altar is of Caen stone, made to Pugin's design with reredos figures of the Elders of the Apocalypse. Its frontal has the Crucifixion, Abel, Noah, Melchisedech and Abraham. The east window's glass originally of 1885 by Wailes was renewed in 1902 and 1912 by Hardman, its theme of the Tree of Jesse retained. The sanctuary walls were faced with Genoese marble and Nottingham alabaster in 1864 under the architect George Goldie. The Venetian mosaics of the Annunciation and the Coronation of Our Lady were presented in 1875. The communion rails of pavonazzo with lapis lazuli panels designed by W.H. Romaine Walker date from 1901. The carved life-size statue of Our Lady of Farm Street by Mayer of Munich was presented in 1861, its later canopy designed by Fr Ignatius Scoles.

The **Sacred Heart Chapel** was erected in 1860 by Henry Clutton, replacing a chapel destroyed by fire. A double arcade of marble shafts separates it from the chancel. It is vaulted with parallel ribs resting on a carved cornice. The walls were lined by G.P. White with polished alabaster broken by inlaid work. The sculpture came from the Lambeth workshop of Thomas Earp: it includes the angels in the blank arcade, and the marble altar inset with panels of brass modelled by Theodore Phyffers, depicting Juda pleading for Benjamin before Joseph (Gen. 44.32-34), Our Lord with Pilate's soldiers, and with St Thomas. Above the altar is a mural by Peter Molitor of the Sacred Heart and saints. Two angels either side of the tabernacle are attributed to J.F. Bentley. Also in the chapel is a bronze gilt tablet to Lady Georgiana Fullerton +1885. The Sacred Heart aisle was extended in 1878 by H. Clutton. The division of its outer bays, by means of blank arcaded screens, forms a succession of chapels. Tierceron vaults throughout enhance the setting. In the chapels are the Stations of the Cross—wood carvings from Austria painted in a uniform stone colour.

The **St Aloysius Altar** of 1883, designed by A.E. Purdie and executed by Farmer & Brindley, has a statue of the saint in the reredos surrounded by figures of angels. In the frontal St Aloysius is shown receiving Holy Communion from St Charles Borromeo.

The **Altar of St Joseph** was designed by Clutton. Its statue in Carrara marble is flanked by wooden panels with the Espousal of Our Lady and the Death of St Joseph painted by Charles Goldie. The outer panels display St Augustine and St Peter (after Crivelli) painted by Miss Gambardella. In the chapel are two windows installed in 1955 in memory of Fr Francis Devas.

In the **Chapel of St Francis Xavier**, the reredos frames a painting of the Death of St Francis by Charles Goldie. Here is also a crucifix of Portuguese workmanship.

The **Chapel of the Agony** was formed by A.E. Purdie in 1905 from the space previously intended for a porch. In 1977 the chapel was adapted as a bookshop.

The adjacent **Altar of Our Lady of Lourdes** was erected in 1887, the architect being Purdie, the sculptor Anstey. The Carrara marble statue was supplied by Thomas Pate of Leghorn. The Assumption window is by Evie Hone.

In the west gallery we note the organ of 1914 by Bishop, restored in 1980. Beneath the gallery the statue of St John Nepomucene was designed by Romaine Walker and sculpted by Charles Whiffen, 1905. The St Antony statue is Italian work in Carrara marble. The west window of 1953 by Evie Hone depicts the Instruments of Our Lord's Passion.

The land to the St Ignatius side eventually becoming available, a comprehensive scheme of an aisle with chapels, and confessionals ingeniously contrived between them, was designed by W.H. Romaine Walker and carried out between 1898 and 1903. Aisle and chapels are vaulted, their ribs of white Corsham stone, the infilling of chalk with bands of blue York stone. The apses are faced with richly sculpted nodding ogee arches. The breathtaking grace of this lavish setting for the altars and statues is truly exceptional. The altars and statues were designed by Romaine Walker, the coloured figures sculpted by Charles Whiffen, the paintings executed by Miss Gambardella. The **Calvary Chapel** is octagonal in plan, with a glazed vault. The altar-piece is a copy of Perugino's Crucifixion. The Man of Sorrows (after Durer) and the Mother of Sorrows, of white marble, were sculpted by J.W. Swynnerton.

The **Chapel of the English Martyrs** has a white marble figure of St Thomas More, of 1905, by C. Whiffen. Within the panelled reredos are painted figures of Ss Elphege, Boniface, Edmund, Winifred, John Fisher, Edmund Campion, John Houghton and Blessed Margaret Pole. The altar bears panels of jasper set in ormolu. Within the chapel is a terra cotta relief of Mater Amabilis, after Della Robbia, given in 1925, the bracket by Eric Gill.

The **Chapel of Our Lady and St Stanislaus**: in the reredos is a sculpted panel of the Annunciation. The frontal is a copy by Legros of the recumbent figure of St Stanislaus in Rome's church of S. Andrea al Quirinale.

The **Altar of St Thomas the Apostle** is of white marble, with panels of fleur de pêche set in ormolu. The reredos is a reproduction of a piece by Cima.

The **Chapel of Our Lady of Dolours**: the altar is of lapis lazuli set in pavonazzo, and the statue was copied by Charles Whiffen from a Spanish model. There are paintings of St John after Verrochio, and of St Elizabeth after Mantegna.

In the aisle between the chapels are statues of Ss Teresa, Margaret, Winifred, Thomas of Canterbury and Ignatius, by Romaine Walker and Charles Whiffen, rising to the challenge of variously coloured marbles. St Frances of Rome is the work of J.W. Swynnerton. During work on the aisle, the exit to Mount Street was constructed, necessitating the loss of the original St Ignatius Chapel.

The present **St Ignatius Chapel**, clerestoried and three bays long, was built allowing room for the exit passage. Its altar, however, of 1888 by Purdie, was carefully re-erected. Numerous niches in its tall reredos display scenes from the life of St Ignatius. Also here are: Our

Lady of Montserrat, a reproduction presented in 1991; St Francis Xavier by C. Whiffen; and the Calvary group designed by Romaine Walker and carved by de Wispelaere.

Bibliography
Kelly, p. 174; Rottmann, pp. 68-81; Eastlake, pp. 476-79; Little, p. 92; Bernard Basset, *Farm Street Church* (London: Society of Jesus, 1948); *Weekly Register*, 5 August 1849; *The Tablet*, 3 June 1843, p. 341; 25 May 1844, p. 326; 4 August 1849, p. 483; 5 November 1887, p. 752; 12 December 1903, p. 924; Br, 8 May 1847, p. 213; 2 June 1849, p. 258; 1 December 1860, p. 772; 8 December 1860, p. 791; 11 May 1861, p. 313; 10 July 1886, pp. 54, 69; BN, 30 May 1884, p. 850; 17 November 1899, p. 656; 5 April 1901, p. 226; 18 December 1903, p. 827; *The Architect*, 21 December 1900, p. 393; 5 April 1901, p. 226; CBR.S, 1980, pp. 54-55; CB, Summer 1987, pp. 86-87; Autumn 1990, pp. 36-38; Autumn 1993, p. 4

French Church, Notre Dame de France, Leicester Place WC2

The *Laity's Directory* during the 1790s enumerated no fewer than eight French chapels, wherein many of the 1,500 exiled French clergy living in London were able to say Mass. Only one of these chapels survived after 1814, that in Carton Street, opened in 1799 and patronised by the French royal family. Eventually its importance was compromised by another French chapel in Leicester Square, so that, owing to dwindling attendances and financial difficulties, Carton Street was closed in 1911.

The French colony having become settled in Soho, Cardinal Wiseman

7. *French Church, Notre Dame de France*

requested the Marist Fathers (who were already developing the Whitechapel mission) to make a new foundation. Fr Charles Faure acquired in 1865 the Rotunda, a large circular structure of 1793–94, designed by Robert Mitchell, in which panoramic views were exhibited. The French architect Louis-Auguste Boileau adapted this for the purposes of a church, using cast-iron columns and rib vaults. Having been opened in 1868, the French church was damaged by bombing in 1940 and repaired by the architects Hall, Easton & Robertson in 1941. After the war it was completely rebuilt to the designs of Hector Corfiato, and opened on 16 October 1955. The builders were C.P. Roberts & Co. The loss of Boileau's ingeniously improvised interior remains a matter for regret.

The curved brick front to Leicester Place has a church hall beneath and domestic quarters above. The triple doorway bears a relief in Portland stone of Our Lady of Sorrows by Saupique, and, in the jambs between the doors, panels depicting scenes from the life of Our Lady by pupils of the Beaux Arts de Paris. Beyond this is a stairway and the church proper. Like its illustrious predecessor, it is circular in plan, and has 12 columns with Doric capitals around the perimeter, forming an ambulatory with gallery over. Off the ambulatory are the west entrance, staircases to the gallery, confessionals, the baptistery (south), the Lady Chapel (north) and the sacristy. The interior is top-lit, from a shallow dome glazed in the centre, over a glazed drum.

The eye is readily caught by the tapestry over the high altar, of Our Lady Queen of Creation, designed by Dom Robert Chaunac-Lanzac and executed at Aubusson in 1954. At its foot is a quotation from Prov. 8.30: 'Cum eo eram cuncta componens; ludens coram eo omni tempore' ('I was with him forming all things; ever rejoicing in his presence'). Flanking the chancel are matching groups of organ pipes, concrete grilles and a pair of ambos, their faces incised with the evangelists and four of the prophets.

The paintings of the Lady Chapel walls were executed by Jean Cocteau in a spare, incisive manner in 1960. They depict the Annunciation, Mary at the Foot of the Cross, and the Assumption. The statue of the Virgin is a copy of a fourteenth-century piece by l'Ecole de Boule de Paris. The font was cut from Vosges sandstone by Les Ateliers de l'Oeuvre Notre Dame de Strasbourg; its relief sculptures of the sacraments and episodes from the gospels were worked by E. Stoll of Strasbourg. In the gallery is a statue of the Virgin and Child, a copy of that in Notre Dame des Victoires, Paris. The Cavaille-Coll organ was rebuilt in 1987 by B.C. Shepherd & Son.

Bibliography
Kelly, p. 245; Rottmann, pp. 134-36; Colvin, pp. 553-54; John Yeowell, *The French Royal Chapels in London* (London: Marylebone Society, 1958); SOL 34, pp. 482-86; BN, 6 September 1868, p. 408; *Architect and Building News*, 13 February 1942, pp. 129-32, 138; AR 101 (1947), p. 111

Harow Road, Our Lady of Lourdes and St Vincent de Paul, 337 Harrow Road, W9

The mission grew out of St Vincent's Home for destitute boys. The Reverend Lord Archibald Douglas acquired the site in 1876, and the chapel adjacent to the home was added in 1879, to the design of John George Hall of Hammersmith. It was early Gothic in style, consisting of unaisled nave and apsidal chancel. The chapel was opened to the public in 1893, and designated a parish church in 1912. Following a decision to build anew, the old premises were demolished in 1972–73, and the present complex of church, presbytery and social centre was erected on an extended site. The church foundation stone was laid by Cardinal Heenan on 3 November 1973, and the first Mass was said in the still unfinished church on 13 May 1975. The architect was Clive Broad, the principal contractors Truett & Steel. A connected group of steel-framed white concrete blocks of varying heights present their faces to the road; these include the tall clerestoried church and its entrance, marked with a series of prominent crosses that proclaim its ecclesiastical character.

Inside, the church is of square plan, beneath a high ceiling with high lighting; three sides of the square extending under low ceilings, and the fourth side containing the sanctuary. The sanctuary is undefined architecturally, apart from being raised in height. There is seating accommodation for about 500 worshippers.

Behind the altar and tabernacle plinth of pavonazzo marble is the abstract reredos by Robyn Denny, in red, purple, green and blue, denoting the unity of cross and altar. The crucifix alongside is from the old church, as are the Stations of the Cross and the statue of St Vincent. The Madonna and Child, in Clipsham stone, and the entrance figure of the Risen Christ in aluminium resin are by Michael Clark.

Particularly admirable is the overall plan of the church with its own ancillary spaces, interconnecting with the presbytery and social rooms. Among these is the parish hall, which may be opened as a westerly extension to the church on major occasions by means of folding screens. Between the two, however, is a neutral space which may be opened to either as a temporary extension.

Bibliography
Kelly, p. 204; Kirk, pp. 67-69; Rottmann, pp. 91-92; Fr G.A. Strain, *Our Lady of Lourdes and St Vincent de Paul* (consecration booklet, 1976); *The Tablet*, 6 January 1883, p. 33; CBR.S, 1972, pp. 240-41; 1974, pp. 188-89

Maiden Lane, Corpus Christi, WC2E

The mission grew out of a school chapel which the Oratorians had founded in Charles Street, Drury Lane. When Canon Keens was placed in charge of the mission, he built this church, opened on 21 October 1874. The cost was £8,000,

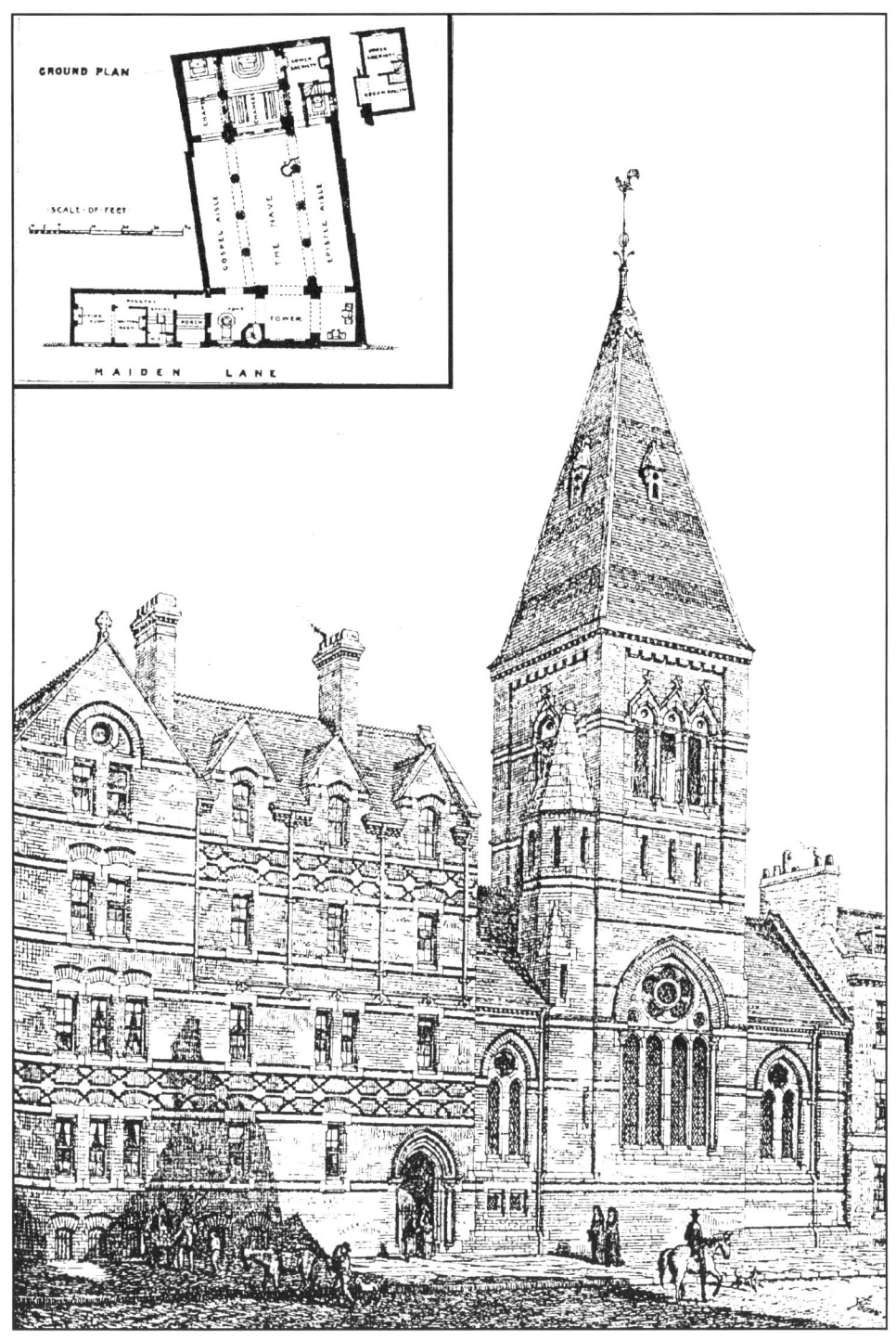

8. *Maiden Lane, Corpus Christi*

F.H. Pownall was the architect, and Messrs Sharpington & Cole of Westminster Bridge Road were the builders.

Pownall laboured here under the difficulty of a restricted site, demonstrated by his L-shaped plan of church and presbytery. The (ritual) west front, of stock brick relieved with bands and interlacings of Staffordshire brick, had to be wrenched away from the succeeding bays. The tower, with its pyramidal roof, nevertheless makes its impact as a symbolic landmark, placed squarely in the centre. To its flanking bays Pownall gave transverse gables, with the overall effect of a western transept.

Owing to local opposition over the question of height, Pownall had to sink the floor of his church some three feet below pavement level. Skirted by buildings on both sides, the interior windows are limited to east, west and clerestory of coupled lancets. Despite these planning difficulties, Pownall produced a cosy Early English interior of baptistery, nave and aisles with alternate circular and octagonal piers, chancel and two chapels. The high altar of Caen stone and marble was sculpted by Thomas Earp. Above it the plate-traceried east window of 1876 depicting Ss Thomas Aquinas, Bonaventure, Catherine of Siena and Juliana of Montcornillion was designed by Percy Fitzgerald in memory of his wife.

To its north, arcaded walls house the Lady altar, whose sculpted frontal presents angels adoring the Blessed Sacrament, and Regina Coeli window. The altar of the corresponding south chapel is in the manner of Thomas Earp; its Sacred Heart statue (and another in the porch) by Mayer.

The Stations of the Cross—freestanding relief carvings—are in memory of Fr J.M. Kearney +1934. The original pulpit and font are of Caen stone. In the nave is a good carved statue of St Genesius, patron saint of actors, and a large St Patrick, installed in 1910. On the west wall are eight casts of the life of Our Lord by Santanella and nearby is a *pietà* of 1869 by Sanson. Above all, however, it is the compact interior that constitutes Pownall's triumph over extraordinary planning difficulties.

Bibliography
Kelly, p. 266; Rottmann, pp. 136-38; Harting, p. 180; P. Fitzgerald, *Corpus Christi Church in Maiden Lane* (1905); BN, 25 April 1873, p. 495; 23 October 1874, p. 488; *The Tablet*, 24 October 1874, p. 534; 26 March 1910, p. 515; *The Universe*, 21 June 1968, p. 1; *Westminster Record*, 18 December 1987, pp. 2-3

Marylebone, Our Lady of the Rosary, Old Marylebone Road, NW1

A school chapel was founded here as an offshoot of the mission of Spanish Place. First, a Spanish nobleman, the Count de Torre Diaz, financed the venture from 1848 by paying for the hire of a hall in Cato Street, in which Fr Joseph Hodgson said Mass on Sundays. Eventually the count and others bought land on which the school chapel was built to Gilbert Blount's design. When opened in 1855, this consisted of a chapel on the ground floor with two storeys of schoolrooms

II. CITY OF WESTMINSTER

above. This building was pulled down after the present church was opened, and the Rosary Hall was erected on its site.

The present church was designed by the architect H.S. Goodhart-Rendel, and, after his death in 1959, it was erected by F.G. Broadbent & Partners, who followed his intentions. The foundation stone was laid on 23 September 1961, and the church was opened on 7 June 1964. The historic style is vaguely Romanesque, executed in modern materials—load-bearing brick walls vaulted in concrete, externally covered with grey-brown Buckinghamshire bricks. The striking front to the road features a broad tower with central doorway, two tall buttresses, a large window above the entrance and lucarnes in the saddleback roof. To left and right are transverse arms. Spare Clipsham stone dressings adorn the lintel and the window surround; and red bricks form a diaper pattern.

9. *Marylebone, Our Lady of the Rosary*

Within the tower a vestibule with oak screen and gallery above leads to the long five-bay nave. This is punctuated by large internal buttresses, pierced to form passage aisles. The buttresses then rise to become transverse roof vaults, their upper reaches pierced by triple round-headed openings. The windows, set high to combat traffic noise, are round-headed in the clerestory, after the manner of the Romanesque church of St Philibert, Tournus.

In the (ritual) north aisle are four built-in confessionals and the baptistery, with wrought-iron rails and a circular font on a base of keeled shafts. In the south aisle are the marble altars of the English Martyrs and St Joseph, with abstract stained glass and statues carved by David Wheeler. Travelling east, the aisle broadens and carries a gallery of two bays. In the nave are the polygonal pulpit, in subdued shades of grey marble, and the Stations of the Cross, rectangular casts executed by the Sisters of St Michael's Convent, Ham Common. East of the nave and aisles is the broad crossing, with non-projecting transepts.

French Romanesque may characterise the nave, but the square-ended chancel with its lancet lights is emphatically English Gothic. Between the series of extremely narrow windows around three sides there is painted geometrical decoration. Above this, the bricks are again laid in a diaper pattern; the tester is based upon a sketch made by Goodhart-Rendel. The principal decoration here is the series of tiled pictures depicting the Mysteries of the Rosary, executed by T. Ledger. Below, the walls are patterned with glazed tiles bearing Marian symbolism. The altar, floor and communion rails are done in marble of various subdued colours.

The gates and the screens to the chapels are of wrought iron. The Lady

Chapel has an altar of varied grey and white marbles, and a cast statue. The Altar of the Sacred Heart consists of varied shades of red and white marbles; its carved statue is the work of David Wheeler.

Bibliography
Kelly, pp. 273-74; Rottmann, pp. 222-24; *The Table*t, 14 July 1885, p. 438; 2 July 1870, pp. 17-18; 23 March 1889, p. 471; 4 November 1899, p. 751; CBR.S, 1958, pp. 57-59; 1962, p. 62; 1965, pp. 38-43; *Building*, 4 March 1966, pp. 113-17

Ogle Street, St Charles Borromeo, W1

The mission began in 1861 when Cardinal Wiseman sent Fr Cornelius Keens to open a chapel of ease to St Patrick's, Soho Square, in a schoolroom in Little Albany Street. This soon became independent of St Patrick's when a school chapel was opened in Howland Mews. With the acquisition of a site in Litle Howland Street (now Ogle Street) a start was made on building the church.

The foundation stone was blessed on 22 August 1862 and the church formally opened on 20 May 1863. The architect was S.J. Nicholl in partnership with T.J. Willson; the builders Messrs Patman & Fotheringham, and the overall cost approximately £4,000. The eventual donors of the freehold were Linda and Arthur Meschini (1921).

Crowded by surrounding buildings, the (ritual) south side faces the street, and the church lacks north and east windows altogether. Stone-built, of Kentish rag, one notes the steeply pitched roofs of nave, transept and lean-to aisle. There is a squat south-west tower, and entrances to the west and south. The transept and west windows consist of lancets surmounted by plate tracery.

Inside, Nicholl reworked the regular Catholic miracle of a religious atmosphere evoked by familiar historical forms. Beyond the small west vestibule with shallow gallery over, one's attention is immediately arrested by the generous width of the nave and chancel (26 feet) beneath a continuous timber barrel roof and uninterrupted by a chancel arch. These are flanked by a wide north and a narrow south aisle, with their corresponding east chapels. Stylistically, the church looks vaguely Early English Gothic; but the plate tracery of the clerestory, the cylindrical ringed piers of the arcades, the square abaci and the bold, simple ornament of the capitals disclose Nicholl's acknowledgement of the wider current interest in Gallic forms.

The glory of the church is the high altar, tabernacle and reredos, of 1870–73 by J.F. Bentley. The reredos is 30 feet high in the centre, its lower wings tiled in two tiers. The altar is principally of Derbyshire marble, its alabaster frontal bearing two quatrefoils painted with incidents in the life of St Charles. The tabernacle, also alabaster, is flanked by slabs of light green marble, and the monstrance throne above it by traceried arcading, with two figures of angels at the extremities. Above the altar are two tiers of panels with full-length figures painted on slate by N. Westlake. In the upper tier appear St Charles, St Mary Magdalen, the Crucifixion, St John and St Francis; in the lower St Edward, St

Peter, the Madonna and Child, St Joseph and St Augustine.

The chancel stalls designed by Bentley and carved by J.E. Knox have disappeared, but the marble communion rails designed by Bentley and executed by J. McCarthy are now sited at the side of the chancel. These arrangements were superseded by the introduction in 1980 of an unusually large altar of Russian teak at the east end of the nave, designed and constructed by Michael Anderson. The nave then became an extended sanctuary with inward-facing seating. In front of this was added in 1984 a font for baptism by immersion. Twelve feet wide, the font is octagonal in shape, with a sunken panel running north–south, and two flights of steps running east–west. The principal facing is of white marble. In the four spandrels at ground level are mosaic symbols of the evangelists derived from St Mark's, Venice; at the crossing below is a square of black marble with an incised gold cross. When not in use, the font may be covered with brass-faced timber panels. The design by Michael Anderson is an orthodox derivation from Early Christian churches. The congregation provided the labour, and the cost was £5,500.

The altar of the vaulted north-east chapel was given by Mrs Grace and T.H. Galton in 1863. Its tall reredos was added in 1902 by A.B. Wall of Cheltenham from designs by S.J. Nicholl. In five canopied niches are four angels holding the Instruments of the Passion, and in the centre a figure of Christ by T. Phyffers. The reredos of the much smaller south-east Lady Chapel consists of Our Lady of Perpetual Help within a niche fronted by slender marble columns; to the left a large Gothic pedestal for the Lady Statue and to the right a smaller one for St John the Baptist. Its alabaster frontal with a vesica containing fleurs de lis was installed in 1879 to Bentley's design.

Also in the south aisle are St Jude, St Charles, and four windows to St Thomas of Canterbury and St Cecilia (1898), St Margaret and St Patrick. In the north aisle are a canopied statue of St Joseph, the Crucifix, c. 1980, by Vanpoulle and St Anthony signed Hillebrand 1896. Here also is a reproduction of Kiko Arguello's The Good Shepherd, and in

10. *Ogle Street, St Charles Borromeo*

the north-west day chapel a reproduction of his Christ and the Lamb. In a basement room is an original mural of The Annunciation by Maurizia Lees.

Bibliography
Kelly, p. 302; Rottmann, pp. 89-91; de l'Hopital, pp. 586-89; *Br*, 17 May 1862, p. 343; 1 April 1905, p. 356; *BN*, 5 December 1902, p. 791; *The Universe*, 9 July 1976, p. 5; *The Tablet*, 22 February 1862, p. 117; 2 August 1862, p. 486; 16 August 1862, p. 518; 6 September 1862, p. 565; 21 February 1863, p. 119; 23 May 1863, p. 326; 4 June 1864, p. 359; 18 June 1864, p. 390; 18 March 1865, p. 164; 29 November 1902, p. 872; *CB*, Christmas 1985, pp. 4-5; Information of Miss J.O. Maynard

Paddington, Our Lady of Sorrows, Cirencester Street, W2

From about 1902, Fr Joseph Worsley of the Oblates of St Charles said Mass in the school. The foundation stone of this modest church adjacent to the school was blessed by Cardinal Bourne on 17 May 1912. In 1916 the removal of the church roof is reported, and the superimposition of a spacious school hall above it. The church was reopened on 14 April 1916. The architect was E.H. Major (of Tasker, Williams & Major) and the contractor was E.H. Roome.

At Christmas 1966 the sanctuary and Lady Chapel were badly damaged by fire, and during the work of repair, Mass was offered in the upstairs hall. The opportunity was taken to adapt the sanctuary to the new liturgy, and new furnishings were installed throughout. The church was again reopened on 25 December 1967.

From the street, the stark exterior of stock brick is relieved only by the red-brick surrounds of doors and windows. Inside, however, all is neat and welcoming, despite the austerity of the structure. For this rather pedestrian interior has a plain tiled ceiling, with heavy beams resting on plain pilasters, and square piers marking the nave and aisles of four bays, with round-headed mullioned and transomed windows.

To the west is a glazed vestibule and organ gallery; to the east a diminutive chancel with plain brick walls and elliptical ceiling. The chancel has matching timber furnishings, and a tapestry to the east wall with a figure of Christ the King. An antependium before the altar, changed with the seasons of the Church's year, is customary. To the south-east is the Lady Chapel, with a large Madonna and Child carved by Dame Mildred, OSB.

The Stations of the Cross are of timber, framed and carved, with a significant detail of each subject emphasised. There are various repository carved statues of the Sacred Heart, St George and St Patrick, and St Joseph in fibre glass.

Bibliography
Kirk, pp. 66-67; Rottmann, p. 91; Br, 21 April 1916, p. 300; *The Tablet*, 25 May 1912, pp. 815-16; 22 April 1916, p. 542; *The Universe*, 29 December 1967, p. 10

Pimlico, Holy Apostles, Winchester Street, SW1

A former Wesleyan chapel in Claverton Street was acquired and opened as a Catholic church in 1917. This was destroyed in an air raid on 16 April 1941

II. CITY OF WESTMINSTER

11. Pimlico, Holy Apostles

and for the next 16 years Mass was said in a studio, a basement garage and in a prefabricated building erected on the site of the old church. In 1948 Fr Edmund Hadfield, a scion of the architectural dynasty of that name, purchased the site of the present church for £7,000. Subsequently he employed the family firm of Hadfield, Cawkwell & Davidson to design the complex of church, hall and presbytery. The foundation stone was laid on 22 September 1956 and the first Mass was said therein on 9 November 1957. Approached from Winchester Street, the unpretentious, symmetrical exterior built of Stamford brick with its (ritual) north-west campanile belies the sheer warmth of the interior. Post-war but pre-Vatican II, the planning is traditional, with nave and aisles of six bays of reinforced concrete arches followed by three bays of chancel and chapels within the same uninterrupted system. The ceiling is of cedar wood, the clerestory and aisle windows rectangular, plus large windows flanking the sanctuary. To the west are the porch, baptistery and stairs to the hall below. Off the north aisle lie the sacristy, confessionals and the altar of St Pius XI.

At the east end are the high altar, the Chapel of St Joseph and the Lady Chapel. All four altars, the communion rails, the tabernacle plinth and the font are of Ancaster stone and Westmorland stone, incised and gilded with images of sacred symbolism, including the 12 apostles along the front of the communion rails. The Stations of the Cross were executed by Philip Lindsey Clark; the crucifix of gilded fibre glass by Charles Blakeman; and the terra cotta figures of Our Lady, St Joseph, St Pius XI and St Teresa by May Blakeman.

Beneath the church is a large well-designed hall, with a stage and galleries around three sides. Its circular, reinforced concrete columns support the portal frames of the church above. At right angles stands the presbytery, with a lower ground floor containing rooms ancillary to the church and hall. Within the angle is a large paved courtyard with a well-tended rose garden, approached by a ramp from Cumberland Street.

Bibliography
Rottmann, p. 14; *The Tablet*, 30 June 1917, p. 831; CBR.S, 1957, p. 84; 1958, pp. 62-64; Rev. Alastair Russell, *Holy Apostles Church Pimlico 1957–1987* (Pimlico; Holy Apostles Parish, 1987)

Queensway, Our Lady Queen of Heaven, Queensway, W2

This church was built in 1868 as the United Methodist Free Church, on the site of a previous chapel of 1828. It was sold in 1909 to the West London Ethical Society, and from about 1946 was occupied by the West London Unitarian Fellowship. In March 1954, the building was bought at auction for £22,000 by Fr Horace Tennant, Superior of St Mary of the Angels, Bayswater, and was officially opened as a Catholic church by Cardinal Griffin on 12 September 1954.

The exterior, of white brick with Caen stone dressings, is Gothic in the Nonconformist manner: that is, the parts arranged with little reference to historic precedent. It is of four storeys, with pointed arches above the doors and windows. Squat matching towers project at either end. On the principal floor a bank of five arched openings with columns and foliage capitals support cusped arches. Above, a four-light window with quatrefoil tracery ascends into the gable, which is flanked by a parapet pierced with quatrefoils.

Inside, the plan is a semi-circle, turned 90 degrees: that is, the flat wall containing the chancel recedes to the right of the entrance. Seating of course runs around the semi-circular chancel, and round two galleries, which are supported by slender cast-iron columns bearing Corinthian capitals. Owing to the irregular relation of the plan to the site, the pointed windows occur in random groups, some of them subdivided, with quatrefoil tracery.

The altar, rails and reredos are all of timber, the reredos with fluted pilasters. Above the altar is a copy of the Rubens triptych in Antwerp Cathedral of the Descent from the Cross, with the Visitation and the Presentation, made in 1879 by Van den Wildenburgh. To the right of the chancel is a bronze of the Risen Christ, of 1981 by Arthur Fleischmann.

Bibliography
The Universe, 8 May 1981, p. 27; Information of Rev. Nicholas Lambert and Rev. Philip Carpenter

St John's Wood, Our Lady, Lisson Grove, NW8

The offer of two wealthy maiden ladies, the Misses Louise and Jessie Gallini, to finance a mission in the neighbourhood of Hanover Square having been declined by Bishop Bramston, the ladies set their hearts upon building a church in St John's Wood, which was sufficiently distant from the chapel at Spanish Place not to diminish attendances there. The contract drawings were dated October 1832, the church was described in the press in 1835, and was opened on 9 February 1836, there having been delays over the question of who should staff it. The ladies favoured the Jesuits, who desired a foothold in London; but Bishop Bramston opposed this, and secular priests were appointed. Within a few years, however, the Jesuits gained a London establishment when they built Farm Street Church.

The Misses Gallini employed J.J.

II. CITY OF WESTMINSTER

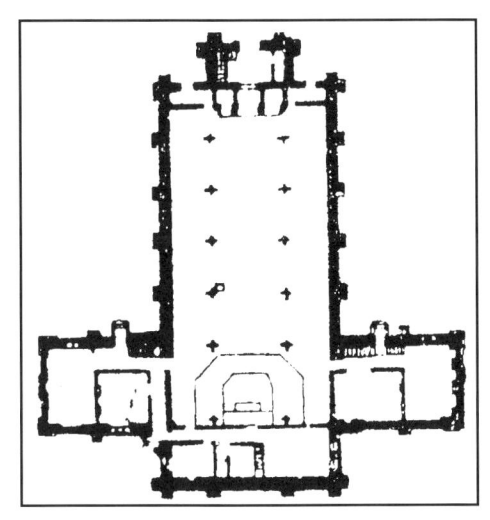

12. St John's Wood, Our Lady, the original plan

Scoles, the leading Catholic architect before Pugin gained prominence. The classical bent of Scoles's training had left him ill-prepared for the Gothic work suddenly demanded, and he had found himself designing Commissioners churches for the Anglicans. In the Commissioners tradition, therefore, Our Lady's Church is symmetrical, spaciously built for a large congregation, and simply detailed in the Early English style, of brick with Bath stone dressings. Decorations are recorded in 1846, and a restoration following a fire in 1884.

The symmetrical plan of nave, aisles and chancel was heavily compromised, however, by Scoles's pseudo-transepts, which were actually modelled as two houses, for the incumbent priest and the Gallini sisters. Following the erection of a presbytery, the houses were transformed into chapels in 1937. The sanctuary was extended and two east chapels were added in 1956, the architects for both these works being Nicholas & Dixon-Spain. The whole church was restored and the sanctuary re-ordered in 1971–75 by David Williams. All the sculpture of this time is by Michael Lindsey Clark.

Beyond the west entrance, which is the width of the nave, the five bays of nave and aisles exhibit single lancet windows and moulded piers with slender shafts, surmounted by quadripartite vaults (albeit of lath and plaster) with rich bosses at the intersections. The chancel was brought west in 1971–75, so that the altar is at the crossing. The new permanent altar has a relief plaque on its front of the loaves and fishes, behind it the tabernacle, both of Ancaster stone. High up on the east wall is Christ in Glory by M.L. Clark, and in the chancel aisles are casts of the Madonna and Child, and St Joseph. There are four stained-glass windows of the 1920s. The north transept Chapel of the English Martyrs has a panelled timber ceiling, plain white walls and a stained-glass window to the Ratcliffe family. The altar is of 1975, its reredos consisting of the crucified Christ and eight panels of martyrs, by M.L. Clark. The south transept contains the organ, 1972 by J.W. Walker, with pipes decoratively exposed

13. St John's Wood, Our Lady

to the crossing. On the south wall is a large stylised painting of the Baptism of Christ, of 1982 by Marek Zulaski.

In the nave is a cast of St Antony, and the Stations of the Cross, rectangular relief sculptures of Ancaster stone. The floor throughout is of African hardwood.

Bibliography
Kelly, p. 343; Rottmann, pp. 254-59; Harting, pp. 266-70; Eastlake, pp. 376-77; Little, pp. 76-77; *Guide*, pp. 243-44; *The Mirror*, 19 December 1835, pp. 417-18; *Br*, 15 November 1884, p. 676; *The Architect*, 27 October 1899, p. 267; *Catholic Gazette*, November 1975, pp. 21-24; *The Standard*, 19 April 1983, p. 12; H. Foley, Manuscript Notes, vol. 3, folios 88-93 in *Archives of the English Province SJ*

Soho Square, St Patrick, Soho Square, W1

Just as the London Road chapel sprang in the 1790s from the need to provide for the growing numbers of Catholic Irish in Southwark, so the mission of St Patrick in Soho was founded to provide a church for these people north of the river. The Irish then formed a far less important element in London Catholicity than they were to do subsequent to the great immigration; but they already numbered several thousands, belonging to the poorest classes living in the back streets and slums in the neighbourhoods of St Giles and Seven Dials.

The prime mover in the establishment of St Patrick's Church was Fr Arthur O'Leary, a priest of the Franciscan order. A committee of subscribers was formed, which in 1791 purchased the lease of the former Assembly Rooms behind Carlisle House in Soho Square. Madame Teresa Cornelys, known as 'The Circe of Soho Square', had taken Carlisle House as a place of entertainment, and in 1761 had erected a new building in the garden, running along Sutton Street behind the house, in which concerts and operatic performances took place. From Madame Cornelys the property passed into the hands of Mr Hoffman, from whom the committee leased it. No change was made to the outside, which was singularly unecclesiastical in appearance, apart from the addition of four porches. Within, however, there were structural alterations to fit the place for ecclesiastical use. It had originally two large rooms, one over the other, which were adapted by breaking through the floor in the middle, making them into one large room. Round three sides the floor was retained, forming galleries. The chapel was opened by Bishop Douglass on 29 September 1792. By 1815 the committee could no longer finance the chapel, and Bishop Poynter undertook responsibility for its financial affairs and the appointment of a chaplain.

After a century, the chapel was ripe for rebuilding, and John Kelly (in partnership with Edward Birchall) was appointed architect. A Yorkshireman by birth, Kelly had served as assistant to G.E. Street for three years. He had a substantial body of work to his credit, including churches at Acton, Chiswick, Kingston and Teddington, when he won this commission in a limited competition. The foundation stone was laid on 18 June 1891, and the church was opened on 17 March 1893, during the rectorship of Canon Langton Vere. The builder was W.H. Gaze of Kingston-on-Thames.

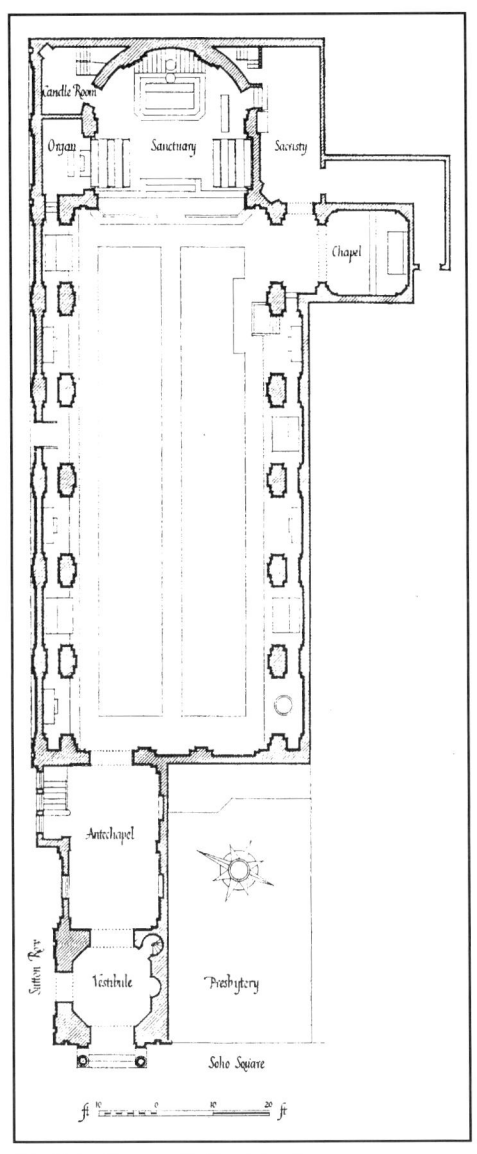

14. *Soho Square, St Patrick, plan*

The finished church is distinguished for its skilful planning as well as for its interior beauty. The trustees had acquired in 1866 the two houses before it facing Soho Square. One of these was demolished to provide additional space for the church of 1893, and the other is now used as the presbytery. As a result of this move, Kelly was presented with a roughly L-shaped space on which to plan his church. Having placed his main entrance beneath the campanile facing Soho Square, he utilised the short western arm as an extended vestibule and ante-chapel.

But before entering, one notes the Italian Renaissance style, realised in red brick with a front of Portland stone. The campanile in five arcaded stages houses the portico with its Corinthian columns and pilasters, its pediment decorated with the Papal arms and above it a statue of St Patrick by Boulton. The north side along Sutton Street is punctuated by blank arcades with Doric pilasters; above the nave are the clerestory and a higher arcaded storey.

Within the octagonal vestibule is a holy water stoup incorporated with a relief *pietà* of Carrara marble, and a cast-iron lamp in memory of J.S.W. Pecorin +1929. Beyond, in the ante-chapel, is the altar of St Anthony with a statue, panels painted by G. Pownall and a frontal of various marbles. Here also is the bas-relief memorial to Fr O'Leary +1802, brought from the old church.

The main interior that follows is an admirable demonstration of Kelly's skill in planning within a restricted site. An apparently aisleless clerestoried nave with a gallery to the west and an apsidal chancel to the east is divided into six bays by stepped Corinthian pilasters and round-headed arches. Between the pilasters are various shallow altars, shrines, confessionals and baptistery. These arrangements are connected with each other by narrow passages. A tantalising ambiguity arises, therefore, whether to regard the arrangements as chapels, or as the bays of extremely narrow aisles. Surrounding the altar, moreover, Kelly's apsidal sanctuary is flanked by space-saving arrangements for the organ, a candle room and a sacristy, all of which interlock in plan as effectively as the pieces of a jigsaw puzzle.

15. *Soho Square, St Patrick, St John Bosco by Anton Dapre*

Rottmann states that most of the altars were re-erected from those in the old church. Scarcely anything is documented, however, with firm dates and artists. Considered clockwise starting from the entrance, the bays contain the following:

1. A *pietà*, by Phyffers, which cost £40; stained glass also depicting St Margaret and St Patrick, 1923.
2. The shrine of St Teresa of Lisieux; above it a painting of Simeon and the infant Jesus.
3. A fine timber confessional of Continental style, with a painting of Joseph's dream.
4. The Altar of the Mother of God, all of timber, handsome Continental work with a handsome statue.
5. Another confessional, similar to (3), but with a differing pediment; above, a painting of the Deposition.
6. The Altar of St John Bosco, of white marble panelled in grey, with a substantial group of St John and pupils, carved by Anton Dapre.
7. In the apse, the former altar is now brought forward, its reredos remaining in situ of white marble with light brown panelling. There are fine altar rails of the same material, with pierced panels. There is a large painting of the Crucifixion, and another of St Mary of Egypt.

The floor and dado are of various marbles. Flanking the chancel are carved statues of the Sacred Heart and St Joseph signed DVP. The organ is by Bishop.

8. To the south is a chapel, domed and larger than the others. with a copy of Murillo's Mater Dolorosa, the Baptism of Christ and St Jerome Emiliani. Its altar was removed in the 1970s.

9. The Altar of the Sacred Heart, of white marble, the reredos with Egyptian capitals and a triangular pediment. The Statue of the Sacred Heart was erected in the old chapel in 1873.
10. The Altar of St Joseph has a painting of the saint with the child Jesus framed by a reredos with red marble columns and Egyptian capitals.
11. In the Altar of Martha, and Mary, the columns and alabaster frontal sculpted with an elaborate diaper design came from the high altar of the old church. The painting is of Our Lord with Martha and Mary.
12. The Altar of Our Lady of Lourdes (called 'modern' in 1926 by Rottmann) with its statue and reredos is all of pure Carrara marble.
13. The baptistery was newly opened in 1930. It contains the Altar of St John the Baptist, of white marble, an octagonal stone font, and a window signed AJS 1921. Nearby is a portrait of St Maximilian Kolbe.

The nave has a barrel vault of timber, deeply coffered and moulded. In the nave is the pulpit, with a marble base and mahogany tester; cast relief Stations of the Cross; and two life-sized angels of Carrara marble holding holy water stoups, of 1875 by Mayer, brought here from St Mary Moorfields in 1966.

Bibliography
Kelly, pp. 360-61; Rottmann, pp. 57-65; Harting, pp. 163-81; Ward, pp. 116-24; Little, p. 159; *The Tablet*, 16 October 1875, p. 499; 20 June 1891, pp. 974-75; 25 March 1893, p. 472; 28 June 1930, p. 876; *Br*, 22 April 1893, p. 305; 11 June 1904, p. 641; SOL 34, pp. 79-80

Spanish Place, St James, George Street/Blandford Street, W1

The mission has grown out of the chapel of the Spanish Embassy. A chapel was erected in Manchester Square in 1793–96 to designs of Joseph Bonomi which was enlarged in 1846 by Charles Parker, and demolished in 1880. The site of the present church was purchased in 1880 for £30,000. Canon William Barry favoured John Francis Bentley as architect of the new church, but in deference to Cardinal Manning he held a competition restricted to Catholic architects. Bentley was not alone in shunning the competition, but nine designs altogether were received. The assessor was James Fergusson, and his choice of the design by Goldie, Child & Goldie was sealed with the approval of both Cardinal Manning and Canon Barry.

Building began and the foundation stone was laid on 17 June 1887. The irregular site dictated a church that was initially broad and short. With the prospect, however, of obtaining land to the east and extending eventually in that direction, the chancel was sited at the west, placing the nave in contiguity to the point of least resistance. Thus, when opened on 29 September 1890, the unfinished church was closed with a brick wall to the (ritual) west. The three westernmost bays of the nave with the

Memorial Chapel and the baptistery were completed in 1914–18 by Edward Goldie, a great-grandson of Joseph Bonomi who had designed the Embassy Chapel of 1796.

As is the case with many town churches, the exterior is uncomfortably close to commercial buildings, the presbytery of 1889 rammed against the transept. The church presents to George Street, however, a varied range of storeys built of Portland stone, ascending from the crypt via confessional and aisle windows, gallery and clerestory, with its flying buttresses. This elevation is punctuated by the unfinished tower, the semicircular staircase to the gallery, the porch and the baptistery, the ensemble making a brave show within a crowded setting.

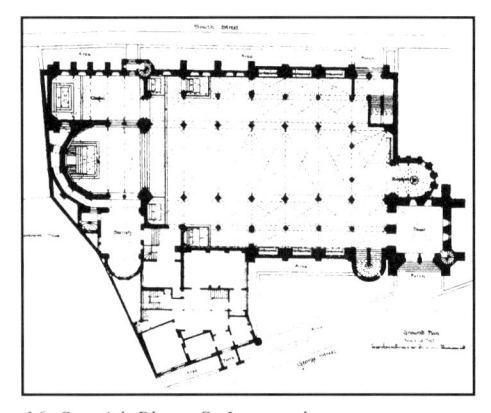

16. *Spanish Place, St James, plan*

Inside, Goldie's statement is immediately clear: namely, a nave flanked by aisles and transepts in the Early English style, with such French Gothic characteristics as the apsidal chancel, the nave piers with attached shafts, quadripartite vaulting throughout and a gallery that extends across the west wall. Goldie's inclusion of double aisles solved the problem of excessive site width. These, together with the wall arcading and the gallery bridges across the transepts, add considerably to the dignity of this handsome, correct interior. Varied materials enhance the effect—the walls of Bath stone, the piers of Hopton Wood, their shafts of Derbyshire marble, the chancel furnishings and the double tier of windows in the apse. Having deferred to Cardinal Manning over the question of architect, Canon Barry saw no reason to refrain from employing J.F. Bentley for the furnishings. There are no less than five altars by Bentley, and other works realised after his death by Thomas Garner. Richest of all is the chancel: its marble and opus-sectile wall-lining designed by Bentley and begun in 1899 displays six panels symbolic of the Eucharist and one of Pentecost. The metal gilt angels above the arcading, the corona and baldacchino are by Garner; the grille to the sacristy by Bentley. The reredos by Garner is of hammered iron, with gilt bronze figures of St James and St Anne. The altar frontal of the Madonna and Child with saints in opus-sectile was by Bentley and John Sears; its marble work executed by Farmer & Brindley. Bentley's communion rails (1892–95) of iron gilt and brass are elaborated with repoussé and pierced designs supporting a frieze inscribed with texts on the Holy Eucharist. The chancel sedilia are by H.S. Goodhart-Rendel. The Lady Chapel has a rich altar of various marbles—Jaune-Lamartine and onyx for the frontal, with Numidian for the super-altar. Within the elaborately carved reredos is set a copy of Murillo's

Immaculate Conception; and the dossal consists of nine traceried panels set with figures from the Old Testament. The altar rails and light fittings also are by Bentley.

Nearby is the small altar of Our Lady of Victories, wholly circumscribed by wrought-iron gilt and brass rails, to Bentley's design. The gradine and super-altar are of cipollino; the frontal and lower reredos of onyx. Within the reredos are five opus sectile panels of the Madonna and Child with angels, painted by Chevallier Taylor. Close to this in the nave is the statue of Our Lady Queen of Heaven, carved locally in 1840, and faced with gold leaf. The backing and canopy are by Bentley, as well as the pedestal of 1894, of Hopton Wood stone inscribed with 'Salve Regina' between moulded buttresses.

Across the nave is the Sacred Heart Altar, its mensa of red marble, its gradine of Languedoc and Hopton Wood stone. Of opus-sectile are the three seraphim in the frontal, and the altar-piece of the Sacred Heart, flanked by the Nativity, the Last Supper, St Peter's Denial and the Doubt of Thomas. Next to this is St Joseph's Altar, of Anglesey marble, and commissioned in 1891. In the frontal is the opus-sectile Flight into Egypt set in a Jura marble surround. The super-altar is of Jaune-Lamartine and the reredos of alabaster, bearing six angels in opus-sectile. On a pedestal within a canopied niche is the life-size statue of St Joseph with the Divine Child, flanked by angels. The marble mosaic pavement and metal rails complete Bentley's design. Before the altar is a memorial brass to Canon Barry +1900, by Garner. Nearby is the pulpit, designed by E. Goldie for Lady Sykes and presented in 1894. It is of alabaster with Purbeck marble shafts, and seated figures of St John and St Paul. The sculptors were Earp and Hobbs; the handrail and gates were by Hart, Son & Peard; the sounding board by J. Marshall; and the dove by T. Garner. Following the completion of the church in 1918, other furnishings were introduced. By Geoffrey Webb are: the large rose window; the baptistery gate, windows and font of Caen stone; the War Memorial Chapel's Stations of the Cross, and three memorial windows. The reredos is of 1925 by J. Arnold Crush.

In the Chapel of the English Martyrs, the reredos is by Geoffrey Webb. Nearby are a statue of St Anne, fifteenth-century

17. *Spanish Place, St James, St Joseph's altar*

German work; a relief of the Virgin, fifteenth-century Florentine work; and the Cardinal Manning memorial window by Bentley. In the gallery is the organ of 1922, designed by Robert L. Hasbury and built by A. Hunter & Sons. The Stations of the Cross—realistic scenes painted on metal against a gold background—were acquired in 1876; the oak frames designed by C.G. Wray and made by G. Leggett. Many such have disappeared during re-orderings of churches, rendering these a remarkable survival of superior work supplied by Mayer of Munich.

Bibliography
Kelly, pp. 366-67; Harting, pp. 132-43; Ward, pp. 98-102; Rottmann, pp. 81-89; de l'Hopital, pp. 544, 561, 565-66, 594-603; Colvin, pp. 125, 620; G.Craven *The Church of St James Spanish Place* (London: Parish of St James,1964); *BN*, 3 July 1885, p. 11; 17 July 1885, pp. 74-75; 31 July 1885, pp. 74-75, 166, 170, 178-79; 7 August 1885, p. 208; 3 October 1890, p. 489, 23 November 1894, p. 737; *Br*, 18 July 1885, pp. 79-80; 1 August 1885, pp. 151-59; 22 May 1886, p. 742; 4 June 1887, p. 847; 11 June 1887, p. 867; 11 October 1890, p. 293; 12 October 1895, p. 258; 5 June 1925, p. 866; *The Tablet*, 7 September 1861, p. 565; 9 November 1861, p. 709; 9 December 1876, p. 755; *The Architect*, 17 July 1885, p. 37; *CBR.N*, 1954, p. 221; *Westminster Record*, 18 April 1986, p. 4

Our Lady of the Assumption and St Gregory, Warwick Street, W1

This church is the descendant of the Bavarian Embassy chapel. The mission was established in 1730 as the chapel of the Portuguese legation in the premises of numbers 23 and 24 Golden Square. The Bavarian Embassy inherited an existing chapel, a small building squeezed in between the backs of the houses that fronted Warwick Street. Count Haslang held the post of Bavarian Ambassador from 1739 until his death. Following the 1745 rebellion, when schools and chapels were everywhere closed for a time, the Bavarian chapel was the only one to remain open. The chapel escaped actual destruction in the Gordon Riots, but a large party of rioters stripped the chapel 'of the various ornaments, books etc., and made a bonfire of them in the street, but did not set fire to the building'.[1] Haslang claimed £1,300 from the Government for damaged linen and vestments, and the chapel was certainly in use again in time for the ambassador's funeral in 1783.

There was a change of ownership when Bishop Talbot purchased the two houses and the chapel in 1788. He assigned the ground behind the houses to the erection of a new place of worship by a committee of lay Catholics while remaining under the control of the bishop, and preserving also nominal links with the Bavarian Embassy. The present church designed by Joseph Bonomi was opened on 12 March 1790, and is of particular interest as the only one to survive on its eighteenth-century site. The elector continued to patronise it until Bavaria became part of the German Empire in 1871, since which time the building has been a diocesan church. Alterations of 1853 included a new altarpiece which incorporated the Assumption by John Edward Carew, and a new ceiling. The west front was partially

---

1. *London Chronicle*, 1–3 June 1780.

remodelled in 1875 by J.F. Bentley, who also added the eastern apse in 1876–77.

With the memory of the Gordon Riots still fresh in Catholic minds, the building committee were at pains not to draw attention to their church and sponsored, therefore, a deliberately unpretentious red brick exterior. There were no ground-floor windows (although two have been interpolated) and the three doors with glazed fanlights (which convey no idea externally that they correspond to nave and aisles) have slits as spyholes beside them, with a view to distinguishing friend from foe. On the upper floor are five round-headed arches, only two of them glazed, and above the three central blank arches is a triangular pediment. The decorative stars and angels were added in 1952 and 1957. The appearance even today is far from being conventionally ecclesiastical, so that the committee may be judged successful in their aim to sponsor a vaguely domestic look.

The interior is almost as restrained as the exterior, the view from east to west particularly conveying an impression of a pre-emancipation Catholic church. It consists of nave, aisles and the apsidal sanctuary of 1875. Ten cast-iron columns with capitals of acanthus leaves support a west gallery that extends most of the way along the north and south aisles. The gallery has eighteenth-century pews and a cast-iron rail. The organ, dating from the 1790s, was last rebuilt in 1960, its case designed by Douglas Purnell and reconstruction by Noel Mander. Above the tall round-headed windows that flank the gallery is a coved, panelled ceiling that may have been altered when it was

18. *Warwick Street, Our Lady of the Assumption, Lady altar*

raised by Bentley in 1875. The apse is divided into three storeys, the lowest dominated by vertical columns of green marble. In the upper storey, pilasters of Sicilian marble punctuate panels wherein are set mosaic figures of Ss Gilbert, Gregory, Joseph, John, Edward and Cecilia. In the semi-dome is a Venetian mosaic of the Coronation of the Virgin with Ss Gabriel and Michael, designed by Bentley and executed in 1910 by George Bridge. The altar of 1914, with its gilt frontal, is now forward, the tabernacle and gradines retained, however. The sanctuary floor is of marble mosaic; the metal rails of fluted columns with medallions at intervals were the gift in 1908 of the Duke of Norfolk, and designed by George Marshall. High in the east wall, above the sacristy door, is

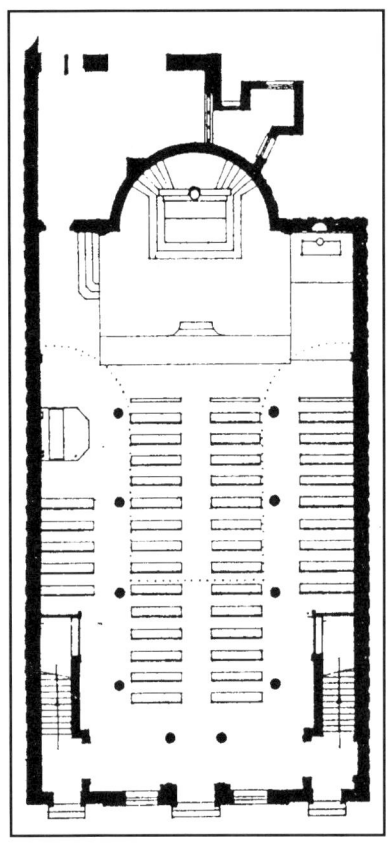

19. Warwick Street, Our Lady of the Assumption, plan

the former altar-piece, Carew's large bas-relief of the Assumption.

South of the sanctuary is the Lady Altar, reconstructed in 1960. Within the Honduras mahogany reredos designed by Douglas Purnell is the life-size statue of the Virgin Immaculate, French work acquired in 1875, flanked by inset panels containing votive offerings. The altar of alabaster bears early mosaic designs by Bentley of the Adoration of the Magi, Our Lady of Lourdes and the Sacred Heart.

In the north aisle is the marble, early nineteenth-century Italian altar that was brought from Foxcote House, Ilmington, Warwickshire in 1958, its panelled reredos designed by Douglas Purnell added in 1966. From the north and south porches staircases ascend to the gallery, with confessionals inserted beneath them. In the south porch is the moulded font, which dates from 1790. Over the west door is a fresco of the Annunciation, and a perspex plaque of the royal arms of Bavaria installed in 1956. The Stations of the Cross, cast tableaux set in oval frames, were acquired in 1956. Also in the nave are statues of St Anthony presented in 1912 by Lady Sykes, and the Sacred Heart and St Joseph, carved in Ulrich, and presented in 1914 by Mrs Claude Watney.

Bibliography
Kelly, p. 417; Rottmann, pp. 65-68; de l'Hopital, pp. 448-52; Harting, pp. 107-13; Ward, pp. 93-98; R.C. Fuller, *Warwick Street Church* (London: Parish of Our Lady, 1956 edn and 1973 edn); J. Britton, *The Original Picture of London* (27th edn, 1823), p. 123; *SOL* 31, pp. 170-72; G. Houghton-Brown, 'The Bavarian Chapel in London', AR, August 1947, p. 67; Br, 1 October 1853, p. 624; *The Tablet*, 15 May 1858, p. 308; 12 October 1918, p. 410

III
Camden

Camden Town, Our Lady of Hal, Arlington Road, NW1

HAL is a small town west of Brussels containing a well-known shrine to Our Lady. This church was founded to serve the Belgians who found refuge in London during the war of 1914–18, and made it their permanent home. The Missionary Fathers of Scheut had a temporary chapel opposite the presbytery from 1921. The present church dates from 1933.

Its (ritual) west front has a tall, impressive brick gable, with tall narrow windows. Below is a triple entrance supported by columns with cushion capitals, and there are three tympana containing sacred symbols in mosaic. On either side are matching domestic bays.

Inside, a low bay with ancillary rooms and a gallery above is followed by a wide nave and an apsed sanctuary. The timber roof consists of transverse pointed arches, with subsidiary rafters between them, containing dormer windows. The tall narrow round-headed aisle windows in varied groups here and on the west front give a hint of Belgian Renaissance work.

The open-plan sanctuary has its altar, ambo, tabernacle plinth and font all matching in Portland stone. To the north is the small, apsed Chapel of Our Lady of

1. *Camden Town, Our Lady of Hal*

Hal. Its carved statue of the crowned Madonna and Child is set within a timber reredos of plain design, with a strong emphasis on perpendicular lines. In the nave is a good set of Stations of the Cross, carved in low relief; and a bronze memorial plaque to Albert I, King of the Belgians +1934, signed Huygelen 1939.

Bibliography
Rottmann, p. 230; *CBR.S*, 1957, p. 297

The Blessed Sacrament, Copenhagen Street, N1

The original church of four bays, opened on 24 June 1916 and the gift of James J. Hicks K.C.S.G., was built to relieve the parishes of Duncan Terrace and Somers Town. The architect was Robert L. Curtis, and the builders E. Lawrence & Sons. Extensions to the church and hall

2. Copenhagen Street, The Blessed Sacrament

below it, which included a new chancel, were effected in 1959 by T.G. Birchall Scott. The façade to Copenhagen Street was of purple brick with red brick arches and dressings. It consisted of a central bay with four banks of triple windows, surmounted by a bell-cote above the gable. This was flanked by two matching round-headed gabled entrances, with five orders of brick moulding.

The interior, in simple Romanesque style, consisted of west baptistery with organ gallery over, flanked by staircases; an unaisled nave of eight bays, and the apsidal sanctuary. Semicircular windows and shallow pilasters marked the bays, beneath the king-post roof. The marble font of 1916, and the high altar of white Pentelicon marble with panels of yellow Siena and Swedish green, and a gold mosaic cross, of 1917, were designed by R.L. Curtis and executed by W. & R. Moore.

At the time of writing, the church was smitten with structural problems that necessitated complete demolition of the (ritual) east end extension and of the presbytery to the right. New planning extensions were in hand by the Solway Brown Partnership.

Bibliography
Rottmann, p. 213; BN, 16 August 1916, p. 163; *The Tablet*, 1 July 1916, p. 13; 24 March 1917, p. 387; *CBR.S*, 1959, pp. 69-70; Information of Mr C. Fanning

Ely Place, St Etheldreda, 14 Ely Place, EC1

St Etheldreda's Church in Ely Place was the first pre-Reformation chapel to be restored to Catholic usage in England. As such, it is as remarkable for its historic associations as for its architecture. It was built about 1300, as the chapel of the London house of the bishops of Ely.

From 1576, a portion of the house and lands was leased to Christopher Hatton, who built Hatton House on part of the land. On Hatton's death, the property passed to his niece, Lady Elizabeth Hatton. In the meantime, the bishop's palace was let between 1620 and 1624 to

III. CAMDEN

the Spanish Ambassador, Gondomar, and Mass was again said in the chapel. When Gondomar left, the chapel was again used for Anglican worship. The Hatton connection ended when Christopher Hatton in 1659 pulled down the house, broke up the grounds, and laid out streets. On 7 June 1659, John Evelyn records his visit:

> To London to take leave of my Brother, and see ye foundations now laying for a long streete and buildings in Hatton Garden, designed for a little towne, lately an ample garden.[1]

In 1772, the Bishop of Ely, Dr Keene, bought a new residence and Ely Place was transferred to the Crown. Soon afterwards, Charles Cole, builder and surveyor, bought the property. He demolished the buildings, leaving only the chapel, and erected the houses in Ely Place. It was Cole's intention that the chapel should serve as the parish church for the occupants of the houses. After having various occupants, including the National Society for the Poor (which erected galleries in the chapel) and the Welsh Episcopalians, the chapel stood empty. When in 1873 the whole of Ely Place was put up for auction in order to settle a dispute between Cole's descendants, the chapel came into the hands of the Catholics.

Meanwhile, the Institute of Charity, commonly known as the Rosminians from the name of the congregation's founder, Fr Antonio Rosmini, had come to this part of London. After vigorously evangelising that part of the Midlands between Leicester and Nottingham, the congregation founded a London mission at Kingsland. At the request of Cardinal Manning, Fr William Lockhart the superior at Kingsland took charge of the missions of Saffron Hill and Baldwin's Gardens. The opportunity of uniting these two missions arose when Fr Lockhart learned in 1873 that the ancient chapel in Ely Place was about to come on the market. Using an agent to preserve his clerical anonymity, Fr Lockhart purchased the chapel for £5,400.

It is in fact two chapels: an upper chapel and a crypt. An extensive restoration was necessary before it could be opened for worship. It was decided to concentrate on the crypt, which could be used while the upper chapel was being restored. Fr Lockhart's architect was Bernard Whelan.

The bases of the supporting posts that upheld the crypt ceiling were replaced by stone. At the same time, the floor was lowered two and a half feet to increase the headroom. An east entrance was formed from Ely Place, and the crypt was opened on 23 June 1876.

3. *Ely Place, St Etheldreda, the upper church*

---

1. E.S. de Beer (ed.), *The Diary of John Evelyn* (Oxford: Clarendon Press, 1955), III, p. 231.

Work then began on the upper chapel. The galleries were removed; the east front had its stucco removed; the north and south windows received tracery copied from the one remaining traceried window; the plaster ceiling was removed and the mediaeval timbers still intact were exposed; coats of plaster were scraped away to expose the shafts that flank the windows; the chancel area was raised above the nave, and an alabaster altar was installed. Exactly three years after the crypt, the upper chapel was proudly opened by Cardinal Manning. There was a restoration in 1935 by Sir Giles Gilbert Scott. Following war damage, the upper chapel was again restored in 1950–52 by J.H. Greenwood. Further work in 1986 by Vernon Gibberd included stone restoration and a review of the lighting.

Entering the upper chapel through the door from the cloister, one passes into the six-bay nave that is divided by a screen one bay from the west. The chancel occupies the easternmost bay. Its moderately sized altar is of plain stone, and the tabernacle is set in the wall immediately below the large east window. Over its five lights is a mass of reticulated tracery, poised at its apex to take off into more complex Decorated shapes. Its glass, made by Edward Nuttgens in 1952, depicts Christ the King surrounded by angels and saints. Flanking the window are statues of Our Lady (cast) and St Etheldreda (carved). The wagon roof has remarkably close-set beams. The eight nave windows all have two traceried lights, with stained glass variously made between 1952 and 1958 by Charles Blakeman, depicting the life of Our Lord on the north side, and Old Testament events on the south, with the arms of pre-Reformation bishops of Ely. Between these windows are crocketed gables, and beneath them standing on corbels eight polystyrene figures of sixteenth-century martyrs with local associations. These were made by May Blakeman in 1962–64.

The oaken screen by J.F. Bentley has five exquisitely traceried bays, with a lateral confessional and staircase to the gallery above. The gallery is cantilevered to the east, with an imitation rib vault complete with bosses. On the frieze are heraldic shields bearing coats of arms. Above it is the organ, neatly divided into two matching sections, of 1897 by Lewis and restored in 1987 by Mander.

The west window by Charles Blakeman was completed in 1964. Its themes are the Redemption, and the English Martyrs. In the antechapel are two good carvings, of the Sacred Heart; and St Peter holding the veil of Veronica, Italian work.

The **crypt** is smaller than the upper chapel, with thicker walls, its windows standing in deep reveals. Six central octagonal stone piers supporting the timber roof effectively divide the space into two naves. Its layout in the 1960s was by Charles Blakeman, who designed most of the furnishings. These include the simple stone altar (placed at an angle) at the west end; the tabernacle and fresco of the Risen Christ (in two arched recesses); the windows, abstract designs with various dominant colours—red, green, brown and blue; and the Stations of the Cross in polystyrene. Also in the crypt is a model of Ely Palace, 1990 by

Joe Pradera; a Madonna and Child signed JAS and AEB; and a statue of St Blaise by La Statue Religieuse of Paris.

Bibliography
Kelly, pp. 214-15; Rottmann, pp. 142-52; de l'Hopital, pp. 645-50; Harting, pp. 114-31; Colvin, p. 229; S.E. Jarvis, *A History of Ely Place* (Camden: Parish of St Etheldreda, 1907); *BN*, 23 June 1876, p. 634; 30 June 1876, p. 686; *The Tablet*, 20 November 1880, p. 660; 3 July 1897, pp. 36-37; CB, Autumn 1988, pp. 57-58; *Westminster Record*, September 1987, p. 4; June 1992, p. 4

Hampstead, St Mary, 4 Holly Place, Holly Walk, NW3

The mission of Hampstead was one of those developed under the influence of French *émigré* priests. As early as 1778 Bishop Challoner noted in a memorandum book: 'Mr Robinson serves Hampstead from Michaelmas for which I am to allow him £20 per annum.'[2] There was a Mass centre at that time in a schoolroom in The Grove, Hampstead Road, belonging to a family called Neal. In 1796 Fr Gerard Robinson moved to the chapel in Marylebone, and the Abbé Jean Jacques Morel arrived in Hampstead where a number of his fellow countrymen had already settled. The mission then was at Oriel House, Church Row. An appeal in the *Laity's Directory* of 1815 stresses the inadequacy of these premises, and the availability of a favourable site on which to build a church. The appeal was successful, and the chapel in Holly Place was opened on 17 August 1816 by Bishop Poynter.

Subsequently, the architect of the west front of 1850 wrote in the *Catholic Handbook* that

> showing signs of a 'falling sickness' Mr Wardell was engaged to prescribe for it, and he added the present front which not only forms a complete buttress and security to the other, but is also of ecclesiastical character... There is a handsome Doric doorway and entablature in the entrance; over which is a niche with a full-size figure, in Caen stone, of the Blessed Virgin, and the whole is finished with a characteristic bell gable.

The figure, six feet high, was executed by Swales and Boulton.

A short vestibule beneath the gallery bears wall tablets to Rev. John Walsh +1859 and Canon Purcell +1900. The nave (said by Rottmann to be a copy of the Abbé Morel's parish church at Verneuil-sur-Avre) is punctuated by three round-headed windows on each side. Its king-post roof was completely renewed as part of extensive restoration work undertaken by the Solway Brown Partnership in 1991. In the nave are the Stations of the Cross of 1953 by G. Masero.

The chancel, side chapels and sacristies were added in 1907 by G.F. Collinson and A.M. Cock. Their decoration by G.L. Simpson of St Martin's Lane from 1907 onwards was still incomplete when Rottmann described the church in 1926. The chancel's entrance arch is flanked by mosaiced octagonal piers bearing Corinthian capitals. Three short bays bear clerestory

---

2. AAW, Z 70.

lights which punctuate the chancel's timber barrel vault; and beneath these windows are six oil paintings of sacred subjects. The walls are panelled with marble revetments and mosaic strips. The altar and the baldacchino of 1935 by Adrian Scott were moved forward when the chancel was re-ordered by Williams and Winkley in 1976. The altar-piece is a painting of the Assumption in the style of Murillo, acquired in 1822. The floor is of Burma teak, supplemented by surplus timber from the restored House of Commons. In front of the chancel is the font, of Sicilian and verde antico marbles. The Blessed Sacrament Chapel to the south is tunnel-vaulted, with a circular top light. Its walls are arcaded by Doric pilasters bearing mosaic patterns. Above its altar is a mosaiced apse for the tabernacle, framed by a reredos of panelled marbles, surrounded in turn by further floral and geometrical mosaic panels. Within the chapel are statues of the Sacred Heart and St Joseph carved by G. Masero; and a carved relief of St Teresa of Lisieux.

The corresponding Lady Chapel to the north is very similar in design, with a tunnel vault bearing two circular lights, and sparingly-applied decoration. In the lunette above the marble altar is a mosaic of the Nativity. Among other artworks, the chapel contains carved figures of Our Lady and St Anthony. Here also is the funeral monument by Wardell of the Abbé Morel +1852, which formerly stood in the entrance. It was removed from there in 1975 to an exterior situation, and brought here in 1991, where it is undergoing careful restoration. Sculpted in Caen stone, this

4. Hampstead, St Mary

Perpendicular-style monument consists of a recumbent figure with a lion and angels. Three quatrefoils along one side contain relief figures.

Its designer, the Gothic-loving Wardell, had found himself unable to Gothicise the west front, but left at least this revived mediaeval table tomb, conscientiously studied in the light of Pugin's influence. Also here is a copy of the National Gallery's triptych by Perugino of the Madonna with Ss Michael and Raphael.

Bibliography
Kelly, pp. 200-201; Rottmann, pp. 244-50; Harting, pp. 263-65; F. Morrall and C. Davies, A *History of St Mary's, Hampstead 1816–1977* (Hampstead: Parish of St Mary, 1977); *Catholic Handbook*, 1857; *Br*, 21 December 1850, p. 610; 24 July 1886, pp. 124, 130-31; *The Tablet*, 17 December 1892, p. 985; 2 September 1911, pp. 391-92; *BN*, 22 November 1907, p. 709; *CBR.S*, 1975, p. 48; *CB*, Spring 1992, p. 60

III. CAMDEN

Haverstock Hill, St Dominic, Southampton Road, NW5

5. *Haverstock Hill, St Dominic, west elevation*

In obedience to Cardinal Wiseman's wish that the religious orders should make missionary foundations in London, the Dominicans purchased three acres of land here in 1862. The priory was built first and its library pressed into service as a temporary public chapel. The foundation stone was laid in August 1863 of a Gothic church designed by Gilbert Blount, but work soon stopped owing to shortage of money. Efforts were made in 1869 to resume building, but when Blount died in 1876, only the ashlar walls of the Lady Chapel and choir had been begun. Charles Alban Buckler was then appointed as Blount's successor. Buckler had good connections with his Dominican patrons, as his three brothers, converts like himself, had all joined the order.

Buckler redesigned the church, but retained Blount's fragment of lower wall at the (ritual) east end. The change from Blount's use of ashlar to Buckler's use of brick may still be observed. We know from the remnant that Blount intended an apsidal chancel and a large south-east Lady Chapel. A note in *The Builder*[7] reveals that it was to have been Geometrical in style, with two west towers, the space between them formed into an open arcaded outer porch.

Buckler's church, opened on 31 May 1883, twenty years after the foundation stone was laid, followed Dominican tradition in planning and elevation. It is one of the largest Catholic churches in London, 200 feet long, 80 feet wide and 100 feet high. In accordance with Dominican custom, the design is as simple as possible, both inside and out. The plan consists of nave and aisles with chapels between the buttresses, apsidal chancel and south-east Lady Chapel. The exterior, of brick with stone dressings, even without a tower makes its own impact by means of the tall narrow nave flanked by aisles, and serried ranks of transverse gables to north and south. Buckler dispensed with towers altogether. His nave and choir are in ten continuous bays, uninterrupted by a chancel arch. A considerable feature is made of Dominican devotion to the 15 mysteries of the rosary, seven chapels to the north and south together with the high altar each being dedicated to one mystery. There are three additional altars in the transeptal south-east Lady Chapel, dedicated to St Dominic, Our Lady and St Joseph.

As Buckler disclosed in a letter to *The Builder*[4] he was at pains to follow Dominican precedents with his design: 'The friars did not despise brick and slate, and some of the most renowned churches of the order in Italy and Belgium are of brick.' He consciously imitated the plans of the Dominican churches at Winchelsea, Antwerp and Louvain, where there is 'no structural chancel, nor a processional way round the apse of the choir, as in cathedral churches and the larger minsters'. He justified his nave roof of timber in imitation of a stone vault by claiming the Dominican church at Ghent as his precedent. The Geometrical west window he derived from the same church, and the 'two-light windows in the apse resemble those of the exquisitely beautiful church of the Dominicans at Louvain'.

The one unpleasing detail of St Dominic's Church is the mean balcony that runs in front of the clerestory. Buckler had designed 'a stone gallery, as at Florence, Valognes, and elsewhere, on corbels, with pierced parapet and coping'. This had been found impracticable on grounds of expense, 'poverty having proved oppressive from the first, and the aim always having been to obtain as much as possible for as little as possible'. Buckler disclaimed responsibility for the substitution of the iron gallery. This was not the first time or the last that poverty was pleaded in prolonging the process of building and in paring down the design of a Catholic church. At St Dominic's, once the church was built, the furnishing and decoration of the 17 side chapels with their altars, was entrusted to private donors, Buckler himself paying for the Chapel of the Annunciation.

Since the Rosary scheme characterises the chapels, it is necessary to comment on these in the correct order,

---

3. *Br*, 19 May 1866, p. 359.
4. *Br*, 7 May 1881, p. 586.

commencing on the left, nearest to the high altar. All are of similar size and layout, with a wrought-iron screen, a two-light window and an altar with a triple-arched reredos beneath a sculpted lunette.

1. **Annunciation**. The donor was C.A. Buckler, the architect of the church. The three panels of the reredos display the Angel Gabriel, the lily flower and the Virgin Mary. Above is the Transfiguration, Buckler's thank-offering for his reception into the church on this feast. Purbeck marble columns support the altar. The window (by J.M. Pearce) also depicts the Annunciation, and includes the donor and his wife. Below it is a cenotaph by Boulton, ornamented with shields bearing the Buckler family arms.

2. **Visitation**. The donors were the Dunn family, whose patron saints appear in the stained glass window. The wrought-iron screen was given by Mr Purselle. In the frontal is the Agnus Dei, and the Visitation appears in the reredos.

3. **Nativity**. The donors, the Lescher family, are commemorated in the window. The infant Jesus, Mary and Joseph are depicted in the triple reredos; and angels bearing shields in the frontal. On the right is a plaque of the Madonna and Child, and a statue of St Pancras, both designed by Aelred Whitacre OP.

4. **Presentation**. The arms of the donor, Countess Tasker +1888 appear in the window. In the reredos is Simeon, with the Child Jesus and his mother. The frontal illustrates Mary's title Rosa Mystica; and in the lunette are figured Ss Catherine, Helen, Anne and the young Blessed Virgin.

5. **Finding in the Temple**. The donor was A.M. Whitham. The subject appears in the reredos in a crowded composition, with a diaper surround here and in the frontal. In the lunette Our Lord crowns St Catherine of Siena. The window depicts Ss Paul, Augustine, Albert and Thomas.

6. **Gethsemane**. The donors of the first sorrowful mystery were the Rosary Confraternity. The altar is supported on columns of Devonshire marble. Above it Our Lord is offered the chalice by an angel, against a background of diaper work. The window is dedicated to the Holland family.

7. **Scourging**. The subject of the chapel's dedication is graphically represented in the reredos, and in the frontal are shields bearing emblems of Our Lord's Passion. The chapel was the gift of Mrs Fortescue, in memory of her husband who gave up much to join the Church. Unlike the other chapels, the window here is filled with glass of grisaille design. Beneath it is a large cenotaph in the style of fourteenth-century examples, with figures of Our Lord, Ss John, Ignatius, Edward and Gertrude. On it is a plaque to Edward Fortescue +1877, by Hardman. The floor tiles bear the family arms. Also in the chapel is the octagonal font, and a figure of St John the Baptist, presented by Edward Currie in 1897.

Crossing to the opposite aisle, one notes on the way the two windows depicting right, St Edward and St Erconwald by Gibbs and Howard; and left, St Hyacinth and St Edmund by J.N. Pearce. Below are the War Memorial 1914–19, lettered by Joseph Cribb; a brass to Fr Austin Rooke OP +1901, by Hardman; and figures of St George and St Patrick.

Continuing on the right, from back to front of the church, the chapel dedications are:

1. **Crowning with Thorns**. The altar is raised on eight columns. In the reredos is Christ seated, by Bilioschi. The gradine bears the Sacred Heart and a trail of thorns. The window of 1885 by J. Beach & Co. commemorates the founder, W.M. Martin-Edmunds. Also in the chapel is a statue of St Anthony by Mayer.

2. **Carrying of the Cross**. In the centre of the reredos is Our Lord, against a diaper background. In the lunette are Abraham and Isaac; and the altar frontal bears trefoils filled with foliage and berries. The window is in memory of Matthew and Susan Liddell of Prudhoe Hall. Between this and the next chapel stands a statue of St Martin of Porres, 1958 by Thomas McGlynn OP.

3. **Crucifixion**. The donors were John and Dorothy Belton. The reredos has our crucified Lord in the centre, with Our Lady, St John and St Mary Magdalen. Diaper work fills the background. In the lunette is the Last Supper; and beneath the altar reposes the figure of the dead Christ. The window bears scenes and symbols of the Passion of Christ. Beneath the window is a tall Lourdes grotto in high relief, with a heavy surround, of 1923 by R.L. Boulton & Sons.

4. **Resurrection**. In the reredos is the Risen Christ against a lively foliage background, flanked by freestanding figures of angels. Beneath the altar are the dismayed guards beside the empty tomb. The window depicts Ss Thomas More, John Houghton and John Southworth. The donors were Lewis Henry Perry and family. Also in the chapel is a small cast of St Paul by W. Theed.

5. **The Ascension** altar has a large group of Our Lady and the apostles all witnessing Christ. The window commemorates the donors, Michael Bowen and family. The screen, with austere detail, is of 1916 by Geoffrey Webb. Between this and the next chapel is the statue of St Peter on a tall pedestal, of 1894 by Peeters of Antwerp.

6. **Pentecost**. Conceptually, this is the most ambitious of the Rosary altars. From the Dove flanked by angels, shafts of fire and light stream downwards onto the faithful gathered in the room in Jerusalem. Within the lunette subdivided into three arches is Christ in Majesty flanked by angels. The window by N.H.J. Westlake memorialises Stephen Perry +1873. A cenotaph with a heavily cusped arch memorialises the Perry and Reddin families. There are brasses to Joseph Perry +1917, and to Emma Perry +1903, signed by Hardman.

7. **Assumption**. In the centre is Our Lady, crowned and attended by angels, against a diaper background. Beneath are the apostles grouped around the empty tomb. The donor was Caroline Leigh. The window was erected to William Leigh +1881, by the Dominicans. Adjacent to the chapel is a statue of St Joan in memory of JHC +1915, by Anthony Foster.

The Crowning of Our Lady is depicted in the five tall windows of the chancel apse, by Hardman. The high altar was designed by C.A. Buckler, with eight mosaic panels showing Dominican saints. Behind is a large altar-piece with a large monstrance throne, worked as 11 stepped arches with crocketed gables. At the sides are pavilions with angelic figures in gabled niches. The altar rails (flanked by statues of the Sacred Heart and St Dominic, 1899 by Boulton) are of carved alabaster and Devonshire Marble. The chancel steps are of St Anne marble. The choir stalls bear carvings of Dominican saints. In the spandrels of the arches are shields bearing the arms of benefactors.

To the left is the altar of St Thomas, with a kneeling figure within a concave frontal, and a seated figure in the reredos, against a facing of patterned foliage shapes: erected in memory of Fr Vincent Monselle OP +1885 and his two Dominican brothers. Behind the altar is the organ by 'Father' Willis. To the right of the high altar is a large transept, three bays wide and two deep, with tall piers bearing eight attached columns and foliage capitals. The transept has three altars:

1. **St Dominic's** altar-piece is a painting of the saint's death, by Philip Westlake. Early English arcading surrounds the altar. In the frontal are St Dominic, a lily and a star encircled by a rosary.

2. **Our Lady of the Rosary** has St Dominic receiving the rosary from Our Lady, sculpted by Boulton. On the altar are mosaic panels of Our Lady, St Pius V and St Antoninus by Salviati of Venice. The tabernacle is by Hardman, and the rose window by Gibbs and Howard. Diapered blank arcading surrounds the altar, which was the gift of Caroline Smith.

3. **St Joseph's** altar is freestanding, and backed by richly diapered blank arcading. The central arch forms a canopy containing a statue of the saint, which rests upon a column of Devonshire marble. Also within the transept is a statue of St Catherine de Ricci.

In the nave is the pulpit, presented by J.W. Randall in 1884. Resting on a cylindrical base with freestanding marble colonettes, it is hexagonal, fronted by open arcades with cusped arches, marble demi-columns and foliage decoration. At the angles are figures of St Dominic, St Antoninus, St Thomas Aquinas and St Vincent Ferrer. The sounding board presented by C.A. Buckler dates from 1895. Finally, the Stations of the Cross: 14 paintings of 1894 by N.H.J. Westlake, the gift of Georgina Black. Realistic and heartfelt, they deserve to be nearer eye level, so that interesting comparisons could be made with those at St Francis, Notting Hill, and St Joseph, Roehampton.

Bibliography
Rottmann, pp. 232-44; Little, pp. 122-23; *Br*, 18 October 1862, p. 754; 15 August 1863, p. 588; 27 May 1865, p. 382; 8 May 1880, p. 588; 12 June 1880, p. 746; *BN*, 10 June 1881, p. 674; 14 December 1894, p. 819; *The Tablet,* 12 August 1865, p. 500; 13 January 1866, p. 21; 3 November 1866, p. 692; 30 October 1869, pp. 697-98; 6 November 1869, p. 729; 11 July 1874, p. 52; 8 August 1874, p. 180; 2 June 1883, pp. 871-73; 23 June 1883, p. 992; 12 March 1887, p. 429; 14 April 1894, p. 592; 2 September 1899, p. 384; 22 May 1915, p. 677

Italian Church, St Peter, Clerkenwell Road, EC1

6. Italian Church, St Peter

The church is in the care of the Pallottine Fathers. Its founding father was Dr Raphael Melia, a priest of the Lincoln's Inn Fields chapel. Perceiving the need as early as 1846 for a church for the Italians gathered in Clerkenwell, he travelled in Italy, Germany and Spain collecting funds with which to build. Wiseman warmly supported the venture, and thought that the church should be extended to other foreigners, under the title of the Church of All Nations. A society of secular priests, the Congregation of the Catholic Apostle-ship founded by Dr Vincent Pallotti, was appointed to take direction of the church. Eventually this dedication was abandoned and the name of St Peter's was adopted, together with the policy of caring mainly for Italian Catholics.

A plot of ground at the top of Hatton Garden was bought in 1852, and a design by Francesco Gualandi of Bologna was published in *The Builder* in 1853. Building was commenced, but not completed, perhaps for want of sufficient funds. Ten years later the scheme was revived successfully with a similar design by John Miller Bryson. The builder was a Mr Fish; the crypt was opened on 25 December 1862 and the church on 16 April 1863. There were decorations in 1885–86 by two Piedmontese artists, Arnaud of Caraglio, and Gauthier of Saluzzo; in 1920 by E.H. Major and Holloway Brothers; and in 1953 by Don Giuseppe de Filippi.

Largely hidden outside by surrounding properties, it is the interior that makes the major impact. Here Bryson

III. CAMDEN 79

drew heavily on such Roman basilicas as S. Crisogono and S. Maria in Trastevere. Larger than average, it has nave and aisles of six bays, broad transepts and apsed chancel and chapels. The Ionic columns of York stone carry a straight entablature. The triforium was designed with two arches to a bay, to give maximum vision and accommoda-tion to the crowds that were expected to throng the High Mass on Sundays. These arches were apparently blocked by 1886, and now bear six paintings of St Peter and St Paul by Gauthier. On the nave ceiling is St Peter with the keys and the cross, and on the front of the arch Pope Pius IX. Also in the nave is the hexagonal pulpit of Sicilian marble raised on a single fluted column.

Beyond the communion rails of varied marbles, punctuated by Corinthian pilasters and worked by Broder, are the chancel and chapels, spatially undivided. The altar of various marbles stands beneath a baldacchino raised upon four Corinthian columns of veined black marble. Within the apse is a large oil painting of the Annunciation, of 1861 by B. Einler of Vienna. Frescoes by Arnaud include the Ascension in the semi-dome, flanked by Isaiah and Jeremiah; and Paradise in the ceiling flanked by angel groups depicting Ave Gratia Plena and Joseph via Maria. The south Chapel of St Joseph has a statue of the saint in a niche above the marble altar, flanked by large mosaic panels of the Holy Family at Nazareth and the Flight into Egypt. The chapel contains an oil painting of the Crucifixion, of 1975 by Cyril Mount. The corresponding chapel dedicated to St Vincent Pallotti is of similar design and contains an oil painting of the Beheading of John the Baptist, and a bronze model of St Peter. Within these two chapels are four large Baroque figures of the Evangelists in terracotta, acquired from the International Exhibition of 1862.

A series of altars and shrines adorn the side walls. Beside the main entrance one marks initially a holy water stoup of Carrara raised on a decorated stem. Then, anti-clockwise

1. The shrine of St Anthony, with a cast statue
2. St Frances, on a marble stand, with a mosaic background
3. A carved statue of St Calogero
4. The Sacred Heart altar, installed in 1893 and restored in 1920, in a shallow recess, with a marble panelled altar, a statue in a niche above it, and walls faced with slabs of Sicilian. The handsome communion rails are delicately punctuated by mini-Corinthian columns.

Past a built-in confessional is the former baptistery, with a mosaic of the Baptism of Christ, and two tablets to Dr Raphael Melia +1876 and Emile Watson Taylor +1879. Then the west gallery with the grand organ constructed by C. Anneessens of Grammont, Belgium, installed in 1884 and restored by J.W. Walker & Sons in 1959 and 1995. Past a *pietà* (in the style of Mayer) the opposite aisle contains

1. A large crucifix
2. The Lady altar in a niche, with a crowned statue of the Madonna and Child. Above the altar are mosaic panels with Ss Catherine and

Francis rendered in opus-sectile
3. A carved figure of St Teresa of 1962 by L.E. Dapre
4. The shrine of St Michael (1977) with a carved figure
5. The shrine of St Lucia with a cast figure

Also around the walls are the Stations of the Cross, cast, in red and gold frames with Renaissance ornament.

The major visible exterior feature is the Italianate loggia in Clerkenwell Road, tactfully added by F.W. Tasker in 1891. It is of brick and York stone, tall and narrow, with three storeys of diminishing height plus a pediment inset with the Papal Arms. A double-arched entrance with doubled Ionic columns and pilasters gives on to a tall two-bayed groin-vaulted portico. Herein are the War Memorial (1914-18) fashioned in marble in 1927 and containing 175 names; and a poignant bronze memorial of 1960 by Mancini to those who perished in 1940 at the sinking of the Arandora Star. Above the entablature is the figure of Christ within a niche that is lively with Baroque detail, flanked by mosaics and lesser statues of St Bede and St George.

Bibliography
Kelly, p. 207; Rottmann, pp. 152-55; Harting, p. 51; Gillow, IV, pp. 561-63; *The Tablet*, 22 January 1848, p. 50; 25 December 1852, p. 819; 5 March 1853, p. 147; 2 August 1862, p. 486; 18 April 1863, p. 245; 28 May 1864, p. 361; Br, 14 May 1853, pp. 312-13; 26 September 1863, pp. 687-89; *British Architect*, 7 July 1893, p. 16; *Westminster Record*, 22 May 1987, pp. 2-3

Kentish Town, Our Lady Help of Christians, Lady Margaret Road, NW5

The Reverend Hardinge Ivers, a convert priest who had been born in Kentish Town and owned property there, opened the first mission in his domestic chapel in October 1846. This was followed in July 1847 by a temporary church in Gospel Terrace dedicated to St Alexis.

The foundation stone was laid in October 1849 of a large church in Fitzroy Place designed by W. Wardell, but this was never completed. Following a dispute over the site, Cardinal Wiseman closed the mission in 1854. A new mission was opened in February 1856 in a temporary chapel in Junction Road, dedicated to Our Lady Help of Christians. Ground for a permanent church was bought in Fortress Road and a design made by E.W. Pugin for a church with schoolrooms beneath. Its foundation stone was laid on 16 August 1858, the basement was pressed into service as a temporary chapel in January 1859, and the church was opened in August 1859. By the 1960s, however, a much larger church was needed. Following a search of the neighbourhood, Fr Bernard Ferry effected an exchange with a Methodist church in Lady Margaret Road. This was originally built in 1864-67 to a design by John Tarring, and included three halls, a flat and a manse. Conversion to Catholic use was carried out by Messrs Burles, Newton & Partners. The present church has been in use since 1970.

Built of Kentish rag, the handsome exterior commands a good corner site at

III. CAMDEN

and bearing Geometrical tracery. The north side has three matching transverse gables, whose upper and lower windows express the internal galleries.

Beyond the west entrance is the broad, spacious interior, five bays long with a narrow, screened east apse. The deep west gallery, extending into the north and south aisles, is supported on slender cast-iron columns which form the aisles, Above the galleries, pointed arches of timber cross the nave beneath the panelled ceiling, and also define the aisles.

To the east of the nave is the raised sanctuary, with plain white stone altar and ambo. In the centre is the Risen Christ, by Vita et Pax, and within the apse is the organ, by Forster & Andrews of Hull, its pipes neatly arranged as three gables. Left and right are the Blessed Sacrament Altar and the font, of matching stone. The south-east window by Carmel Cauchi, to Jim Breheny, is of abstract design, and beside it is Our Lady Help of Christians, carved in wood. In the nave are the Stations of the Cross, attractive bas-relief carvings; the Sacred Heart, and the Madonna and Child.

7. Kentish Town, Our Lady Help of Christians

the junction of Falkland Road and Lady Margaret Road. The west front expresses the interior nave and aisles, with its prominent north-west tower and octagonal spire with three tiers of dormers, and its gabled south bay. The buttressed front has a central entrance consisting of double doors with attached colonettes beneath an arch enfolded in turn within a tall sculpted gable. Above it the west window is of seven lights, transomed,

Bibliography
Kelly, p. 234; Rottmann, pp. 230-32; *The Tablet*, 10 July 1847, p. 439; 27 November 1847, p. 757; 6 October 1849, p. 628; 16 February 1856, p. 101; 27 February 1858, p. 131; 3 July 1858, p. 420; 28 August 1858, p. 548; 15 January 1859, p. 36; 20 August 1859, p. 533; 27 August 1859, p. 547; 25 November 1876, p. 691; 21 October 1916, p. 548; *Br*, 6 October 1849, p. 478; *BN*, 17 January 1868, p. 53; *CAR*, 1850, pp. 115-16; *The Universe*, 22 August 1969, p. 2; 19 December 1969, p. 3; *CBR.S*, 1971, pp. 325-28

Kilburn, Sacred Heart of Jesus, Quex Road, NW6

In 1864, Cardinal Wiseman requested the Oblates of Mary Immaculate to make a foundation in London. Their mission was opened at number 1, Greville Road on 2 February 1865, and a temporary church was soon established nearby. Fr Robert Cooke purchased five acres of land in 1866 on which to build a church and priory by the architect Edward Pugin. The priory was ready in that year, and its library then served as a public chapel. Edward Pugin died in 1875, and the Decorated church he had designed was erected by his brothers, Peter Paul and Cuthbert, in partnership with G.C. Ashlin. The builders were Merrett & Ashley of London Wall.

The foundation stone was laid on 3 June 1878, and the partially complete church was opened for use on 8 May 1879. It then consisted of four bays of nave and aisles.

Building was completed in 1898–99 under the brothers Pugin; the contractors being S. & H. Roberts of Islington. The church had then six bays of nave and aisles, apsidal chancel, side chapels and three new confessionals projecting from the north wall.

To accommodate the large congregation, the west narthex was added in 1959, to designs of the architects Gordon & Gordon. The considerable overflow persisting, the south aisle was widened in 1963 almost to the width of the nave, a broad transept was constructed on the site of the chancel and chapels, and the sanctuary was rebuilt further east. The

8. *Kilburn, Sacred Heart of Jesus*

architects of this work were F.G. Broadbent & Partners. The large Perpendicular window in the south transept is clearly a thoughtful inclusion in a later phase of Gothic by the architect in charge, Mr John Kirby.

Notwithstanding its chequered building history, the exterior of yellow brick with Bath stone dressing presents a harmonious view from the corner of Quex Road and Mazenod Avenue. The tall gabled nave dominates, with its large traceried window; and gathered around it like offspring are the narthex, the hefty south aisle with its own porch, and the transept in the distance.

The narthex is large, undecorated and top-lit, with a pre-cast marble tiled floor, and reinforced concrete ceiling. The openings of the west wall were considerably enlarged, to provide an unobstructed view of the interior from here. Inside the church proper there is an organ gallery followed by nave and aisles, transept and chancel. The north arcade has columns of polished Bessbrook granite, with capitals and bases of Portland stone. Above them are shields sculpted with sacred symbols, and surrounded by grapes, wheat and foliage decoration. The clerestory, two windows to a bay, is filled with quatrefoil and sexfoil shapes in Edward Pugin's experimental manner, rather than conventional traceried lancets. The scissor-beam roof is of pitch pine. The south aisle has three wide bays with massive square chamfered piers, which do not correspond to the north aisle nor to the clerestory. Next come the transept, with taller arches to the nave, and the shallow chancel with its fine Gothic crucifix. The panelled ceiling over transept and chancel is decorated with sacred symbols, of Jesus, Mary and the Evangelists. The sanctuary furniture is of plain white stone, sparsely decorated with incised panels—the altar with a stylised cross, the ambo with an eagle, the font with a dove. On the east wall is the Last Supper, of 1967 by Arthur Fleischmann, rendered in a combination of sculpture and painting on sheets of perspex. To the north, the Sacred Heart shrine bears a similar panel of the Lamb of God.

The elaborately sculpted Lady Altar to the south was executed by Boulton & Sons in 1899 to the design of the architects. In its frontal is the Annunciation; in the reredos, panels bearing the Nativity and the Flight into Egypt flank a central niche containing a statue of Our Lady. Also in the south transept is a cast *pietà*.

The Stations of the Cross consist of low relief, unframed carvings. There are 14 stained glass windows in the church. Rottmann[5] attributes the second, third and fourth in the south aisle to Hardman, Westlake and Mayer repectively. The sixth is signed Hardman 1992.

Bibliography
Kelly, p. 235; Rottmann, pp. 250-54; BN, 28 December 1866, p. 877; 16 May 1879, p. 552; 21 October 1898, p. 591; 20 October 1899, p. 510; Br, 8 January 1876, p. 27; 15 June 1878, p. 629; The Architect, 8 June 1878, p. 350; 8 February 1879, p. 83; The Tablet, 20 October 1866, p. 662; 22 December 1866, pp. 805-806; 10 May 1879, p. 595; 14 October 1899, p. 632; CBR.S, 1959, pp. 66-67; 1963, pp. 39-41; 1965, pp. 54-55; The Universe, 17 March 1961, p. 3

---

5. Rottmann, pp. 253-54.

Kilburn West, Immaculate Heart of Mary, Stafford Road, NW6

The pressure of the post-war Catholic population on the church of the Sacred Heart became so great that in 1948 Fr Philip Danaher bought this former Methodist church dating from about 1880, in which he established a Mass centre. Two years later it was designated a chapel of ease and dedicated to the Immaculate Heart of Mary, with Fr Danaher in charge.

A solid building of brick with stone dressings, the church proper rests upon a basement storey five bays long, with rectangular side windows. The (ritual) west front is of three bays with arched entrance and side windows, and a triangular pediment. Built on to the opposite end are the presbytery and extensive premises of the 1980s designed for community and parochial use.

Inside the church, the space is subdivided into an ante-chapel of two bays which can be thrown open by means of a folding screen. Then comes the principal space so arranged as to be inviting, comfortable and intimate. Opposite the ante-chapel is another screen that can be opened on Sundays to gain ancillary accommodation from the attached community hall. Thus the church is extendible in two directions: a useful development in planning not observed in churches elsewhere. The altar is placed in the centre of the rectangle's long side, and in consequence no seat is far away from it. The chancel furnishings—altar, lectern and tabernacle stand—are all of timber and of simple design. Behind the altar are three windows with matching geometrical motifs.

Other furnishings are few and chaste: a large statue of the Immaculate Heart of Mary and another statue of the Sacred Heart; and the Stations of the Cross—of timber, each frame together with the subject within it carved in one piece.

9. *Kilburn West, Immaculate Heart of Mary*

Bibliography
Centenary Brochure of the Oblate Fathers in Kilburn (1965); A. Vaughan Williams, *Church of the Sacred Heart* (Kilburn: Oblate Fathers, 1965).

Laxton Place, St Anne Laxton Place, Longford Street, NW1

A school for Catholic girls was built in Little Albany Street in 1853, and used as a school chapel from 1857. This was replaced in 1938 by a new church in Seaton Place designed by T.H.B. Scott. When the whole area was replanned in

III.　CAMDEN

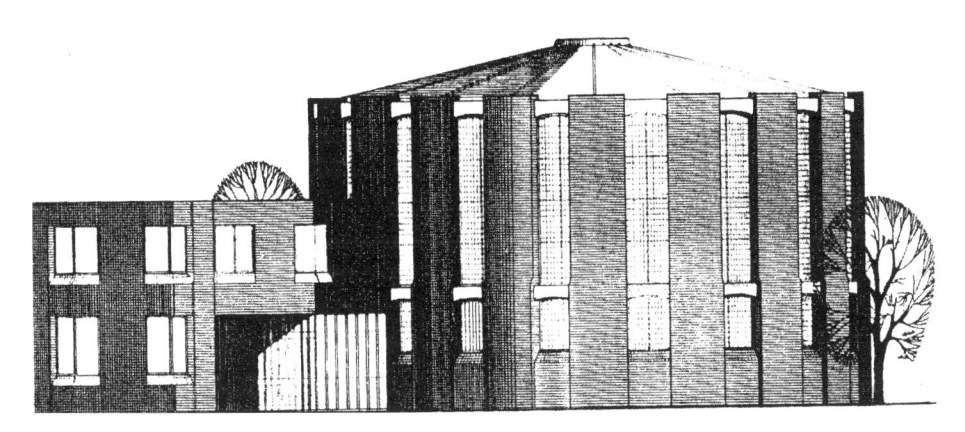

10. Laxton Place, St Anne, west elevation

the 1960s, a new site for the present church and presbytery was provided by the developers. The foundation stone was blessed by Cardinal Heenan on 30 May 1970, and the church designed by Scott and Jaques was opened in the same year.

The church with matching presbytery stands on the corner of Laxton Place and Longford Street, facing R.C. Carpenter's Anglican church of St Mary Magdalene of 1852. Its curved walls are of dark-coloured brick in two shades, one employed for the buttress-like members, the other ancillary to the tall intervening windows. This agreeable vertical rhythm is enhanced by the curvature of the overall plan. Converging pre-stressed concrete portal trusses support a copper roof. Inside, the convenience of the plan is immediately recognised, with the altar against the longer south side opposite the entrance, and the whole space free from intervening supports. Here, the 17 tall windows come into their own, with the soft glow of tinted glass installed in the 1970s. The shallow concrete vault is supported by girders crossed in scissor fashion.

The church furnishings are few and unobtrusive. Only the altar is of stone, the remaining sanctuary furnishings being of timber. There is a fine carved crucifix from Italy. The Stations of the Cross, painted on metal, were acquired from La Sagesse Convent, Golders Green, on its closure in 1978.

Bibliography
Rottmann, pp. 228-29; *CBR.S*, 1966, p. 46; *Guide*, p. 256

Lincolns Inn Fields, St Anselm and St Cecilia, Kingsway, WC2

The precursor of this church, the Sardinian Chapel, was probably the best known of all the embassy chapels. It was in existence, however, long before it became an embassy chapel. During the reign of James II, a house in Lincoln's Inn Fields was occupied by priests of the Franciscan Order, who also built a chapel. This was on the south side of Duke Street, leading into the west side of

11. Lincoln's Inn Fields, Ss Anselm and Cecilia

the square. Following the flight of James II in 1688, the London mob attacked the chapel, but was repulsed by the military. When the Franciscans withdrew, removing whatever goods they could, the mob moved in and destroyed the chapel.

By 1700 numbers 53–54 were in the occupation of the Portuguese Ambassador. The probability is that soon after 1688 the embassy occupied the restored buildings. Then by 1715 a Sicilian embassy chapel was here. The Duke of Savoy exchanged his kingdom of Sicily with the Emperor for the kingdom of Sardinia in 1720, so the Sicilian Chapel of 1715 was almost certainly the same establishment as the Sardinian Chapel. It is first referred to as the Sardinian Chapel in 1722. A serious fire destroyed the chapel in 1759, but it was restored within three years. A well-known print of Bishop Challoner shows him preaching in this chapel, behind him the chancel with its reredos painting of the Deposition. The chapel was again wrecked in the Gordon Riots of 1780, its furnishings carried out to a bonfire by a rabble bent on destruction. Afterwards compensation was awarded by the Government and the ravaged interior was repaired and reopened in February 1781.

In 1798 the ambassador closed the chapel and proposed to let the house. Bishop Douglass, Vicar Apostolic, was able, however, to obtain the property. The bishop's steps to reopen the chapel are recorded in his diary:

> 1799, Jan. 2nd. The Chaplains of Lincoln's Inn call upon me. We considered upon and determined that the ambassador should be written to, and requested to grant the Bishop and Chaplains leave to open the chapel again, for they knew that the congregation would support by subscription and donations among themselves.

The move was successful; the embassy became a clergy house, and the chapel was reopened on 13 August 1799. It functioned as a missionary church under the name of St Anselm's from 1852, adding the dedication to St Cecilia in 1866.

When the thoroughfare of Kingsway was driven through the previous maze of tiny streets west of Lincoln's Inn Fields, the old church in Sardinia Street was one of the many buildings that had to be demolished. An alternative site on which to build was provided, inconveniently long and narrow, but fronting Kingsway. By the disposal of the Sardinia Street site in 1902, Cardinal Vaughan was not only able to purchase the new site in Kingsway and erect a church upon it, but he was also able to place some £10,000 to the credit of the Westminster Cathedral Building Fund.

The foundation stone of the present church was laid on 10 June 1908, and the opening took place on 6 July 1909. F.A. Walters was the architect, and James Smith & Sons of Norwood were the builders. The church was damaged by enemy action on 11 September 1941. The west front and south aisle were rebuilt in 1954, under the direction of Stanley Kerr Bate of Walters & Kerr Bate, architects. Following a fire on Christmas Day 1992, the church was closed, and officially reopened by Cardinal Hume on 24 March 1994. The restoration included improved electric lighting, recolouring of the sanctuary canopy, and installation of the thanksgiving window. Outside, the window tracery was modified, and a segmental pediment was substituted.

Always interested in experiments in historic styles, Walters supplied here an early Renaissance design 'as being most in accord with the traditions of the old church'.[6] He by-passed, however, the Renaissance type of City church realised by Wren, and looked instead to the Continent. The requirements of the London County Council necessitated a west front wholly of Portland stone, and of an equal richness to the other buildings in the street. Walters provided a façade to the nave in two storeys containing the principal entrance and an upper window. The entrance was flanked by coupled Ionic pilasters, with the arms of St Anselm above the door. Above rose a mullioned and transomed window with lateral pilasters surmounted by a compound pediment in which segmental and triangular elements interlocked. The exterior effect was that of a scaled-down version of such Baroque churches as S. Michel, Louvain, of 1650–70, by the Jesuit architect Peter Huyssens. Here were the early seventeenth-century characteristics that the occasion seemed to require.

Considerably brightened by the restoration of 1993–94, the interior faced with Bath stone consists of nave of seven bays with west gallery, chancel with lateral passages leading to the sacristies, and a short but wide south aisle. Natural lighting comes from the west window (1994 by Shades of Light) and the clerestory, with two lights to each arcaded bay. The roof is of pitch pine, divided at each bay by large arched ribs which rest on stone shafts with carved capitals.

Above the passages that flank the chancel, the organ is housed in one of two galleries which are connected by a rood loft for which a precedent can be found in the church of St Etienne du Mont in Paris. Although the visual parallels are not close in detail, the general idea of a shallow arch carrying a bridge with a rood over it is indeed similar. So here was another early Renaissance prototype that Walters required to characterise his design. Yet another was the capitals of the chancel arch that Walters 'studied from those in the chancel built by Blessed Thomas More at Chelsea Church'.[7]

The altar has been moved forward.

---

6. *The Tablet*, 17 July 1909, p. 115.
7. *The Tablet*, 17 July 1909, p. 100.

12. Lincoln's Inn Fields, Ss Anselm and Cecilia

The tabernacle stands before the reredos which is almost plain in its lower part, except for two roundels bearing the Instruments of the Passion. Above this is a sculpted group of the Coronation of Our Lady, flanked by St Anselm and St Cecilia. This and all other sculpted work was carried out by Earp & Hobbs of Lambeth. Several furnishings were brought from the old church: the oval marble font with mahogany cover; the organ of 1857; the arms of the House of Savoy; and south of the chancel a large painting of the Deposition variously stated to be a copy by Rigaud of Beaumont's original, or a copy by Benjamin West of Spagnoletto's original destroyed in the Gordon Riots.

In the south aisle is the Sarcophagus-shaped Lady Altar also brought from the old church, and statues of the Queen of Heaven and the Sacred Heart. Off the aisle are the chapel of St Thomas More, with a wooden altar and a carved figure; the altar of St Joseph, of white marble with a mosaic reredos of the saint holding a model of the church; and built-in confessionals. In the nave are small altars of St Antony and St Jude, a statue of St Teresa; a bronze cast of St Peter; and the Stations of the Cross, relief work cast and painted, signed ADB 1909. A memorial to Mgr Francis Bartlett +1992 incorporates the sculpted Colonna Crucifixion after Michelangelo.

Bibliography
Kelly, pp. 250-51; Rottmann, pp. 138-42; Harting, pp. 22-54; Ward, pp. 86-93; J.H. Harting, *History of the Sardinian Chapel* (Paternoster Row: Washbourne, 1905); J.K.A. Farrell, *The Church of St Anselm and St Cecilia* (Kingsway: J. Scholles, 1967); *CRS* 11; *BN*, 3 October 1902, p. 468; 19 June 1908, p. 904; 23 July 1909, p. 115; *Br*, 22 October 1898, p. 357; 7 April 1906, p. 370; *The Architect*, 19 November 1909, p. 328; *AR*, September 1910, p. 120; *The Tablet*, 18 August 1855, p. 518; 20 June 1857, p. 388; 29 August 1857, p. 548; 3 October 1857, p. 629; *Westminster Record*, April 1994, p. 1

Somers Town, St Aloysius, Phoenix Road, Eversholt Street, NW1

The parish and church are the descendants of one of the eight French chapels enumerated in the *Laity's Directory* during the 1790s. The Abbé Louis Chantrel opened a chapel in 1798 at number 6, Garden Gate at the corner of Brill Place, Skinners Street, in part of the Somers Town scheme developed by

13. Somers Town, St Aloysius

the architect and speculative builder Jacob Leroux. Meanwhile, the Abbé Guy Carron, a priest indefatigable in missionary fervour, appeared on the scene. Carron had already opened three churches, a hospital, an orphanage, a library and several schools during his four years on the Isle of Jersey. Moving to London in 1796, he opened schools and catechism classes, a house for aged priests, a seminary for clerical students and a chapel in Conway Street, with a Providence whence soup and provisions were distributed. Carron settled in Somers Town in 1799, and when the Abbé Chantrel returned to France in 1802, Carron strove to keep the mission alive for the use of English Catholics, as well as the few remaining French. A chapel dedicated to St Aloysius was opened on 8 April 1808. Its architect may well have been Leroux, since he was on hand. Rectangular in plan with galleries on three sides, there were modifications in 1830 which may have included the addition of the west front with its pediment and Tuscan pilasters. 'The building is interesting as a good example of church architecture of the time when English Catholics were emerging from penal laws into the happy epoch of the Second Spring.'[8]

By the 1960s there was desperate need for a larger church, and the foundation stone of the present church was laid on 15 January 1967. With seating for 500 and costing £150,000, the new church was formally opened on 19 May 1968 during the rectorate of Fr Arthur Welland. The architect was A.J. Newton of Burles, Newton & Partners; the contractors were Messrs Marshall-Andrew & Co. The Faithful Companions of Jesus gave the site, and their new convent was built on the site of the old church and presbytery.

The buildings on their corner site comprise presbytery and church with a social centre beneath. Externally, the bold juxtaposition of straight and curved elements forms an agreeably composed ensemble.

Inside the spacious entrance (served by a ramp as well as steps) the interior is revealed through glazed doors. Within the rectangular site the central space

---

8. Kelly, p. 362.

consists of an elliptical drum supported on columns, containing the chancel, and seating arranged fanwise. An ambulatory surrounds the ellipse, giving access to the chapels, baptistery, confessionals and sacristy. The altar stands in the centre of the 'long' side, beneath a top light. Between the drum and its ceiling is a continuous ring of abstract stained glass, by Whitefriars. The ceiling is of parana pine from South America. The church floor is of Genoa green terrazzo, and the sanctuary floor of Sicilian white marble. The sanctuary is lightly furnished, with altar and ambo of Rosso Levanto marble. Over all is the figure of the Risen Christ carved by Vigilio Prugger. To the right, the Blessed Sacrament is reserved in an apsidal recess decorated with sacred symbols displayed on irregular ceramic shapes, by Adam Kossowski. The altar is of Portuguese marble.

Proceeding around the ambulatory, one observes the Lady Chapel with its marble altar and bronzed fibre glass cast of Our Lady, Mother and Image of the Church, by Gordon Beningfield. Beyond shrines with cast figures of the Sacred Heart and Our Lady of Lourdes, there is the Chapel of St Joseph, containing a History Corner, which holds memorials and well-modelled busts of the Abbé Guy Carron +1821 and Jean François de la Marche, Bishop of St Pol-de-Leon +1836.

Next to the entrance is the baptistery, of circular plan with roof lighting, a window by Whitefriars and the font, a monolith of Portland stone, its circumference lightly fluted.

Along the north wall are five windows designed by John Lawson of Goddard & Gibbs. Their subject matter, the Glorious Mysteries of the Rosary, is depicted large and uncluttered. Also here are fibre glass statues of St Aloysius and St Patrick, by G. Beningfield.

Bibliography
Harting, pp. 240-53; Ward, pp. 53-55; Kelly, p. 362; Rottmann, pp. 224-28; J. Molloy and J. Head, *St Aloysius Somers Town 1808–1958* (Camden: St Aloysius Church, 1958); *The Tablet*, 15 June 1850, p. 381; 13 October 1860, p. 645; *CBR.S*, 1965, pp. 58-59; 1968, pp. 28-30; *The Universe*, 20 January 1967, p. 5; 8 March 1968, p. 6; 24 May 1968, p. 2; *Westminster Record*, June 1992, p. 5

Swiss Cottage, St Thomas More, Maresfield Gardens, NW3

The parish was founded by Fr Bernard Whelan, incumbent from 1938 to 1956. His long, narrow church was the former studio of the artist Philip de Lazlo. The present church, founded by Fr Paul Thompson, was ingeniously fitted into the presbytery garden, and the old church was converted into a parish hall. Bishop Casey blessed the foundation stone on 15 October 1967, and Cardinal Heenan opened the new church on 20 April 1969. Gerard Goalen was the architect; Ove Arup & Partners consulting structural engineers; and John Murphy & Sons the contractors.

The approach from the road is via a broad porch and steps, sandwiched between the presbytery and the hall. Behind the porch, all that one can see of the rest is a segmental brick wall

14. *Swiss Cottage, St Thomas More*

surmounted by the concrete-framed clerestory. Over the centre is a bell-cote and cross. Within the porch, which is glazed to the interior, there is a marble holy water stoup in memory of Fr Whelan, and a life-size bronze figure of St Thomas More.

The nearly-elliptical plan of the main interior places the altar and the main entrance along two long walls to the north and south, ensuring clear, close visibility from all parts. Eighteen slim fluted columns support the clerestory and gallery. Above them thick reinforced concrete rafters running north to south support the roof. There are textured brick panels in the lower walls, as well as absorbent materials in the ceiling, designed to limit sound reflection.

The altar and ambo raised on steps are of Grecian marble. The major focus, however, is the crucifix by David John. Its bronze figure on a steel cross has its arms intentionally elongated, to suggest the embracing love of Christ. Three clerestory windows above the sanctuary are filled with abstract stained glass.

To the left of the chancel is the Blessed Sacrament Chapel, with top lighting and an altar of white marble. Near the main entrance is a carved statue of St Anthony, and in the five-sided Lady Chapel a Madonna and Child by Mayer.

Bibliography
CBR.S, 1966, pp. 40-41; 1967, pp. 38-39; 1968, pp. 50-53; 1969, pp. 28-31; *Hampstead News*, 17 September 1955, p. 1; *Express and News*, 25 April 1969, p. 7

IV
Greenwich

Abbey Wood, St Benet, Abbey Grove, SE2

THE name of the locality is derived from Lesnes Abbey, an Augustinian house founded in 1178 by Richard de Lucy, and dedicated to St Thomas of Canterbury. The monaster y was suppressed by Cardinal Wolsey in 1524.

The Congregation of the Filles de Jesus established a convent in 1904 on the south side of Woolwich Road, bordering on Brampton Road. Their chapel was served from Plumstead, and was open to the public.

The present church dedicated to St Benet Biscop and built to the design of Benedict Williamson was opened in August 1909, but was not formally separated from Plumstead until 1939. Miss Frances Ellis was the benefactress.

Standing within a row of terraced houses, the church with its attached presbytery is built of London stock brick. The modest (ritual) west front has a round-arched central entrance, a triple window with tubby columns, and a lower string course. The porch was extended to left and right in the late 1980s, at the time when the sanctuary was reordered.

The interior plan is of nave and sanctuary. There are round-headed side windows along four nave bays and in one chancel bay. A restoration of 1962 under the architects Bernard F. Moss & Partners included the introduction of a lower panelled ceiling and external maintenance.

1. *Abbey Wood, St Benet*

The furnishings are few and tasteful. They include the carved Crucifix, a Madonna and Child, St Joseph, and the Stations of the Cross worked in relief and dating from the restoration of 1962.

Bibliography
Kelly, p. 45; T. Coyle, *The Church of St Patrick Plumstead* (London: J.H.Morris, 1969) pp. 17, 20; Information of Fr Edgar Dunn

IV. Greenwich

Abbey Wood, St David, Finchale Road, SE2

The parish was founded from St Benet's, at that time under the care of Fr Michael Collins. From 1960, Mass was said in the hall in Grovebury Road; and from 1963 in the school in Mottisfont Road. The present church was opened in 1964. It is part of the Thamesmead Christian community, a local ecumenical project that includes the Church of England, the Methodist Church and the United Church.

2. *Abbey Wood, St David*

The present structure was originally designed as a two-storey parish hall, and in the course of building it was modified into a permanent church. The organ gallery is a remnant of its original upper storey. The adjacent site formerly intended for the church is now occupied by parish rooms. The church exterior is a plain brick rectangle, with a large relief of St David flanking the main entrance, and vandal-proof glass panels on the (ritual) north side.

Inside, there is a vestibule with ancillary rooms and a deep gallery above. Beyond this there is the wide nave, with walls and flat ceiling bright with a mainly white decor. Cylindrical structural columns form a narrow, glazed south aisle. In the windows opposite are narrow stained glass bands of abstract design, supplied from Dublin.

In the nave there are good carved statues of the Madonna and Child, and St Joseph; and the smaller Stations of the Cross, of agreeable opus-sectile work by Hardman.

The chancel, built within the same structural system, is visually narrowed within a timber frame. Prominently sited on its far wall is a large Christ the King beneath a tester which is geometrically panelled in pastel shades. The altar, tabernacle stand and ambos are all admirably assembled, not in the customary timber or marble, but in small rusticated blocks of English limestone.

Bibliography
Information of Rev. Patrick Fox

Blackheath, Our Lady Help of Christians, Cresswell Park, SE3

In 1870, the Reverend Dr William Todd purchased Park House for use as an orphanage, and built a chapel on the site of the present St Mary's Hall. Abutting Park House he also built a two-storeyed school with refectory and playroom. In due course, Rome permitted the patrons and supporters of the orphanage to hear Mass in the chapel. The mission created thereby was formally established by

Bishop James Dannell in 1873. The present church, built at the expense of Charles Butler, was begun in 1890, and opened by Bishop John Butt on 1 July 1891. A.E. Purdie was the architect, Smith & Sons of Norwood were the builders, and the cost was reported as £4,147.

Tucked away along Cresswell Park, the church is a delight both inside and out. Plainly, money was not stinted on the design or the materials. The result is a throwback to the kind of authentic Gothic sought by Pugin in the 'forties and Wardell in the 'fifties. The exterior, of Kentish rag and Monks Park dressings, presents a picturesque composition to the north-west approach. It includes a square clock tower which grows into an octagonal bell turret, a central entrance beneath a large traceried window; and a low octagon. Beyond the front is the receding parade of clerestory and north aisle windows, and in the distance the gable of the north-east chapel.

Inside, the magic is sustained with the familiar concept of a Gothic church as a worthy setting for artists' skills. The nave and aisles, of four bays, have piers of circular plan with foliage capitals and moulded arches. The clerestory has three lights in each bay; each aisle window is of three lights, traceried. The nave has a scissor-beam roof. There is an organ gallery, built-in confessionals on the south side, and the former baptistery, a charming octagonal room which now houses a shrine to Our Lady.

Beyond their respective arches, replete with lush foliage sculpture, are the sanctuary and chapels. The chancel is two bays deep, with a polygonal apse containing windows of paired lights. The original altar is retained, with its frontal panels depicting the Lamb of God flanked by angels, separated by marble columns. The tabernacle is of marble, and set within a gorgeous reredos. This consists of two panels of the Annunciation and the Assumption worked in high relief, flanking the monstrance throne. At the extremities are niches with statues of angels. Over all is a series of arches surmounted by three crocketed spires raised on openwork gables. This and the remaining sculpted work in fourteenth-century style was executed by D.N. Smith of Clapham. For the forward altar and matching lectern, designs of plain stone were wisely chosen.

3. *Blackheath Village, Our Lady Help of Christians*

The south-east Chapel of the Sacred Heart has an altar of wood, its frontal and reredos extensively panelled and decorated with painted figures of saints. Between this chapel and the chancel is the font, octagonal and raised upon marble columns, with sculpted symbols set inside quatrefoils along its sides. To this and the corresponding chapel on the north side there are rails and gates of wrought iron. The Lady Chapel's sculpted altar is a smaller version of the high altar, with a frontal of marble columns framing panels that contain Marian symbols within foiled shapes. The relief panels of the reredos show the Nativity and the Flight into Egypt set beneath gabled arches. Above, there is a statue of St Joseph flanked by statues of angels.

In the north aisle is the redundant pulpit, raised on an octagonal base. At its sides are the symbols of the Evangelists within panels punctuated by marble colonettes. Around the church are 18 stained-glass windows of good quality, many of them memorials. On the walls are the Stations resembling the work of Mayer, painted on metal in oaken arched frames.

Bibliography
Neil Rhind, *Blackheath Villages and Environs 1790–1976* (Blackheath: The Bookshop Limited, 1993), I, p. 51; Kelly, p. 85; *Our Lady Help of Christians Centenary History* (Cresswell Park: C.J. Henderson, 1973); *The Tablet*, 27 June 1891, p. 1010; 11 July 1891, p. 66; BN, 3 July 1891, p. 32

Charlton, Our Lady of Grace, Charlton Road, SE7

In 1903 some Oblate Sisters of the Assumption, expelled from France owing to the law against religious associations, bought a large house, High Combe, as their convent. Their chaplain was Fr Benedict Caron; Miss Frances Ellis was a benefactress. Their chapel in the bow-fronted ground-floor room was opened to local Catholics, and became the cradle of the parish, warmly encouraged by Bishop Bourne, and developed by the Augustinians of the Assumption, who remained until 1989.

The foundation stone was blessed on 27 August 1905, and the church was opened on 8 September 1906. The exiled religious employed a French architect, Eugène-Jacques Gervais (1852–1940). His experience designing public buildings in Bordeaux led Gervais to design a church of somewhat theatrical splendour, quite unlike other contemporary London Catholic churches. Costing £5,000, Our Lady of Grace was not cheap, but fine decoration was not spared. The builders were Jones & Sons of Erith. The exterior, of stock brick with stone dressings has a tall (ritual) west front, with a columned and gabled entrance, a round window heavily cusped, and an arched, gabled niche with a statue. Lean-to buttressed aisles flank the entrance. From the presbytery side, one views the symmetrical south aisle, buttressed and plainly windowed, with the sacristy forming a transeptal feature.

Inside, the Romanesque style is seen to undergo a nineteenth-century French interpretation, with emphasis on clear space and strikingly colourful decoration.

4. Charlton, Our Lady of Grace

Beyond the west gallery with its cast-iron rail and organ by Mander, are the nave and aisles of five bays. Scagliola columns with Corinthian capitals support round-headed arches. Above these is a triforium consisting of foiled circles bearing emblems derived from the Litany of Loreto. Higher still is a band of stylised foliage, and Ionic pilasters mark each bay. The decor of soft blues, greens and light grey was inspired by the London sunset.

There is no clerestory, but a tunnel vault to the nave, and high circular windows and groin vaults to the aisles. Off the north aisle are added ancillary compartments, which include a Lady Altar with carved relief statue. Also in relief are the Stations of the Cross, acquired in the 1960s, and set high on the walls. Other carved statues include St Patrick and St Teresa; the Sacred Heart and St Joseph, signed DVP. The benches and pulpit are attributed to Fr Gregory Chedal. The pulpit has five panels of Our Lord and the Evangelists dated 1924. Even more elaborate than the nave is the polygonal chancel with its upper blank arcading of double and triple arches, above them the decorated foiled circles continuing from the nave. On the reredos is a Byzantine painting of the Madonna and Child, and above this a large open arch. Here was originally 'a beautiful picture of Our Lady, erected over the high altar. The queen of Heaven is depicted advancing from the clouds bearing in her arms the Most Holy Redeemer.'[1] Now, however, the focus of the interior is the carved Crucifixion with

---

1. *The Tablet*, 15 September 1906, p. 419.

IV. Greenwich

figures of Our Lady and St John standing within the arch, with concealed lighting derived from the surrounding apse which projects to the east. A similar if grander panorama appeared in old St Mary Moorfields church of 1817–1903. There the architect John Newman derived his inspiration from the church of St Sulpice in Paris. Perhaps Eugène-Jacques Gervais had the same source in mind when designing this example at Charlton.

Bibliography
Kelly, pp. 120-21; *The Tablet*, 7 October 1905, p. 599; J.G. Smith, *Charlton* (Charlton: J.G. Smith, 1975), pp. 217-34

Eltham, Christ Church, 229 Eltham High Street, SE9

The church is in the care of the Canons Regular of the Lateran. The mission was commenced in 1870, and a church in the classical style was opened in 1890. The present church was begun in 1911 and opened on 8 November 1912. The nave and aisles were not then built to their intended length. Their western completion was begun in 1935 and the finished church was reopened on 23 February 1936. The architects were Canon A.J.C. Scoles and his nephew Geoffrey Raymond.

The exterior presents a highly symmetrical west front to Eltham High Street, consisting of nave, flanking crenellated aisles and matching porches, all of yellow brick laid in English bond for this impressive essay in the Perpendicular phase of the Gothic Revival.

Its plan consists of nave and aisles of five bays, with side chapels and apsidal sanctuary. At the west is a five-light window of the Risen Christ with saints, and an extra narrow bay with low arches punched into the responds. The main

5. *Eltham, Christ Church*

piers, of cruciform plan, are chamfered with mouldings which rise to the apex of each arch, uninterrupted by capitals. There is no clerestory, and the clear structural outline is finally emphasised by the simple panelled ceiling. Within the aisles are north and south entrances, built-in confessionals and three-light windows with Perpendicular tracery and tinted glass. The cast Stations of the Cross consist of painted tableaux within ogee arched frames.

Off the south aisle is St Joseph's altar, polygonal with a carved statue and two windows signed by H. Clark. The Lady Chapel similarly bears on its marble altar a carved figure of the Madonna and Child, and a three-light window.

The marble altar is preserved to the rear of the chancel, and a modern altar stands in front. Within the polygonal apse are five windows illustrating the advent of Christ. These and all the stained glass windows are the work of Harry Clark Studios of Dublin.

The north-east chapel of the Blessed Sacrament has a marble altar, its frontal heavily incised with cusped quatrefoil shapes, a Gothic panelled reredos and tester, and a window to Fr A. Smith, CRL, +1981.

South of the church is the priory of 1963 by F.G. Broadbent & Partners, with a sculpted roundel of Christ in Glory on its west gable, 1964 by James Butler.

Bibliography
Kelly, pp. 166-67; *The Tablet*, 28 October 1911, p. 713; *BN*, 15 November 1912, p. 703; *CBR.S*, 1963, pp. 92-95; 1965, pp. 70-73

Eltham Well Hall, Ss John Fisher and Thomas More, Well Hall Road/Arbroath Road, SE9

The mission was founded in 1929, and the church built in 1936 to the design of J. O'Hanlon Hughes. Standing on a prominent corner site, the compact exterior built of stock brick reads as nave and aisles with a sturdy east tower housing sacristies, and a pair of matching west towers which are diagonalised to the nave.

Within the entrance is a glazed narthex with a gallery above. Beyond it the rectangular space comprises nave and sanctuary in one, without the structural interruption of a chancel arch. The ceiling is lower at the sides, however, supplying the concept of aisles unsupported by piers. The clerestory consists of narrow lancet lights, and within the shallow pointed ceiling are glazed circular openings.

The chancel, slightly recessed to the east, the Blessed Sacrament Chapel and the baptistery are neatly dovetailed into the nave and into each other with clean, clear structural lines.

The altar, tabernacle plinth, sedilia, ambo and font are all of matching white stone partially faced with marble. On the sanctuary are stylised relief sculptures of St John Fisher and St Thomas More. In the centre is a large carving of the Risen Christ. The Stations of the Cross consist of elegant tableaux of cast metal mounted on wooden crosses. To the south is a minuscule Lady Shrine, with a window signed '1988 David me fecit'. Overall, this church deserves full marks for its thoughtful, uncluttered planning in the idiom of the 'thirties, with its respectful backward nod to pointed Gothic arches.

Greenwich, Our Lady Star of the Sea, Crooms Hill, SE10

From 1791 the Catholic architect James Taylor occupied Park House in Park Vista, to the north of Greenwich Park. Immediately behind the house, Taylor added a chapel for the use of the Catholic seamen at the Royal Hospital. This was opened by Bishop Douglass on 10 November 1793. With the advent of the railway, however, the chapel had to be demolished in the 1870s. In the meantime, the pastor of the chapel, Fr Richard North, felt the need for a larger building. With the help of a grant from the Admiralty, he succeeded in building Our Lady Star of the Sea, which was opened on 9 December 1851. Its style is fourteenth-century Decorated, the design by William Wardell.

6. *Greenwich, Our Lady, Wardell's elevation*

The exterior, of Kentish rag with Caen stone dressings, is dominated by the (ritual) west tower. This rises prominently above the houses in Crooms Hill, with its angle buttresses, a corner staircase and tapering spire with two tiers of dormers. The aisle roofs are lean-to, and expose the clerestory windows of four foiled circles and triangles, irregularly spaced above six aisle bays, in the manner of Wardell's recent church at Clapham. The principal entrance is via the base of the tower, and once within the nave, the impact of the conventional Puginian plan is evident, with nave and aisles of six bays, chancel and side chapels.

The nave has octagonal piers of Purbeck marble carrying plain moulded capitals and arches with head-stops including Ss Gregory, Augustine, Winifred and Dunstan; and King Ethelbert. Formerly in the nave was a Caen stone pulpit of the reading-desk type, in the style of Pugin's pulpit of 1848 at St Thomas's, Fulham. Since the church is rich in furnishings, a clockwise account may be the most useful.

Left of the entrance is the baptistery, encompassed by a stone screen with wrought-iron gates. The octagonal font of Caen stone is incised with sacred symbols, including those of the evangelists. Here also are two windows of the 1920s.

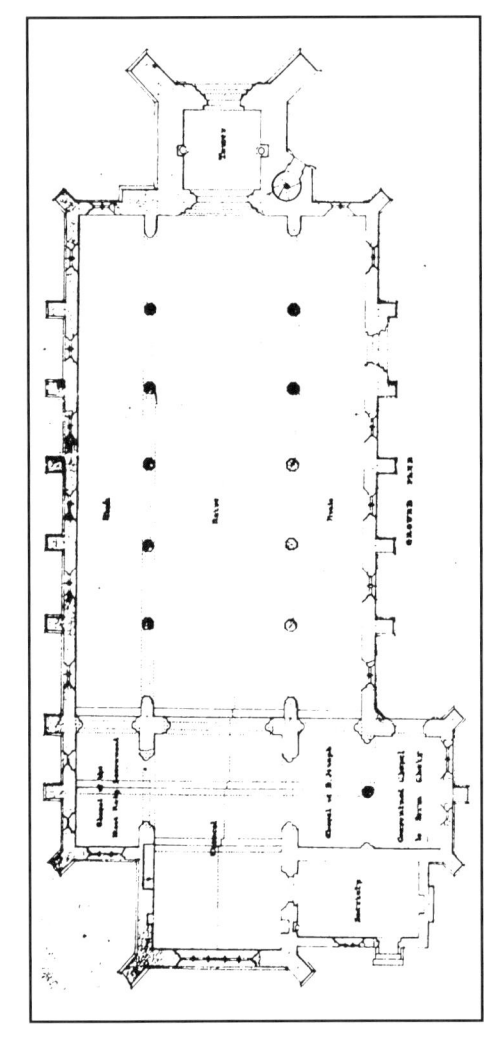

7. Greenwich, Our Lady, Wardell's plan

Along the north aisle, St Joseph's altar has a low stone surround and a figure of white statuary marble. Also in the aisle are two windows of the 1940s.

Much of the decoration of the chancel and the Lady Chapel (originally dedicated to St Joseph) was designed by A.W.N. Pugin. Above the Lady Chapel altar is a large reredos with the Blessed Virgin and angels within a large arch. The sacristy projecting to the left was originally designated for the organ and also as the oratory of a religious community. Between the Lady Chapel and the sanctuary is the Perpendicular-style tomb of Canon Richard North +1860.

A remarkable survival in a Catholic church is the screen before the chancel, of Caen stone, in three bays, traceried with foiled circles. Above it is the Calvary, its central figure of oak and the two Marys of stone. Before it are the communion rails, patterned with shields within vesica shapes, and a marble balustrade. To the left is the statue of Our Lady Star of the Sea, in a large niche with a pinnacled canopy above and seated figures supported by slender marble columns below. There is a modern altar of Sicilian marble, and the original Caen stone altar shown at the Great Exhibition also survives. Sculpted within its frontal are the Coronation of Our Lady, the Annunciation and the Visitation. Above a richly carved cornice, the chancel ceiling consists of 36 panels bearing monograms of the Blessed Virgin Mary. There is a stone sedilia, and set in the tiled floor a memorial brass to Canon Richard North +1860 and his brother Canon Joseph North +1885. Beyond a small fretwork screen is the Blessed Sacrament Chapel, its altar raised on columns and its panelled frontal recessed. The tabernacle is flanked by diaper work. The ironwork and stained glass of this chapel and the high altar are by Hardman.

Built out from the adjacent aisle is the Sacred Heart Chapel. Edward Pugin had made a design for a chantry chapel at this church for Stuart Knill as early as 1855.

However, the present chapel, of Kentish rag with floor and roof of oak, is recorded as newly opened in September 1891. Above a marble frontal with a mosaic Agnus Dei, the Gothic detailed reredos has a central figure of the Sacred Heart, and in the panelled remainder are angels, shields and much diaper work. Opposite the altar is a cenotaph, with a sculpted crucifix and marble memorial tablets, to Canon Michael O'Halloran +1921. There is a window to Canon John Sheen +1937, and a low rail with marble balustrade.

The choir loft, inner porch, confessionals, panelling of the nave and aisle ceilings and the organ were installed during a restoration of 1965 by Myles and Deirdre Dove.

Bibliography
Kelly, pp. 194-95; CAR, 1850; *The Ecclesiologist*, 1855, p. 150; *Kentish Mercury*, 13 December 1851; *Br*, 18 August 1849, pp. 390-91; 19 May 1855, p. 229; *The Tablet*, 9 September 1848, p. 580; 25 August 1849, p. 532; 24 November 1849, p. 737; 13 December 1851, p. 792; 25 September 1852, p. 611; 26 September 1891, p. 517

Greenwich East, St Joseph, Pelton Road, SE10

The privately owned chapel in Park Vista which the Catholic architect James Taylor had opened in 1793 was closed following the opening of Our Lady Star of the Sea Church in Crooms Hill, in 1851. However, the spiritual needs of the growing and mainly Irish Catholic population plainly required a mission in east Greenwich, and therefore the old chapel was reopened in 1868. Already much too small for comfort, it was highly inadequate in other ways, and had to be closed permanently in 1876 to make way for the railway extension.

8. *Greenwich, St Joseph*

From that time, Mass was said in the upper storey of the school that Fr Wilfrid Wallace had built in Pelton Road in 1871.

The permanent church was raised during the rectorate of Fr Augustine Boone. Its foundation stone was laid by Bishop James Dannell, and the church was formally opened by Cardinal Manning on 25 May 1881. W. Smith of Kennington was the builder, and Henry John Hansom, District Surveyor of Battersea, and a son of the more famous Joseph Hansom, was the architect of both school and church. The estimate was £4,335, without the tower, which has never been completed.

The church has a reasonably good site which furnishes views of the exterior from the north and the west. The materials are brick with Bath stone dressings, and the style is the Early Decorated phase of Gothic. The major feature of the west front is the four-light traceried window. Of minimal impact, however, are the blocked central door, and the truncated north-west tower with its own north entrance. Alongside this is a fully modelled entrance with two orders of colonettes supporting a gabled arch. Viewed from the north-east, the overall composition is pleasantly varied, especially by the windows of aisle, clerestory, apsed chancel and lower side chapel.

Beyond a west narthex, which is glazed to the nave and has a gallery above, the plan consists of three bays of nave and aisles, with chancel and two side chapels. A narrow outer south aisle has the appearance of being constructed as an afterthought to the rest. The nave arcade of three bays has circular piers with attached shafts and moulded capitals, clerestory and panelled timber wagon roof. The windows bear Early Decorated geometrical tracery above pairs of lancets in each aisle bay, and pairs of two-light windows in the clerestory.

The sanctuary, consisting in plan of five sides of an octagon, has a marble altar and tabernacle in situ, as well as a forward altar of timber. Behind it hangs a large carved crucifix against a mosaic background. There are three stained glass windows, and the church retains its altar rails, which are flanked by carved statues of Our Lady and St Joseph.

The Chapel of the Sacred Heart has a marble altar with the pelican and Instruments of the Passion on the frontal; a timber Gothic reredos with crocketed gables, and the Sacred Heart statue in a central niche. The Lady Chapel altar is similar to the other two, its front lightly decorated with Gothic panels, and a statue within a niche of Our Lady of Lourdes.

In the north aisle is a large crucifix, mounted against a background of linenfold panelling. There is a fine marble font, consisting of a square base below an octagonal stem with Gothic blank arches, and a bowl decorated with roundels bearing symbols of the evangelists. Around the bowl are Christ's parting words to the disciples from Mt. 28.19. There are very fine Stations of the Cross, painted on metal and acquired in the 1870s, possibly copies of Belgian work.

Bibliography
Kelly, p. 195; Edgar Dunn, 'The Return of Catholicism to East Greenwich' in *The Southwark Record*, (March 1966), pp. 12-27; *BN*, 3 June 1881, p. 655

Kidbrooke, St John Fisher, Kidbrooke Park Road, SE3

The mission was founded and served from Blackheath in 1961, and the present church was opened by Archbishop Cowderoy on 30 April 1964. The architects were Bingham, Towner & Partners. It became an independent parish in 1968. The church is built on a spacious site, the south aisle with its porch facing the road. Balancing the porch is a tall square campanile with saddleback roof, in four storeys, with mosaiced panels between the windows. It is built in two shades of brick laid in English bond. Above the entrance is an imposing statue of St John Fisher standing before Rochester Cathedral, his coat of arms on a panel below.

Beyond the extensive porch, the interior demonstrates that as late as the

IV. Greenwich

9. Kidbrooke, St John Fisher

1960s the Gothic Revival was still not quite extinct. The plan is straightforward, with broad nave and aisles of three bays, sanctuary and north chapel of the Blessed Sacrament. There are piers of square plan supporting pointed arches, lacking, however, mouldings and capitals, in a minimal Gothic-flavoured manner. The aisle and north clerestory windows also are Gothic-derived, subdivided into groups of lights with shallow pointed tops. The ceilings are tiled. The altar, ambo, chair and font are of Portland stone on bases of brick, providing a nice contrast of materials. The circular font is panelled with blank arcades, and decorated with the arms of St John Fisher.

There is a quantity of good-quality wood carving—the large Calvary on the east wall; the painted Madonna and Child; and the Stations of the Cross in relief. Flanking the sanctuary are sculpted statues of St John Fisher and St Thomas More.

Bibliography
CBR.S, 1966, p. 98

Plumstead, St Patrick, Hector Street, SE18

The mission was founded in 1890 by Fr Thomas Whelehan, under the direction of Bishop John Butt. Initially, Mass was said in a room in the Sussex Arms in Plumstead Road. A site in Coupland Terrace was found for a temporary building, and here a school chapel existed from March 1891. The church (with schoolroom beneath) in Conway Road to the design of F.A. Walters was then built, and opened on 7 August 1893. The presbytery was added in 1906. The mission was designated a parish in 1923.

In the 1960s, needing a larger church to accommodate increased numbers of worshippers, Fr John Morris negotiated the purchase of St Paul's Anglican Church in nearby Hector Street. Erected in 1901 to the design of William Basset Smith, St Paul's Church was already closed, owing to dwindling congregations. Since it was a consecrated building, an Act of Parliament was required before the change of use could take place. The necessary legislation was completed by October 1968, and St Paul's, renamed St Patrick's Church, was formally opened on 4 July 1969. Only the austere north side may be viewed conveniently from Hector Street. Of red brick with spare stone dressings, the exterior is dominated by its clerestoried nave and west bell-cote, with the lower chancel, transept, north aisle and west entrance gathered around it. The historic style is early Decorated.

Its interior is scarcely less austere. There are four bays of nave and aisles with narrower chancel; the piers of square plan with demi-columns to the faces, following the model of Heckington Church. The arches are brightened with alternate stones of different colours. There are two clerestory windows to a bay, and a high mansard roof with intermittent tie-beams.

Various furnishings brought from the old church brighten the interior, struggling bravely, however, against the cold, mechanical detailing of the structure. The old altar of 1925 now sits harmoniously against the original panelled reredos, beneath a five-light Decorated window of 1920. In the south

10. Plumstead, St Patrick, Church of 1893

aisle, the Lady Altar has two handsome carved statues of the Madonna and Child, and St Joseph. In the north aisle is the modest War Memorial in Sicilian marble, executed in 1920 by W.E. Smith; a cast of St Teresa, made in Lisieux; and a statue of the Sacred Heart acquired in 1930, made by La Statue Religieuse of Paris.

At the west end are the octagonal font standing on four marble columns; four stained glass figures inserted into the west window; a cast of St Anthony; and a cast pietà acquired in 1930, signed J. Strosl of Chelsea. Around the church are the Stations of the Cross, cast reliefs in quatrefoil frames; and the 15 Rosary windows, installed in the old church in 1960.

Bibliography
T. Coyle, *The Church of Saint Patrick Plumstead* (London: J.H. Morris, 1969); Kelly, p. 315; *The Universe*, 1 March 1968, p. 16; 7 June 1968, p. 12; 11 October 1968, p. 2; 11 July 1969, p. 2; *Catholic Herald*, 7 June 1968, p. 2; 18 July 1969, p. 6

Plumstead Common, The Holy Cross, The Slade, SE18

Erected in 1950 to the design of Archard, Worrow & Hardy, this partly pre-fabricated structure was intended as the parish hall of a future church to be built on the adjacent lawn. The church continued to be served from Plumstead until 1967. Originally the presbytery was number 23, The Slade, but in 1973 the parish was bequeathed number 27 next to the church. In 1979–80 this was converted to a presbytery, linked to the church by a building containing a parish room and extended porch. The church was decorated at the same time. Fr Ernest Becher's architects were Myles and Deirdre Dove; the builders were Purl & Balderstone. In 1982, Myles Dove arranged for the original asbestos roof of the church to be replaced by corrugated metal with improved insulation, by Kenmead Ltd. The simple interior consists of five uninterrupted bays of nave and chancel, with plain rectangular windows. The altar, tabernacle plinth and ambo are all of wood, tastefully matching. Also in wood are the carved Crucifix, statues of the Sacred Heart, Our Lady of Lourdes, St Joseph and the Stations of the Cross.

Bibliography
CBR.S, 1980, pp. 61-63; Information of Mr Myles Dove

11. *Plumstead Common, Holy Cross*

Shooters Hill, St Joseph, Herbert Road, SE18

A former Methodist church built in 1886 was acquired and opened for Catholic use in 1970. The original architect was J.K. Cole, and the builder E.G. Covil.

Of red brick with Portland stone dressings, the church commands a corner site, straddling Herbert Road and Paget Rise. Here the tower in three stages with its octagonal spire, the west apse and the south transept contribute a series of asymmetrical emphases to the overall composition.

Inside, however, the planning is rigidly symmetrical in the Nonconformist manner. The apsidal former baptistery with matching north and south porches is followed by the unaisled nave, a pair of shallow transepts and the polygonal sanctuary. The style is free Gothic, treated with more exuberance than was then customary in Catholic work. Thus the nave bears a spectacular hammer-beam roof, its principal elements lacking, however, collar and king-posts, but supplied with compensating struts. The nave windows are of two lights with quatrefoil tracery above, bearing small panels of tinted glass inset with symbols of the apostles. There are stained glass lancets also in the sanctuary, and wheel windows in the north transept and the west gable.

All of the chancel furniture is of timber. Particularly noteworthy here is the hexagonal tester with Gothic detailing above the altar. There is a statue of Our Lady high in the north transept; and small relief carved Stations of the Cross. The organ was built by A. Hunter & Son of Clapham.

Woolwich, St Peter, Woolwich New Road, SE18

There was a mission from 1816 in St Mary Street, where a large hall served as a chapel. To obtain funds to build a new church, Fr Cornelius Coles appealed to wealthy Catholics in 1841, Daniel O'Connell appearing on the subscription list. Within a month, a grant by the Board of Ordnance of freehold land on which to build a church enabled Fr Coles to proceed with confidence. The church was begun in the spring of 1842, and opened on 26 October 1843. This was the first church in London by A.W.N. Pugin.

The contract excluded the chancel, and the projected south-west tower has never been built. The front displays a large traceried window over the west door, but continuous financial straits are indicated by the lean-to roofs of the aisles, and the use of brick rather than stone. Inside, however, the space is generous, and charged with atmosphere. Here are the customary Pugin features in archaeologically correct forms. Nave and aisles are of six bays, the piers quatrefoil in plan, with plain moulded capitals. The nave has a scissor-beam roof. There are two-light windows to the aisles, bearing varied tracery designs. The two westernmost bays are occupied by a large porch with ancillary rooms, confessionals, and a gallery above.

IV. Greenwich

The chancel and south-east chapel were added in 1889, to the design of F.A. Walters, in the style of the Decorated period that characterises the earlier portions. Pugin's original altar and window were transposed to the new chancel. The altar frontal displays angels in arched niches. The reredos, the work of Jans of Belgium, was installed in 1892 at a cost of £105. A forward altar of Portland stone, with a base of variously coloured English stones, was added in 1993, together with a matching lectern and chair. In the altar frontal is the Lamb of God, and on the lectern are the keys of St Peter. Alongside the chancel arch there are pinnacled niches containing statues of St Joseph and St Patrick.

The Altar of St Joseph was erected in 1905, its Gothic frontal and reredos heavily diapered. The window installed in 1909 was designed by N.H.J. Westlake. Before it stands the font, designed in Pugin's manner, with sacred symbols sculpted within its eight deep panels. The corresponding Lady Chapel is part of the original building. Its Gothic altar and reredos are panelled and decorated with scenes from the life of Our Lady, and its three-light window dedicated to Sancta Maria. At the chapel's entrance, within a large Gothic niche, there is a statue of the Virgin and Child of the type supplied by Mayer. Also, evidently by Mayer, are the Sacred Heart statue and the Stations of the Cross, oil paintings acquired from Southwark Cathedral in 1895.

In the south-east bay there is the shrine of St Teresa, dating in its present form from 1943, and a carved St Antony within an elaborate portalled frame. In

12. *Woolwich 1, St Peter*

the porch there is a bronze model of St Peter on a sturdy marble plinth, Roman work of 1878 by E. Balmes.

Bibliography
Kelly, pp. 447-48; Rev. Michael Clifton, *St Peter's Church Woolwich* (London: Rev. Ronald Pepper, 1979); *CD*, 1842, p. 14; *BN*, 16 August 1889, p. 238; *The Tablet*, 10 July 1909, pp. 66-67

Woolwich, St Catherine Laboure, 698 Woolwich Road, SE7

The mission was founded by Canon William Monk in the 1950s to serve the area between St Peter's and Our Lady of Grace at Charlton. The canon acquired the present site, and the church was opened in 1961. A parish hall of almost equal size to the church was also built at the rear. The architects were Walters & Kerr Bate.

The exterior of stock brick with Bath stone dressings and pantile roof presents a wide front with recessed arms to the road. This front is in fact the (ritual) south side. The entrance on the left is approached by steps. The fenestration consists of a series of convex pointed lancets with wide mullions between them. We shall see this shape again.

Once inside, the plan is revealed as a compact rectangular nave which will seat 250 worshippers. The sanctuary in a wide recess faces another recess which houses a confessional and the wind porch. There is a gallery to the left, and the Blessed Sacrament Altar to the right. Over the nave there is a queen-post timber roof, and over the sanctuary a lean-to roof, with a central gable.

All the furnishings are of matching timber design—altars, tester, ambo, benches. Their panelled surfaces quietly echo the quaintly arched shapes of the windows. This distinctive shape is also seen above the piscina and the holy water stoups. On the sanctuary are the carved Crucifix, Blessed Virgin Mary and St Catherine Laboure. The octagonal arcaded timber font bears a plaque with a relief Madonna and Child dated 1974. The Stations of the Cross are also carved, in small rectangles with demi-scenes in low relief. This intimate interior gains an added charm from the uniform good taste displayed in all its matching parts.

Bibliography
Rev. Michael Clifton, *St Peter's Church Woolwich* (London: Rev. Ronald Pepper, 1979); *CBR.S*, 1961, pp. 134-37

13. *Woolwich 2, St Catherine Laboure*

V
Hackney

Clapton, St Scholastica, Kenninghall Road, E5

1. *Clapton, St Scholastica*

THE mission was founded from Kingsland by the Institute of Charity. From 1862 the chapel was a rented room in the London Road. Meanwhile, St Scholastica's Retreat, a charitable foundation for poor and reduced Catholics of either sex, of sixty years or over, was founded by William and Elizabeth Harrison, and endowed from the estate of their brother Robert Harrison and Charlotte Scholastica his widow.

The foundation stone was laid on 24 September 1861, the architect being E.W. Pugin and the builder Mr Oxborn of Clapton. The buildings comprised dwellings for forty people and a common hall. The first part was opened in 1862; the second part was built in 1864–67; and the building was finished in 1874. In 1879 the rented chapel was given up, and the Reverend Robert Swift moved his quarters from London Road to Kenninghall Road, where the common hall of St Scholastica's Retreat was pressed into service as a chapel. Its reversion to the role of reading room in 1882 indicates that the 'fair sized school chapel adjoining the building'[1] was opened at this date. The school chapel still survives as the parish hall.

The present church was built for Fr E.G. Chadwick, with increased seating accommodation in view. The foundation stone was laid on 29 September 1962 by Cardinal Godfrey, and the opening took place the following year. John E. Sterrett and B.D. Kaye were the architects, and Pitchers Ltd of Holloway were the builders.

The eye-catching (ritual) west front, of brick and Portland stone has a triple-gabled entrance beneath a six-light window, flanked by multi-windowed semicircular projections which mask the aisles. Behind this is the narthex with gallery over. To one side of the narthex is the repository, to the other the day chapel of St Benedict, with windows of coloured glass, a timber altar and a figure of Christ Resurrected. Beyond are the nave and aisles, of seven bays, clearly delineated by piers of square plan which support shallow straight-sided arcade arches. The aisle windows are also arched, beneath transverse pointed ceilings. The clerestory windows are rectangular, beneath a flat ceiling.

The sanctuary, one bay deep and projecting into the nave, has an altar facing the people. This and the side altars, the paving and the steps are all of Travertine marble. The altar furniture is of timber, including the organ of 1963 by J.W. Walker & Sons. Beneath a panelled tester the reredos consists of a large timber frame containing the crucifix hung against a red damask curtain. The side altars are of similar design and materials. That to the left has a sculpted statue of the Sacred Heart; that to the right the Virgin and Child, and also a carved figure of St Scholastica. To the rear of the nave, mounted on a corbel of Sicilian marble is another similar statue of St Antony with the Child Jesus.

Bibliography
Kelly, p. 133; Rottmann, pp. 203-204; *Br*, 1 October 1864, p. 732; *The Tablet*, 27 September 1862, p. 613; 26 October 1867, pp. 675-76; 26 August 1882, p. 353; *CBR.S*, 1965, pp. 48-50

Clapton Park, St Jude, Blurton Road, E5

The mission was founded from St Dominic's, Homerton, following the purchase of this former Methodist church of 1885, and was established as a separate parish in 1965. The brick exterior is unprepossessing, with a central door at the top of a flight of steps, and symmetrical pointed windows.

The interior is better than the exterior, as is generally the case. Its simple rectangular plan embraces nave and sanctuary without any structural division. Above the (ritual) west entrance there is a spacious gallery with organ by A.P. Mander. On each side of the nave are three round-headed windows, above them a scissor-beam roof.

Within the sanctuary the altar and tabernacle stand are of marble. To the sides are four windows with symbols of

1. Rottmann, p. 204.

V. HACKNEY

the Evangelists in bright pastel colours, by Carmel Cauchi. On the rear wall and also by Cauchi is a relief in fibre glass of the Blessed Virgin Mary, executed with admirable economy of line; and an oval relief bust of St Jude, set in a mosaic frame of blue and gold. Also in the church are figures of St Martin and St Rita; and Stations of the Cross carved in relief, in the 1960s style of Burns and Oates.

Bibliography
The Universe, 14 March 1980, pp. 7, 15; Information of Keith Stoakes

Hackney, St John the Baptist, King Edward's Road, E9

The earliest note found refers to the existence in 1842 of a temporary chapel in London Lane, opposite St Thomas's Square. The first priest associated with this enclave of Moorfields territory was Fr Joseph Fernandez Herrezuolo. It became an independent mission in July 1843, the pastor then being Fr John Lecuona who was to build the permanent church. In 1845 a site in the Triangle was purchased for £760, and the church designed by William Wardell was opened on 7 February 1848. This modest church consisted of nave, north aisle, chancel and sacristy, and cost £2,000 to build. Contemporary reports stress that the architect and his clients desperately wanted to erect here the first Catholic spire in London. Funds being limited, however, they contented themselves with a large westerly bell-cote which they termed a spire, illustrating it in *The Tablet* in 1848. A south aisle was added in 1861–62 by the architects T.J. Willson and S.J. Nicholl. Sadly, the church suffered severe damage in the Second World War, and had to be replaced.

The present church, designed by Archard & Partners, was opened by Bishop George Craven in 1956. Its exterior, of brick with a tiled roof, has an

2. *Hackney, St John the Baptist, 1848*

3. Hackney, St John the Baptist, 1956

interestingly varied silhouette viewed from King Edward's Road, with nave, lower south porch and chapel, and the stout tower overtopping the chancel. Towards the road, the tower displays a bas-relief figure of St John the Baptist. The dignified west front has a recessed central door, a tall window and a bell-cote, all within a compact vertical composition.

Inside, this design of the 1950s is strongly traditional in character, although employing contemporary structural techniques. Thus its wholly traditional plan consists of a west vestibule, nave and aisles of five bays, sanctuary flanked by chapels and south porch. The vestibule is glazed to the nave and in the gallery above is the organ reconstructed by Henry Willis & Sons in 1956. Here the large stained glass window of the Crucifixion may be studied at close quarters. Transverse arches of reinforced concrete curved from floor to apex suggest the Gothic tradition, and define the nave bays. In each bay there are rectangular clerestory windows installed in 1988, with differently coloured panes in geometrical shapes by John Lawson of Goddard & Gibbs. Shades of green, blue or orange predominate in each window. Attached to the piers are the fine Stations of the Cross, small unframed groups of figures carved in high relief, of 1938 by Anton Dapre of Burns, Oates & Washbourne. The window in the south aisle is by Michael Kelly.

The sanctuary's ample dimensions are modified by a polygonal panelled screen standing before the east wall. Behind it lighting from a concealed source illuminates the crucifix. Before it the matching chancel furniture is of timber, the altar with a relief carving of loaves and fishes, the lectern with Alpha and Omega.

Adjacent to the south porch is the Blessed Sacrament Chapel, with small rectangular windows that bear multi-coloured panes in random shapes, by Goddard & Gibbs. The tabernacle, faced with opus-sectile decoration, dates from 1988, the work of Michael Burke of Dublin. The corresponding Lady Chapel north of the sanctuary has the addition of top lighting, but is otherwise plain in decor. Attention is thus appropriately concentrated on the crowned Virgin and Child, pre-war work by Anton Dapre.

Bibliography
Kelly, p. 197; Rottmann, pp. 204-205; *Br*, 18 March 1848, p. 137; 29 June 1861, p. 452; *The Tablet*, 31 December 1842, pp. 727, 855; 14 June 1845, p. 373; 18 March 1848, p. 179 (illus.); CD, 1842–45; *The Ecclesiologist* 5 (1848), pp. 327-28; *The Catholic Handbook*, 1857; *CBR.S*, 1956, pp. 38-40; 1972, pp. 193-95

Homerton, Immaculate Heart of Mary and St Dominic, Ballance Road, E9

The mission was founded on 2 February 1873 by Fr George Akers at 21 Sydney Terrace, a school chapel being erected the following year. The foundation stone was laid on 23 September 1875, the church was opened on 29 October 1877, and the campanile was completed in 1883. The architect was C.A. Buckler, and the builder W. Kell of Windsor. The church was severely damaged by enemy action on 9 March 1941, only the walls and campanile being left standing. It was rebuilt in 1955–57, the architect being John E. Sterrett. The Montfort Missionary priests have had charge of the parish since September 1983.

At a time when the Gothic style was popular and widespread, Buckler the architect designed this church, perhaps at the behest of Cardinal Manning, in conscious imitation of the Early Christian churches of Rome. From Ss Nereus and Achilles he derived the general plan, particularly the arcade of six bays; and from S. Maria della Navicella he copied the three east apses and the details of the west front.

The exterior is all of brick—London stock mostly, with bands of red to define the numerous arches. The west front is nicely composed, with the campanile of five storeys balancing the church proper. This has a projecting portico of five bays faced with Portland stone, one of its arches housing a statue of St Dominic. Above these are the clerestory windows and triangular pediment, derived from S. Maria della Navicella. The south side visible from Ballance Road shows the aisle with tiny windows set in a blank arcade, and the corresponding series of clerestory windows.

Inside, the Early Christian narthex is now subdivided, forming repository, entrance and confessional. There are two windows to St Cecilia and St John the Baptist. Beyond this are the nave and aisles with a gallery over the first bay. The piers are of rectangular plan, with pilasters on all four sides. The arcade and clerestory arches are round-headed throughout. In the clerestory are 15 windows depicting the Mysteries of the Rosary, by Goddard & Gibbs. The

4. Homerton, Immaculate Heart of Mary and St Dominic

design for the nave ceiling, with its lighting fixtures set within stars inside diagonalised panels, dates from the rebuilding of 1955–57.

The sanctuary, Blessed Sacrament Chapel and Lady Chapel are all similar to each other, with marble altars and marble-faced apses with mosaic-decorated domical vaults. Differing, however, in detail they are unified by the altar rails, also of marble with three sets of wrought-iron and brass gates. This unity is further enhanced by the crucifix, Sacred Heart and Blessed Virgin, all three carved by Ferdinand Stuflesser of Ortisei. Also by Stuflesser is a series of carved statues in the nave, consisting of Michelangelo's *pietà*, St Dominic, St Teresa, St Peter, St Joseph, St Antony and St Patrick. The total effect is one of fluent manipulation of space, achieved by traditional planning and elevation, beautified moreover by the consistent use of marble, mosaic and timber.

Bibliography
Kelly, p. 217; Rottmann, pp. 200-203; G.L. Vere, *Random Recollections of Homerton Mission* (London: Burns Oates, 1912); *The Tablet*, 23 August 1873, p. 241; 25 September 1875, p. 403; 2 October 1875, p. 434; 3 November 1877, p. 563; 5 July 1884, p. 36; *BN*, 14 December 1894, p. 819; *The Lamp*, 10 March 1894, pp. 146-49; *CBR.S*, 1957 pp. 57-58

Hoxton, St Monica's Priory, Hoxton Square, N1

The church is in the care of the Augustinian friars. Founded in the twelfth century, the order had numerous houses in England prior to the Reformation, the most prominent in London being the church and hospital of St Bartholomew the Great. In pursuance of his policy of encouraging the orders to work in his diocese, Cardinal Wiseman invited the Augustinians to return to London. The order purchased a house in Hoxton Square and under Fr Michael Kelly building proceeded rapidly. With E.W. Pugin as architect and Mr Oxborn of Clapton as builder, the foundation stone was laid on 20 September 1864, and the church was opened on 4 May 1865.

Edward Pugin's design is highly symmetrical both inside and out. The (ritual) west front presents to Hoxton Square a buttressed central entrance beneath a five-light Decorated window, and a substantial bell-cote, all flanked by narrow-windowed lean-to bays which denote the aisles. The materials are principally London brick, with discreet bands of red and blue brick, and Bath stone dressings.

Through a glazed vestibule, the symmetry is again perceived in the plan of nave, aisles and chancel. The nave is

V. HACKNEY

5. Hoxton, St Monica

eight bays long, the first bay occupied by a choir gallery, with organ by Bishop. The most remarkable feature is that nave and aisles are separated by piers and arches of timber (pitch pine) which support the clerestoried stage of sexfoil windows, and the scissor-beam roof. Timber arcades notwithstanding, Edward Pugin scored a notable first here, by reducing the aisles to the width of access passages. This planning development in Gothic Revival work had been initiated by G.E. Street in 1863 at All Saints, Clifton, whence Edward Pugin may have obtained the idea, using it here for the first time in a Catholic church. This seeming improvisation was to become a widespread feature of church planning.

The sanctuary is narrower than the nave, with a rose window and narrow lateral windows. The altar of timber was designed and executed by Mayer & Company in 1875. Its reredos is preserved in situ, and has painted panels between Gothic niches with gabled faces, terminated above by turrets and pinnacles. The paintings display the Last Supper and St John giving Holy Communion to Our Lady. The altar table is now detached and placed forward. Its panelled frontal depicts emblems of the evangelists.

To the right is the Lady Chapel, added in 1880 by the architect John Young. Its window depicts the Immaculate Conception, the Annunciation and the Visitation. Set in the marble altar is a painting of Our Lady of Good Counsel after the original at Genazzano.

Around the walls are the Stations of the Cross, reliefs in oaken frames by Mayer; St Joseph, 1882, also by Mayer beneath a timber Gothic canopy, and St Antony, 1964 by L. Widmer. Opposite these are the Sacred Heart within a canopy by Mayer, St Nicholas of Tolentino, and St Teresa by La Statue Religieuse. Adjacent to this group is a memorial tablet to Fr Michael Kelly +1914; and a bronze cast of St Augustine, 1979 by CS OSB.

Bibliography
Kelly pp. 220-21; Rottmann, pp. 208-10; *Br*, 8 October 1864, pp. 745-46; *The Dublin Builder*, 15 October 1864, p. 213; *The Tablet*, 16 July 1864, p. 455; 24 September 1864, p. 614; 22 October 1864, p. 677; 18 December 1875, p. 786; 25 December 1875, p. 819; 18 December 1880, p. 787; 25 March 1882, p. 471

Kingsland, Our Lady and St Joseph, Balls Pond Road, N1

The foundation was made by Fr William Lockhart of the Order of Charity, with the opening of a chapel at 83 Culford Road on 22 April 1855. By July 1856 an adjoining warehouse had been acquired, and after conversion by W. Wardell

6. Kingsland, Our Lady and St Joseph

opened as a church with a school beneath it, on 29 September. Following extensive remodelling by E.W. Pugin, the church was reopened on 24 February 1860. This was superseded by the present church, which was formally opened by Cardinal Heenan on 12 April 1964. The architect was Wilfrid C. Mangan.

Of brick with stone dressings, the front to Balls Pond Road is wisely designed to catch the eye by means of a sturdy tower which rises a step above the porch and organ loft. Beneath a pyramidal roof the tower has two tall transomed windows with a cross superimposed on them. Below this is a triple entrance, and in the tympana are relief sculptures of the Holy Family and Alpha and Omega.

Beyond a spacious porch with organ gallery above it is the broad, unaisled nave, seven bays long, its elliptical ceiling marked by curved transverse beams. On either side of the nave there are windows divided into groups of three lights, whose stepped arrangements echo that of the main front. In the nave there are built-in confessionals. The Stations of the Cross in opus-sectile and mosaic were made in 1963 by Hardman.

The sanctuary, two bays deep and narrower than the nave, has a marble altar with panels of verde antico, and above the tabernacle a large crucifix. Beside the chancel arch are carvings of the Sacred Heart and St Antony.

To the left of the chancel is the Shrine of St Joseph, its statue sculpted by Michael Lindsey Clark. To the right is the spacious Lady Chapel with a marble altar and a sculpted relief of the Virgin and Child, again by M.L. Clark. Also in the chapel are carved statues of St Teresa and St Martin de Porres.

Bibliography
Kelly, pp. 236-37; Rottmann, pp. 210-11; *The Tablet*, 28 April 1855, p. 262; 14 July 1855, p. 438; 5 July 1856, p. 421; 4 October 1856, p. 628; 11 February 1859, p. 101; 3 March 1860, p. 133; 21 September 1872, p. 370; *CBR.S*, 1962, pp. 66-67

V. HACKNEY

Manor House, St Thomas More, Henry Road, N4

The church, presbytery and basement were designed by Buries Newton the architects as a single unified entity. The brick front to Henry Road presents surfaces of various heights, some of them recessed, consonant with their various interior functions. The walls of the church are distinguished by a cross entwined with the Crown of Thorns, and a roundel depicting St Thomas More.

The church was opened on 29 June 1975. Beyond the entrance, the main congregational space is squarish, with the altar in the middle of one side. To its (ritual) south is a large day chapel with provision for separation by means of a screen. The tabernacle is common to both components. There is another screened ancillary space to the west, allowing accommodation to be maximised as required. The walls have concrete piers forming panels with brick infill, and several narrow vertical windows. Overhead, a gabled timber roof admits concealed lighting to the sanctuary.

The altar furniture is of timber; the organ is by Johannus. Behind the altar is a collage of the Risen Christ by Joy Aurus, and a ceramic crucifix, perfectly proportioned to its setting, of 1950 by EMB. The Stations of the Cross, canvas paintings of 1970 by A. Swkowska, are strikingly evocative, with reds and blues dominant against sombre grey backgrounds. Their quality matches the excellent clarity of the planning.

Bibliography
Information of Rev. Aidan Sharratt

Fr Ethelred Taunton built a temporary

Stoke Newington, Our Lady of Good Counsel, Bouverie Road, N16

church which was opened on 12 January 1888. The foundation stone of the present church, designed by T.H.B. Scott, was laid on 2 April 1927. The unfinished church was opened for use on 2 October following, the former church serving as its nave. The present nave was constructed in 1936.

The exterior built of brick places the church firmly within the neo-Romanesque style. Its tall front has a central entrance projecting slightly, a series of stepped arches marking the doorway, and in its gable a plaque depicting Our Lady of Good Counsel. Higher still is a circular window, and all is flanked by the narrow ends of the aisles. The south side exhibits a varied composition, which includes the gable to the gallery, the clerestory and the octagonal crossing tower with its tiled roof. At its side is the shallow south transept, and the lower Lady Chapel which was added later.

Inside, the plan consists of nave with passage aisles, transept and crossing, sanctuary and chapels. The elevation realised on this plan amounts to a competent, dignified achievement. The nave is four bays long, with organ gallery over the first bay. The arcade piers are circular, with block capitals bearing incised linear definition. Above the clerestory with its pairs of windows to each bay is a king-post roof. From beneath the tower one can mark the transition from a lower square plan to a higher octagon, managed by means of corner arches which are lit by narrow windows, and above them an ingenious timber roof.

Over the marble altar there stands a conspicuous baldacchino, raised on four marble columns with carved capitals, its arched stone roof decorated with incised Celtic motifs. The chapel to the left has an altar of timber, with a carved figure of the Virgin and Child. In the transept hangs a carved Gothic Crucifixion triptych.

The north-west baptistery has an octagonal font, its faces decorated with cusped rectangles. On the wall hangs a cast of the Baptism of Christ. In the nave is a carved figure of St Antony, and the Stations of the Cross, low relief casts, seemingly influenced by the spare style of Eric Gill's Stations at Westminster Cathedral. To the south, behind a glazed screen, is the Chapel of Our Lady of Good Counsel, its altar within a setting of white marble and ceramic tiles in blue and various paler hues. The statue is of 1907 by K. Bortrievikz.

Bibliography
Kelly, p. 375; Rottmann, p. 218; Consecration booklet (1976); *The Tablet*, 21 January 1888, p. 213; Information of Mr S.J. Peter

7. Stoke Newington, Our Lady of Good Counsel

VI
Hammersmith and Fulham

Brook Green, Holy Trinity, W6

THERE has been a mission at Hammersmith since 1669, in which year four nuns of the Institute of the Blessed Virgin Mary from Munich established a house and school there with its own chapel which the local populace could attend. Despite many vicissitudes, the community survived under the aegis of the Vicars Apostolic, and finally moved to Teignmouth in 1865. In the meantime, the convent chaplain, Fr William Kelly, had established a neighbouring mission at Fulham where the church by Pugin was opened in 1848. By this time Hammersinith also was ready for its own public church. This was founded in Brook Green by Fr Joseph Butt.

Cardinal Wiseman presented the ground; William Wardell was the architect, Messrs Bird the builders, and the contract price (excluding the spire) was £20,000. The Countess Tasker was a generous benefactress here and elsewhere. 'At Brook Green she not only built the girls' school at her own cost, but paid off the debt upon the church amounting to £4,000, with the first cheque drawn after attaining to the property left her by her father.'[1] The foundation stone was laid by Cardinal Wiseman on 8 May 1851 and the church

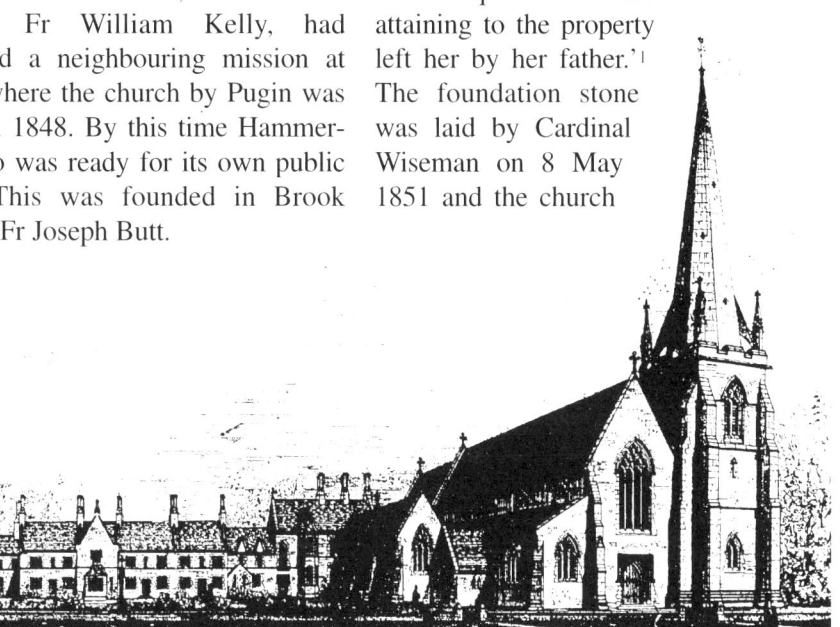

1. *Brook Green, Holy Trinity, Wardell's tower design*

1. *The Tablet*, 24 March 1888, p. 498.

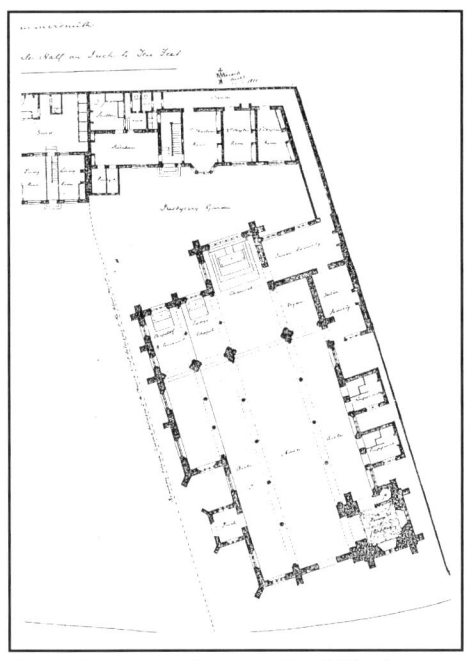

2. Brook Green, Holy Trinity, Wardell's plan

opened with considerable pomp on 26 July 1853. The materials are Kentish rag with Caen stone dressings. The adjacent St Joseph's Almshouses were also designed by Wardell, engendering a pleasingly unified composition. Behind the church St Helen's Girls and Infants School was built in 1862 to the design of J.J. Scoles. The children removed to the new Sacred Heart School in 1894 and the old building has long served as parish rooms. The church spire was erected in 1871 by J.A. Hansom, who refined Wardell's parapet, lucarnes, flying buttresses and fenestration at the bell stage with a simpler outline. The west entrance was embellished in 1872 by the priest architect Canon A.J.C. Scoles. The presbytery, formerly two semi-detached houses, was rebuilt in 1963 by Messrs Westmore & Partners, P.J. Mabley being the architect in charge.

Decorated Gothic of the fourteenth century, the design represents something of a high-water mark among Wardell's London churches. Some 120 feet long and 65 feet wide, the church consists in plan of nave, (ritual) north and south aisles, outer north aisle, chancel, three chapels, north porch and south-west tower.

The six arcade bays of the nave include the west vestibule with gallery over. 'The architect has given us a welcome novelty in the way of flooring. It is formed of wood instead of earthenware, this giving all the comfort of wood with the good effect of the other.'[2] The floor has since been renewed and carpeted. The nave piers are octagonal, with plain moulded capitals and moulded arches. In the arcade spandrels are painted medallions of figures with Christian symbols. A similar painting of the Crucifixion over the north entrance is signed Fenton 1862. The clerestory consists of small two-light windows in each bay. The timber roof has projecting brackets on corbels which support angels playing musical instruments, alternating with kings bearing Christian symbols.

The chancel is two bays deep, and paved with Minton's encaustic tiles. Its roof repeats the angels of the nave. The Calvary above the chancel arch dates from 1892, by Peter Paul Pugin. The east window, 1853 by Hardman, cost £250. It has 12 scenes of the Passion of Our Lord, and tracery emblematic of the Trinity. The altar was moved westward in the 1970s. The reredos now bears the tabernacle on a marble stand, flanked by six saints in niches, with diaper work beneath. The inner north chapel has a

2. *The Tablet*, 30 July 1853, p. 483.

panelled ceiling and elaborate foliage capitals. Its window is of 1854 by Hardman, restored after war damage, 1944. Its reredos has the Coronation of the Blessed Virgin Mary with Ss George and Teresa; in the frontal are the Magi offering gifts to the Infant Jesus.

The outer north Chapel of the Blessed Sacrament was donated by Countess Tasker. The reredos designed by J.J. Scoles in 1854 depicts the Finding of the Cross by St Helen and Constantine, with the Holy Eucharist, the Nativity and the Crucifixion in the frontal. The east window showing the Last Supper (1855) and two memorial windows to Joseph and Louis Tasker are by Hardman. In the outer north aisle is the brass to Fr Joseph Butt (+1854), formerly in the chancel.

3. *Brook Green, Holy Trinity, Wardell's interior design*

Three windows by Mayer depict the Ascension, the Resurrection and St William. The inner north aisle windows depict the Sacred Heart, Our Lady with Ss Patrick and Julia, and Our Lady with Ss Robert and Lucy, by Mayer. The large west window depicts the Blessed Trinity with Ss Stephen, Joan of France, John Fisher and Thomas More, and was installed in 1887.

Beneath the tower is the baptistery, a tall room with a lierne vault with foliage bosses, and in the centre boss the Baptism of Our Lord. The octagonal font has angels and symbols of the evangelists carved into its faces. The elaborate timber canopy with its eight paintings of angels and saints, was designed by Wilberfoss and executed by Thomas Orr. In the south aisle Wardell designed two large built-in confessionals; there are also three windows by Mayer, who also supplied the Stations of the Cross. Wardell designated the space at the aisle's east end for the organ; but by 1857 the chapel of Ss Joseph and Paul was in this spot, and a west gallery had been erected to house the organ. The chapel's altar, designed by J.J. Scoles has relief sculptures of the conversion of St Paul and the Flight into Egypt. Its window of St Paul is of 1854, by Hardman.

Bibliography
Kelly, pp. 199-200; Rottmann, pp. 111-16; Harting, pp. 182-208; A. White, *History of Holy Trinity Church Hammersmith* (London: The Universe, 1903); *The Catholic Handbook*, 1857; Evinson; *Holy Trinity Brook Green Centenary Souvenir*; CBR.S, 1964, p. 504

Fulham, St Thomas of Canterbury, Rylston Road, SW6

The mission was founded from Hammersmith in 1842, when Fr William Kelly opened a school and Mass centre in a rented room in Parsons Green Lane. Fr Kelly then acquired a plot of land on which to erect a church, cemetery and school. He was assisted by Mrs Elizabeth Bowden who wished to build a church in memory of her late husband, and undertook to bear the complete cost of the work. The foundation stone was blessed by Bishop Griffiths on 16 June 1847, and the church was opened by Bishop Wiseman on 30 May 1848. The architect was A.W.N. Pugin, and the builder George Myers.

St Thomas's is conveniently placed for those wishing to study a complete Pugin church in London. It must be remembered, however, that it was built as a country church in what were then the market gardens of Fulham Fields, and since the 1880s has been forced into the role of a town church, surrounded by extensive housing.

The materials are Kentish rag with Caen stone dressings, the style transitional Decorated Gothic of about 1250 to 1300. The three gables of the east end face the road, and the church entrances are via the south porch and the north transept. The best exterior view is from the cemetery to the west, whence the tower and spire (142 feet high) may be seen, as well as the graves of numerous clergy, nobility and gentry of the nineteenth century. The attached presbytery of stock brick, also by Pugin, stands to the north.

The interior is easily read, with nave, aisles, chancel, two chapels and south porch. The arcade of six bays runs continuously through nave and chancel. The piers are circular in plan, with plain moulded capitals. A pair of octagonal piers marks the original division between chancel and nave. The present altar and retaining wall are of Portland stone. The reredos of the original high altar remains, as well as two side altars, the font and the stone lectern from which Newman preached at the opening of the church. All of these were then in place, having been designed by Pugin and supplied by Myers.

4. *Fulham, St Thomas*

VI. Hammersmith and Fulham

5. *Fulham, St Thomas*

The altar of the north chapel has lost its mensa, in the interests of conserving space. Its frontal now fixed to the wall bears the eagle and the chalice, symbols of St John the Evangelist. The reredos has sculpted panels of the saint suffering torture, and writing his gospel. In the vicinity is the statue of St Thomas of Canterbury, the gift of its carver Anton Dapre, a quondam parishioner. Here also is the octagonal font, at its foot the symbols of the evangelists. These are repeated in the upper panels, and augmented with the dove, the lamb, foliage and IHS.

The corresponding south chapel's reredos depicts the Coronation of Our Lady in splendid high relief. In the frontal are angels bearing the arms (left to right) of Pope Pius IX, St Thomas of Canterbury, Pope Pius XII, St Thomas's family and Mrs Elizabeth Bowden.

The four windows at the east end were installed by Hardman in the 1860s, to designs of John Powell. The chancel window, however, was damaged by wartime bombing, and the five saints were renewed in 1947 by Goddard & Gibbs, but its tracery glass is original. The small south window depicts with restrained assurance the Flight into Egypt and the Holy Family at Nazareth. The large west window with its reticulated tracery was designed by N. Westlake, and installed in 1896. Its vigorous scheme depicts the Immaculate

Conception surrounded by the seven archangels, figures of the Old Testament, and patron saints of the donors, the Roskell family. During reordering in 1970 by Bartlett & Purnell, the former sacristy was opened to the north aisle, forming a transept. In the gallery above it is the organ, reconstructed in 1969 by Mander. During redecoration in 1980, the eight Celtic crosses in the chancel ceiling were copied from Pugin's *Glossary of Ecclesiastical Ornament*.

Bibliography
Kelly, p. 182; Rottmann, pp. 53-55; Little, pp. 86-87; D. Evinson, *St Thomas's Fulham* (Hammersmith: Fulham and Hammersmith Historical Society, 1976)

Hammersmith, St Augustine, Fulham Palace Road, W6

The church is in the care of the Augustinian friars, and was founded from Hoxton, where the order has been settled since 1863. In answer to Cardinal Vaughan's request, the Augustinians proceeded to fill a missionary gap with a foundation in West Kensington. Prior Raleigh and Fr Condon set up a temporary presbytery and chapel in a house, number 71 Comeragh Road, opening the mission on Easter Day 1903. Subsequent arrangements to purchase a plot of land on which to build a church fell through, and a fresh start was made in Fulham Palace Road. Here, a temporary iron church with accommodation for 250 people was opened on 16 September 1903. This was later superseded by the present church. The priory was ready for occupation in 1914. The church foundation stone was laid on 25 March 1915, and the formal opening took place on 14 October 1916. The architect was Robert Curtis, and the builder A.E. Symes of Stratford. Curtis provided a large church in the neo-Romanesque style, of purple grey bricks with bright red brick dressings, and roofed with Welsh slates. The external emphasis is concentrated on the west front, where the round-headed openings of doors and windows, five at ground level, three on the upper storey and one forming a central niche are assembled into an overall triangular composition. At the corners there are lightly scaled pavilions designed to mask the lean-to roofs of the aisles. The central concentric arches of the main entrance are sculpted

6. *Hammersmith, St Augustine*

with foliage and symbols of the Eucharistic. These and the statue of the Virgin and Child were worked in Portland stone by R.L. Boulton of Cheltenham.

Immediately inside is a narthex glazed to the nave, and two ancillary rooms with a gallery housing the organ by Bishop & Son. The main interior is planned with nave and broad processional aisles of six bays, chancel and two side chapels. The aisle and clerestory windows are all round-headed, the roof of pitch pine braced with additional tie-rods. The nave piers are circular in plan, with capitals bearing symbols on four faces of incidents in the life of Christ, sculpted by Boulton. There is no chancel arch, the system of nave bays extending uninterrupted into the sanctuary. Around the apse is a blank arcade, with pilasters rising to a ribbed vault. The altar, ambo and font of Carrara marble were installed in 1988 during renovations undertaken by the Arvanitakis Partnership.

The Lady Chapel to the north was given a new altar and renewed marble decor in 1960 by D. Plaskett Marshall. At the same time the apse was opened to a new east nave constructed as part of extensive parochial buildings at the rear of the church. Owing to falling numbers, however, the apse wall was restored in 1988, and the east nave was put to other parochial uses.

To the south is the chapel of St Nicholas of Tolentino, an Augustinian friar of the twelfth century. Its altar of Carrara marble was supplied by Edmund Sharp of Dublin in 1920. Flanking the altar are freestanding niches on plinths of Sicilian marble, housing statues of St Nicholas and St Augustine. In the frontal there is a marble crest with symbolism of the Blessed Sacrament and St Augustine, and in the floor is a chalice executed in mosaic. The window depicting St Nicholas is a memorial to the Tyler family, 1952. On the altar steps of Italian dove grey marble is a remnant of the altar rail, made by Boulton and installed as a memorial to Prior Reid, founder of the church. The reredos picture of St Nicholas was painted by Fr Edward Foran. By him also are the Stations of the Cross, colourful works with a strong perspective feeling.

Near to the south-east chapel is St Anthony executed in ceramic. Various statues are placed around the church—the Sacred Heart, St Patrick, St Joseph (by BOW), St Augustine, St Teresa and St Rita of Cascia by La Statue Religieuse.

Bibliography
Kelly, p. 182; Rottmann, pp. 116-18; Evinson, pp. 51-53; *The Tablet*, 3 April 1915, p. 446; 21 October 1916, p. 546; *CBR.S*, 1961, pp. 81-83

Parsons Green, Holy Cross, Ashington Road, SW6

Fr William Kelly of Hammersmith had a Mass centre and school in Parsons Green Lane in 1842–48, which became the nucleus of St Thomas's mission. The permanent mission of Parsons Green was established when Canon C.J. Keens opened a school chapel in Ashington Road in June 1884. The architect of this building (which still stands, as Holy Cross School) was Francis W. Tasker;

7. Parsons Green, Holy Cross

the builders were Messrs Stimpson. The school occupied the upper floor, the chapel the ground floor. In 1887, however, the school took over the whole building when a temporary iron church was opened nearby.

The permanent church of the Holy Cross was not built until 1924, this and the Church of Our Lady in Stephendale Road both being paid for by Mr Edward Eyre. The architects were Fr Benedict Williamson, who supplied sketch plans, and T.H.B. Scott, who provided detailed plans and overall supervision. The foundation stone was laid on 19 January 1924 by Bishop Butt, and the church was formally opened on 21 December following by Cardinal Bourne. A west extension designed by Thomas Birchall Scott, son of the original architect, was constructed in 1956. This comprised one bay of nave and aisles with gallery over, and a narthex.

The exterior presents to the south-west a nice arrangement of parts, including a longish nave and aisles, to which are added transepts, narthex and the tall west front with its bell-cote and statue. The principal material is Hampshire Cottage brick, with added dressings of Portland stone. The style is derived from Romanesque, with a sparing added use of Egyptian capitals and moulded corbels.

Within the narthex there is a copy of Michelangelo's Bruges Madonna and Child. Glazed doors lead to the nave and narrow passage aisles, of five bays with a west gallery. The system is wholly traditional—round-headed arches raised

VI. HAMMERSMITH AND FULHAM

on piers of square plan which bear Egyptian capitals, and corbels for the soffits of the arches; no clerestory, but high rounded windows in the aisles; a king-post roof and two built-in confessionals. A slightly projecting transept leads to the chancel and chapels. The sanctuary has much panelling work of differently coloured marbles. The high altar was designed and installed by Fenning of Fulham in 1958; above it is a crucifix framed by a corbelled arch. The south Chapel of the Sacred Heart has a similar marble panelled altar. On the south wall is a tall plaque carved with figures of the four evangelists. The north-east Altar of Our Lady Queen of Peace has a statue of the Madonna and Child. Its reredos in mosaic was erected in memory of those who died in the war of 1914–18.

The Stations of the Cross are signed M. Chantral 1922; and at the west end of the south aisle there is a small window to St Thomas More.

Bibliography
Kelly, p. 311; Rottmann, pp. 49-52; Evinson, pp. 64-65; *The Tablet*, 27 December 1924, p. 868; 20 October 1928, p. 526; *Fulham Chronicle*, 26 October 1956, p. 9

Polish Church, St Andrew Bobola, Leysfield Road, W12

The Polish community had only one church in London, in Islington, until this was acquired in 1961. The new English Presbyterian Church, erected in 1870 by Perry Brothers to designs of Edmund Woodthorpe was bought for £10,000 and opened for Catholic use on 8 December 1961. The architect for the conversion was Alexsander P. Klecki.

The exterior remains a staid, stone-built Victorian Gothic piece, with a centrally placed (ritual) west tower in four stages, a wide aisleless nave, tall transepts and ancillary eastern extensions both old and new.

The main entrance through the tower gives direct access to the nave, and from the vestibule a glazed screen gives an unobstructed view of the altar. Above the vestibule is an organ gallery; then the nave of five bays with Early English windows of coupled and tripled lancet lights. Over the nave there is a hammer-beam roof, the hammer-beam system fashioned into a quadripartite arrangement in the east bay over the chancel.

The furnishings designed by the architect include the altar, pulpit, candlesticks and rails; Christ the King of aluminium on steel, with a bronze crown; the Stations of the Cross and the large reredos representing the Martyrdom of St Andrew Bobola in panels of ciment fondu with a bronze cold-cast finish. The nave windows of the 1980s are variously signed A. Klecki and Janina Baranowska.

A further building stage involved the construction of a south aisle with Blessed Sacrament chapel and baptistery, and the construction of a hall to the east.

Bibliography
Architect and Building News, 26 December 1962, pp. 951-54; *The Universe*, 15 May 1981, p. 27

Shepherds Bush, Holy Ghost and St Stephen, Ashchurch Grove, W12

The customary pattern of missionary development was repeated in this expanding suburb of Hammersmith when in June 1889 Fr Arthur Pownall opened a room as a first chapel at 33 Askew Crescent. Fr Bernard Pownall joined the mission in the same year, and succeeded his cousin as rector in 1892. With the financial assistance of the Hon. Charles Petre, he erected a school chapel in Rylett Road, which was opened in May 1892. Afterwards, the chapel was enlarged, and then superseded by an iron church in the playground. This temporary church being quite inadequate, plans were made by Canon Scoles for a new church on the model of St Augustine's, Stroud Green, on a site in Ashchurch Grove.

When the foundation stone was laid on 29 March 1903, the intention was to leave the north aisle for future completion. However, when the incomplete church, consisting of nave, south aisle and sanctuary, was opened on 5 April 1904, arrangements were already in hand for the remaining aisle and chapel to be provided. The cost of this work and of the high altar was defrayed by Mrs Charlotte Elizabeth Petre. By this time the priest architect Canon Scoles was in partnership with his nephew Geoffrey Raymond. The general contractor was John McManus of Hammersmith, the altar was installed by A.B. Wall of Cheltenham, and the overall cost was in the region of £6,000.

Romanesque had been the intended style,[3] but what emerged was yet another Gothic design. The highly symmetrical triple-gabled façade of red brick and Portland stone is clearly delineated by means of buttresses. It bears tall windows with cusped lancet lights, and Gothic plate tracery with quatrefoils punched into the surrounding stone. Above the doors are relief sculptures of the Holy Ghost and St Stephen, and in the centre a statue of the saint beneath a Gothic canopy.

8. *Shepherds Bush, Holy Ghost and St Stephen*

Internally, the church bears the traditional features of a deep chancel and aisles wide enough for congregational seating, two aspects of the long neglected Puginian ideal. Reading the plan from west to east, one sees a vestibule with

---

3. *The Architect*, 29 May 1903, Supplement, p. 20.

organ gallery; nave and aisles of five bays with octagonal piers and two-light clerestory windows; the tall, deep chancel; north-east Lady Chapel; south-east Sacred Heart Chapel; and off the north aisle a series of shallow recesses with shrines, baptistery and confessionals. The most arresting feature is the marble reredos with paintings of saints in arched panels; above these a turreted and pinnacled monstrance throne surrounded by paintings of angels, and higher still a quatrefoil stained glass window. The marble pulpit has on its faces relief sculptures of saints; the Stations of the Cross consist of small carvings in high relief; the large mural of St Stephen on the south wall was painted by Gary Hier in 1978; and the Lady Chapel's north window was designed by Veronica Whall in 1948.

Bibliography
Kelly, p. 353; Rottmann, pp. 125-26; *The Tablet*, 2 July 1895, p. 36; 12 January 1901, p. 75; 10 August 1901, p. 225; 8 March 1902, pp. 391-92; 29 May 1903, p. 871; 9 April 1904, p. 594; *Br*, 6 June 1903, p. 595; 23 April 1904, p. 443; *BN*, 12 June 1903, p. 815; 8 April 1904, p. 534; 22 April 1904, p. 581; *West London Observer*, 20 July 1978, p. 14

Stephendale Road, Our Lady of Perpetual Help, SW6

This church was opened on 17 December 1922 by Cardinal Bourne. It had the same architects as the nearby Holy Cross Church, Parsons Green, namely Fr Benedict Williamson in association with T.H.B. Scott, and both churches were paid for by Mr Edward Eyre.

The severe exterior of grey stock bricks is best viewed from the north (ritual west). The walls are sheer to the parapets, unbroken by a single moulding. The eye is caught therefore by the tall north-west bell-tower with its statue of Portland stone and its pyramidal copper roof. There are two recessed entrances with Portland stone capitals, and a rose window in the gable.

Inside, the impact is made by the generous disposal of space—three tall round-arched bays to the nave and chancel, with tall narrow aisles. There is a king-post roof to the nave. The original oak lining of the organ loft, piers and walls has been modified by inserted plywood panels. The piers, lined to a height of six or seven feet, are of square plan with capitals reminiscent of early Florentine designs. There are tall, arched windows high above the aisles. Off the

9. Stephendale Road, Our Lady

south aisle there is an arcade of four bays, with various shallow ancillary spaces.

The former stone altar and rails have been removed, and also the painted Crucifixion. The reredos remains, however, with pilasters supporting an entablature which in turn carries six pedestals beneath a triangular pediment.

The Lady Altar also remains, similar in design to the former high altar, its frontal decorated with a cross, alpha and omega. The style of these and of other sacred symbols, and of the pilasters, is in Williamson's Egyptian manner. The reredos is distinguished by a picture of Our Lady of Perpetual Help. Matching the overall decor, and obviously designed by the architects are the Stations of the Cross carved in stone, and the benches supplied by Bennett.

Bibliography
The Tablet, 23 December 1922, p. 860; *Westminster Cathedral Chronicle*, 1923, pp. 25-26

White City, Our Lady of Fatima, Commonwealth Avenue, W12

The church hall formed the nucleus of the mission founded by Fr Thomas Daniel in 1951. The foundation stone was blessed on 20 February 1965, and the church dedicated to Our Lady of Fatima at Cardinal Heenan's behest was opened on 15 August 1965. The architect was Wilfred Cassidy, the builders Walker Symondson Ltd.

Situated on the corner of Commonwealth Avenue and Canada Way, the church is prominent while blending with the neighbouring school and council housing. It is of London stock brick, with extended dressings of Portland stone to the (ritual) west front. This makes its ecclesiastical impact by means of a triple-arched entrance with mosaic

10. *White City, Our Lady of Fatima*

designs above the doors, a Venetian window above, and a square Italianate north-west tower. The long north and south lines are broken on each side by projections for aisles, confessionals and transepts.

One enters a west vestibule with glazed doors, ancillary rooms and organ gallery. This is followed by a wide nave and narrow aisles. There are seven piers (lacking capitals), and tall round-headed windows in each bay of aisle and clerestory. At the west end are a series of built-in confessionals. The roof bears in each bay a single arched principal which is corbelled into the wall, its weight then descending to the aisle piers.

The two easternmost bays have a shallow transept containing the chancel, and shrines to Our Lady of Fatima and the Sacred Heart. On the chancel are a large new tabernacle plinth, altar and baptismal font in Portland stone. Further to the east an arch encloses a shallow semi-domed recess. The Stations of the Cross, sombre in dark blues and browns, were painted on wood by John Watts.

Bibliography
CBR.S, 1966, p. 34; 1980, pp. 80-90

VII
Islington

Bunhill Row, St Joseph, Lamb's Passage, EC1

ST JOSEPH'S School Chapel in Bunhill Row is listed in the Catholic Directory from 1850. Later the establishment migrated to Golden Lane for two years, after which a new building was opened on 1 December 1856. The chapel, within the mission of the pro-cathedral of St Mary Moorfields in Finsbury Circus, was built above two schoolrooms designed by Edmund J. Kelly of 23 Thavies Inn, in a plain, unassuming Gothic, with a rectangular nave, an apse containing the altar, and north and south porches. This was replaced in 1901 by the present building. Here, the chapel is at basement level, beneath three storeys of a former school building. The names of the architect and builder have not come to light, nor the precise date of its opening. Following its restoration by Messrs Fetherston Construction Ltd after years of neglect and damaging reordering, the church was formally dedicated by Cardinal Hume on 14 October 1993.

The church is well signposted, and, despite being tucked away, the entrance is further emphasised by a prominent classical arch, built in 1993 to the design of the architect Anthony Delarue. Within its triangular pediment are the papal tiara and keys, and rising above is a cross flanked by pineapples, the symbol of friendship. A flight of steps descends to the church. En route are 14 wrought-iron crosses, designed by the architect and made in France. One enters the church through a small vestibule containing an eighteenth- or early nineteenth-century water stoup from one of the previous chapels. The statue of St Joseph above the entrance door was the gift of the parish of St Mary, Chelsea.

The church has a simple interior, clear and concise, rectangular in plan with two shallow pilasters dividing nave and sanctuary. Beneath the panelled ceiling, the walls are arcaded, some bays glazed and others blind. The round-headed arches were dictated by a series of stained glass windows dating from the 1820s, and brought from the old St Mary Moorfields church after it was pulled down in 1899. Two of these now grace the sanctuary, depicting the Agony in the Garden and the Good Shepherd. Two more, the Descent from the Cross and the Death of St Joseph, were destroyed by enemy action in the 1940s.

There are several cast statues, and modern cast Stations of the Cross given by subscription, which replaced the original nineteenth-century German stations in the 1980s. This was a sad loss. A Grotto of Our Lady of Lourdes was built at the time of the restoration in 1993. Its statue comes from the old school. Its hanging lamp is nineteenth-century French work. In the nave there is a handsome eighteenth-century font of black marble, perhaps from the original Moorfields Chapel, with a new Baroque-style cover.

Bibliography

Kelly, pp. 108-109; Rottmann, pp. 162-64; *The Tablet*, 12 April 1856, p. 229; 6 December 1856, p. 771; 3 September 1864, p. 565; *CB* 35 (September/October 1995), pp. 48-49

Clerkenwell, Ss Peter and Paul, Amwell Street, EC1

A school founded from Lincoln's Inn Fields by Fr John Hearn became the nucleus of this mission in July 1842. Bishop Griffiths appointed two Spanish priests, whose chapel was a room in a disused workhouse in Saffron Hill.

The present church, designed by John Blyth, had been erected for the Countess of Huntingdon's Connexion in 1835. When its congregation diminished, it was put up for auction and was purchased by the Catholics for £2,300. It was opened as a Catholic church on 13 June 1847.

The (ritual) west front has a central door and flanking windows with Ionic pilasters and an entablature. There are two side doors. The upper storey consists of a central Venetian window flanked by two round-headed windows, with balustrades resting on corbels.

The inside consists of a large rectangular hall. Above a west vestibule glazed to the interior there is a deep west

1. *Clerkenwell, Ss Peter and Paul*

gallery with wrought-iron Gothic rails extending along the sides, supported by cast-iron columns with Corinthian capitals. Owing to the gallery, the multi-paned windows run in two storeys, rectangular below and round-headed above. There is a flat plaster ceiling, panelled and coffered.

There is no architectural division for the chancel, but a feature is made of three tall round-headed arches defined on the east wall by Corinthian pilasters. The chancel furniture is all of timber by Ormsby of Scarisbrick, with some applied relief carvings—Emmaeus for the altar, symbols of the evangelists for the lectern and an ear of wheat for the tabernacle stand. There is a fine Ortisei-type crucifix. Also on the chancel are cast statues of St Peter and St Paul, signed Hall, Paris. The Blessed Sacrament is reserved to the left, beside it a cast statue of the Blessed Virgin Mary.

The Stations of the Cross, painted in oils on canvas, have the appearance of Victorian studio work, perhaps by Mayer. There are four windows bearing stained glass, all in the same post-1945 style. They contain St Martin of Porres, St Teresa of Lisieux, St Anthony and St Vincent Pallotti, signed CE.

Bibliography
Kelly, p. 135; Rottmann, pp. 155-58; W.J. Pinks (London: Charles Herbert, 1881), *The History of Clerkenwell*, pp. 174, 578; *Is. Chapels*, pp. 24-25; *Architectural Magazine* 3 (1836), p. 41

Highbury, St Joan of Arc, Highbury Park, N5

The first church was a Nissen hut opened in Kelross Road on 13 October 1920. This was extended in 1925, but as the congregation continued to grow, the church remained permanently inadequate in size. A Carmelite convent had been founded here in 1918, and following war damage it was closed in the 1950s, the site thereby serving for a new church.

The foundation stone was laid by Cardinal Godfrey on 30 May 1961. The church was blessed by the parish priest Fr Robert Tollemache on 19 April 1962 and formally opened by Bishop Cashman on 23 September following. The architects were Messrs Walters & Kerr Bate; the contractors Whatt Builders of Streatham. The materials are two-inch Dutch bricks laid in five courses of stretchers to one course of headers, with dressings of Bath and Clipsham stone.

An impressive west front faces the road, a high gable presenting to the view a seven-light, neo-Perpendicular window in three tiers. To the right is the presbytery, and to the left the tall campanile, with massive angle buttresses and narrow louvres. Poised above its open top is a copper-covered pyramidal roof, its finial a radioactive lightning preventor, the first of its kind in England.

Inside, the plan is seen to be traditional, with narthex, nave and aisles, transepts, chancel and side chapel. The nave is dominated by its transverse arches, but the banks of windows in groups of seven, with their tiny convex-pointed arches throughout aisles and clerestory throw a respectful nod

2. Highbury, St Joan of Arc

towards the character of late Gothic. Within each window are two stained glass panels bearing sacred symbols, 44 of them in all, designed by A.E. Buss of Goddard & Gibbs. The narthex is glazed to the nave, and above it is a gallery with organ by J.W. Walker & Sons. In the nave are carved Stations of the Cross, in the 1960s style of Burns Oates. To the south of the nave is the baptistery, with octagonal stone font, and fibre-glass relief decoration in memory of L.G. Parisi +1966.

Low circular arches give on to the passage aisles, which contain built-in confessionals. The aisle furnishings include a carved crucifix, statues of St Patrick and St Antony, and another set of Stations of the Cross, framed coloured prints by Ian Howgate. In the south transept is the Sacred Heart Altar; in the north transept the Altar of St Joan of Arc, with a perspex statue of 1962 by Arthur Fleischmann.

The sanctuary, two bays deep, arched and vaulted in concrete, has marble steps and matching ambos of Ancaster stone to left and right; two wooden altars and a large carved crucifix. To its north is the Lady Chapel, glazed to the sanctuary. Its original altar in Belgian black marble has a monogram 'M' in the frontal. The piscina is inset with mosaic in blue and gold. By Ferdinand Stuflesser are the tall carved statues of the Madonna, and St Joseph the Worker.

Bibliography
Rottmann, p. 218; *CBR.S*, 1959, p. 51; 1963, pp. 61-63; 1964, p. 45; *Is. Chapels*, pp. 83-85; *Catholic Herald*, 21 September 1962, p. 5

The Passionist Fathers have been in

Highgate, St Joseph, Highgate Hill, N19

London since 1848. From their house at Hyde near Edgeware they purchased in 1858 the Highgate property which included a house, office and a site for a church. A small temporary church was built in 1859 by John and Edward Bird of Hammersmith who also furnished the plans. This proved to be too small, and the Fathers determined to build a new church 'spacious and practical, one of the simple and severe character which should distinguish a Passionist church and from the designs of E.W. Pugin'.[1] This was opened for use in 1861 and completed in 1863. In 1875 the Fathers rebuilt their monastery in stages on the site of the old house, employing F.W. Tasker as architect. In 1880 they undertook an extensive decoration of the church, under the direction of Albert Vicars. Then, surprisingly, the Passionists obliterated their decorations with a complete rebuilding of the church. The foundation stone was laid on 24 May 1888, and the present church, to Vicars's design, was opened on 21 November 1889. Considering the generous size of the new church, the Fathers took the unusual course of not employing a general contractor; they literally carried out the work themselves, Brother Alphonsus acting as superintendant under the general supervision of the architect.

The church that Vicars designed is Romanesque in style, brick-built with stone dressings. Placed on an acute-angled corner site, the front of the nave has five stepped arches in its gable, a large wheel window and an arched entrance with the Espousal of the Virgin in the tympanum, flanked by St Peter and St Paul. The design is dominated however by the east dome, 138 feet high to the top of the cross. This is balanced by the domed north-west tower, 108 feet tall.

Inside, the Romanesque design is clothed with extravagant Italianate furnishings and decoration. An entrance bay with gallery above is supported by piers with capitals displaying musical instruments. Beyond an arched, glazed screen are the nave and aisles of six bays. The circular piers bear Corinthian capitals, whose foliage blends with symbols of Our Lord's Passion. Above a panelled stage, round-headed clerestory windows with stained glass figures penetrate the elliptical ceiling, and in between the windows are painted figures of saints. The multi-panelled ceiling was decorated by N.H.J. Westlake with figures of angels and verses of the *Te Deum*.

3. Highgate, St Joseph

1. *The Tablet*, 22 January 1859, p. 52.

The wedge-shaped site dictated a broadening of the church from west to east, so that the succession of chapels and confessionals off the aisles becomes progressively deeper. Off the left aisle is the shrine of the *pietà*; adjacent to it a painting of the Crucifixion. Behind a six-bay arcade is the spacious Lady Chapel, with a post-war marble altar and rails. The reredos consisting of three mosaic panels has in the centre Our Lady sculpted in Carrara marble against a gold background, flanked by the Annunciation and the Coronation. Next is the Chapel of Passionist Saints, with a domed ceiling and a painting by M.A. Laby of St Paul of the Cross kneeling in prayer. This chapel leads us to the sanctuary.

Since the limitations of the site precluded transepts, the architect was forced to fashion his dome over the sanctuary rather than above a crossing. The happy outcome is the greatest interior prominence given to the sanctuary, where the sumptuous baldacchino and altar of 1904 by Edmund Sharp of Dublin are brilliantly lit from above. The steps are of Sicilian, and the sanctuary floor is laid with mosaic. Above the baldacchino are frescoes to left and right of the Nativity and the Death of St Joseph. A forward altar of marble and sandstone by Gerald Murphy of Burles, Newton & Partners was installed in 1964. To this was subsequently added the matching ambo in memory of Sylvester Ijoma Oti +1988, with the Passionist symbol incised on its front. Near the ambo hangs a canvas of the Holy Family, presented by Sir Charles Santley.

The south chancel chapel has above its altar a pedimented arch containing a statue of the Sacred Heart, and a canvas of the Crucifixion. Along the south aisle there are eight windows with stained glass roundels containing sacred symbols.

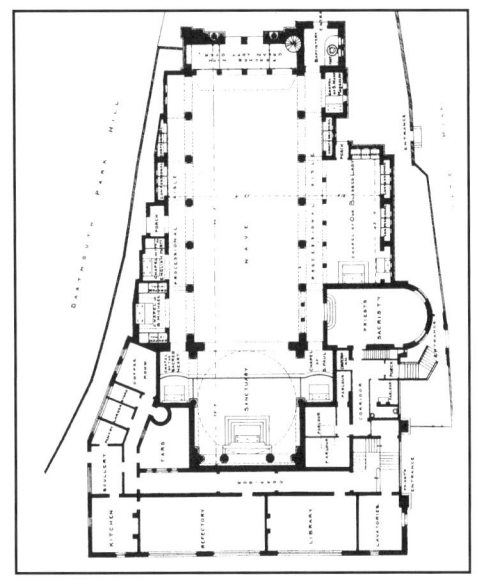

4. *Highgate, St Joseph, plan*

The aisle contains the chapel of St Michael—a memorial to the Rev. Michael Watts Russell +1875—with marble altar and rails exhibited at the Paris Exhibition of 1889. Its frontal has relief figures of angels, and St Michael stands above. Next to this is the Martyrs' Chapel, with marble altar and rails, and a painted reredos depicting Forty Martyrs of England and Wales.

In the aisles are the Stations of the Cross, large painted relief carvings with foliage surrounds, by F. Devriendt, installed in 1886. In the nave is the font, of stone with marble columns and symbolism in relief on its eight faces. Nearby is the hexagonal oaken pulpit and tester with carved relief panels of the Holy Family, a memorial to Elizabeth Tooley +1937.

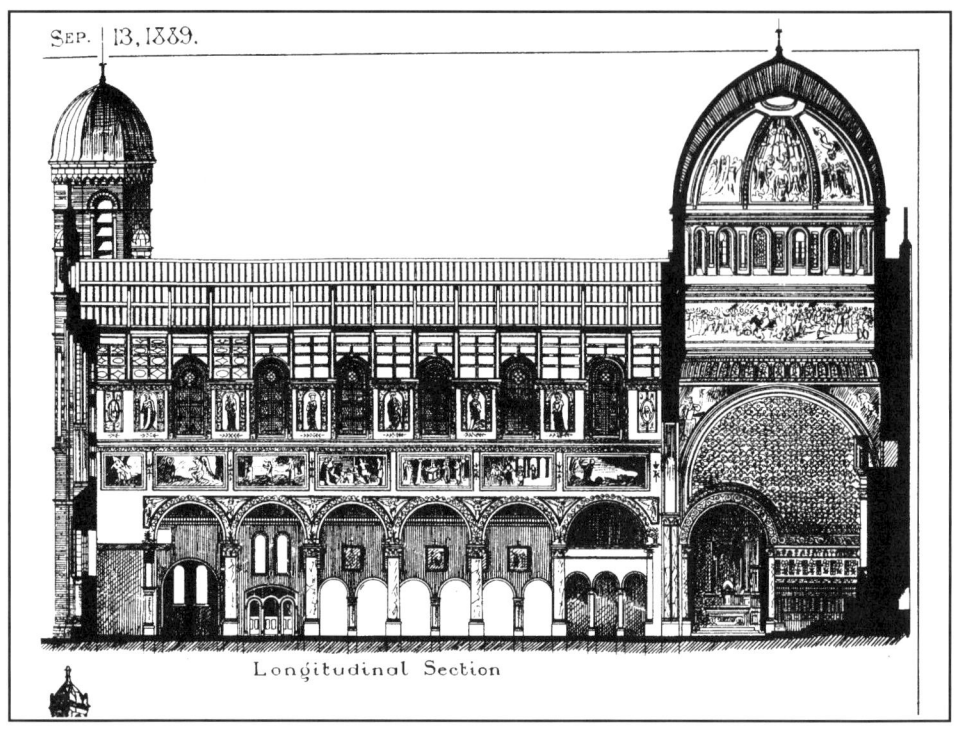

5. *Highgate, St Joseph, section*

Bibliography
Kelly, p. 213; Rottmann, pp. 216-18; The Tablet, 10 July 1858, p. 437; 11 February 1860, p. 85; 2 June 1860, p. 342; 27 April 1861, p. 268; 4 May 1861, p. 278; 17 August 1861, p. 517; 18 September 1880, p. 370; 20 February 1904, pp. 311-12; Br, 25 September 1880, p. 397; BN, 11 August 1874, p. 214; 1 January 1875, p. 8; 19 June 1875, p. 559; 13 September 1889, p. 350; CD, 1905, p. 120; CBR.S, 1960, p. 67; Westminster Record, 15 January 1988, p. 4

Holloway, Sacred Heart of Jesus, Eden Grove, N7

The mission was founded in December 1854 from St John the Evangelist, Duncan Terrace, by Canon Oakeley, initially at 5 Albany Place. By March 1855, premises were rented at 19 Cornwall Place, which served as a school during the week and as a chapel on Sundays. Following an enlargement owing to the numbers attending, this was formally opened on 11 June 1855. By this time there were two schools, established by the munificence of the Countess of Shrewsbury and Mrs Canning. In 1868 Canon Keens was given charge of the mission. By March 1869, he had secured a site for a church and schools, at a cost of £1,500. The foundation stone was laid on 5 August 1869, and the church was opened by Archbishop Manning on 18 August 1870. F.H. Pownall was the architect of the Early English design, and the builders were Messrs Carter of Holloway Road. The cost was in the region of

£7,000. The sanctuary was remodelled in 1961 by Archard & Partners. Its new high altar was blessed by Bishop Cashman on 7 March 1961.

The (ritual) west front, flanked by schools and presbytery, is asymmetrical,

6. Holloway, Sacred Heart

with a lean-to aisle roof to the left, and a stout tower to the right, with a porch at its foot. Pownall's design for the tower had three storeys with a pair of lancets, a tall bell-stage with paired bell openings, and a saddleback roof. The omission of the upper parts is a real aesthetic loss. To the nave there are two tall lancets and a cusped wheel window; to the aisle a two-light window with a heavily cusped trefoil. In the centre is the War Memorial, 1914–18, by Jones & Willis.

Inside, the walls of red brick are relieved by bands of black brick and stone dressings. The plan consists of nave and aisles, sanctuary and side chapels. The nave is five bays long, with circular piers of blue pennant stone bearing lush foliage capitals donated by Mr Holland, and sculpted by Farmer & Brindley. The clerestory consists of paired and single lancets in alternate bays.

The west gallery was added in 1961. Its stained glass window illustrates the Mysteries of the Rosary. Beneath is a bronze figure of St Peter by Froc-Robert, Paris. The baptistery has wrought-iron rails and a vase-like font, a monolith of alabaster. Overlooking it is a stained glass window of the Baptism of Our Lord.

Along the left side there are three recesses, originally for built-in confessionals, and the Sacred Heart shrine with a carved statue. In the opposite aisle there are three windows depicting St Thomas More, St Edmund Campion and Bl. Margaret Pole; alternating with statues of St Antony, St Patrick and a carved St George. There are fine Minton tiled floors to the nave and aisles; and the Stations of the Cross, painted relief tableaux carved by Anton Dapre are mounted in gold Gothic frames.

All three altars and their steps are now renewed, all of marble with a generous use of Sicilian, that is white marble bearing irregular bluish veins. Each has its own tasteful appeal. The Lady Altar has oatmeal coloured panels and the legend 'My soul glorifies the Lord'. The centrepiece is a Madonna and Child made in 1924. Also here is a dignified St Joseph, carved work by Vanpoulle. The two-light window depicts the Annunciation and the Nativity.

The sanctuary is two bays deep, its altar of Sicilian with mosaic decoration. The reredos, a tall panel of verde antico framed in white, displays the Crucifix, the figure mounted on a cross of black marble. The window by Hardman illustrates devotion to the Sacred Heart. Other windows are attributed to Thomas Grew, artist and choirmaster.

Finally, the Blessed Sacrament altar is constructed of various light-coloured marbles. Inset above the tabernacle is an embroidered Risen Christ flanked by 'I am with you always'. The subjects of the traceried window are St Joseph's Dream and the Flight into Egypt.

Bibliography
Kelly, p. 216; Rottmann, pp. 214-15; *Is. Chapels*, pp. 97-99; *The Tablet*, 20 January 1855, p. 38; 24 March 1855, p. 181; 28 April 1855, p. 262; 16 June 1855, p. 373; 10 October 1891, p. 595; 26 March 1892, p. 512; 21 July 1894, p. 104; *BN*, 21 May 1869, p. 457; 18 June 1869, p. 557; 13 August 1869, p. 138; Br, 14 August 1869, p. 655; 17 September 1870, pp. 752-53; *CBR.S*, 1961, pp. 94-95

Islington, St John the Evangelist, Duncan Terrace, N1

The mission was founded from Moorfields. In order to serve the growing Catholic population of Islington, a school chapel was built in 1839, to designs of J.J. Scoles. The foundation stone of the present church was blessed by Bishop Griffiths on 27 September 1841, and the church was opened by him on 26 June 1843. The architect was again Scoles, the builder Mr Tiernan of Somers Town.

Scoles's neo-Norman design was severely castigated by Pugin in *The Dublin Review*, in which he called for a rebuilding of Islington's mediaeval Gothic church. Joseph Hansom, however, powerfully defended Scoles's church in the pages of *The Builder*, of which he was then editor, pointing out that Catholicism had other 'beautiful forms, styles and adaptations in store for us'.[2] The design is, in fact, an inspired adaptation in Norman terms of the plan initiated in Rome's church of the Gesu in 1568 by Giacomo Vignola, involving a broad nave flanked by a series of chapels between the buttresses.

When opened in 1843, the church's twin towers were incomplete. The

7. Islington, St John the Evangelist

[2]. *Br*, 1 April 1843, p. 98.

(ritual) west front was finished in 1870, with towers and spires differing (on Canon Frederick Oakeley's decision), not only from each other, but from Scoles's design. Otherwise, the façade is symmetrical, having a central round-headed doorway with double angle shafts and the Papal Arms in the tympanum, three upper windows and wheel window in the gable. Flanking this are the towers with tall angle shafts. Each has an arched doorway, two stages of single narrow openings, bell stage and a pyramidal roof. The south tower is taller than the north, owing to the interpolation of a tier of blank arcading beneath the bell stage. The War Memorial, 1914–19, of Portland stone with Carrara panels was sculpted by M. and R. Moore. The interior consists of a large rectangular nave of five bays flanked by chapels, and apsidal sanctuary. The west gallery was built to J.J. Scoles's design and an organ installed in 1861. The present organ by J.W. Walker dates from 1963.

The vestibule was glazed to the nave in 1884. Above the nave's arcaded walls is the clerestory, ten red and blue bordered arched windows on each side, beneath a roll moulding supported by Corinthian columns. Each pair of windows is now punctuated by the principals of the hammer-beam roof, which replaced Scoles's original roof truss during a renovation by F.W. Tasker in 1884.

The church has been continually enriched by paintings. The earliest decoration soon after the opening was the Transfiguration in the semi-dome of the apse by S. Aglio, renewed in 1963. To this, Edward Armitage added a fresco of Christ and the Apostles in 1861–62, now obliterated. Also within the apse are three niches containing statues of Ss Peter, James and John. At ground level there is a series of blank arches. These surround the marble- and mosaic-decorated frontal and tabernacle of the old altar. Before it is a light, stone altar with moulded supports, and at its front are sacred symbols worked in mosaic.

The chapels now claim our attention, beginning on the right with the Lady Chapel. This is recorded as decorated by

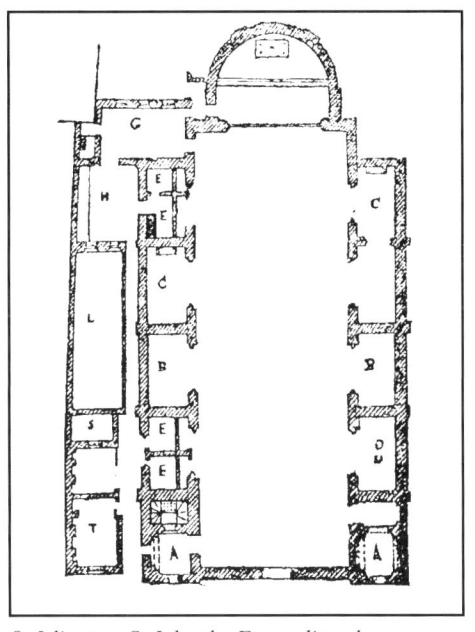

8. *Islington, St John the Evangelist, plan*

Pitman & Son in 1883. Behind its marble balustrade, the altar and frontal are raised on columns. There is a handsome tiled floor, and around the walls blank arcading defined by Corinthian columns. The statue of Our Lady comes from Munich, and is probably the work of Mayer.

The Chapel of St Joseph was erected during Canon Tynan's rectorate between the wars. The statue of the saint presented by Cardinal Bourne once stood in St Mary's Church in Horseferry Road. On the rear wall are memorial tablets to Canon Leopold Pycke +1921; Mgr Henry Grosch +1923; Canon Frederick Oakeley +1880; and James Joseph Hicks +1916.

The Chapel of St Francis was furnished in 1882 to designs of the architect J.J. Connelly. The altar's frontal is a blank arcade in Gothic style with marble infill; the mensa of Siena; behind it a mosaic panel of red and white roses growing from the same bush; higher still, Gothic panels infilled with foliage patterns in blue mosaic; and finally an entablature of red Mansfield stone with a bracket supporting the statue of the saint, which stands before a frescoed background. The altar step and the chapel floor are of Sicilian marble, dated 1882 with the initials (of the donors?) PS and TS. Opposite the altar, a fresco of St Francis and his companions before Pope Innocent III, of 1859 by Armitage, was repainted by him on canvas in 1887. The artist preserved the general plan of the original, but restudied heads, hands and draperies. Another Armitage canvas of St Francis and St Dominic dates from 1882. Next comes the baptistery behind cast-iron rails, with marble-faced walls and paved with tiles. The font is raised on a stout base, its faces sculpted with sacred symbols. On the walls are frescoes of Christ raising Lazarus, signed GA 1910; the Baptism of Christ, in monochrome tints by Charles Beyaert of Bruges; and a painting of the Conversion of Hermogenes, after Mantegna's fresco in the Eremitani church in Padua, signed Holt 1921.

On the left side of the church is the Blessed Sacrament Chapel, whose walls were originally painted by H.T. Bulmer in 1855. The altar and tabernacle, of alabaster and marble, were designed by Goldie and Child, and sculpted by Thomas Earp in 1872. Before it is a small altar formerly in the nave in the 1960s. The remainder of this side is taken up by built-in confessionals. Scoles's design placed the penitent outside the screen, in Continental fashion, but later developments here and elsewhere soon placed the penitent inside a closed compartment. In the nave are the very fine Stations of the Cross acquired in 1884: fourteen oil paintings in oaken frames copied by Charles Beyaert of Bruges from the originals in Antwerp Cathedral done by J. Hendrix and F. Vinck in 1865–66.

Bibliography
Kelly, p. 229; Rottmann, pp. 211-13; J. and G. Basto, *Scrapbook* (London: St John the Evangelist Church, 1993); *Dublin Review*, February 1842, pp. 139-42; *Illustrated London News*, 1 July 1843, pp. 4-5; *BN*, 11 February 1870, p. 126; 5 August 1870, p. 104; 3 May 1872, p. 363; 16 September 1892, p. 407; *The Architect*, 3 May 1872, p. 363; 7 June 1887, p. 14; 26 August 1887, p. 130; *The Tablet*, 9 October 1841, p. 655; 1 July 1843, p. 406; 12 March 1859, p. 166; 15 October 1859, p. 660; 26 May 1860, p. 326; 9 March 1861, p. 155; 28 September 1861, p. 613; 21 June 1862, p. 390; 12 July 1862, p. 438; 26 July 1862, p. 470; 2 August 1862, p. 486; 27 April 1872, p. 526; 9 June 1877, p. 725; 3 December 1881, pp. 911-12; 8 July 1882, p. 63; 9 December 1882, p. 952; 21 April 1883, p. 632; 8 November 1884, p. 751; 20 August 1887, p. 312; *CD*, 1903, p. 116

VII. ISLINGTON

Polish Church, Our Lady of Czestochowa and St Casimir, Devonia Road, N1

The Polish mission commenced in 1904 with a chapel in Cambridge Road, Bethnal Green. The following year a sailors' home erected in Shadwell in 1856 under Prince Albert's patronage was leased by Cardinal Bourne, and adapted as a church and centre for the Polish population of east London. The community migrated to the present church in Islington in 1930. Here, the acquired premises were formerly the New Church College, erected in 1852 from designs of Edward Welch. Subsequently, a scheme published in 1915 for a church in Victoria Park, Hackney designed by Percy Lamb was not carried out.

The front to Devonia Road comprises three sections, a tall gabled centre separated from lower matching domestic quarters by buttressed spiral staircases beneath octagonal turrets. In the centre is the chapel's Perpendicular west window above an arched and gabled doorway. All is in the Tudor style, of brick with Bath stone dressings.

Beyond an arched stone screen the plan consists of nave and chancel, with a substantial Lady Chapel to the right of the nave. From the vestibule, steps lead to the choir gallery and the organ of 1874 by G.M. Holdich.

There is a king-post roof to the nave, penetrated by clerestory lights with patterned coloured glass. These and the (ritual) east window are of 1952–53 by Stanley G. Higgins. Other glass by Lowndes & Drury dates from 1939–45 designs of Adam Bunsch.

There is no structural division between nave and chancel. Behind a forward wooden altar the original reredos remains, with a wide ogee arch, two angels in the spandrels and a cornice entwined with vine leaves, executed in 1879 by Martyn & Emms of Cheltenham, from designs of Alexander Payne. The inset tabernacle is a memorial to Cardinal Bourne. To the left of the altar there is a gallery with Gothic detail corbelled out of the wall.

In the nave are sculpted statues of the Sacred Heart and St Antony Pomoz; and in the chapel St Stanislaus Koska and St Andrew Bobola. Also in the nave are the Stations of the Cross, bronze, of 1945 by J.Z. Henelt.

Bibliography
Kelly, p. 76; Rottmann, pp. 171-73; *Is. Chapels*, pp. 53-57; Br, 5 November 1915, p. 330; *Intellectual Repository*, August 1852, pp. 315-16; January 1853, pp. 36-37; March 1874, p. 142; December 1879, pp. 534-36

Tollington Park, St Mellitus, Tollington Park, N4

The mission was founded in 1925, and served from St Peter-in- Chains, Stroud Green. A temporary chapel built by Canon John Mostyn was opened in Everleigh Street in 1938. Finally, a Nonconformist church was acquired by Canon George Groves in 1958, and following adaptation for Catholic use by

9. *Tollington Park, St Mellitus*

the firm of Gordon Reeves, was opened in 1959. This had been the New Court Congregational Church, foundation stone 11 November 1870, designed by C.G. Searle & Son, built by Dove Brothers and opened in 1871.

It is an imposing Classical design, prominently situated on the corner of Tollington Park and Fonthill Road. The (ritual) west front is five bays wide, with a central projecting narthex of three bays, complete with Corinthian columns, entablature and triangular pediment. Within the narthex are three doorways bearing segmental pediments, with circular windows above. Along the side walls three tiers of windows are divided by Doric pilasters, and crowned by an entablature.

The interior consists of a large rectangular room, seven bays long, with no special architectural division for the chancel. The ceiling is double coved, and has panels decorated in grey and white. A large west gallery with a cast-iron and timber balustrade extends along the sides, supported on slender cast-iron Corinthian columns. Owing to the gallery, the side windows are in two tiers, rectangular below and round-headed above. Within the gallery is the organ, 1920 by A. Hunter; and two windows, the Good Shepherd of 1877, and Our Lady surrounded by children, 1907 by Wm G. Langford.

Below, the chancel and chapels are lightly raised on steps. The chancel is backed by a blank arch composed of fluted Corinthian piers and columns. In the rear wall is a central doorway defined by Corinthian pilasters and a triangular pediment; above it a series of trellised blank arches. The furnishings of the three altars are all of timber. The Blessed

Sacrament Altar has a timber reredos in which Doric pilasters create panelled spaces. There is a large crucifix over the high altar, and a Madonna and Child on the Lady Altar, carved with admirable economy of line. The Stations of the Cross are interesting and unusual, consisting of figures sparingly incised on stone panels, with a measure of very low relief, and lightly coloured in pastel shades. Harry Ibbertson was the artist.

Bibliography
Is. Chapels, pp. 80-81; *Islington Gazette*, 2 August 1963

Upper Holloway, St Gabriel, Holloway Road, N19

The mission was founded from St Joseph's, Highgate, with a church built in 1928. When this was made over to the diocese in 1938, Cardinal Hinsley united it with Tollington Park mission, to form the joint parish of St Mellitus and St Gabriel, with Dr John Mostyn as the first parish priest. When St Gabriel's was made a separate parish in 1964, Canon George Groves purchased the site of the present church.

Bishop Casey blessed the foundation stone on 6 May 1967, and the church was opened by Cardinal Heenan on 17 December the same year. Gerard Goalen was the architect, Noel O'Connell the structural engineer, and Marshall Andrew & Company the contractors.

'The fortress-like quality of this church has been dictated by its position on a noisy trunk road.'[3] The exterior is indeed anonymous, and unglazed except for the porch and repository in St John's Villas. In Holloway Road there is a self-effacing entrance, and next to it two modest apses. For the rest, all is sheer windowless wall, of austere grey brick and broadmarked concrete.

Once inside, the contrast with the exterior is extreme. Past a well-lit porch glazed to the interior, one enters a large rectangular space, its corners comfortably curved. The flat panelled ceiling rests on 18 piers which define the ambulatory extending around three sides. The lower walls are indeed windowless, but daylight enters through windows above the ceiling, and is reflected off the walls into the main space below. The altar stands in the centre of the long side, facing the main entrance. Five banks of benches fill the congregational space which is raked, the efficient plan ensuring that every seat has a clear view, none being more than 40 feet from the altar.

The wide sanctuary is most tastefully furnished. The altar, lectern, chair and font are all constructed of plain stone of greenish tint, and designed with rectangular and curved elements artfully juxtaposed. Slightly recessed between piers there are bronze figures of the Risen Christ, the Madonna and Child, and angels surrounding the tabernacle.

To the left there are two shallow apsed shrines, with similar smaller figures of the Sacred Heart and St Gabriel. The ambulatory walls are marked by tall blank arches; and here hang the Stations of the Cross, rectangular bronze panels bearing starkly

---

3. *CBR.S*, 1966, p. 30.

represented relief figures in stylised settings. Just why this church is so comfortable both to body and spirit may be explained by its being, as it were, all of a piece. That is, the perceived totality of plan, structure and furnishings surely points to 'a directness of sense and taste rarely met'.[4]

Bibliography
Parish of St Gabriel's (booklet on the official opening, 1967); *Catholic Herald*, 21 September 1962, p. 6; *The Universe*, 12 May 1967, p. 2; 22 December 1967, p. 9; CBR.S, 1968, pp. 50-51; *Westminster Year Book*, 1969, pp. 200-201

---

4. *CB*, October 1960, p. 13.

VIII
Kensington and Chelsea

Bayswater, St Mary of the Angels, Moorhouse Road, W2

AN Oratory was projected here in 1848, but not carried through. However, a mission begun in 1849 thrived, and a school chapel was erected in 1851 to the design of Thomas Meyer. Meyer also designed the large Gothic church initially called St Helen's, after its patroness Mrs Helen Hargrave. The foundation stone was laid on 2 December 1851, but having reached the height of the aisle parapets, this ambitious work stopped for want of funds. Subsequently, Cardinal Wiseman appointed Manning here, as superior of the newly introduced Oblates of St Charles; work was resumed under Manning's kinsman, the architect Henry Clutton, and the church was opened on 2 July 1857.

Manning was committed to what he found already built at Bayswater. His attitude to Gothic is exposed, however, by one of the Oblates:

> Monsignor Manning had no love for Gothic architecture; if he had had in his hands the building of the church from its foundation, no trace of Gothic would have appeared in the design; but the building was too far advanced to be transformed into anything like an Italian church. He, however, made an attempt by hanging curtains over the beautiful tracery of the Gothic windows, and placing oil paintings of Saints where stained glass was intended to glow with light and many colours. After his consecration and removal to Archbishop's House at Westminster, he did not object to the wishes of the community that the original plan should be carried out; so gradually the curtains came down, and some very beautiful works of art in stained glass took their proper place.[1]

1. *Bayswater, St Mary of the Angels*

1. Kirk, p. 9.

Originally the church consisted of nave, aisles, chancel, north and south chancel chapels and the base of the south-west tower. The materials are Kentish rag with Bath stone dressings; the steps of Cragleith stone and the nave piers of Portland. However, the church was greatly extended by J.F. Bentley, who virtually doubled its size. Bentley's additions were the tower's belfry stage (1864); the outer north aisle containing the altars of the Sacred Heart and St Joseph (1868–69); the outer south aisle and Lady Chapel (1872–74); the south-east chapel of Ss Helen and Mary Magdalen (1876); and the two north-east chapels of the Holy Ghost and St Charles.

Meyer's engraving of 1852 shows a most impressive designated group of church, school and presbytery, clearly conceived under the strong influence of Pugin. Despite the absence of the spire, the upper reaches of the tower, the crocketed spirelets and the gables included by Meyer in such profusion, the present-day exterior viewed from Needham Road still exhibits a strong presence, with its banked stone masses of windowed confessionals, aisles and nave rising in succession.

Inside, the plan is quite conventional, except for the double aisles. The nave is seven bays long, its piers consisting of clustered columns, with a west gallery, and clerestory of spherical triangles containing various geometrical designs. At the north-west angle is the former baptistery with railings and gates of wrought iron, of 1868 by Bentley.

The high altar was supplied in 1914 by Jones & Willis. Its reredos of alabaster has panels of the Presentation and Finding in the Temple, St Ambrose and St Charles. The frontal has the Sacrifice of Melchizedek and the Supper at Emmaeus. Forged-iron screens separate the chancel and the east chapels. To the north, the Chapel of the Holy Ghost has an altar of alabaster framed with marble panels. This, together with the mosaic pavement and screen adjoining the chapel of St Charles, is of 1912 by George Power.

The chapel of St Charles was built in 1887 under Bentley. Its altar of 1903 was designed by F.W. Tasker; the reredos (of panelled stone and Connemara marble) by Hardman & Powell. An oaken aumbry in its north wall was designed by Bentley, to house the chasuble of St Charles. In the outer north aisle is the shrine of St Joseph, 1874 by Bentley, its reredos and frontal paintings by Westlake. The aisle also contains a north porch and two early built-in confessionals, with customary fireplaces for the comfort of hard-working priests. Immediately south of the chancel is the Chapel of St Helen and St Mary Magdalen, with its altar of 1876 by Bentley. The sacristy is adjacent, and so is the Lady Chapel, of 1872–74, with furnishings by Bentley. The altar and reredos are of Carrara marble, with relief foliage sculpture attractively highlighted in gold. The wrought-iron grille dates from 1876. The outer aisle consists of a twelve-bay wall arcade forming four built-in confessionals.

The church is rich in stained glass designed by Bentley and executed by Lavers, Barraud & Westlake. The windows include the north aisle, two lancets to St Joseph, 1871–75; Chapel of St Charles east window 1888, and three two-light windows to the English Martyrs 1893; Chapel of the Holy Ghost, Pentecost window 1888; Chapel of St Helen and St Mary Magdalen, two lancet lights 1875; the Lady Chapel, two windows depicting Eve, Ruth, Judith and Esther. In the south aisle designs by Bentley are recorded for the window of St Anthony, 1875, and two more windows of 1880. Other stained glass windows are: the chancel Coronation of Our Lady by Jones & Willis; and in the north aisle a three-light window to John Hungerford Pollen +1902, depicting the Virgin and Child, St Vincent de Paul and St John the Evangelist; designed originally by Pollen himself for the Chapel of Studley Royal, and adapted after his death as a memorial window.

Bibliography
Kelly, p. 71; Rottmann, pp. 93-100; Kirk, pp. 1-28; de l'Hopital, pp. 366-67, 377-88, 525-26, 529, 539-41, 558; *The Tablet*, 31 May 1851, p. 346; 6 December 1851, p. 772; 20 August 1853, p. 531; 1 December 1855, p. 756; 16 May 1857, p. 308; 14 November 1857, p. 724; 21 November 1857, p. 740; 22 June 1872, p. 785; 6 December 1873, p. 733; 22 November 1890, p. 809; *The Architect*, 4 December 1903, p. 368; *Br*, 17 January 1857, p. 45; 30 September 1851, p. 595; *Illustrated Times*, 18 July 1857, pp. 61-62

Chelsea 1, St Mary, Cadogan Street, SW3

The first church was founded by the Abbé Jean Nicolas Voyaux de Franous, a French *émigré* priest. It stood at the corner of Pavilion Road, where now stands number 105 Cadogan Gardens. It was erected in 1812 at a cost of £6,000 by the architect G.J. Wigley. The sanctuary was added in 1850 by J.J. Scoles, and a chapel in 1860 by E.W. Pugin. By 1875 the lease was running out and the chapel was moreover hopelessly inadequate to the mission's needs. A plot on the opposite side of Cadogan Street had been acquired for a new church; adjacent to it was a small cemetery with a chapel erected in 1845 to A.W.N. Pugin's design.

Canon Richard Mullen had employed J.F. Bentley to design an altar and pulpit in 1863–64. Inevitably, Bentley was his choice as architect of the new church. Cardinal Manning blessed the foundation stone on 12 July 1877, and opened the church on 1 May 1879. The builders were Messrs Braid; the style is Early English.

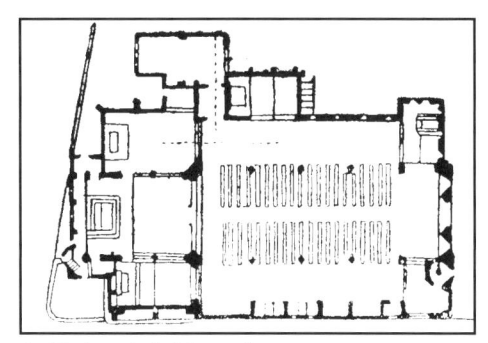

2. *Chelsea 1, St Mary, plan*

For approximately £10,000, Bentley provided a church seating 500. But economy took its toll, and the exterior is quite plain, with facings of white stock brick, red tiles and a sparing use of stone. The principal face, to the north, reads as

3. Chelsea 1, St Mary, exterior

west entrance, aisled and clerestoried nave, transept and chancel with a shorter north-east chapel. A south-west tower was planned but not erected.

Inside, however, the effect of light and space belies the plain exterior. Bentley provided a short nave of four bays, and achieved the desired effect of length by surrounding it with aisles, chancel and a west narthex. A transept is unobtrusively inserted into the north aisle without interrupting the flow of the nave arcade. To the narthex he attached western extensions which he utilised as porch and baptistery. He also cleverly incorporated A.W.N. Pugin's cemetery chapel as the south-east chapel of his church, and had E.W. Pugin's chapel of 1860 rebuilt here. We begin our description with these.

The chapel by E.W. Pugin is three bays long, and is connected to the south aisle by arcading with attached marble columns. It has a stone rib vault, with big bosses sculpted with the Mass, the Resurrection and the Blessed Virgin; the vaulting ribs supported on eight columns of Galway marble standing on polished alabaster bases. The walls are panelled with Sicilian and Devon marbles, and high up are four cinqfoil windows of 1860 by John Powell. The tabernacle is of polished alabaster inlaid with spars and other coloured marbles, its door made by Hardman. The monstrance throne and reredos (supported by marble and porphyry columns) are surrounded by angels holding the instruments of the Passion, while the frontal of Caen stone displays the Adoration of the Lamb. All the stonework was executed by Farmer & Brindley. The altar rails date from 1932. A confessional is built into the west wall. On the south side are memorial tablets to the Tussaud family.

4. Chelsea 1, St Mary, Pulpit

To the south-east of the chancel is the cemetery chapel of 1845 by A.W.N. Pugin. The altar reredos has five panels and the frontal has five angels sculpted in high relief. There is a three-light east window and a scissor-beam roof. The organ (of 1964 by J.W. Walker) is housed in the chapel.

The nave piers are of octagonal plan, with attached keeled shafts. The clerestory has two cusped lancet lights to a bay, beneath the wagon roof. The pulpit of 1864, designed by Bentley and brought from the previous church was sculpted by Phyffers. It is of alabaster and Derbyshire marble with mosaic decoration and bears five figures painted by Westlake of Our Lord, St Gregory, St Ambrose, St Jerome and St Augustine. Also by Westlake are St Peter and St Paul on the piers of the chancel arch. The statue of the Sacred Heart by Mayer was installed in 1908.

The chancel, faced with ashlar from Corsham Down is two bays deep, with blank arcading around three sides, its angels sculpted by Henry McCarthy. The clerestory is of five lancet lights with a storey of blank arcading beneath it. The east window consisting of four cusped lancets has double tracery before it. The rood of Christ the King was designed by Bentley. Beneath it is the marble altar standing on four plain columns, the tabernacle to the east on a marble plinth.

In the north-east chapel is the altar of 1864 from the old chapel, designed by Bentley and sculpted by Phyffers. It has an elaborate tabernacle and frontal, the latter with three sculpted panels surrounded by mosaic work, of the Annunciation, the Coronation of Our Lady and the Nativity. Between them are figures of Abel, Noah, Abraham and Melchisedech. The chapel has a three-light east window and two two-light north windows with double tracery. Adjacent to this chapel in the north transept is a large statue of Our Lady beneath a canopied shrine of carved wood, designed by Bentley in 1894. Next to it is a praying figure, sculpted in high relief, the memorial to the Abbé Voyaux +1840.

The north aisle bears a series of chapels between the buttresses, the system not consonant with the nave bays. From east to west there is a built-in confessional followed by the shrine of St Anthony of 1906; the Shrine of Our Lady of Lourdes, 1906; Our Lady of Sorrows, 1927, containing a scale model of Michelangelo's *pietà*; and finally a confessional constructed in 1927.

Beyond a cast-iron grille a single narrow bay forms a western transept containing the baptistery to the south, and the entrance from Cadogan Street to the north. The font comes probably from the old chapel of 1812–79; the baptistery's west windows are signed by Paul Quail, 1989. The Stations of the Cross were erected in 1909 by Mayer.

Bibliography
Harting, pp. 253-62; Kelly, pp. 123-24; de l'Hopital, pp. 380-81, 396-402, 529-30; Rottmann, pp. 17-22; Little, pp. 153-54; W.J. Anderson, *A History of the Catholic Parish of St Mary's, Chelsea* (Cadogan Gardens: St Mary's Church, 1938); *CAR*, 1850, p. 106; *BN*, 30 November 1860, p. 915; 21 December 1860, p. 980; *Br*, 1 December 1860, p. 722

Chelsea[2], Holy Redeemer and St Thomas More, Cheyne Row, SW3

Although the Church of St Mary already existed in Chelsea, the Mission of the Holy Redeemer was opened by Canon Cornelius Keens at the request of Cardinal Vaughan, to serve the poor in the western part of the borough. Canon Keens possessed a remarkable facility for pioneering new missions: 'His life's work deservedly earned him the name of "the church builder" '.[2] This church was his eighth and last.

Canon Keens chose as his architect Edward Goldie, who had worked with his father George Goldie on their Gothic masterpiece of St James, Spanish Place. Following his father's death, Edward Goldie had built the Gothic church of St Thomas at Wandsworth, but it seems that, at Chelsea, a Renaissance design was uncompromisingly required. At the time of its opening, two versions of the church were illustrated in the building press. The earlier design consisted of nave, aisles, octagonal domed crossing and chancel, somewhat in the style of Wren's church of St Stephen Walbrook. This had to be modified, partly on the grounds of cost, but principally because the site had been reduced owing to street-widening proposals of the London County Council. Goldie's executed design lacks therefore aisles and crossing. The foundation stone was laid on 7 June 1894, and the church was opened on 23 October 1895. The church is built of red brick with Bath stone dressings, and has a lead-covered roof. The outside is unremarkable except for the handsome portico with its Ionic columns and pilasters and its broken pediment, flanked by oval windows. In the pediment are the arms of St Thomas, 1952 by Peter Watts. Above are a large Venetian window and triangular pediment. The three windows received glass in 1991 by Shades of Light of Wimbledon.

Internally, the plan consists of nave and chancel without aisles. The west

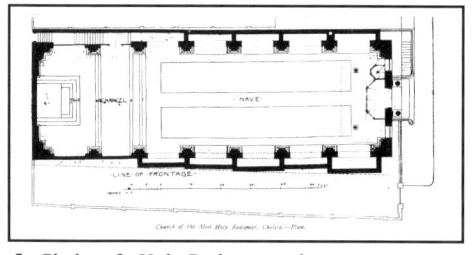

5. *Chelsea 2, Holy Redeemer, plan*

2.*The Tablet*, 22 July 1905, p. 149.

gallery with porch and narthex occupy one bay, the nave four bays and the chancel two. The gallery is of Kaurie pine; its organ by G.M. Holdich. There is no structural division between nave and chancel, the sum of the parts therefore comprising seven harmonious bays. These are divided by Ionic pilasters with Bath stone plinths, which form a recess for a shrine or altar in each bay. High above these, large round-headed windows penetrate the coved, panelled ceiling. The sanctuary was rearranged in 1970 by Bartlett & Purnell. Its floor levels were altered and relaid with black and white tiles; the altar was moved forward and re-erected on plinths of verde antico and Siena marble. Behind it is a large canvas of the Holy Redeemer flanked by statues of St Peter and St Paul. The Blessed Sacrament is housed on the north side within a marble shrine. The marble ambo dates from 1972. Next to it is a statue of St Thomas by Enzo Plazzotta.

On the north side is the altar of St Thomas More, erected in 1935, with the saint's arms above a carved statue framed by pilasters and a broken pediment which contains the Lamb of God and the papal tiara flanked by angels; the shrine of St Francis (after Corregio) flanked by statues of St Antony and St Teresa by S. Ercoreca; the Sacred Heart (1896 by F.J. Curley); and the *pietà* of 1909 by Mayer. On the south side is the Lady Altar, with a copy of Murillo's Virgin and Child; and the

6. *Chelsea 2, Holy Redeemer, interior*

shrine of St Thomas More, with a copy of the Holbein portrait. Mounted on the pilasters are the Stations of the Cross, miniatures by G. Ruggeri.

Bibliography
Kelly, p. 123; Rottmann, pp. 37-38; Little, pp. 158-59; Br, 19 October 1895, p. 270; 2 November 1895, p. 318; 16 November 1895, pp. 358-59 (illus.) *BN*, 10 May 1895, p. 649; 25 October 1895, p. 612; *The Tablet*, 1 August 1896, p. 193; 20 February 1897, p. 313; *Academy Architechture*, 1893, p.106 (illus.); 1895, II, p. 13 (illus.).

Fulham Road, Our Lady of Dolours, 264 Fulham Road, SW10

The church is staffed by the priests of the Servite Order. Although founded in the thirteenth century, the Servites did not come to England before the Reformation, or indeed before 1864, in which year two Italian members arrived in Chelsea. Initially they began their mission in a house in Stewarts Grove.

The Oratory parish having grown to unmanageable dimensions, a division was effected in 1867, and the Servites were given charge of west Chelsea and south-west Brompton. They moved to a larger house, number 78 Park Walk; then took a house in Netherton Grove, and fitted up an adjacent school as a chapel. With the advent of the hospital, they had to relinquish these premises, and so took their present house, number 264 Fulham Road. There they erected a temporary church in the front garden, and commenced the permanent church behind the house. Fr Philip Bosio the superior chose J.A. Hansom & Son as his architects. Fr Pyritheus Simoni wrote of J.A. Hansom:

> He has lately built three magnificent churches, one in Manchester for the Jesuits, one at Boulogne, and one at Arundel for the Duke of Norfolk, and at present he is working on another large and beautiful one for the Jesuits at Oxford. As he has not yet built a church in London he is, it appears, putting his heart into it, and is doing his best, as he tells us, to make it something worth seeing.[3]

The foundation stone was blessed by Archbishop Manning on 19 June 1874, and the church was opened by Manning, now a cardinal, on 19 September 1875. Hansom's Early English design was for a high clerestoried nave flanked by aisles, a long apsidal chancel, side chapels and aisle recesses. The builders were George Grimwood & Sons; the fittings of pitch pine were made by George Hammer. The material is brick with exterior dressings of Ham Hill stone, and interior dressings of Corsham Down stone; the nave piers are of Freeman's Cornish granite with polished detached shafts.

J.A. Hansom having died in 1882, his son J.S Hansom designed the pulpit of 1883, and the magnificent reredos of Caen stone constructed by George Porter of Chelsea, with statues by Boulton of Cheltenham, and the tabernacle by Hardman. Sadly, these were taken down when the chancel was reordered in 1976. The altar has been retained, however, in a forward position, and the tabernacle is now located in the north-east Lady Chapel. Thus the stained glass in the apse is now more easily seen. Its central window was designed by W. Tipping of Edith Grove, and installed in 1877 by Clayton & Bell.

The Lady Chapel was extended to the east by J.S. Hansom in 1890, at a cost of £1,115. Of Caen stone, coloured marbles and alabaster, its altar has an elaborately sculpted reredos and frontal depicting the

7. *Fulham Road, Our Lady of Dolours*

3. G.M. Corr, *Servites in London* (Newbury: The Servite Fathers, 1952), pp. 56-57.

VIII. KENSINGTON AND CHELSEA

Seven Sorrows, with statues also of Our Lady, the Seven Holy Founders and St Philip. The chapel has its own nave and miniscule aisle of five bays, its arcades very generously decorated with a riot of foliage sculpture and diaper work in the spandrels, clerestory windows with double tracery and a tall double-arched openwork screen to the chancel. But most remarkable are the wayward shouldered arches that were to become a regular fingerprint of J.S Hansom's work.

Proceeding along the north aisle we pass the Sacred Heart Altar, installed in 1889, of Caen stone with marble columns, in the style of J.S. Hansom. Next is the richly marbled altar of St Mary Magdalen, designed and executed in 1895 by J.W. Swynnerton. The kneeling figure in strong relief is of Serravezza marble; the background of rich Siena giallo antico; the enclosing arch is pinkish grey, known as fior di Persico; the altar stone, super-altar and steps are of Carrara marble. Crossing to the south aisle, the former chancel chapel retains its reredos with relief carvings in five panels, and frescoes of the Seven Holy Founders, 1885 by Fr Simoni. To the east of this chapel is the choir gallery, the organ by Henry Jones. The tall arch between the chapel and the chancel is occupied by a most unusual strainer arch, after the manner of those installed around the crossing of Wells Cathedral in 1320, to support the tower: that is, beneath a regular Gothic arch, another inverted arch is inserted. Since the reason for it here is scarcely structural, one can only assume that J.S. Hansom introduced it in a spirit of light-hearted playfulness.

From here, the south aisle is occupied by the altar of Servite Saints, bearing in its reredos a series of panels painted by Fr Simoni; the altar of St Joseph, its wooden gilt statue by Antonio Buletti, and supplied by Mayer, the four reredos scenes from the life of St Joseph painted by L. Galli; and the Calvary altar of 1895, with columns of delicate blue onyx, the altar and wall in richly toned alabaster, designed by J.S. Hansom, the figures by Mayer. Also along the aisles are series of sculpted corbel heads.

Eventually the approach from road to church was built up. The priory front costing £1620 was designed in 1879–80 by J.A. Hansom & Son, and built by Frank Wilkins. Next to it a stout belltower with an arched entrance is followed by an Early English colonnade of nave and aisles, ten bays long. Between this and the church proper is a large narthex of three bays, with triple aisles on each side of its nave, yielding a forest of columns whose shouldered arches support quadripartite vaults. All of this is of 1894 by J.S. Hansom, its patron being Charles Robertson. Within the narthex is a marble *pietà* by J.W. Swynnerton (a memorial to Fr Antonine Apollini +1900), bronzes of the Redeemer and St Peter, 1872 by Mayer, and a copy of the Holy Face after Lorenzo di Credi, of 1895 by John Shirley-Fox, in a frame of gilt and alabaster. Below the altarino are the emblems of the Passion in gilt; the arched frame is filled with variously coloured marbles; the steps of black marble veined with white. The whole was designed and arranged by Leonard Stokes.

The baptistery was constructed west

of the narthex in 1925. It has a bronze font by Miss Barker and Miss Brown, and bronze tableaux set in its walls. The Stations of the Cross are comparatively recent: carved in mezzo-relief and painted in pastel shades. There are also about 30 stained-glass windows in the church, including the apostles in the clerestory, and the west Te Deum window, commemorating the canonisation of the Seven Holy Founders in 1888.

Here in his only London church, J.A. Hansom surely succeeded in his aim at something worth seeing.

Bibliography
Rottmann, pp. 43-49; G.M. Corr, *Servites in London* (Newbury: The Servite Fathers, 1952); *Br*, 27 June 1874, p. 553; 21 April 1883, pp. 540-41; *BN*, 22 October 1880, p. 470; 6 July 1883, p. 32; *The Tablet*, 25 September 1875, p. 402; 16 June 1877, p. 758; 21 January 1883, p. 150; 19 May 1883, p. 790; 30 June 1883, p. 1018; 4 August 1894, p. 183; 20 April 1895, p. 625

Kensal New Town, Our Lady of the Holy Souls, Bosworth Road, W10

Following his work for them at Bayswater and Notting Dale, the Oblates of St Charles invited J.F. Bentley to design a complete new church. A tentative beginning had been made in 1862 with the hire of a cottage for Mass, followed by a larger house, and in 1872 a school chapel. An iron church in Absalom Road, designed by Bentley, succeeded this, and served until the permanent church was opened, on 13 April 1882. Bentley's brief to design a church seating 500, in the plainest manner possible, included a proviso that 'It must be strictly Roman, without pointed arches or stained windows.'[4] By the time Cardinal Manning laid the foundation stone, however (24 May 1881), Bentley had won the Oblates over to his own idea for a church in the Early English manner. It was given the dedication of Our Lady of the Holy Souls, owing to its proximity to St Mary's Cemetery, whose chaplaincy belonged to the Oblates. Stimpson & Co. were the builders, and the cost was £5059—very little for a church on this scale.

The tall shell of red bricks relieved by horizontal bands of Bath stone dominates the surrounding streets, with its nave and chancel of the same height, lean-to aisles and the transeptal arrangement of the organ loft. Above the west entrance are three tall lancet lights, slightly recessed between buttresses, the arrangement repeated in the gable. On the corner an octagonal bell turret surmounted by a brick spirelet effectively masks the lean-to end of the south aisle.

The interior is pervaded by a similar clarity of line. The nave of six bays is

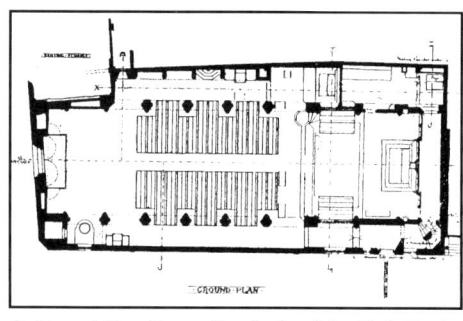

8. *Kensal New Town, Our Lady of the Holy Souls, plan*

4. De l'Hôpital, p. 404.

flanked by processional aisles, whose plain surfaces were intended to receive commemorative tablets. The piers are more complex than those employed by Bentley at Chelsea St Mary's, having keeled shafts to east and west, chamfered pilasters to the aisle and the same with added triple shafts to the nave, rising to clerestory level. The clerestory bears coupled cusped lancets, deeply recessed. Above it is a wagon roof; beneath it the De Profundis was painted in 1907, now obliterated but deserving of restoration. The north wall has a series of recessed arcade bays, placed in irregular relationship to the nave. Here, the Sacred Heart Shrine, formerly part of the Holy Ghost Altar, is now the only feature in the church designed by Bentley, its panels painted by John Stacey of St John's Wood.

North of the chancel stands the Lady Chapel. Here and south of the chancel are two large, glazed, traceried, arched screens. The chancel, three bays deep, has two cusped lights to each clerestory bay, and a wagon roof. There is a forward marble altar, behind it the tabernacle on a marble stand. South of the chancel is the organ, in a timber gallery not intended by Bentley to project so far. On the east wall is a large, panelled timber reredos of 1889, carved, painted and gilt, formerly 50 feet high, designed by Fr Arnold Baker, and painted by him and friends. Since 1978 the church has been in the care of the Augustinian Recollect Friars.

9. Kensal New Town, Our Lady of the Holy Souls, exterior

Bibliography
Kelly, pp. 232-33; Rottmann, pp. 123-25; de l'Hopital, pp. 402-407; Little, p. 154; Kirk, pp. 29-52; The Tablet, 14 September 1872, pp. 340-41; 23 March 1889, p. 471; Information of Mr P. Howell

Kensington 1, Our Lady of Victories, 235A High Street, W8

The mission sprang indirectly from the French exodus. The Abbé Charles de Broglie established in 1794 a school for the sons of French exiled noblemen at Kensington House (near the site of the Royal Albert Hall). Here the few local Catholics were able to hear Mass in the domestic chapel. The school was closed in 1806, but the chapel continued in use owing to the efforts of the English congregation. A new chapel recorded as a plain rectangle was erected in Holland Street in 1812. Enlarged with a new chancel in the 1830s, this served until the opening in 1869 of the major church designed by George Goldie. Our Lady of Victories then took the title of pro-cathedral from St Mary Moorfields, and held it until the opening of Westminster Cathedral. Goldie's French Gothic design was 140 feet long, and comprised nave and aisles of six bays, sanctuary with apsidal end, two side chapels, sacristies, baptistery and confessionals. Sadly, all this was destroyed by enemy action in 1940.

The foundation stone of the present church was blessed by Cardinal Godfrey on 23 March 1957 and the church was opened on 31 October 1958. The

10. Kensington 1, Our Lady of Victories

architect was Adrian Gilbert Scott and the builders Messrs Holliday & Greenwood. Outside, only the (ritual) west front is visible—of brick with a Portland stone arched entrance surmounted by a statue of Our Lady of Victories executed by Messrs Albion of Merton. Before this a screen fronts the road, consisting of a stone arch and a statue of Our Lady of Victories, survivors from the previous church.

Within, above the entrance is the organ gallery; to the north a repository converted from the former baptistery; and to the south the Chapel of the Martyrs. The chapel's altar has statues of Our Lady of Walsingham by Siegfried Pietzsch, Ss John Fisher and Thomas More, Margaret Clitheroe, Thomas of Canterbury, Alban and Edmund Arrowsmith, by Vincent Dapre. To mark the bicentenary in 1994, eight canvases were rendered in emulsion by Peter Lyall. Executed in theatrical style, they display in the ceiling the Assumption; then clockwise on the walls: Our Lady of Walsingham; St Alban; two angels; St Thomas More; Ss Edmund Arrowsmith and John Southwell; St John Fisher; and martyrs at Tyburn.

The nave is five bays long, with internal buttresses pierced to form passage aisles, stone dado work to a height of 12 feet and a pointed roof ceiled beneath the apex. The nave windows consist of double lancets crowned with octofoil tracery. All the glass is by Charles Blakeman. Off the north aisle are built-in confessionals, and in the south aisle is a large crucifix of Bavarian workmanship, formerly over the high altar. The Stations of the Cross are a survival from the previous church. To the north of the chancel stands the timber pulpit and to the south the font of sandstone matching the surrounding fabric. High in the east wall is the Resurrection of 1988 by Michael Clark. Between the chancel and the chapels are screens glazed and barred, their ironwork by Porter. The south-east Lady Chapel is extremely elegant. It has a striking tent-like panelled ceiling, decorated in varying shades of blue. There is a neo-Gothic reredos framing a vesica which contains Our Lady of Victories with rays extending around her, restored in 1991 by Michael Madsen. The corresponding Chapel of the Sacred Heart is comparatively austere, with abstract glass and a statue by Mayer, also restored in 1991 by Michael Madsen. This, together with new sacristies, meeting room and domestic accomodation, was completed in 1971. The architects then were Messrs Archard & Partners.

Bibliography
Kelly, p. 233; Rottmann, pp. 107-11; Harting, pp. 214-17; Eastlake, pp. 349-50; Little, pp. 210-11; *SOL* 37, p. 68; *BN*, 17 May 1867, p. 348; 12 June 1868, p. 389; 16 April 1869, p. 349; 7 May 1869, p. 420; 5 January 1872, p. 15; *Br*, 9 May 1868, p. 332; 11 July 1868, pp. 507, 511; *The Architect*, 2 October 1869, p. 166; *AR*, January 1942, p. 16; *CBR.S*, 1957, pp. 38-39; 1958, pp. 74-75; 1959, pp. 43-44; 1971, pp. 318-20; *CB* 36 (November/December 1995), pp. 60-61

Kensington 2, Our Lady of Mount Carmel and St Simon Stock, Kensington Church Street, W8

The Order of Mount Carmel was introduced into England by St Simon Stock in 1240. After the Reformation, Carmelite priests laboured continuously on the English mission. It was Fr Herman Cohen whom Cardinal Wiseman singled out to found a Carmelite monastery in London. The original foundation in 1862 was in a house in Kensington Square. Needing larger premises, the Fathers acquired in 1863 Newton House in Duke's Lane and a disused school which they adapted as a chapel. Decorations in the Italian Gothic style were superintended by G.J. Wigley, and the altarpiece was painted by Westlake. Ground for a permanent church was purchased in 1865, and the church to Edward Pugin's design was opened in 1866. This church sadly suffered severe damage in the war of 1939–45, and has since been replaced.

The present church, to designs of Sir Giles Gilbert Scott, Son & Partner, was opened in 1959. The commanding exterior viewed from Church Street presents a tall (ritual) west front of brick with spare stone dressings, and a tall three-light window with a glazed tympanum above it surmounted by a bellcote. A west transeptal arrangement is formed by the north and south entrances. Beyond are glimpses of steeply pitched lean-to aisles with transverse gables above the chapels, and a tall clerestory.

Immediately inside, the west entrances flank the former baptistery and the organ gallery within the first bay. Nave and chancel co-exist in seven continuous bays, their masonry encased in stone to a height of ten feet. The structure is based upon six tall transverse arches which visually dominate the nave. Above these arches are a clerestoried space and the flat, raftered ceiling. At ground level the internal buttresses are hollowed to form access passages to the nave. On the tympana of these openings are mounted the Stations of the Cross,

11. Kensington 2, Our Lady of Mount Carmel

cast tableaux dominated by gold and blue, signed A. Stafford and variously dated between 1960 and 1965.

The passage aisles are punctuated to north and south by alternate shrines and built-in confessionals between the buttresses. On the north side are the Infant of Prague, St Teresa of Avila, the Sacred Heart and the north-east Lady Chapel. On the south side are St Teresa of Lisieux, St John of the Cross and St Joseph.

The chancel is of one bay, with an altar of stone and marble. To the east a deep recess contains the tall, wooden panelled reredos, neo-Perpendicular in concept, containing the Virgin and Child supported by angels, and episodes from the life of Our Lady. These are the Flight into Egypt, the *pietà*, the Espousal, the Annunciation, the Assumption, the Coronation, the Journey to Bethlehem and the Adoration of the Maji.

Bibliography
Kelly, pp. 233-34; Rottmann, pp. 100-107; *The Tablet*, 17 October 1863, p. 661; 6 May 1865, p. 277; 22 July 1865, p. 452; 28 July 1866, p. 470; *BN*, 20 July 1866, p. 488; 15 December 1905, p. 827; *Br*, 6 June 1874, p. 487; *Architects' Journal*, 8 May 1958, p. 686

Notting Hill, St Francis of Assisi, Pottery Lane, W11

Following the success of their foundation at Bayswater, the Oblates of St Charles planted missions at Notting Hill and at Kensal New Town. One of the Oblates, Fr Henry Rawes, was given charge of the Potteries (later called Notting Dale and now Notting Hill), and there at his own expense he built the church of St Francis which was opened on 2 February 1860. His first architect was Henry Clutton, whose assistant on the site was the young John Bentley.

Clutton's exterior, of stock brick with sparing bands of Staffordshire blue brick, is severely simple provincial French Gothic of the thirteenth century. Fr Rawes then decided to add a baptistery, south west porch, presbytery and school, and entrusted these works to Bentley. The baptistery formed a western extension to the (ritual) north aisle, and here Bentley was the first person to be baptised, on 16 April 1862, taking Francis as his baptismal name.

VIII. KENSINGTON AND CHELSEA

The plan consists of west narthex with gallery over, baptistery with tribune of 1882 above, nave of three bays, a wide north aisle giving the church a double-naved appearance, chancel and north-east Chapel of Our Lady of Dolours, slanted south to flank the chancel apse, owing to the restricted site. The nave and aisle have roofs of timber, with tie-beams and braces; the chancel, Lady Chapel and baptistery have quadripartite vaults.

The chancel consists of one bay with an apsidal east termination. The high altar and reredos of 1863 are of alabaster inlaid with marble and glass mosaic. The engraved tabernacle door is richly encrusted with enamels and jewels; the frontal has an oblong panel depicting the Dead Christ; the reredos is painted with figures of Abel, Noah, Abraham and Melchisedech; the throne is supported on the Hound of Heaven, and the canopy is surmounted by a pelican. The piscina, designed by Walters, was installed in 1917. The altar rails have disappeared, but the small pulpit is preserved on the south side.

The Lady Chapel is two bays deep, with a shallow terminal apse. Its altar is of alabaster, the mensa with paintings by Westlake of archangels, Our Lady of Sorrows and four busts of Virgin Martyrs. The chapel walls are tiled, and above are depicted in encaustic on slate the Seven Dolours of Our Lady, three of which form the reredos. The piscina is of alabaster. Also in the chapel is the Altar of St John the Evangelist, designed by Bentley and sculpted by Earp. Westlake's first paintings for Bentley are the reredos, of St John giving Holy Communion to Our Lady, and the frontal, of St John and Daniel. At the chapel's entrance is an alabaster inlaid offertory box, designed by Bentley and installed in 1863.

12. *Notting Hill, St Francis of Assisi, Baptistery*

The nave and north aisle are separated by octagonal piers. Here, also by Westlake, are the Stations of the Cross of 1865–70, realistically portrayed groups painted on slate against a neutral green background; note especially the first three next to the Lady Chapel. In the aisle, beneath an elaborate canopied niche of marble and crystal designed by Bentley, is the statue of the Blessed Virgin of 1870, sculpted by T. Phyffers, the gift of Westlake. Off the aisle are the sacristy and a built-in confessional.

To the west of the aisle is the baptistery of 1861 by Bentley. According to Eastlake:

> The baptistery, as the production of a young architect then little known to fame, was much admired. There is a breadth and simplicity about the design which distinguished it from previous work, as well as from much that was executed at that time.[5]

Eastlake goes on to notice the thirteenth-century French character of the details, the stone vault of its two bays, carried on shafts of red and Irish green marble, with richly carved capitals. Some carving was completed in 1907 by Hardman. The iron grilles and gates and two wall panels were added by Osmond Bentley betwen 1907 and 1910. The font of 1861–62 consists of a red granite basin mounted upon a base of alabaster and green marble columns, raised on a tiled platform. The oaken cover of 1865 was executed in the workshops of T.C. Lewis the organ builder; it was designed and given by Bentley as a thank-offering for his conversion. Into the north wall of the baptistery Bentley cleverly slotted a built-in confessional; and in the narthex next to the baptistery is the statue of St John by Blanchard, on a marble corbel designed by Bentley.

According to the *Building News* of 1863, all the stained glass then installed was designed by Bentley and Westlake, and executed by Lavers & Barraud. These may include the two cinqfoil windows containing angels in the chancel, and two lancets in the Lady Chapel. In the baptistery are two windows of St John the Baptist and St Charles Borromeo, designed by Bentley and installed by Lavers, Barraud & Westlake in 1872. Others are St Elizabeth (1886), St Francis (1926) and St Augustine in the nave; and St Agnes and the Good Shepherd in the north aisle.

The sanctuary was decorated in 1864, and again in 1872–73 by Westlake. The church was decorated by John Whitby from designs by Bentley in 1896. The Lady Chapel was redecorated in 1915 by Osmond Bentley. Further redecorations took place in 1926 by G.N. Watts and in 1960 by A.J. Sparrow. Under these attentions, the original painted decoration has all but disappeared; note, however, in the chancel vault two angels surviving from Westlake's work of 1872–73. The church was again redecorated while undergoing reordering by Williams & Winkley in 1984. A freestanding temporary altar was then given a platform near the edge of the sanctuary. Several stained glass windows were re-leaded, and since Bentley's original elaborately patterned surfaces had long since been painted out, the interior was redecorated to a new colour scheme. At the same time, a sculpted bust of St Francis by Arthur Fleischmann was erected on a corbel in the forecourt.

---

5. Eastlake, p. 321.

St Francis's church retains much of the beauty intended by its founders. This is largely due to the retention of its permanent furnishings which are here recognised as worthy of preservation, their continuing presence not necessarily in conflict with the mind of the Church. Would that this much wisdom had prevailed more widely.

Bibliography
Rottmann, pp. 118-23; de l'Hopital, pp. 350, 369-77, 528, 563; Eastlake, pp. 320-21, 404-405; Kirk, pp. 53-70; *SOL* 37, pp. 352-55; *BN*, 20 January 1860, p. 43, 16 January 1863, pp. 44-45; *Civil Engineer and Architects' Journal*, 1 August 1862, pp. 248-49; *The Ecclesiologist* 25 (1864), p. 151; *The Tablet*, 27 June 1896, p. 1031; *CB*, Easter 1984, p. 58; Information of Mr Peter Howell

The Oratory, Immaculate Heart of Mary, Brompton Road, SW7

The Oratory was introduced into England by John Henry Newman, following his ordination in Rome in 1847. His foundation at Birmingham still flourishes, and a London foundation was made at Charing Cross by Newman's disciple Fr Faber. The Fathers moved to Brompton in 1854. In accordance with Newman's advice that 'no one will give us money for a house, while it is comparatively easy to collect for a church', the Fathers resolved to be content with a temporary church.[6] Thus the house, the Little Oratory and a temporary church were erected first, to designs of J.J. Scoles. In 1875 a plan by F.W. Moody for a permanent church was considered but later dropped. Then in 1876 Herbert Gribble, a gifted young draughtsman in the South Kensington office of J.A. Hansom & Son, published a suggested design for a large Oratory church. This triggered the competition for a new church, which the Fathers held in 1878, with Alfred Waterhouse as professional assessor. The instructions to architects specified the style of the Italian Renaissance; the church was to cover the whole of the space available—340 feet by 130 feet; a sanctuary 60 feet deep, a nave not less than 50 feet wide, six lateral chapels besides a large chapel to the east of the sanctuary, space for several confessionals and an entrance on the west side. After receiving Waterhouse's report, the Fathers awarded Gribble the first prize and Henry Clutton the second. *Building News* published Gribble's modification of his competition entry, which he called his 'Selected Design'. In plan it is very similar to his earlier published version, consisting of nave and aisles of three bays, with chapels in each bay, north and south transepts, apsidal chancel and large south-east chapel. Gribble retained the passage aisles and the generous provision of side chapels. He also took the opportunity to simplify the line of the dome and added two west towers.

The foundation stone was laid on 29 June 1880, the contractors being Messrs Shaw of Westminster. The walls were completed by March 1882; and the vaulting of the nave and transepts and the construction of the inner dome by March 1883. Gribble later disclosed that his choice of concrete as the material of the vaults was influenced by its use in the ancient temple of Minerva Medica in

---

6. Fr R.F. Kerr, 'The Oratory in London', *The Oratory Parish Magazine*, November 1926, p. 208.

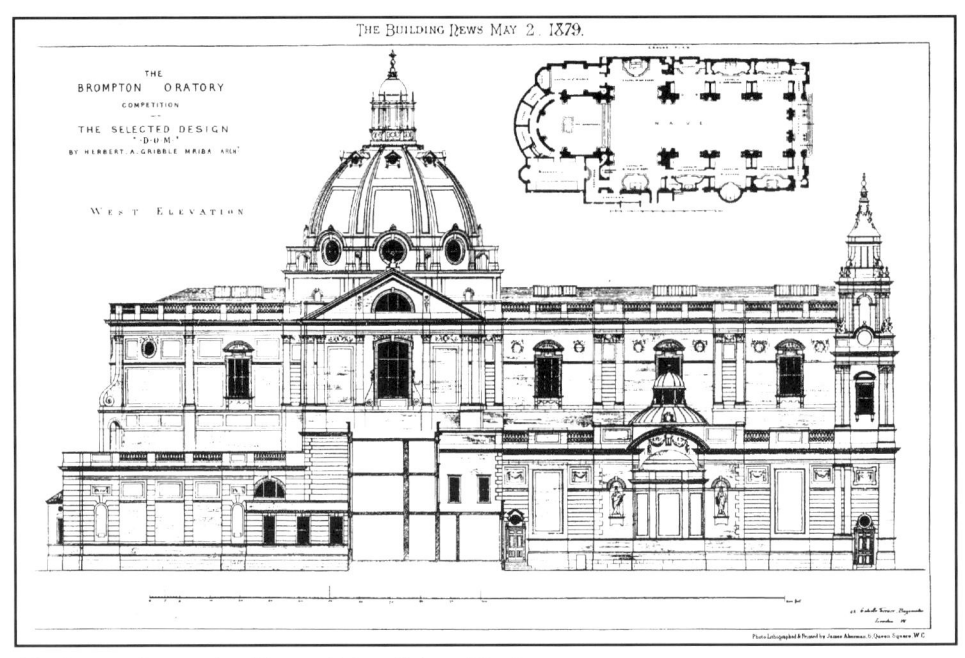

13. Oratory, Immaculate Heart of Mary, Selected Design

Rome. There a pentagonal shape 75 feet in diameter surmounted by a concrete cupola was Gribble's inspiration for the 51-foot wide nave and 53-foot diameter of the dome in the Oratory. He described how he first filled the four haunches in the nave bays, and when the concrete there was set, how he completed the saucer domes with layers of diminishing thickness. Similarly, the infilling of the dome was contrived by a continuous ring of six-inch thickness, laid in a spiral manner 'as one would wind the cord around a boy's top'.[7] The unfinished church was opened on 25 April 1884. The west façade was built in 1890, but minus Gribble's proposed towers. After Gribble's death, the outer dome was added in 1895–96 by George Sherrin. The lantern was designed by Edwin Rickards, a clerk in Sherrin's office. The monument to Cardinal Newman of 1896 was designed by Bodley & Garner; the statue is by L.J. Chavalliaud.

Despite the piecemeal process of its completion, the exterior, of Portland stone, is most striking. The façade, with doubled columns to the narthex and the pedimented nave gains rather than loses from its lack of west towers. The side view offers a series of emphases to the eye, by means of an apsidal chapel, upper balustrades, pedimented transept windows and the dome. Gribble's perspective of the interior had been remarked as 'one of the most elaborate and ably got up' in the competition.[8] His vision of the interior was designed to evoke the type of Roman Renaissance church initiated in the Gesu built in 1568–84. There, Vignola the architect had contrived a combination of both

---

7. *BN*, 13 April 1885, p. 518.

8. *BN*, 28 June 1878, p. 643.

VIII. KENSINGTON AND CHELSEA

centralised and longitudinal planning schemes, domed over the crossing, with shallow transepts and an extended nave with chapels in each bay. The Gesu scheme was extremely influential, among its progeny being the Chiesa Nuova. There, St Philip had insisted on a spacious church, and at Brompton the Fathers conceived their church in similar generous dimensions.

The coupled pilasters that punctuate the nave bays of the Gesu are also echoed here, with the added refinement of coupled columns complementing them within the arched openings. Gribble's provision of natural light by means of the clerestory was supplemented by means of circular lights incorporated in the dome, following the Gesu and the Roman church of S. Andrea delle Valle.

The **nave**, at 51 feet, is claimed as the third widest in England (after Westminster Cathedral and York Minster). Against the piers are Corinthian pilasters of the Devonshire marble favoured by Gribble. The large series of the Twelve Apostles in Carrara marble by Giuseppe Mazzuoli (1664–1725) after being ejected from the Duomo at Siena, were acquired for the Oratory in 1895. Much of the rest results from the decoration of 1930 by Commendatore C.T.G. Formilli. By him are the stucco panels of the Stations of the Cross, 12 recumbent figures in the spandrels of the arches representing the principal virtues, and groups of cherubs over each arch. Venetian-made mosaic panels depicting saints connected with St Philip flank the clerestory windows; on the west wall portraits of Newman and

14. *Oratory, Immaculate Heart of Mary, exterior design*

Faber. In the vault are large panels with angels holding Instruments of the Passion. The spandrels beneath the dome bear large mosaic figures of the four evangelists. The clerestory stained glass windows depict the arms of principal benefactors of the church. Also in the nave are the pulpit of 1930 by Formilli and the statue of St Peter copied from that in St Peter's, Rome. Cast in bronze, with a chair and pedestal of white and multi-coloured marbles, this majestic and authoritative figure was installed by Messrs Burns & Oates in 1903.

The **chancel** is one bay deep, with an apsidal termination. Its decorations were designed in 1888–90 by J. Cosgreave. The walls are lined with various marbles, principally Languedoc. The floor, of various inlaid woods, and the stalls inlaid with ivory were brought from the former church and were the gift of the Duchess of Argyll. The high altar of marble and gilt is by B. Pozzi. Above it is a cartouche with a gilt heart by Sir Edgar Boehm. The supporting angels are Italian work. Also by Pozzi are three large paintings of incidents in the life of St Philip. The communion rails, also from the former church, are of Sicilian and Siena marbles and the gates are of metal gilt. The two seven-branched candle-holders designed by William Burges were the gift in 1879 of the Marquess of Bute.

In time for the centenary celebrations in 1984, a complete new decoration of the interior took place, designed to unite disparate elements of earlier work. The principal architectural members were given a stone colour carefully matched to the original; to decorative elements (such as mouldings, corbels, dentils and paterae) rich reds, strong blues and gilding were applied; and to the lower frieze and transept doorcases a false marbling imitating the dark green cipollino that surrounds Blessed Sebastian's altar. The **chapels**, north side, west to east, are listed below.

1. **Chapel of the Sacred Heart**. The altar and reredos were designed by Gribble, modelled on the Scuola di S. Giovanni, Venice. The statue of the Sacred Heart is in Carrara marble. The chapel was decorated about 1935 by Geoffrey Webb. Also herein is the shrine of St Anthony, with a life-size statue of Carrara marble.

2. **Chapel of St Joseph**. Here a projecting apse contains the altar from the former church, designed by Scoles, 1861, and the statue of St Joseph, Belgian work of 1884. The chapel was decorated (1964) by Andrew Carden.

3. **Chapel of the Seven Dolours**. The altar, severe in character, of black and white marbles, designed by Gribble, was the gift of the Duchess of Norfolk. The altar-piece, Our Lady of Sorrows, was commissioned at Rome by Fr Faber from Ferenc Szoldatits. In the lunette is a copy of the Entombment by Francia.

4. **Chapel of St Philip**, north transept. The large altar given by the Fifteenth Duke of Norfolk, was designed by Gribble and executed by Farmer & Brindley. Beneath the pediment is an alto-relievo of the Death of St Philip by Girolamo Moneta. Flanking this are bas-reliefs of incidents in the life of the saint by Laurence Bradshaw. The altar-piece is a copy of Guido Reni's portrait of St Philip. Left and right are St Matthew and

St John, attributed to Guercino. In an apse nearby is the altar of Blessed Sebastian Valfre. The altar was installed when the church was opened. Its marble surround was added in 1902–1903 by Farmer & Brindley to designs of Thomas Garner, employing principally dark green cipollino and lighter verde antico, with margins of white pavonazzo. Cream statuary marble dominates the carved string course, with rosso antico added for the cartouches.

The **chapels**, south side, east to west, are listed below:

1. **Chapel of St Wilfrid**. The chapel was donated by Mrs Elizabeth Bowden in memory of Fr Faber, whose remains were transferred here from Sydenham in 1952. The decoration was by J. Cosgreave, the walls of Mexican onyx, and the entrance columns of Connemara marble. The principal altar in the east apse was the central part of the high altar of Maestricht Cathedral, and dates from c. 1710. The statue of St Wilfrid is by Codina Langlin. On the south side is a painted copy of Our Lady of Good Counsel at Genazzano. On the north side is the shrine of St Cecilia, the figure in Carrara marble a copy of Stefano Maderna's in S. Cecilia in Trastevere; the painting above it after Raphael. Near the entrance are the altars of the English Martyrs and St Teresa of Lisieux, 1938 by David Stokes. The marble bas-relief of St Teresa by Arthur Pollen; the triptych of the martyrs by Rex Whistler.

2. **The Lady Altar**, south transept. Bought in 1884, the large altar, 21 feet high and 40 feet wide, came from the Dominican Church at Brescia. With its profusion of inlaid marbles and Carrara statues, it was constructed in 1693 by Francesco, Domenico and Antonio Corbarelli. The statue of Our Lady of Victories came from the Oratory in King William Street, Charing Cross. St Rose of Lima and St Pius V are by Orazio Marinali, and the rest of the figure sculpture (including St Dominic and St Catherine of Siena) is by Thomas Ruer. Two statues of angels now in the organ gallery, overlooking the chapel of St Mary Magdalen are by Santo Calegari.

15. Oratory, Immaculate Heart of Mary, interior

3. **The Calvary**. Following a fire in 1950, new figures were carved by Enid Fenton-Smith. The organ in the gallery above was renewed by J.W. Walker & Sons in 1954, to specifications of Ralph Downes.

4. Chapel of St Mary Magdalen. The decoration is by J. Cosgreave. The altar and reredos of Devonshire marble were designed by Gribble, with columns of Derbyshire alabaster; the Venetian mosaic panels of scenes from the life of the saint, by A. Capello of Chelsea, 1883–84; the bronze gates by Starkie Gardiner. At the sides are statues of St Teresa and St Camillus, copies of those in St Peter's, Rome. Here also are two confessionals on the Antwerp model.

5. Chapel of St Patrick. The chapel walls are of Irish marble. The altar, previously in the old church, came from Naples. Its superstructure of Sicilian and Siena marbles was designed by Gribble. The paintings of St Patrick, St Brigid and St Columba are by Pietro Pezzatti of Florence; the Circumcision and the Presentation perhaps by Frans Floris of Antwerp.

In the **baptistery** is the font, a reduced version in red African breccia of that in Orvieto Cathedral, of 1406 by Luca di Giovanni. Its stem is of Derbyshire alabaster; the supporting lions of Carrara; and the cover of bronze, by Starkie Gardiner.

Despite the piecemeal character of its structure, furnishings and decoration, the Oratory remains one of the most attractive churches in the land. The church, handed down to our generation through the watchful care of the Oratory Fathers, fully justifies Gribble's claim that 'Those who had no opportunity to see an Italian church had only to come here to see the model of one.'[9] The sheer opulence, however, of its high Renaissance character regrettably precluded its being widely imitated.

Bibliography
Kelly, pp. 103-104; Rottmann, pp. 22-37; Little, pp. 141-43; Fr E. Kilburn, *A Walk Round the Church of the London Oratory* (Covent Garden: Sands and Co., 1975); Fr C. Napier, *The London Oratory* (Brompton: The Oratory Church, 1983); H. Gribble, 'How I Built the Oratory', *Merry England*, 5 (1885), 260-72; *BN*, 3 March 1876, p. 218; 24 May 1878, p. 520; 28 June 1878, p. 648; 12 December 1879, p. 719; 30 September 1881, p. 426; 2 December 1881, p. 724; 7 September 1894, p. 338; *Br*, 29 June 1878, p. 665; 3 July 1880, p. 33; 18 December 1909, p. 676; *The Tablet*, 3 July 1880, pp. 19-20; 5 April 1884, p. 550; 3 May 1884, p. 711; 23 September 1899, p. 513; 4 April 1903, p. 551; *CB*, Christmas 1984, pp. 60-63

St Charles Square, St Pius X, 79 St Charles Square, W10

The mission was founded in 1937, drawing on the territory of Notting Hill and Kensal New Town parishes. Initially, services were held in the college chapel of the Society of the Sacred Heart. The chapel opened in 1908 was designed by Percy Lamb who had been Clerk of Works under J.F. Bentley during the building of Westminster Cathedral. However, the college was destroyed in 1941, and after restoration the chapel became the parish church in 1955.

The church is of substantial size, consisting of nave and chancel, 68 feet by 30 feet. To the south of the chancel is a transept, designed originally for the accommodation of worshippers, but now cast as an extension to the parish hall.

---

9. *Br*, 15 March 1884, pp. 386-87.

The building is styled in the manner of English seventeenth-century Renaissance work, in red brick, with high arched windows. Internally, there is an organ gallery in the westernmost bay, and a low passage constructed in 1954 to the south. In each bay there are wide arched windows bearing figures of 11 saints by John Trinick. Between them corbels support broad ribs that subdivide the plaster barrel vault, which has in each bay a central geometrical figure with a foliage surround. The chancel arch is dominated by fluted Ionic pilasters; the entablature and pilasters are repeated in the chancel. This consists of a single square bay with a saucer-domed vault and angel frescoes. At the sides are Diocletian windows (following Westminster Cathedral) and on the north further frescoes of saints. Most prominent, however, is the fine reredos, with marble panels rising to a monstrance throne and figures of the Virgin and Child in a pedimented niche, surrounded by angels. The Stations of the Cross, small freestanding tableaux, are signed FST.

Bibliography
BN, 26 June 1908, p. xiv; *Br*, 2 January 1948, p. 17

IX
Lambeth

Brixton, Our Lady of the Rosary, Brixton Road, SW9

MISS Frances Ellis provided the site and church of St Helen in Robsart Street, opened in 1905. Small, in the Romanesque style, and built of London stock brick, it was in the customary manner of the architect F.W. Tasker. A Lady Chapel was added in 1938 by J. O'Hanlon Hughes. After the Second World War, the diocese acquired the redundant Brixton Independent Church. This had been built by Myers & Son in 1869–70, to designs of Arthur J. Phelps. Following restoration and adaptation by Justin Alleyn and John Mansel, the church was opened for Catholic use in 1953.

The church is well sited on the west side of Brixton Road, near to Stockwell Park Walk. The style is Early English, realized in red brick with dressings of stone and dark blue bricks. Above the (ritual) west entrance there are three stepped lancets beneath the gable. To the left may be seen the lean-to aisle, fronted by a chamfered baptistery addition. To the right is a bold square tower in three storeys, buttressed and crenellated, with lucarnes in its topmost storey.

Beyond an ante-chamber there are four bays of nave and aisles followed by aisled transepts and the apsidal sanctuary. The slender cast-iron piers formerly supported galleries, all removed now except for that in the western bay. The upper arches of the arcade, and the barrel roof, are all of timber. There are lancet windows throughout, mainly grouped in twos and threes. In the south-west corner is the Good Shepherd window, of 1928 by W. Aikman.

In the apse is the plain stone altar. The crucifix above the tabernacle depicts Christ the King. In the north transept there is an altar of marble, and several cast statues—the Madonna and Child, St Teresa, St Patrick and St Antony. There are Stations of the Cross, also cast, coloured, and mounted in Gothic frames.

Bibliography
SOL 26, pp. 125, 130-31; AAS

Brixton Hill, Corpus Christi, Trent Road, SW2

The mission was founded from Camberwell by Fr Hendrick van Doorne. He initially took a freehold house and land between Lambert Road and Hayter Road

IX. LAMBETH

1. Brixton Hill, Corpus Christi

and renamed it Corpus Christi House. The first Mass there was said on 3 June 1881. The possibility of building a church at the back was discussed, but difficulties of light and air arose. Bethel House in Brixton Hill with its huge garden in front and behind was therefore bought as a more suitable site, and Corpus Christi House was sold to the Sisters of Notre Dame. J.F. Bentley made plans for a large Decorated church, and the foundation stone was laid by Bishop John Butt on 14 June 1886. The contractors were Messrs E. Lawrence & Sons. The sanctuary and side chapels were erected first, but, on their completion, considerations of finance brought a halt to building. Reluctant to incur more debt, Bishop Butt formally opened the unfinished church on 12 June 1887. The transepts were not added until 1904, after Bentley's death. A temporary wall closes the existing church, which would be more than doubled in size had the nave and aisles been built. During refurbishment in 1983–84, a new entrance and parish hall were added, to designs of Messrs Hall & Riley. Since 1980 the church has been in the charge of the Society of Jesus.

Tall and compact, of red brick with stone dressings, the east front to Brixton Hill displays the many-windowed chancel gable, with two storeys of lancets below its three major windows. Flanking these are the matching chapel gables, with five-light traceried windows and octagonal turrets at the corners. From the side roads, the sanctuary and transepts, dignified and well pulled together, stress the aesthetic loss of the unbuilt nave.

The furnishings of the truncated interior, consisting of sanctuary, chapels, transepts and crossing are now rearranged, affording maximum seating around the sanctuary. A major consequence is that the polychrome altars from Belgium have disappeared from the side chapels, and wooden altars now stand at the transept extremities.

The high altar and reredos were designed by Bentley. The altar is of Hopton Wood stone, its frontal faced with Siena marble and inlaid cipollino. The tall, panelled reredos contains the Baptism of Christ, the Descent from the Cross and the Resurrection, worked in opus-sectile. To the sides are tiled panels above a base of cipollino. At the extremities, turreted niches contain angels sculpted in Carrara marble. The altar rails of brass, furnished by the Bentley firm, survive. Behind the altar is an ambulatory which allows arcading in front of the windows, a feature previously included by Bentley at Chelsea St Mary's. The three major windows above the altar are filled with stained glass, renewed since the original glass was installed. The seven windows beneath these, however, retain their glass installed in 1899 to Bentley's designs. They contain figures of St Evaristus, St Stephen, St Peter, St John the Baptist, St Paul, St Henry and St Charles Borromeo. Of the four windows in the former Lady Chapel, two have lost their stained glass except for the tracery. The two survivors contain figures of Eve, Sarah, Rachel, Miriam, Deborah and Ruth beneath scenes from the life of Our Lady.

Adjacent to the foregoing is the north transept, with its stained glass windows of 1911 by Osmond Bentley. Beneath these is the altar of St Joseph, wholly of timber. Its panelled reredos has figures of the saint with the child Jesus in a central niche. From left to right appear St Peter, St Mary Magdalen, St Lucy and St Edward the Confessor. Matching this is the south transept, with similar windows designed by Osmond Bentley and installed in 1910.

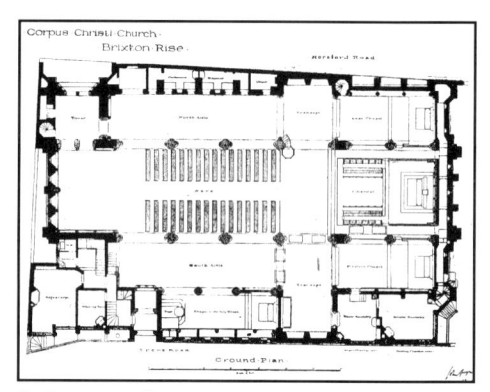

2. Brixton Hill, Corpus Christi, plan

The altar also is of similar design, with a carved reredos depicting Our Lady, crowned, with her Son in a central niche. To the left is the Nativity, to the right the Coronation of Our Lady, carved in high relief. Nearby is a carved statue of St Antony. Adjacent to the transept is the choir loft, with organ by W. Ginns of Merton. Also in the church are the Stations of the Cross, painted on metal and framed; and the font, 1888, of marble, continental work, with octagonal stem and bowl above a sturdy base.

Bibliography
Kelly, pp. 101-102; de l'Hopital, II, pp. 407-19, 541-44; Rottmann, pp. 278-84; Little, p. 154; *SOL* 26, pp. 100-102; Information of Mr P. Howell

Clapham, Our Immaculate Lady of Victories, also known as St Mary's, Clapham Park Road, SW4

The first Mass in Clapham since the Reformation was said on Christmas Eve 1847 by Bishop Wiseman in the house known as St Anne's, and owned by the Daughters of the Heart of Mary. Thereafter, until the Redemptorists came to Clapham, Mass was offered, at least on Sundays, in the Sisters' chapel. When Fr de Held and Fr Petcherine arrived, they said Mass there daily for about two months, when they opened the chapel in their new residence. Their domestic chapel was plainly inadequate to their missionary needs, and the Fathers lost no time in commencing a permanent church adjacent to their residence. Designs were obtained from William Wardell for a Decorated Gothic church, and building began. The foundation stone was laid on 2 August 1849 and the church was opened by Wiseman, now a cardinal, on 14 May 1851.

3. Clapham, Our Lady of Victories

Constructed of Kentish rag with Caen stone dressings, the church then consisted of nave of six bays and chancel, with (ritual) south aisle and chapel of St Alphonsus, and north aisle with sacristy plus a porch at the foot of the tower. The chancel, chapel and porch had lierne vaults, the rest being roofed of timber. The sturdy tower, three storeys tall, was given bells, claimed as the first post-Reformation peal in a Catholic church. It is surmounted by a broach spire with lucarnes in two storeys.

Subsequent building history is more complex than is usually the case. J.F. Bentley (who lived in the parish) designed and built the Lady Chapel projecting from the north aisle in 1886. The north transept (and new clergy house) also by Bentley were begun in 1892. The house was ready by the end of 1893; the transept by March 1895. The Chapel of St Gerard Majella and two adjacent confessionals were built in 1910, to designs of Bentley's son Osmond. In front of it the outer south aisle was added in 1928–29 by the architect Bernard Cox. Meanwhile, the War Memorial outside, consisting of a crucifix with Gothic detail and a record of names, had been erected in 1920, to designs of Giles Gilbert Scott. The various parts are now described in detail, roughly in the order of building.

The nave has piers of quatrefoil plan, with keeled faces and slender cusped shafts in the angles, and head corbels for the hood moulds of the arches. Above the arcade, the clerestory consists of three pairs of two-light windows. These are evenly spaced, but fail to bear a regular relationship to the arcade arches, a wayward feature that Pugin would scarcely have approved. Above the chancel arch a fresco of the Last Judgment executed in 1854 by J. Settegast of Coblenz was replaced in 1920 with a copy on canvas by J. Linthout.

The sanctuary retains its furnishings designed by Wardell. The altar is of stone, the seven panels of its frontal sculpted with angels and scenes of Our

Lord's Passion. The reredos consists of three niches containing the throne in the centre, with figures of Jesus and Mary to left and right. Above the niches are gables and pinnacles, all extravagantly crocketed. Between them are angels in smaller niches, holding quatrefoils with the Instruments of the Passion. To the right are the sedilia and piscina, also richly decorated with crocketed gables and nodding ogee arches. High on the side walls are statues of the four evangelists with Jeremiah and St Teresa. The great east window is of six lights with Decorated tracery. The theme of its stained glass is the Coronation of the Virgin surrounded by angels and saints. To the right of the chancel arch is the stone pulpit, its faces incised with circles containing cusped quatrefoils inset with figures of Ss Mark, John and Luke. To the left, and mounted on the arch, is the statue of Our Lady of Victories, carved and coloured. Beneath it is the octagonal font, with busy sculpture designed by Wardell. Its stem is detailed with diaper work. The faces of the bowl have crocketed gables inlaid with floral motifs, with more diaper work in the spandrels, and ornamental cresting.

Off the north aisle is the exquisite Lady Chapel, built and furnished in 1886 by Bentley. The carefully detailed altar has a panelled frontal with scenes of the Nativity, the Deposition and the Presentation painted on slate. In the reredos are seven angels within panels, bearing Instruments of the Passion. Above is a triptych containing a picture of Our Lady of Perpetual Help. The floor is tiled; the ceiling panelled and decorated with angel figures and Our Lady's titles. The three windows celebrate the Old Testament types of Our Lady—Eve, Sara, Rebecca, Rachel, Deborah, Ruth, Abigail, Esther and Judith. Adjacent to the chapel is the angel window, 1894, signed by Bentley.

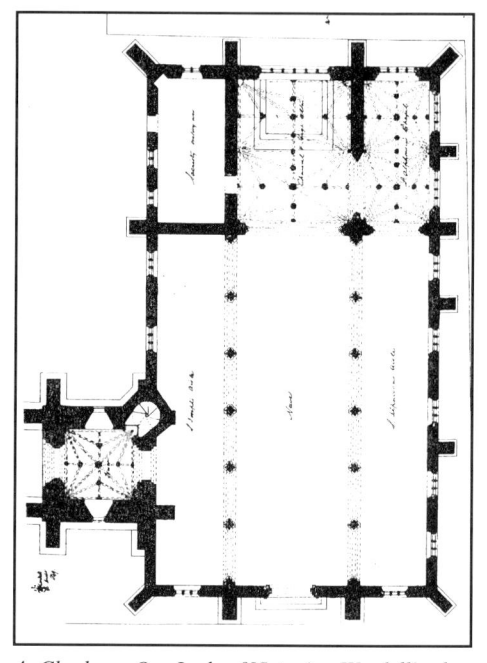

4. Clapham, Our Lady of Victories, Wardell's plan

Bentley's north transept, four bays long, is double aisled, with barrel roofs of timber resting on rounded piers with moulded shafts. It was erected in 1893–95. The head corbels of the nave arcades are repeated on the capitals here. Above the entrance is a crocketed ogee arch sculpted on the wall in Bentley's inimitable manner. The wrought iron railings and light fittings are also to Bentley's design. Projecting from the transept is the altar of St Joseph designed by Wardell, formerly in the north aisle and re-erected here. Its mensa is a solid slab of Sicilian marble. Beneath it the stone frontal sculpted in three panels depicts the death of St Joseph flanked by angels. The super-altar consists of seven panels sculpted with foliage set within quatrefoils. The reredos above it has a figure of St Joseph with Jesus in a central niche. To the left is a relief sculpture of the Espousal; to the right the Nativity. Designed by Bentley are the floor tiles, the rails of wrought iron and brass, and the windows. As soon as the transept was complete, the west gallery was enlarged by Bentley, to house the new organ built by A. Hunter and inaugurated in 1895.

A carved statue of St Gerard Majella was erected in May 1905, to mark his canonisation. It was not until 1910 that adjacent land was acquired on which to build St Gerard's chapel. J.F. Bentley having died in 1902, the architect was his son Osmond. The carved statue of the saint stands in a central niche over the altar, flanked by painted panels representing incidents in the saint's life. Below these are panels containing diaper work richly painted. The frontal has the appearance of textile work. It consists however of various inlays—mother-of-pearl, ivory, wood—worked into stylised floral patterns. The wrought-iron screen also was designed by O. Bentley. The window on the right, with scenes from the life of St Gerard dating from 1899, was designed by J.F. Bentley.

More land was obtained in 1928, enabling the construction of the outer south aisle. At about the same time, the organ was moved to its present site, displacing the chapel of St Alphonsus, and the organ gallery was demolished. A new chapel was constructed next to the tower entrance, wherein the altar of St Alphonsus was re-erected. The chapel is now hidden by a Confessional, but its reredos survives here. Designed by Wardell and dating from the opening of the church, it displays events in the life of the saint sculpted in bas-relief. Its altar table raised on marble columns now serves in the sanctuary. Its statue of St Alphonsus, carved by Mayer, now stands in a recess in the outer south aisle. The windows in the chapel and that in the adjacent aisle (1930) were designed by Sr Margaret of the Carmelite Convent of Woodbridge. The canted oaken front to the confessional was designed by Harrison & Cox of Birmingham, and carved by Robert Bridgeman of Lichfield.

Bibliography
Kelly, p. 133; Rottmann, pp. 284-91; de l'Hopital, pp. 383; 452-58; 538-39; 558-59; G. Stebbing, *History of St Mary's Clapham* (Covent Garden: Sands and Co., 1935); Little, pp. 134, 153; *The Catholic Handbook*, 1857; *BN*, 1 February 1861, p. 94; *The Tablet*, 29 April 1905, p. 664; *CD*, 1933, p. 64; Information of Rev. H. Parker

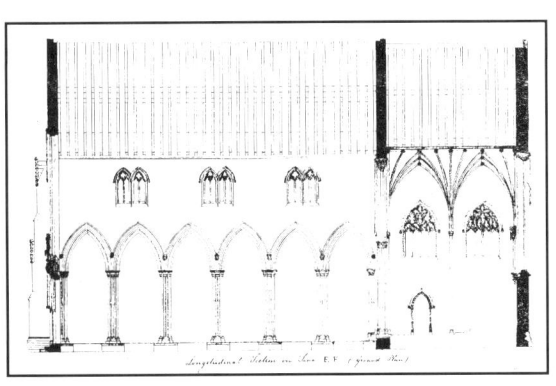

5. *Clapham, Our Lady of Victories, section by Wardell*

Clapham Park, St Bede, Thornton Road, SW12

In 1903 Miss Frances Ellis donated Hyde House to the diocese. Here St John Berchmans School was opened for boys destined for St John's Seminary at Wonersh. A mission was also opened, and the first Mass was said in the house on 8 September 1903. B.W. Kelly recorded the number of resident students as 'about sixteen'. The school was apparently closed when the adjoining church was opened on 27 April 1906. The large, handsome house now serves as the presbytery.

The church is built in the customary plain style of Ellis churches, and cost £2,000. The building application dated 7 December 1905 does not reveal an architect, but the builder is named as E.B. Tucker of Lavender Hill. The chancel and the (ritual) west front have both been extended.

The approach from Thornton Road is quite picturesque. Through a lych gate and past a neat lawn a drive leads to the church entrance. Of yellow stock brick, the west front is two-storeyed, with broad pilasters, a broken pediment of Portland stone and three round-headed windows. At ground level, an ample open porch (containing a statue of St Bede) projects, the whole arrangement firmly reminiscent of Early Christian work. Inside, there is a broad aisleless nave of six bays divided by pilasters,

6. Clapham Park, St Bede

with high semicircular windows, a timber barrel vault and a west gallery; the chancel of two bays, and the south-east Lady Chapel.

The altar is of light grey marbles, with IHS let into a central mosaic panel. Above the tabernacle is a circular stained-glass window of Christ in Majesty. The Lady Chapel has an east apse with a glazed semi-dome, housing the altar of white and blue marbles, with an enamelled tabernacle and a statue of Regina Coeli by Mayer. Also in the chapel are carved statues of St Joseph and St Antony. The baptistery with its octagonal font, and a confessional are sited to the south of the nave. In the nave there are a carved crucifix, the Sacred Heart by Stuflesser, and the Stations of the Cross—stylised figures cast in bronze by R. Gourdon.

Bibliography
Kelly, p. 133

Norbury, St Bartholomew, Hepworth Road, SW16

This is recorded as one of the Ellis churches, and the first Mass here was said on 20 September 1908. The architect was Fr Benedict Williamson.

The original church consisted of the sanctuary, the transept with its two chapels, and about ten feet of the nave. Fr Alex Trew completed the church in 1929, with the nave extension, the baptistery and the narthex. Additions for Fr James Carolin completed in 1974 included the retro-chapel east of the chancel, the repository at the west end and new sacristies. At the same time, the Blessed Sacrament Chapel was refurbished with a vaulted ceiling of fibrous plaster, the Shrine of Our Lady was installed, and the west gallery of reinforced concrete received a new organ with two batteries of pipes flanking a new circular window. The architects for this work were Broadbent, Hastings, Reid & Todd; the contractors Whyteleafe Ltd.

7. Norbury, St Bartholomew

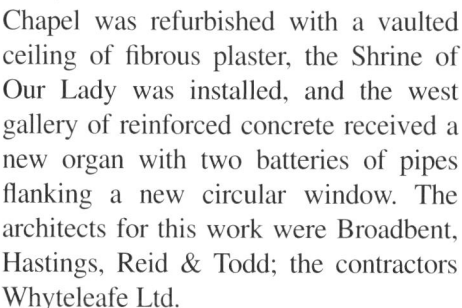

The exterior is of plain stock brick with minimal stone dressings. There is a large window in the west gable, and below it three matching doorways to the nave and aisles. In contrast with this symmetry, the aspect to the south is agreeably broken with projections made by the transept, the entrance lobby and the foyer to the parish centre constructed in 1978.

The interior is of Romanesque derivation, with nave, crossing, transept and chancel. To the east, the retro-chapel, added in 1974, is reminiscent of the Lady Chapel customary in major mediaeval churches. Beyond a glazed narthex the two bays of the nave carry broad round-headed arches borne on square piers with thinly moulded capitals lightly rusticated along their surfaces. Above the arcade are the clerestory and king-post roof. Off the north aisle are the polygonal repository, the baptistery with octagonal stone font of 1929, and built-in confessionals.

The altars of the Blessed Sacrament Chapel and Our Lady's Shrine (of 1974) bear mosaic reredoses with appropriate symbolism. These and the high altar (of 1978) are all constructed of Siena marble. The altar rails are happily extant, of a simple wrought-iron and timber design. The windows throughout are round-headed or circular, many of them filled with stained glass. Particularly striking here are two triple groups: in the south transept the Nativity, and in the north transept the Last Supper, of 1981 by Hardman. The Stations of the Cross and the Lady Statue are cast; in the retro-chapel are tastefully carved statues of St Joseph and St Bartholomew; and in the nave the Sacred Heart carved by Mussner G. Vincenzo of Ortisei.

Bibliography
CBR.S, 1974, pp. 178-79; 1978, pp. 44-45; Information of Rev. James Carolin

Norwood West, St Matthew, Norwood High Street, SE27

The foundation stone was laid on 20 September 1904, and the church was opened on 30 March 1905. Miss Frances Ellis was the benefactress, according to Archbishop Amigo's Visitation Reports. The architect was probably F.W. Tasker, according to the Survey of London, volume 26. It is indeed in Tasker's customary plan of nave, aisles and chancel. The church was lengthened by two bays at the east end in 1937. Following damage by enemy action in 1940, the west end was rebuilt in 1949–50. The architect for this work was D. Plaskett Marshall. Subsequent structural reorderings took place in two stages. In 1972, under the architect W. Stone, some of the piers were removed so that the altar could stand in the raised centre of the south aisle, the facing congregation extended to its left and right. Then, in 1984, Derek Phillips added the narthex entrance opposite the altar. At some point, long horizontal windows were inserted into the aisles.

The exterior is mainly of brick, its visual emphases being the north and west fronts. The north addition (with three glazed gables) is neatly contrived beneath the same roof as the north aisle. The two-storeyed west front, with a tall round-headed arch stepped to the nave, bears between two windows a statue of St Matthew sculpted by Joseph Cribb.

The interior layout is an interesting demonstration of improved congregation-oriented planning. The original arrangement of nave, aisles and chancel of six bays, with plain square piers, clerestory and tiled ceiling, has been turned clockwise by 90 degrees. The font introduced in 1986, the lectern (1989) and the altar (1992) appear to be a matching set of the same marble. Also of 1992 are four stained glass windows depicting the evangelists, in deep blues and reds. To the left of the altar are the Stations of the Cross, of fibre glass, grouped all together; and to the right a carved statue of St Patrick. In the Blessed Sacrament Chapel there are statues of the Risen Christ and St Matthew, installed in 1980 and carved by Mussner Vincenzo of Ortisei.

8. *Norwood West, St Matthew*

Bibliography
SOL 26, pp. 14, 179; Southwark Diocesan Visitation Reports; Information of Canon J.P. Devane

Stockwell, St Francis of Sales and St Gertrude, Larkhall Lane, SW4

The church was begun in 1902 and opened in 1903. It is in the Romanesque manner of the architect F.W. Tasker. It is also typical of the numerous churches erected in south London about this time—of modest size, brick built and financed by Miss Frances Ellis. The (ritual) west front facing Larkhall Lane has a gabled nave and slightly recessed lean-to aisles. There is a large circular window beneath the gable, a feature characteristic of F.W. Tasker's churches. Between the original north and south porches a modern extension with a glazed roof has been added.

Inside, there is the traditional plan of nave, aisles and sanctuary. The church was renovated in 1991–92 by the architect William Thuburn. The former arcade piers of square plan have been replaced by tall, hollow, metal cylinders, free from capitals, which support an entablature on either side. The entablature itself is composed of timber struts arranged in a continuous grid of triangles. Above this there is a timber barrel roof to the nave, and flat ceilings to the aisles. Also new is the gallery over the entrance, with a meeting room glazed to the nave. The original rectangular windows are high, each subdivided by a stocky mullion between the panes. The circular windows in the re-entrant angles are also original. Within the projecting sanctuary the marble altar is especially fine, the proportions of the supports and the spaces between them all standing in well-considered relation to each other. Along the table front is incised 'Unigenitus Dei qui est in sinu patris'.

9. Stockwell, St Francis of Sales and St Gertrude

Over the tabernacle there is an economical representation of Calvary, with starkly stylised figures carved by Robert Kiddie of Newark. To the right there is the Shrine of Our Lady of Lourdes, its statue executed by Duport of Bruges.

Also in the church is a figure of the Sacred Heart, and a cast of St Antony of 1895. Around the walls are the fine modern Stations of the Cross, 14 canvas paintings, as dramatic in execution as they are colourful in concept.

Bibliography
Kelly, p. 374; *SOL* 26, p. 83; *The Tablet*, 8 October 1904, p. 594

Streatham, The English Martyrs, 2 Mitcham Lane, SW16

The mission commenced when the Poor Servants of the Mother of God established a convent at Russell House, Streatham. The first Mass was said here on 6 May 1888 by Canon McGrath of Camberwell. The present church adjacent to the house was built piecemeal as funds became available. The foundation stone was laid by Bishop John Butt on 4 May 1892, and the nave, aisles and southwest tower were opened by Cardinal Vaughan exactly one year later. The style is fourteenth century Decorated. The architect was A.E. Purdie; the builders Lorden & Sons of Tooting Bec; and the major benefactor was Robert Measures. The tower and spire were completed on 1 January 1894. The completed chancel was opened on 16 June 1897.

In 1931 the Russell House convent was rebuilt, and the opportunity was taken to straighten the wall of the southeast chapel which stood adjacent to it. The architect for this work was Frank Geary and the builders were Messrs Greenwood. During a redecoration of about 1952, the nave ceiling was embellished with the names of English martyrs. In the 1960s, adjacent land was acquired, and the north-east transeptal chapel was added. Opened in 1965, its architect was Thomas Sibthorp. The church was reordered in 1986 for Fr David Sheehy by the architect D.L.S. Phillips.

The church is well sited on the corner of Tooting Bec Gardens and Mitcham Lane. The exterior of Kentish rag with

10. *Streatham, English Martyrs*

Bath stone dressings is further enhanced by its proud broach spire with its bands of Portland stone. This stands to the (ritual) south-west. On its faces are mounted statues of St Anselm and St Thomas of Canterbury. The west front has a five-light window with Decorated tracery above a triple entrance. The central doorway is gabled, and in its tympanum is a sculpted representation of the Child Jesus in the Temple. Inside is a lobby glazed to the nave, containing a memorial tablet of marble to the first rector, Fr William Lloyd +1912. Above the lobby is the organ gallery with its large window celebrating the life of St Thomas More. The organ of about 1900 by T.C. Lewis of Croydon was completely rebuilt by R. Rust & Sons of Norwood in 1974.

To describe the main interior as nave and aisles of five bays plus chancel and chapels would be to ignore its sumptuous character. The generosity of Robert Measures added to the professional insight of A.E. Purdie together generated a splendid interior remarkably superior to that of the average church. This was achieved by the additional furnishings, particularly statues, stained glass and altars.

The circular piers of the nave arcade carry deeply carved capitals with generous foliage and floral details. Above them is the clerestory of three lights to a bay, and in the panelled ceiling numerous names of English martyrs. In the spandrels between the arcade arches are mounted statues of the better-known sixteenth-century martyrs. There is more sculpture in the aisles—to the south a Calvary and the Good Shepherd; to the north Ss Peter, Patrick, Gregory and Leonard. The Stations, mounted within ornate Gothic frames, also extend the effect. To these the numerous windows by Hardman add their contribution.

The chancel and chapels are three bays deep, with more complex piers of quatrefoil plan and keeled shafts supporting tierceron vaults. The reordered sanctuary has a forward altar of limestone from Chichester Cathedral Workshops, ingeniously supported on two inverted metal arches. The high altar dating from 1897 was sculpted by A.B. Wall of Cheltenham. Its setting is a tour de force of thematic detail. The central throne is flanked by two tiers of niches, all topped by spires and crocketed gables, and containing figures of Ss Thomas of Canterbury, Edmund, Alban and Winifred. Between these and the alabaster tabernacle, the reredos is arcaded to left and right. Clearly visible behind its arches are sculpted reliefs of many martyrs in procession. Below these are panels containing monograms set in diaper work.

The panelled frontal bears relief sculpture of the Crucifixion flanked by the deaths of John the Baptist and St Stephen. Above the piscina to the right are the sculpted heads of Robert Measures and Mary his wife; and above the aumbry to the left are Fr William Lloyd and one of the Measures daughters. There is more sculpture still, in the spandrels of the arches, on the north side Ss John the Baptist, Gabriel and Peter; and on the south side Ss Andrew, Michael and Paul. The six clerestory windows hold figures from the Old Testament, and the seven-light traceried east window celebrates the life of St John Fisher.

To the right is the Chapel of the Holy Spirit with its window dating from 1932. It now houses the baptismal font, a piece superior to customary designs, with a circular base supporting slender marble columns grouped in threes, which in turn support a hexagonal bowl bearing sculpted scenes from the life of Our Lady.

To the left of the sanctuary is the shrine of the Queen of Martyrs. On a plinth stands the statue of Our Lady holding a crown of thorns. This and the nearby statue of St Margaret Clitherow are the work of Michael Clark. There is a five-light window with reticulated tracery. Around the shrine are magnificent brass communion rails, formerly before the high altar.

The transeptal chapel of the Sacred Heart, opened in 1965, is a spacious rectangular room. Intentionally designed in the manner of the earlier parts, its ceiling is panelled like that of the nave, and decorated with names of the martyrs. Its windows were constructed to the same size as those in the nave clerestory, and now house many of the stained glass figures of martyrs removed from the nave. Its principal feature is the large wooden altar by de Wispelaere of Bruges, used at the opening of the church in 1893. Its reredos stands in two tiers. Relief panels of Jesus and the Children and the Return of the Prodigal Son are flanked by statues of saints.

Above these is the Sacred Heart in a central niche supported by crocketed gables, and the four evangelists. In the frontal is the Last Supper, flanked by St Bernard and St Margaret Mary. Bordering the altar are two statues of St John Houghton and Bl. John Storey formerly in the nave and brought here in 1974, as well as the alabaster statue of the Madonna and Child.

Bibliography
Kelly, p. 380; G. Brine, *English Martyrs Streatham* (Streatham: Malthouse Press, 1993); *BN*, 13 May 1892, p. 686; 5 May 1893, p. 623; 19 May 1893, p. 690; *The Tablet*, 6 January 1894, p. 34; 19 June 1897, p. 991; *CBR.S*, 1962, pp. 124-29; 1965, p. 70; *Streatham News*, 5 February 1932; 21 October 1932; 28 October 1932

Streatham Hill, Ss Simon and Jude, Hillside Road, SW2

The first Mass in the church was said on 27 July 1906. The site, church and presbytery were the gift of Miss Frances Ellis and the architect was Clement Jackson. To the rectangular aisleless nave the chancel was added in 1937; and, to provide extra accommodation, the gallery was added in 1960. Underpinning took place in 1988–89 under the direction of Keith Mascarenhas of Southern Dry Wall Construction. During a thorough restoration and reordering in 1988–90, a new (ritual) west entrance and new sacristies on the south side were built. The architect for this work was Derek Phillips; the contractor Harry Nolan of Collinstown Construction Company. The result of all this is a warm, bright, compact interior.

The church is built of London stock brick. Its two-storeyed west front has a projecting Tuscan gable, beneath it a large Diocletian window, in the manner of examples at Westminster Cathedral. At ground level is the projecting entrance with its glazed gable, added in 1990. Inside, one sees the beauty of 11 stained glass lights, displaying a comprehensive group of saints and luminaries of the Church. In one of the ante-rooms is a statue of St Anthony, English work.

The main interior consists of nave of three bays with its deep west gallery and king-post roof, followed by the chancel, one bay deep. Here the altar is of Cornish stone, standing on four circular supports reused from the previous altar. Behind it the column supporting the tabernacle is of Balmoral granite. Its base and capital are of Cheshire sandstone, as is also the base of the pulpit. The woodwork is of English oak. These British materials adorn this church much more readily than the Continental examples frequently encountered elsewhere. The crucifix is of the nineteenth century, and the statues of Our Lady and St John carved from tree trunks are seventeenth-century Netherlands work. On the north side of the chancel is the Bradford Ahlborn computer organ. Finally, there are two east windows to the Good Shepherd and Ss Simon and Jude, of 1990 by Andrew Taylor. Also by him are the stained glass windows in the nave, the Lady Shrine and the entrance.

In the nave are cast statues of the Sacred Heart and St Teresa; a bas-relief plaque of St Martin of about 1920; St Jude, German carved work; and St Joseph by Philip Clark. The Stations of the Cross, well-detailed groups of figures carved by Anton Dapre, were installed in 1944. The five candelabra, the exterior gates and railings were wrought by Tim Hallett of Hale.

Bibliography
Michael Coffey, *Ss Simon and Jude*, (Streatham Hill: Catholic Chuch, 1990)

11 *Streatham Hill, Ss Simon and Jude*

Vauxhall, St Anne, Kennington Lane, SE11

Through the initiative of Bishop John Butt, Mass was said from 1886 onwards in the school in Vauxhall Walk, and from 1892 in the new school in Harleyford Road. Credit for building the church rests almost entirely with Fr (later Bishop) W.F. Brown, who was in charge of the mission for 60 years. Fr Brown adopted the well-tried policy of completing the shell using funds in hand, and leaving the provision of altars and other furnishings for the future. He succeeded in erecting the shell, accommodating 700 worshippers, but exclusive of further embellishments, for £10,000.

With such fine churches in mind as Buckfast Abbey and the Sacred Heart at Wimbledon, Fr Brown chose F.A. Walters as his architect. The builders were Goddard & Sons of Farnham and Dorking. The foundation stone was laid on 3 November 1900; the church was in use from January 1903, and was formally opened by Archbishop Bourne on 26 October following. The rood, pulpit and altar rails were added in 1906; the high altar the following year. The chapel off the (ritual) north aisle, with a parish room above it, and the north-west tower were added in 1907.

Walters met Fr Brown's wish for a large and dignified church with this Gothic design. Not a church that Pugin would have recognised as Early English, it belongs to that refined and functional type of late Gothic that Walters was trying to develop. Clearly it is designed from the inside. Beyond the west entrance with the baptistery on the left, the nave is of five bays, with pitch pine roof, narrow passage aisles with pairs of tall lancet windows, and piers of octagonal plan, without capitals. The easternmoat bays of the nave are canted inwards, producing a strong eastward drive. Owing to the irregularity of the site, the north transept is larger than the south, and neatly houses the organ (of 1903 by Bishop & Son). The chancel is deep, and flanked by chapels with coupled arches.

12. Vauxhall, St Anne

The chancel now has a forward altar, of 1982, in plain verde antico. The original altar of 1903 remains for all to admire. It is of alabaster with marble inlaid panels, above it a figure of Christ the King. The multi-arched reredos with its sculpted decoration is surmounted by a carved baldacchino. High in the left wall is the carved organ case. These and the chancel walls are brightly decorated in red, blue and gold, with repeated patterns of fleurs de lys and quatrefoils. Blending with all this are the painted figures of the chancel rood.

The south-east Lady Chapel has similar decoration to grace its otherwise simple sandstone altar of 1911, with its panelled reredos and figure sculpture. In the chapel are two stained glass windows of 1912 by N.H.J. Westlake. The north-east Altar of the Sacred Heart of 1919 has a similar panelled reredos with figure sculpture and bright stencilled decoration.

Beyond an iron screen off the north aisle is the Requiem Chapel. The frontal and reredos of its altar consecrated in 1928 are again subdivided into panels, with much figure sculpture denoting the Trinity and All Souls. On its north wall is a set of Stations of the Cross, relief work cast and painted, and around the walls much stencilled decoration. The rood, pulpit and communion rails, all designed by Walters, were installed in 1906. Also in the nave are statues of the Madonna and Child, St Antony, a *pietà*, and St Joseph of 1919 by Walters.

All of the foregoing Walters expressed externally with a quiet economy of means that nevertheless produced an impressive statement. He concealed the narrowness of the aisles beneath the pitch of the roof. He wisely refrained from bringing his tall west front up to the line of the pavement, but set it back flush with the adjacent presbytery, and provided at ground level a deeply recessed porch with a flanking baptistery.

The climax of the red brick exterior is the north-west tower, with its sparing use of stone dressings, and its faces in two tiers of paired lancets, flanked by tall, flat buttresses, the whole surmounted by a saddleback roof. Here, Walters arrives at a type of tower that he appears to have sought for some years: a tower highly individual, yet consonant with the rest of his design. Altogether, Walters achieved in St Anne's, Lambeth, a church of truly noble simplicity.

Bibliography
Kelly, p. 407; Little, pp. 162-63; *SOL* 26, pp. 39-40; W.F. Brown, *Through Windows of Memory* (Covent Garden: Sands and Co., 1946), p. 25; *BN*, 16 November 1900, p. 722; 30 October 1903, p. 604; *The Architect*, 6 February 1903, Supplement, p. 17; *The Tablet*, 7 July 1906, p. 27; 18 October 1919, p. 506

Waterloo, St Patrick, Cornwall Road, SE1

To answer the desperate need for Catholic schools in the district around Waterloo, a school chapel was founded here in 1897. The land cost £3,000 and the buildings the same figure. Two school buildings of two storeys were erected, the chapel being in the upper room of one of them. The new schools were blessed by Cardinal Vaughan on 1 November 1897, and Mass was said in the chapel for the first time on Sunday 7 November. The mission was served initially from St George's Cathedral. In 1915 Fr Philip Hemans took quarters in Cornwall Road, and St Patrick's district was separated administratively from the cathedral. Since 1964 the parish has been in the care of the Friars Minor Conventual.

The church occupies the first floor of the western building. Its stock brick front to Cornwall Road in three narrow bays has a gabled centre with a bell-cote on the right. A large circular window is flanked by smaller blind circles. Lower still are a pair of round-headed windows and the domestic-looking entrance. The name of the architect is not recorded, but some of these features are in the customary manner of F.W. Tasker.

Upstairs, the church is a modest rectangular room divided into six bays which include the gallery and the sanctuary. The flat ceiling is chamfered, and along the sides are rectangular windows singly and in pairs.

The timber altar is supported by coupled colonettes standing before a Gothic panelled frontal with a central IHS monogram. The reredos is striped in red and gold. There are cast statues of the Sacred Heart, the Blessed Virgin, St Patrick and St Joseph, signed Regall Bros. In the nave there is a carved figure of St Antony.

Bibliography
Kelly, p. 418; Bogan, pp. 302-303; 325; The Tablet, 6 November 1897, p. 752

X
Lewisham

Beckenham Hill, The Annunciation, Dunfield Road, SE6

THE primary school was opened in 1928 and Mass was said there by a priest from Sydenham. From 1934 a wooden building served as a church, and Fr Desmond Coffey was the parish priest. The foundation stone of the present church was laid on 19 October 1963, and the church was consecrated on 26 August 1964. Raglan Squire & Partners were the architects.

The imposing exterior has a circular core, consisting of a tall polygonal drum of brick, roofed with copper. Each facet has a glazed gable, and alternate sides project slightly. In the centre of the drum is a crown-like lantern; and around its perimeter is a lower storey, interrupted on the south side, where three stout turrets flank two doorways, in a manner reminiscent of a barbican.

Inside, the plan is easily read. The tall drum has the altar at its centre, and on its circumference is the tabernacle opposite the entrance, with four banks of benches filling the main space. Square brick piers with elliptical arches mark the 12 bays. High up are triangular windows, and a triangular folded timber roof repeated in each bay. In the centre is the base of the lantern.

The altar and tabernacle stand are raised on masonry plinths. The credence, font and chair are all of matching timber. Behind the tabernacle a curtained screen conceals the organ, of 1865 by J.W. Walker. The wide ambulatory houses several altars, of the same construction as the high altar, and of matching marble. Flanking the entrance are two apsidal chapels, one to Notre Dame de Sacre Coeur, the other to St Augustine, with a fine sculpted statue crafted with a commendable economy of line that matches its setting. Other altars are dedicated to: St Patrick; St Teresa of Lisieux, each with a carved statue; the English Martyrs; and St Joseph. Here and there the building materials are varied by narrow windows bearing stained glass of random colours within geometrical shapes. On the piers hang the Stations of the Cross, carved in low relief.

Brockley, St Mary Magdalen, Howson Road, SE4

The mission was established with the opening of the schools by Bishop John Butt in September 1895. A room in the boys' school served as a chapel until the

1. Brockley, St Mary Magdalen

church was erected by the diocesan builder, Mr Romain, from the design of the architect Young Bolton. The foundation stone was blessed on 9 July 1898 by Bishop Francis Bourne, and the church was opened on 16 March 1899. It has been in the charge of the Augustinians of the Assumption since 1906.

Following serious damage sustained during an air raid, reconstruction was carried out in the late forties, and the west front especially is much changed, the central bank of windows being replaced by a doorway, and windows substituted for two flanking doors. Consequently, the west front is reminiscent of concert hall or theatre architecture rather than church designs of the period. Of red brick and in two storeys, it has a central pedimented bay surmounted by a cross, and in a niche below it a statue of St Mary Magdalen. The recessed flanking bays are each crowned by a cupola on an octagonal drum. The side view displays five matching windows sandwiched between the taller main front and the lower chancel roof. The concept, therefore, is an interesting example of the round-arched style that was to characterize so many new churches in Southwark diocese during the next decade.

Beyond the entrance bay with its organ gallery resting on Corinthian columns, is the unaisled nave with its elliptical plaster ceiling. The round-headed windows bear panes of variously coloured glass. The chancel is narrower than the nave, and flanked by the Lady Chapel and the sacristy. The original marble altar by Fr Gregory Chedal is preserved, with a sculpted Calvary forming the reredos, and the Last Supper in the frontal. The design is punctuated by niches with statues by Verrebout. There is a forward altar with matching chancel furnishings of timber.

The Lady Chapel also has a timber altar, above it a statue of the Virgin and Child. Adjacent to it is the octagonal stone font. In the nave there are cast relief Stations of the Cross; and statues of the Sacred Heart, St Joseph, St Antony, St Teresa, St Peter and St Vincent, the last two by La Statue Religieuse of Paris.

Bibliography
Kelly, pp. 102-103; Baker, p. 58; *The Tablet*, 16 July 1898, p. 116; *Westminster Cathedral Chronicle*, 1912, p. 79; Parish archives

Catford, Holy Cross, Sangley Road, SE16

The church was founded from Lewisham, and was opened by Bishop Amigo on 14 September 1904. The donor of the site, church and presbytery was Miss Frances Ellis, and the architect was F.W. Tasker. The exterior of brick and Portland stone was described by The Tablet as 'a plain and unpretentious structure'. The (ritual) west gable with its rose window attempts a brave show, however, amid the terraced houses of Sangley Road. Beyond the wide porch (added in 1949), the visitor is immediately impressed by the well-polished brightness of the interior. The plan is a Greek cross, marked by pilasters and an entablature, and ceiled with a groin vault of timber. There are shrines within the re-

2. *Catford, Holy Cross*

entrant angles. This compact arrangement does much to render the church intimate and inviting.

The sanctuary of 1924 has three pilastered bays, a king-post roof and a round window depicting angels adoring the Sacrament. Its furniture is all of marble—tabernacle stand, sedilia, altar, lectern and font. Across the chancel arch there is a rood with carved figures flanking the crucifix.

To the left is the Sacred Heart Shrine with a statue by Mayer, and a canvas of Our Lady of Perpetual Help by Calafati. The corresponding top-lit Lady Altar and frontal is of marble, with a base and columns of stone. Its Madonna and Child statue is by Mayer. Near to the entrance is the Lourdes Shrine, with figures of Our Lady and St Bernadette.

Around the broad nave are the Stations of the Cross, brightly coloured canvases in oaken frames. Also in the nave there are two prominent niches with Renaissance features, containing figures of St Patrick and St Agnes by Mayer.

Bibliography
Baker, p. 57; Kelly, pp. 119-20; *BN*, 16 September 1904, p. 416; *The Tablet*, 17 September 1904, p. 472; *Br*, 24 September 1904, p. 321; *CBR.S*, 1961, pp. 128-29

Deptford, The Assumption, 131 High Street, SE8

The mission was founded in 1842 by Fr William Marshall, and a school chapel was opened in Old King Street the following year, the gift of Canon Richard North, rector of the Greenwich mission. The foundation stone of the present church was laid on 22 June 1844, and the nave was opened for use about a year later. The cost was £2,000, and Canon North was architect as well as patron. The chancel and Lady Chapel were opened on 15 December 1859, both designed and financed by Canon North. The sacristy, west gallery and presbytery were added at the same time.

Only the (ritual) west front, of London stock brick with Portland stone dressings is visible from High Street. It presents a symmetrical arrangement of four buttresses which define a central triple-arched window flanked by single lancets, and their corresponding entrances. To the right is a porch in keeping with this, added c. 1980.

The interior echoes throughout the Early English phase of Gothic, with tall lancets each side of the nave and a straight-ended chancel. The timber roof incorporates both king-post and hammerbeam elements in its principals. A likely local precedent for this choice of style may have been Holy Trinity Church, Bermondsey, opened since 1835.

Catching the eye is the prominent chancel arch with its copious foliage-sculpted capitals and corbelled plinths. These are matched by sculpture over the sacristy door, with Descendit ad Infernos in the tympanum, beneath an ogee arch and statues of St Michael and angels.

The chancel is almost square in plan, with three clerestory lights to each side, and a wheel window depicting the Assumption. It has modern matching

3. Deptford, The Assumption, detail of sculpture

furniture of timber, and the old altar is still in situ. This was installed in two stages: first the actual altar with its frontal panels of the Annunciation, the Nativity and the Assumption; and above this the tabernacle and monstrance throne. Then in 1884 came the reredos, exhibited at the Paris Exhibition in 1878, and presented by Canon Joseph North.

To a height of about six feet it has extensive diaper work of terracotta. Above this is a series of niches, occupied by figures of angels bearing symbols of the Passion, with Our Lady in the centre. At each end are traceried and canopied buttresses. The reredos was sculpted by Earp, Son & Hobbs, and the design is attributed to F.A. Walters.

To the right is the Lady Chapel, with a carved statue of Our Lady of Lourdes, and St Bernadette. This was furnished as the Sacred Heart Chapel by F.A. Walters in 1886. Its altar is diapered and panelled, and in the frontal is a vesica containing the emblem of the Sacred Heart.

Various permanent furnishings remain to be noted. The west window depicting Our Lady of Victories, St Michael and St Martin, all within three large lancets; in the porch the carved crucifix presented in 1871; the carved Stations of the Cross in their Gothic frames; the nave statues of Ss Patrick and Michael, and the Sacred Heart by Mayer.

Bibliography

Kelly, pp. 152-53; Rev. John Kenny, 'A Part of Deptford' Past and Present (Deptford: Rev. James McGillicuddy, 1992); *The Tablet*, 22 June 1844, p. 390; *Br*, 27 December 1884, p. 876; AAS; RIBA drawings collection

Forest Hill, St William of York, Brockley Park, SE23

The mission was founded from Brockley, with a gift from Frances Ellis sufficient to supply a small church and presbytery. The foundation stone was laid in 1905, and the church was opened by Bishop Amigo on 3 May 1906. The chancel, aisles, vestibule and gallery were added in 1931 by Wilfrid Mangan. The church was reoriented when in 1986 a new chancel was built out from the old north aisle, by the architects Williams & Winkley. The former sanctuary then became a meeting room, screened from the nave by a folding partition, and capable of supplying overflow congregational space. Above it a large hall extends over the first bay of the nave. Entering via the vestibule, one finds the sanctuary is on the left, with a wide band of seats spreading across the nave, close to the altar and uninterrupted by supports. The original orientation of the nave is still discernible, with its king-post roof, its elliptical windows, and the gallery over the vestibule.

The chancel extension is a steel and timber-framed structure, with matching decor, wide and visible from all parts. Its panelled roof is gabled in the centre. In the gable is a circular mullioned window containing abstract stained glass by Goddard & Gibbs, the design of John Barber, a parishioner. The sanctuary furniture of matching stone includes altar, credence table, lectern and font, by David John. To the right is the Blessed Sacrament Altar, all of marble, mainly Sicilian.

Facing the high altar, the former aisle serves as an ambulatory giving access to all parts of the nave. It has a round-arched arcade, with marble columns between the piers. On the piers hang the Stations, plain black wooden crosses, their subjects lightly incised in gold. In the south-west corner are statues of the

4. *Forest Hill, St William of York*

Sacred Heart and Our Lady of Victories, carved by Mayer.

Outside, it was felt that the street façade should not be altered, and thus the 1986 reorientation has had minimum impact. In the neo-Romanesque style current in 1906, the façade is of brick (laid in Flemish bond) with stone dressings. Most prominent is the Tuscan gable fronting the nave, and its large round-headed window; beneath it a buttressed porch with a columned entrance and a tympanum. To left and right are the asymmetrical additions of 1931. It would be useful to know who was the original architect.

Bibliography
Kelly, p. 180; *CB*, Winter 1986, p. 39; Brockley parish archives

Lee, Our Lady of Lourdes, Burnt Ash Hill, SE12

The mission of St Winifred's in Effingham Road was served from Blackheath from 1892. It was separated from Blackheath in 1910 on the opening of a church in Manor Lane. This was superseded by the present church built in Burnt Ash Hill to the design of Francis Panario. Its foundation stone was blessed on 25 March 1939 by Bishop William Brown and the opening took place on 24 December following. Approaching the church from Burnt Ash Hill, one sees a solemn Early Christian type front, brick-built, with an imposing triple-arched window, a lean-to ante-chamber, and an Italianate north-west tower.

Inside, Early Christian characteristics prevail, with round-arched arcades and windows throughout. The nave is of five bays with narrow passage aisles. Above the arcade are tall clerestory windows and a queen-post roof. Around the apsidal sanctuary there is an ambulatory with an arcade of verde antico columns, their capitals busily detailed with ecclesiastical symbols. The original privileged altar with its tabernacle is preserved beneath an imposing baldacchino. This consists of four marble monoliths with Corinthian capitals, its roof depicting Our Lady surrounded by angels. The altar before it is of stone raised on marble piers. The communion rails are of stone inset with panels of verde antico, and a coping of pavonazzo.

Two chapels flank the sanctuary. The north chapel's altar is of varied marbles including Sicilian and verde antico. In the reredos a figure of the Sacred Heart in opus-sectile is set against a gold mosaic background. The south chapel's altar is of similar design, its reredos bearing a pietà in opus sectile. Also in this chapel is a carved figure of St Bernadette and a canvas of the Betrothal of the Virgin.

Beneath the west gallery is the baptistery, its font rising from a square

5. *Lee, Our Lady of Lourdes*

base through a superstructure of sandstone projections enclosing marble panels which match those of the communion rails and the pulpit. The Stations of the Cross are cast, as is the figure of St John Bosco by Vanpoulle. Also in the nave are figures of St Teresa carved by EGD, and St Joseph by Mayer.

Bibliography
Baker, p. 57; H. Pragnell, *The Styles of English Architecture* (London: Batsford, 1984), p. 150; *The Tablet*, 22 October 1910, p. 672; *CD*, 1893, 1911

Lewisham, St Saviour and Ss John the Baptist and Evangelist, Lewisham High Street, SE13

Founded from Blackheath in 1894, the mission commenced with Mass in a house in Marley Road. A school chapel followed in 1898. The foundation stone was laid on 24 April 1909 by Bishop Amigo, who also opened the church on the following 16 December. 'The church is a quaint and interesting specimen of the Roman style freely treated according to the designs of Messrs Kelly and

6. *Lewisham, St Saviour*

Dickie.'[1] The builder was F.J. Bradford of Leicester, and the cost was £2,000.

When opened, the church consisted only of narthex, nave with narrow aisles, apsidal sanctuary and Lady Chapel on the north side. By 1914, however, the north aisle confessionals, the Altar of St Patrick, the ambulatory, high altar and pulpit were all installed. The new Lady Chapel dates from 1917–18; the Altar of St Joseph from 1921. The Sacred Heart Chapel was constructed in 1924; the extended south aisle and the campanile were built in 1928–29.

The exterior, strongly resembling that of Claude Kelly's earlier church of St Vincent, Clapham, presents only its west front to view. It is built of Dutch bricks with tiled courses. A lean-to projection containing ancillary rooms introduces an Ionic columned doorway with mosaic decoration in its tympanum, and a Tuscan gable of oak. Prolific statuary consisting of a Calvary (1919), St Peter, St Patrick and the Sacred Heart (1991) leads upwards to a circular window below another Tuscan gable. To one side is the tall brick campanile. It has incised pairs of arches at its faces, then a double-arched unglazed storey, and finally a quadruple plinth bearing a statue of Christ the King. At a height of 126 feet it is altogether a most prominent landmark.

None of this prepares us for the interior, an impressive Romanesque design. The first of the six nave bays

---

1. *The Tablet*, 18 December 1909, p. 978.

comprises a narthex with organ gallery above. The arcade arches are supported by tapering Doric columns of Nailsworth stone. The vaulted roof is penetrated by tall clerestory windows. The chancel is also arcaded, with an ambulatory bearing Corinthian pilasters, and further enriched with a ceiling fresco of The Transfiguration, c. 1916 by Hugh Chevins. The altar is of Carrara marble, its reredos panels carved with swags against gold mosaic backgrounds. What really arrests the visitor, however, is the sheer wealth of marble decoration throughout the church—mostly panelling to the walls, and a clear illustration of the influence of Westminster Cathedral. The Renaissance detail of the altars and statues also exhibits varied marbles, especially Sicilian, that is, white flecked with blue.

In the north aisle, east to west, is first the Lady Chapel, with marble panelling around the altar. In a niche above it is the Madonna and Child, by La Statue Religieuse of Paris. One window has Our Lady with St Anne dating from 1957; the other has Our Lady of Lourdes of 1935 by Arthur Orr. Along the aisle is the altar of St Joseph, its statue in a columned niche with a pedimented Ionic arch; St Patrick's altar, the figure worked in mosaic beneath a Corinthian arch with a broken pediment; a series of confessionals; and the Lourdes shrine, a low narrow space panelled with marbles and mosaics that frame the statue. Next to the entrance is the former baptistery, with two fine windows portraying the Presentation and the Baptism of Christ.

In the broad south aisle is the Sacred Heart Altar, with its statue set in an apse with concealed top lighting. The effect is further enhanced by two Ionic columns of marble, said to have come here from Westminster Cathedral. The marble facing of the aisle is thorough, interrupted only by the Stations of the Cross, inset panels of opus-sectile work reminiscent of the works of Eric Gill and Joseph Cribb; and by four stained glass windows of English Martyrs, of 1935–37, by Arthur Orr.

Bibliography
Kelly, pp. 247-48; Baker, p. 58; *Br*, 3 April 1909, p. 419; 15 May 1909, p. 590; *BN*, 24 December 1909, p. 948; *The Tablet*, 1 May 1909, pp. 714-15; 21 March 1914, p. 456; 13 October 1917, p. 466; 26 April 1919, p. 526; *CD*, 1936, p. 164; 1938, p. 202; *CBR.S*, 1978, p. 64; 1979, pp. 20-23; 1980, p. 19

Sydenham, Our Lady and St Philip Neri, Sydenham Road, SE26

Following a temporary church of 1872, the first permanent church was opened in part in 1882. Designed in thirteenth-century terms by F.A. Walters, this was completed in 1912. However, the church was destroyed in an air raid in September 1940, and services were subsequently held in a wooden hut in the presbytery garden. The foundation stone of the present church was blessed by Bishop Cyril Cowderoy on 8 December 1957, and the church was opened the following year. Its tower was completed in a simplified version of its original design in 1961. Messrs Walters & Kerr Bate were the architects, and Messrs Adams

Brothers of Croydon were the contractors.

The exterior is of Sussex brick, with stone dressings to the rectangular windows. Its traditional plan consists of a Latin cross with nave, transepts and chancel. A lantern rises above the crossing, and angle chapels project from its base. The bell-tower terminates the north transept. This and the lantern have pyramidal roofs.

7. Sydenham, Our Lady and St Philip Neri

The sum of these parts is a well-proportioned interior, whose principal virtue is clarity of vision. A contributory factor here are the ingenious arches of reinforced concrete, which intersect about the crossing without obstructing the view of the chancel.

The high altar, its steps, pulpit, ambo and rails are of various marbles, and generous use is made of Westmorland dark green slate. The angle chapels are artistically similar to each other in design, with their reredos figures fashioned in opus-sectile within a mosaic setting. Various symbolic colours proliferate: for example, red characterizing the altars of the Sacred Heart and the English Martyrs. Verde antico and pavonazzo are also used extensively in the altars and shrines. The south transept window by Goddard & Gibbs depicts the death of St Philip Neri. In the north transept is a gallery housing the organ of 1977 by Mander. The Great Organ is mounted on the gallery rail, behind the player; the Positive Organ above the keyboards. The case is of oak.

Bibliography
Kelly, p. 387; Baker, p. 58; *CBR.S*, 1959, pp. 98-102; 1961 p. 93

Sydenham, The Resurrection of the Lord, 165-169 Kirkdale, SE26

The mission was founded from Our Lady and St Philip Neri, and the church was built in 1974. The architects were Broadbent, Hastings, Reid & Todd, the partner in charge being D.A. Reid. The structural engineers were Norman Crossley & Partners. The overall plan is an irregular hexagon, which is not apparent outside. From the main entrance on the corner of Kirkdale and Sydenham Park, the yellow brick structure broadens as it regresses, the exterior walls marked here and there by buttresses and narrow strips of glass bricks. Over the entrance there is a small parish room, and facing the road a bas-relief in fibre glass and cement of the Risen Christ, partially swathed in bands of cloth, with forearms raised, by Stephen Sykes.

Inside the hexagon, the chancel, nave and entrance are formed in line. To left and right of the nave are angular ranges which contribute to an overall fan-shaped congregational space. The sacristy is off left, and to the right is a small space with a security grille, designated as a day chapel or weekday porch. The roof is irregularly pitched over the nave and chancel, with transverse concrete ribs. To the sides other ribs form pointed arches, all the rectangles that result being panelled or glazed.

The chancel furniture is all of matching timber; its crucifix with its soft outlines is by Elizabeth Reid. The tabernacle niche has a surround of dark green Westmorland slate bordered with gold leaf. The fibre-glass statue of the Madonna and Child is signed CS 1983; and the epoxy resin Stations of the Cross are signed MC 1985.

Bibliography
CBR.S, 1974, pp. 166-67

XI
Southwark

Southwark, Cathedral of St George, Lambeth Road, SE1

IN the eighteenth century there were Mass-houses in Southwark in which worship took place in private, although this was technically illegal under the penal laws. The situation is exemplified by the case of the Rev. John Baptist Maloney who in 1767 was arrested for saying Mass in Kent Street. He was sentenced at Kingston Assizes to perpetual imprisonment, which was commuted after four years to banishment. By the 1780s a large number of Catholics, many of them Irish, were gathered in that part of Southwark called the Borough, where they were without a chapel or a resident priest. From 1787 they were served by the Revd Thomas Walsh, an alumnus of Douai College, with regular Mass in a hired room in Bandyleg Walk. Within two years, however, the chapel was too small for the numbers attending. Bishop James Talbot authorised a committee to collect for the purposes of a chapel and a house, and appointed the Revd John Griffiths to the care of the mission. A site was procured on the London Road in St George's Fields, and plans were drawn by James Taylor, a Catholic architect. The chapel and house, still unfinished, were both pressed into service in March 1790. The passing of the Toleration Act gave an added impetus to the subscriptions, and the completed chapel was formally opened in March 1793.

Taylor's design was Georgian with a broad nave and a flat ceiling, and a single altar, whose reredos was a copy of Murillo's Crucifixion. Gothic arches were introduced in 1808, the first use of Gothic in a London Catholic chapel. With its curious mixture of styles, this chapel served the Southwark mission until it was superseded by Pugin's great church of 1848.

St George's was the brainchild of Fr Thomas Doyle, a priest of the

1. *Southwark Cathedral, Pugin's second design*

London Road chapel from 1829. Conscious of the severe overcrowding inside the chapel, and a permanent overflow of people unable even to enter during Sunday Mass, Fr Doyle obtained the permission of Bishop Griffiths to proceed with his plan of building a major church. Fr Doyle extended his collections from the chapel to the rest of London. When he appealed to other parts of England, the plan was dismissed as 'Fr Doyle's folly'. Undeterred, he went begging in Europe, enlisting the interest and aid of foreign royalty. The English aristocracy also were contributors. Fr Doyle's humorous progress reports which appeared almost weekly in the pages of *The Tablet* for many years monitored the length and difficulty of the struggle. By 1838 there was sufficient money in hand to begin, and the planning committee obtained a design from A.W.N. Pugin which they rejected, however, as too expensive. A new committee then called for competition designs from four architects—Pugin, John Buckler, Edward Foxhall and J.J. Scoles. The terms specified a church, clergy house and two schools. 'Pointed Architecture' was required, and 'solidity of construction' was preferred to 'Ornamental Architecture'.[1] The successful design was chosen avowedly because it contained the greatest space. It turned out to be Pugin's. Fr Doyle obtained a site for £3,200 consisting of a triangle of land in St George's Road—the very spot on which Lord George Gordon had harangued his anti-Catholic crowd in 1780. Messrs Myers & Wilson were appointed builders, and work began on 8 September 1840. The foundation stone was laid at a private ceremony on 26 May 1841. Several times the money almost ran out and Fr Doyle undertook three more begging visits in Europe, cheerfully reporting his progress in letters to *The Tablet*. Bishop Griffiths prudently declined to open the church until every penny necessary was in hand. When he died in August 1847, however, Wiseman his successor determined on an early opening, which took place on 4 July 1848.

Pugin's rejected design had been for a cruciform church with a central tower on a grand scale. His realised design was no mean feat, being the largest church that Catholics had erected since the beginning of the revival, and comparatively the most magnificent. Its plan then (and now) consisted of a long nave flanked by aisles of almost equal height, chancel and side chapels, and a large west tower containing the entrance. Pugin's solution to the perennial Catholic problem of economy was to subdivide his plan into relatively narrow compartments which required no great height of wall or breadth of roof. Consequently, he dispensed altogether with a clerestory. The chancel, however, was rich, with a pavement of encaustic tiles, stalls for 40 clerics, carved stone sedilia, screen, altar frontal and reredos, a ceiling resting on angel corbels and stained glass by Wailes. The perspective view of Pugin's interior is undeniably impressive, with its long arcade, the variously traceried windows and the rood screen all contributing to a highly ambitious concept.

Pugin's view of the outside is better in the engraving than in the reality. Of his

---

1. St George's Cathederal, *Minute Book of the New Catholic Church and Schools in Southwark*.

proposed tower and spire 320 feet high, only the substructure of the tower was built to a height of 60 feet. But it was to the design of the spire that Pugin had evidently applied his ability, and the result suffers in the execution. Moreover, walls of yellow brick with Bath stone dressings make litle aesthetic contribution, so that the exterior impact relies on the differing heights of its parts and on the varied tracery of the windows.

On the night of 15–16 April 1941, the timber roof was fired by an incendiary bomb and the whole cathedral was gutted. Services were held in the Notre Dame Convent and in Amigo Hall pending restoration. Work commenced in August 1953 under the architect Romilly B. Craze and the builders Higgs & Hill, and the formal reopening took place on 4 July 1958. The cathedral was changed in several ways. For Pugin's slender nave piers with attached shafts, piers of more substantial profile were substituted. The nave walls were heightened and a clerestory was introduced beneath a panelled ceiling of flatter pitch. A transept was wisely constructed in the second bay from the chancel arch. An access passage at clerestory level bridges the transept somewhat in the manner of Spanish Place and Westminster Cathedral. The aisles were given skeleton vaulting with panelled infill. Beyond a triple arch a substantial day chapel was introduced at the east end of the the south aisle, and a baptistery next to the west entrance. Portland stone was used for the exterior, Painswick for the interior.

From the galleried entrance containing the organ by John Compton and the Coronation of the Virgin window by H. Clark, a clockwise tour takes one along the north aisle, with its row of confessionals built between the buttreses. Above their doors are the Stations of the Cross, stark, rectangular bas-relief casts set high. The roofs of both aisles are octopartite, with flying ribs and panels designed by Robert Hendra and Geoffrey Harper. From the aisle one may study the clerestory windows, with neo-Perpendicular tracery that Pugin would not have recognised. Along the north aisle are two table tombs, to Provost Thomas Doyle +1879 with a recumbent effigy supported by angels within a cusped arch backed by diaper work; and Archbishop Amigo +1949, plain with a recumbent figure. The window above by Goddard & Gibbs commemorates the visit of Pope John Paul II on 28 May 1982.

2. *Southwark Cathedral, interior*

Behind a wrought-iron screen by Hardman is the Blessed Sacrament Chapel, its Pugin altar carefully restored. The altar rests on four piers fronted by praying angels, behind them a panel displaying the Lamb of God surrounded by angels. The reredos is panelled also, above its tabernacle a crucifix within a niche. The panel to the left contains Melchizedek as priest and king; that to the right the miracle at Cana. Adjacent to this is the Knill chantry of 1856–57 by E.W. Pugin, four bays long, with mini-buttresses bearing crocketed gables, and between them openwork traceried arches surmounted by eight figures of angels. Inside, delicate arcade shafts bear capitals with birds and foliage shapes that support the octopartite vaulted roof. The exquisite altar frontal is subdivided into three panels containing vesica shapes bearing sacred monograms within busily entwined foliage. The reredos has within a niche the Virgin and Child with saints, flanked by angels. The floor is paved with encaustic tiles.

The sanctuary now stands forward of the chancel arch, within the first nave bay. It underwent rearrangement by Austin Winkley in time for the Papal visit in 1984. This involved the repositioning of the cathedra, with a new high altar and ambo, all in marble and stone, together with a wrought-iron screen and painted fabric by Alan Evans and Sue Ridge. Above the chancel arch is the Crucifixion with Our Lady and St John, sculpted by Alfred Banks. Beyond it is the east window, nine lights depicting the Crucifixion and saints, by H. Clark. The richly gilded ceiling panels were designed and painted by Robert Hendra and Geoffrey Harper. The doorway to the sacristy is a Pugin survival, with angels in the spandrels.

To the right is the chapel of St Peter and English Martyrs, with a central statue in the reredos supported by Blessed Margaret Pole, Venerable John Griffiths, St Augustine Webster and St Philip Howard. Adjacent to the wrought-iron screen is a statue of St Michael signed HY.

To the south of the south aisle stands the Lady Chapel of substantial size, three bays long with large neo-Perpendicular windows. Its altar protected by a gate of wrought iron has a canopied niche bearing a figure of the Virgin and Child, Flemish work of the eighteenth century. Between the Lady Chapel and the south aisle is the Petre chantry, 1849 by Pugin for the Hon. Edward Petre +1848, freestanding and containing a table tomb with a top of black marble. The altar frontal has a seated Madonna with angels; the reredos a Crucifixion with angels and saints. The floor is paved with encaustic tiles. Along the aisle the Talbot Chapel was begun in 1854 and completed as the Relics Chapel in 1905, and now houses the statue of St Patrick.

Adjacent to this is St Joseph's Chapel. Plans for a memorial chapel to Samuel Weld +1851 not being carried out, the Chapel of St Joseph was erected here in 1890. Pre-war windows to St George and St Alban flank the altar with its statue of St Joseph. The chapel has a tierceron vault, with angels carved in the bosses. Also here is the frontal of the Pugin high altar of 1848. Having been encased in the post-war high altar, it was rediscovered during the reordering of the sanctuary in

1989 by the architect Austin Winkley. Of Caen stone now set in Bath stone, the frontal consists of three quatrefoil bas-relief panels depicting the Transfiguration, the Resurrection and the Ascension. Flanking the west door is the baptistery added in the post-war restoration by Romilly B. Craze, of octagonal plan with an octagonal font, and a figure of the Risen Christ in stained glass.

Bibliography
Kelly, pp. 365-66; Rottmann, pp. 259-70; Eastlake, pp. 154-56; Harting, pp. 151-62; Ward, pp. 110-15; Little, pp. 45, 81, 94-96, 202-203; Bogan; *SOL* 35, pp. 72-75; AAS; *St George's Cathedral Minute Book; Gentleman's Magazine*, 1840, II, p. 68; 1844, I, pp. 180-82; 1848, II, pp. 192-93; *The Tablet*, 29 May 1841, p. 351; 8 July 1848, p. 425; 16 February 1856, p. 101; *Br*, 9 September 1848, pp. 439-40; 11 January 1946, pp. 33-35; *AR* 91 (1942), pp. 27-28; *CBR.S*, 1956, p. 19; 1957, p. 30; 1958, pp. 37-39; *CB* 36 (November/December 1995), p. 38

Bermondsey, Dockhead, The Most Holy Trinity, SE1

As long ago as 1773, Fr Gerard Shaw, chaplain to the Spanish Embassy, gave £500 to Bishop Talbot specifically to found a church at Bermondsey. The first chapel in Salisbury Lane was destroyed by the Gordon rioters in 1780, but was rebuilt. By the 1830s, the old chapel was so crowded that steps had to be taken to provide a new church. The Baroness de Montesquieu, the English-born wife of a French émigré gave £5,000. The new church owed its existence to Fr Peter Butler, who had volunteered to work in this mission of 9,000 souls. Fr Butler acquired a new site in Parker's Row, where the church designed by J.J. Scoles was erected in 1834–35. In Early English Gothic, an idea of how it looked may be gained from an inspection of another Scoles church, Our Lady's at St John's Wood. Sadly, the church was hit by a V-bomb on 2 March 1945, and totally destroyed. The present church was built in 1957–60 during the rectorship of Canon Owen McManus. The architect was H.S. Goodhart-Rendel, and following his death in 1959 the church was completed by Messrs Broadbent & Curtis. The foundation stone was laid on 16 June 1957 by Bishop Cowderoy. Consecration took place on 24 May 1960.

3. *Bermondsey, Holy Trinity, 11th Station by A.C. Brown*

The large, dignified church dominates the angle of Dockhead and Jamaica Road. Stylistic features may be identified from several sources—Renaissance symmetry, Gothic planning and a suggestion of the Diocletian windows of

Westminster Cathedral. Like the cathedral, it is mainly of brick, with extensive pattern-work involving grey-brown Buckinghamshire bricks combined with reds and Staffordshire blues. Even from outside, the plan is easily read—a west entrance recessed between two matching towers, hexagonal in plan, rising to 12-sided louvered storeys with conical roofs; the massive nave with its tall many-mullioned windows, followed by the taller transept and the chancel. Along the south side are the sacristies, and projecting confessionals with a balustraded roof.

Inside, all is light, bright and welcoming. The nave of five bays is followed by the transept of two bays (partially hidden from the nave by solid wall), the sanctuary and side chapels. All is vaulted in concrete. Over the first bay is the gallery with organ by J.W. Walker & Sons. Beneath the gallery is the shrine of the Sacred Heart, with wrought-iron gates and statue of the Sacred Heart by Mayer. Also here is the baptismal font, of plain, circular, stone construction, its base composed of Doric pilasters. The nave piers are cruciform in plan, placed so as to form narrow passage aisles, all the seating thereby being central. On the north side is the semicircular pulpit, in two shades of stone. Most remarkable are the Stations of the Cross, of 1971 by Atri Cecil Brown, rectangular framed sculptures composed in detail, and enamelled in blue, red and gold. The scale is small but the technique is monumental. The sanctuary walls are panelled in stone, in two tiers. The altar, now moved forward, and the ambo are of stone in two shades. Against the east wall the tabernacle plinth is supported by three piers faced with tiles bearing sacred symbolism. Above the tabernacle the reredos is panelled with sculpted reliefs representing the Nativity, Christ with St Peter, and Pentecost.

The south-east Lady Chapel contains a statue of the Madonna and Child in Carrara marble and an elderly brass stand for votive candles, an unusual survival. The corresponding north-east chapel of the English Martyrs has two medallions flanking the crucifix, depicting Tyburn and the Bull 'Regnans in Excelsis' issued by Pope Pius V in 1570. The altar rails, of stone with wrought-iron gates, are wholly intact.

Bibliography
Kelly, pp. 74-75; Rottmann, pp. 270-74; L.E. Whatmore, *The Story of Dockland Parish* (1960); *The Architect*, 27 October 1899, p. 267; *The Tablet*, 28 May 1910, p. 862; *Catholic Herald*, 18 March 1983, p. 10; *CBR.S*, 1958, pp. 92-93; 1960, pp. 76-77; *CB*, Autumn 1989, p. 10

Bermondsey, Our Lady of La Salette and St Joseph, Melior Street, SE1

The mission began in 1848 in a rented room in Webb Street. This was superseded by the present church in Melior Street, opened on 2 May 1861. The architect was Edmund J. Kelly of 23 Thavies Inn, and the builder was John Cowland of Portland Road, Notting Hill.

The façade to Melior Street is styled in the Early English phase of Gothic. It consists of a gabled front to the nave, with a transeptal feature to its right. The materials are stock brick, with dressings of brick alternating with stone imparting a polychrome effect. The lowest courses are wholly of stone giving way to brick, which suggests a change of intention, perhaps for financial reasons. The entrance was modified in 1936. The architects F.A. Walters & Son introduced in the tympanum the weeping figure of Our Lady of La Salette as she first appeared, flanked by shields bearing sacred symbols. The quatrefoil windows are original, as are the lancets and circular windows above the entrance.

The interior consists of an unaisled nave and a broad apsidal sanctuary. To the (ritual) north is a blank arcade of five bays, indicating a designated but unbuilt aisle. High in the south wall there are seven lancet windows. Above the entrance is the gallery, with stained glass celebrating the seven sacraments in the wheel window. Each principal of the nave's timber roof consists of a collar beam supported by struts. Around the apse are nine lancet windows, the central trio with stained glass depicting Calvary. The wall beneath is marble-faced and arcaded with slender piers and cusped arches. The marble altar was inaugurated in 1927, F.A. Walters & Son being the architects. Its frontal is arcaded, and bears a central relief of the Lamb of God.

Behind is the reredos, with a central niche flanked by four arched panels containing sculpted symbols of the Evangelists. To the left of the sanctuary stands the pulpit, also of marble and polygonal in plan, with diapered surfaces.

There are two chapels. Near the entrance is the chapel of the Sacred Heart, with the feeding of the multitude sculpted in its altar frontal. Along the north side is the chapel of Our Lady of La Salette with altar and rails of matching stone. Its reredos has a central figure of Our Lady, flanked by panels with relief sculptures of her first appearance, and her discourse with the children. The chapel's walls are panelled in variously coloured marbles, clearly influenced by Westminster Cathedral.

Around the church are numerous statues, among them casts by Mayer of the Holy family and a pietà. The Stations of the Cross are unframed relief carvings in the 1950s manner. Beneath the gallery is a large memorial brass to Fr Simon McDaniel +1899, who erected this church. Adjacent to this is an ornate votive candle-holder with a marble table, and its supports, candle brackets and so on, all wrought of brass.

Bibliography
Kelly, p. 276; Bogan, pp. 117, 245; AAS; Information of Stephen Welsh

Bermondsey South, St Gertrude, Debnams Road, SE16

The site for the church was acquired by Bishop John Butt in 1892, but building was not begun until 1902. Fr Martin Gifkins commenced the mission on 13 September 1903, and the church was formally opened on 11 November following. F.W. Tasker was the architect, and Mr Romaine was the builder. Miss Frances Ellis was the donor.

The symmetrical west front is of plain

stock brick. It has a central circular window, mullioned and transomed, beneath the gable, and flanking porches with stone tympana over the doors. To the left is the presbytery, also of brick.

The plan is a Greek cross emphasised by a high cornice and a groin vault of timber. Within the re-entrant angles are four spaces with much lower ceilings, which house two shrines and two porches. To the west is a gallery, with organ by R.F. Stevens maintained by Rushworth & Dreaper. Facing the gallery is the broad sanctuary, with a marble altar and tabernacle stand, and a carved crucifix. Flanking the sanctuary are the shrines of Our Lady and the Sacred Heart. In front there are statues of St Joseph and St Gertrude, standing on corbelled plinths above inset ceramic tiles which bear sacred symbols. Also in the church are figures of St Patrick, St Thomas More and St Antony. Around the walls are the Stations of the Cross carved in low relief, coloured, and well proportioned.

Bibliography
Southwark and Bermondsey Recorder, 21 November 1903, p. 7; Kelly, p. 75

Southwark Borough, Precious Blood, O'Meara Street, SE1

Bishop John Butt pursued his policy of subdividing the area served from St George's Cathedral by supporting school chapels in the surrounding districts of Borough, Vauxhall, Walworth and Waterloo. Of these, Borough was the first to receive a permanent church. The foundation stone was blessed by the bishop on 27 September 1892. The architect was F.A. Walters, the builders James Smith and Sons of Norwood, and the first rector Canon William Murnane. The cost of the site was £4,000, and the contract price for the church and presbytery was £7,000. Since 1981 the parish has been in the charge of the Society of the Divine Saviour, known as Salvatorians.

Little of the exterior can be seen, apart from the facade in O'Meara Street. Here the west front, wholly of stock brick, is perfectly symmetrical with Romanesque details. Two tall, slender bell-cotes border a large round central

4. *Borough, Precious Blood*

window. The two bells were installed in 1956 by the Whitechapel Foundry. Smaller windows articulate the remaining wall above the central entrance with its stepped arches. To one side is the Lourdes shrine appointed in 1957. The reposeful Lady statue executed in Sicilian marble stands within a niche lined with Norfolk flint. Its Baroque surround worked in Dartmouth stone is exuberant with intermittent rustication, scrolls and a pierced pediment.

At the church's planning stage, Walters predicted that 'It will be of an extremely simple and severe style of Romanesque or Norman, somewhat like the earliest portions of the Abbey of St Albans' (*The Tablet* 3 October, 1891, p. 556). Although this is true, the interior is nevertheless a joy to enter, warm, welcoming and uncluttered by busy detail. Alongside the entrance are ancillary rooms beneath a large gallery two bays deep. The nave is seven bays long with aisle windows in pairs, and large circular clerestory windows. In each principal of the timber roof, hammerbeams support a King-post truss.

In the north aisle is a carved figure of St Joseph. In the corresponding bay of the south aisle is the Lady chapel, with a plain alter, and a carved Madonna and Child. Around the walls are the striking terracotta Stations of the Cross, 1893 by Mathias Zens, in deep relief with some figures freestanding. Beyond the nave non-projecting transepts are followed by the apsidal sanctuary. In the south transept is a carved figure of St Antony signed DPV.

Within the sanctuary there is a forward altar table. The original plain stone altar with its tabernacle has been retained. It is distinguished by its timber baldacchino. Raised on four supports, the upper part is balustraded in two stages, one square, one octagonal and surmounted by a pyramidal roof, wholly reminiscent of those baldacchinos in Rome's churches of S Lorenzo and S Giorgio.

Bibliography
Kelly, pp. 90-1; T. Mariapa, *Centenary of the Church of the Precious Blood* (Borough: L. Talbot, 1992) *BN* 2 October 1891, p. 486; 9 October 1891, p. 524; 24 June 1892, p. 882;*The Tablet*, 4 June 1892, p. 912; 11 June 1892, p. 953.

Camberwell, Sacred Heart, Camberwell New Road/Knatchbull Road, SE5

'The mission was opened on Easter Monday 1860, when Mass was said at De Crespigny Lodge, Denmark Hill, by Fr Claude Bernin of Lyons.'[2] There was a subsequent chapel at Chepstow Cottage; another in Thomas Street later called Becket Street; and a temporary church opened in 1863 and enlarged in 1864. This was superseded by the first church on the present site, opened by Bishop James Dannell on 12 August 1872. In twelfth-century Gothic style, it was designed by C.A. Buckler and built by Mr Fanthorpe of Notting Hill. This church was enlarged in 1891 by the architect F.A. Walters and the builder Thomas Gregory of Clapham Junction. Sadly, it was destroyed by enemy action on 8–9 October 1941.

The foundation stone of the present church was blessed by Bishop Cowderoy

2. Kelly, p. 114.

5. Camberwell, Sacred Heart

on 19 April 1952, and the opening took place in 1953. The previous church had lain parallel to the railway, but the new church now turned its back upon the viaduct. In order to exclude railway noise still further, its architect D. Plaskett Marshall artfully reduced the width and height of the nave in stages towards the sanctuary.

The exterior viewed from Knatchbull Road is of red brick with spare dressings of Portland stone at roof level. The (ritual) west front is completely blank towards the railway viaduct. There is a tall rectangular north-west campanile, and entrances at either side.

Inside, the structure is easily read, with five stages that are progressively reduced in width. These bays have tall, rectangular clerestory windows, and an arched roof of concrete correspondingly reduced in height. The upper walls are faced with red brick. At ground level, a series of arcades formed by rectangular marble-faced piers further extend the space into chapels and other ancillary areas.

From the entrance, the first stage supports a large gallery containing the organ rebuilt in 1962 by Rushworth & Dreaper and completely refurbished in 1993. Flanking this stage is the baptistery, with a marble-faced octagonal font and three stained glass windows. The second stage is level with the entrances. The third stage houses on the left the shrines of the Sacred Heart and St Antony; and on the right confessionals and the shrine of St Teresa of Lisieux. The fourth stage houses substantial chapels dedicated to Our Lady and St Joseph. Finally comes the sanctuary, its floor raised, and flanked by arcades leading to sacristies.

The altar, tabernacle plinth and communion rails are all of Irish marbles. The reredos is of maple framed with mahogany. The most arresting feature is the crucifix, prominently framed between the tester and the altar. Also noteworthy is the lectern, carved with an eagle and figures of the evangelists at its four faces; and the Stations of the Cross by Burns Oates, of opus-sectile set against a gold background.

This church is remarkable not only for its ingenious plan, but for the consistent good taste exhibited in its furnishings. Here, the extensive use of marble facings on the piers and elsewhere, the uniform timber of the shrines and altars, and their carved figures together conspire to make the whole artistically greater than the sum of its parts.

Bibliography
Kelly, p. 114; BN, 16 August 1872, p. 130; 19 May 1876, p. 492; 14 November 1890, p. xvi; 23 October 1891, p. 600; Br, 24 August 1872, p. 674; The Tablet, 9 July 1881, pp. 73-74; CBR.S, 1959, pp. 88-91

Dulwich East, St Thomas More, 380 Lordship Lane, SE22

The Franciscans from Peckham evangelised the district, beginning with Mass at number 40, The Gardens in 1879. Soon afterwards Five Elms in Lordship Lane was acquired as a monastery. They converted the stables and coach house into a chapel, where Mass was first said on 1 June 1879. This chapel was succeeded by a new school chapel on the site in 1883. In accordance with their itinerant apostolate, the Franciscans eventually relinquished the mission, which was administered by the Benedictines of Downside from 1892. The present site was acquired in 1907, and a presbytery built to the design of J.N. Comper.

The church designed by Joseph Goldie and built by Messrs Goddard of Dorking was begun in December 1927 and formally opened on 20 May 1929. The side chapels were built in 1934 and the baptistery in 1935. On 13 July 1944 the presbytery was destroyed and the church was rendered unsafe by a flying bomb, and services had to be held in the old school chapel. The necessary restoration began in 1948. The presbytery was rebuilt to the design of Russell Vernon, and the church was reopened for use on 15 February 1953. The Benedictines had relinquished the mission in 1923, and the first diocesan parish priest was Fr James O'Donoghue (1923–61), to whom fell the work of building the church and its subsequent restoration. Designed in the manner of fourteenth-century Gothic, the exterior of Bargate stone with Bath stone

6. *Dulwich East, St Thomas More*

dressings catches and holds the eye. The front to Lordship Lane is symmetrical, with a traceried central window of six lights, above it a crucifix and a bell-cote, and below it a broad projecting porch, triply compartmented, with stepped flat roofs. Along the sides are series of nave windows, with double-gabled transepts in the distance.

Inside, the plan consists of a broad nave five bays long, its windows of three lights with geometrical tracery, its hammer-beam roof of Oregon pine; transeptal chapels and a chancel three bays deep. Its panelled ceiling is decorated with sacred symbols dating from a restoration of 1963; its walls panelled in oak in two tiers, linenfold below and Gothic motifs above. There is a forward altar of plain stone, and adjacent to it the font, octagonal with incised panels.

The rear altar acquired in 1928 came from Hales Place near Canterbury, where it was intended for a religious community. Its reredos bears an extravagantly sculpted iconographical scheme probably devised by its patron Miss Barbara Hales. Three large niches gabled and pinnacled hold the monstrance throne and statues of Ss Martha and Mary Magdalen. In between these, four relief panels are dedicated to St Teresa, St Catherine of Ricci, St Mary Magdalen of Pazzi and St Juliana Falconieri.

To the left is the Sacred Heart Altar. The frontal bears an incised cross decorated with foliage details. Its triple-panelled oaken reredos by A.J. Robinson encloses canvases of the Sacred Heart, St Margaret Mary and Blessed Claude de la Colombiere, signed GFH 1963. Corresponding to this is the Lady Chapel, renewed in 1970 to designs of John Kirby and at the cost of the Knights of St Columba. Wrought-iron rails enclose a pavement of Purbeck freestone and the altar of Ancaster stone. The oak reredos and candlesticks were carved by A.J. Robinson; and the Madonna and Child statue in 1933 by Freda Skinner. Also in the chapel is the window to St Columba by Patrick Pye. Near the church entrance is the former baptistery, renewed in 1963 and now a repository, with wrought-iron gates. In the nave are carved figures of St John Fisher and St Thomas More by Anton Dapre; the polygonal pulpit with carved traceried panels, serving as a lectern; and the strikingly superior Stations of the Cross, unframed relief carvings lightly decorated with gold, carved in 1929 by Anton Dapre.

Bibliography
Kelly, p. 159; Michael Smith, *The Dulwich Catholics 1879–1973* (Dulwich: Rev. J. Kenny, 1973); *CBR.S*, 1973 p. 183

Dulwich Wood Park, St Margaret Clitherow, Kingswood Drive, SE19

The mission was founded in 1952 by Fr Alfred Cole, with a Mass centre in a house in Kingswood Drive, and from 1962 in the church hall. The present church was built in 1974, the architect being A.J.H. Stalley of Broadbent, Hastings, Reid & Todd.

The church stands on a gently sloping

site, adjacent to the presbytery, which was built in 1966. Externally the walls are of dark russet hand-made bricks; the roof of dark grey interlocking concrete tiles. Viewed from Kingswood Drive, the north side presents a range of tall, narrow, rectangular windows along the nave and transept, and above the crossing a prominent pyramidal feature with a cross at its apex. Inside, the plan is in the form of a 'T'. Beyond a shallow west entrance with a gallery over, the nave is followed by the chancel at the point where the transepts divide to left and right. Above the altar, the roof is pyramidal, and glazed. The walls are plastered, and painted in light colours, and the ceilings to the nave and pyramid are finished in fissured acoustic tiles. This bright effect within a comparatively small space generates a close, intimate atmosphere which pervades the interior.

The furnishings are few, and blend well with the structure. The altar is of white marble, given by Mrs Murray in memory of her mother. There is a sculpted figure of Our Lady of Banneau given by the Catholics in the local Cheshire Home; and a carved St Margaret Clitherow given by the priest on his retirement. The Stations of the Cross, the gift of St Matthew's, West Norwood, are Belgian work of about 1850–70, painted in oils on canvas backed with zinc and restored by Mrs L. Murray.

7. Dulwich Wood Park, St Margaret Clitherow

Bibliography
CBR.S, 1974, p. 253

Herne Hill, Ss Philip and James, Poplar Walk, SE24

In October 1904, *The Tablet* noted that a mission was wanted at Herne Hill. The foundation stone is dated 1905, and the church was opened late in 1906. Both church and adjoining presbytery were the gift of Miss Frances Ellis. The names of the architect and builder are not recorded. Outside, this familiar type of standard rectangular aisleless nave-cum-chancel stands commandingly astride Poplar Walk and Lowden Road. It is all of stock brick with dressings of Portland stone laid in alternate large and small blocks. The west front bears a large circular central window above a sturdy entrance with a tympanum and flanking windows. Between this and the presbytery is the church hall, lower and slightly stepped back, with a similar entrance.

Long-standing plans to build a new church were finally dropped in 1979 in favour of reordering. Immediately inside, one finds that the church has been reoriented—the altar now standing in the centre of the south side. It faces an

XI. SOUTHWARK

8. Herne Hill, Ss Philip and James

arcade originally intended to form a north aisle where in fact a hall abutted the church. The arches were removed, and the hall was brought into the ambit of the church, providing extra accommodation on Sundays by means of folding screens. At the same time a glazed entrance lobby and confessional were formed. The architects of these works were Messrs Tomei & Mackley of Croydon; the builders Messrs F. & F.H. Higgs.

The walls are now painted, and the customary Ellis church king-post roof is intact. The sanctuary has a permanent altar and tabernacle plinth of stone, with panelled reredos and ambo of hardwood. The tabernacle, carved figures of the Risen Christ, Our Lady, St Joseph and the Stations of the Cross, south German work in limewood, were supplied by Ormsby of Scarisbrick. The rose window, a glass block design with a range of blues dates from 1979. Following the dedication of the altar by Archbishop Bowen on 20 May 1981, the high-level windows to Lowden Road were supplied with multicoloured blocks depicting the seven sacraments, these and the earlier window all being designed by Dom Charles Norris of Buckfast. The organ, by Hill, Norman & Beard of Crouch Hill, was acquired in 1982, and installed on its high-level platform adjacent to the entrance, its oak console being at ground level.

Bibliography
Kelly, p. 211; *The Tablet*, 8 October 1904, p. 594; SOL 26, p. 153; Southwark Diocesan Visitation Reports; *CBR.S*, 1978, p. 67; 1979, pp. 31-32; 1980, pp. 48-50; *CB*, Easter 1984, pp. 76-77; Information of Rev. Peter Clements

Kennington Park, St Wilfrid, Lorrimore Road, SE17

Miss Frances Ellis purchased the land for the diocese, and had a stable converted into a chapel. This was opened on 2 October 1904, and was served from the cathedral. The sanctuary of that chapel is now the sacristy of the present church, which was begun in July 1914. The aisle was first used on 11 June 1915, and the church was opened on 7 November following. F.A. Walters was the architect, and Goddard & Sons of Farnham and Dorking were the contractors. The building cost £5,000, which was defrayed by Mr Henry Smail of Wimbledon. The church was badly damaged through enemy action on 16 November 1940, and restored in 1948–49.

The exterior is a modest essay in Gothic of the late Perpendicular period, realised in appropriate materials of red brick with stone dressings. The (ritual) west front has a six-light traceried window above a shallow projecting porch which is flanked by single-light windows. To the left there is a sturdy tower in four storeys. This has its own west porch, above it a statue of St Joseph and two storeys of windows. The third stage is gabled to the sides, with its centre carried up to an embattled parapet and a Hertfordshire spike.

The interior plan consists of nave and chancel in a continuous flow of five bays, plus the north aisle and Lady Chapel. The arcade piers are octagonal, with moulded capitals supporting wide arches. There are clerestory windows to the left, and Perpendicular traceried windows to the right, beneath a shallow panelled timber ceiling.

9. Kennington Park, St Wilfred, detail of sculpture

This otherwise correct but modest interior is distinguished by the generous detail applied to its two altars. Both are correctly in period, with characteristic Perpendicular panelling applied extensively to vertical surfaces. The panels in turn are infilled with decoration, particularly cusped arches, quatrefoils and foliage. No names of artists have come to light, but the architect F.A. Walters was perfectly capable of designing this decorative detail, and Messrs Jones & Willis are likely candidates for its execution.

There is a forward altar of timber, but its predecessor (which cost £400 in

1915) has wisely been retained. Its panelled frontal is inset with sacred symbols. Flanking the tabernacle there are cusped circles inset with shields which display the Instruments of the Passion. The reredos consists of five tall blank arches; within corbelled niches there are figures of St Wilfrid, St Augustine of Canterbury, the Lamb of God, St George and St Thomas of Canterbury. The communion rail of stone with a marble balustrade contains within its panels shields bearing sacred symbols. To its right is the polygonal pulpit, its faces sculpted with cusped arches and floriated quatrefoils. A traceried arcade leads to the north aisle and Lady Chapel. Here the marble altar stands upon corner supports of square plan, decorated with traceried panels each bearing a white rose resting upon foliage. The reredos is inset with three niches: in the centre a relief representation of Our Lady supported by angels; to the left figures of St Anne with her daughter Mary; and to the right St Joachim. Between the niches there are sculpted tiers of angels. The marble altar rails are panelled, with floral motifs set within quatrefoils. The gates are of brass.

In the aisle there are three marble plaques: to Henry Smail +1915, to whose memory the Lady Altar was given; in memory of those who died in the Great War of 1914–18; and to the parish church, following its consecration on 14 June 1960 by Bishop Cowderoy. In the nave there is a carved statue of Our Lady and other cast statues. The Stations of the Cross, casts in high relief, were installed in 1921 at the expense of the parishioners. Beneath the tower is the tiny baptistery. The font stands behind wrought-iron gates, and has sacred symbols sculpted within quatrefoils on its eight faces.

Bibliography
Kelly, p. 290; BN, 3 July 1914, p. 10; Br, 8 January 1915, p. 43; The Tablet, 11 November 1905, p. 797; 19 June 1915, p. 811

Nunhead, St Thomas the Apostle, Evelina Road, SE15

The mission was founded from Peckham Rye, and the church was opened on 5 November 1905, Fr Peter Ryan being the first rector. The house, site and church were given by Miss Frances Ellis. No architect is recorded, but the original church is in the general manner of F.W. Tasker's churches, in this case a plain brick rectangle four bays long, with a projecting entrance in Hollydale Road. Inside, the whole of this now forms the sanctuary, which is in consequence exceptionally broad and deep. It retains its wheel window above the porch, and its timber roof with a king-post truss. The altar is of Sicilian marble, other furnishings being of timber or brick. With dramatic effect, the wall facing the altar was taken out, and a rectangular, low-ceilinged nave was added in 1972 by the architects Wilman Partnership. With no pretentions to aesthetic merit, the new nave is nevertheless superbly functional—a spacious rectangle with generous seating accommodation in full view of the altar.

Among other sacred furnishings there is a Risen Christ done in fibre glass, and a superb set of Stations of the Cross, frameless, and carved in 1924. Supplied by Burns, Oates & Washbourne, they are unsigned, but are clearly the work of Anton Dapre at his best.

To the east of the church is the old parish hall, still in use, and to the west another larger hall, contemporaneous with the nave. It is a pity that the church exterior does not make a better visual impact. Viewed from Evelina Road, it is impossible to distinguish its ecclesiastical character from the secular additions, owing to the overall rendered finish.

Bibliography
Kelly, p. 299; AAS

Peckham, Our Lady of Sorrows, Friary Road, SE15

The church is in the charge of the Capuchin Franciscans. An Italian priest, Fr Aloysius, on his way to Toronto in 1851, broke his journey in London and chanced to meet Cardinal Wiseman. Wiseman's characteristic invitation to make a missionary foundation in London was accepted. Owing, however, to various administrative delays, the foundation was not made until 1854, and then south of the river, in the diocese of Dr Thomas Grant, Bishop of Southwark.

The familiar pattern of parochial development with its own architectural overtones through house, temporary church and permanent church took place in Peckham. The first chapel, adapted from a coach-house and stable, was

10. *Peckham, Our Lady of Sorrows*

picturesquely known as 'The Hole in the Wall'. Then a wooden chapel preceded the permanent church and monastery. The foundation stone was laid on 6 July 1859, but, owing to building delays caused by shortage of funds, the church was not opened until 4 October 1866. E.W. Pugin was the architect, and the builders were initially Mr Kelly of Kingsland, and latterly Mr Smith of Ramsgate.

The exterior is an imposing edifice commanding the corner of Friars Road and Bird in Bush Road. Built of stock brick with intermittent bands of dark blue brick and stone dressings, it reads as nave and chancel, with a lean-to aisle. A squat south-west tower doubles as a porch, with a mosaic of Ss Peter and Paul above its door. The tall east gable next to the friary is relieved by its large round window, by a statue of St Francis and by the War Memorial with its carved crucifix.

Inside, the broad nave and chancel are built in eight continuous bays, and flanked by aisles and side chapels. The arcade piers are circular in plan, with moulded capitals; the roof is a timber barrel vault. The westernmost bay is glazed to the nave, and houses the organ gallery, raised on a single elliptical Caen stone arch of 30-foot span. Along the walls there are confessionals built between the buttresses (as at St George's Cathedral) and pairs of lancet windows in each bay.

The chancel walls are extensively faced in marble. The forward altar of stone dates from 1966. The old altar remains, its frontal of marble panelled with five cinqfoils. Above it are five narrow lancets surmounted by a large circular window. There are two matching ambos, and altar rails happily preserved, with wrought-iron gates, marble colonnettes supporting Gothic arches, and a marble balustrade.

The south-east Lady Chapel now has its altar forward. Its reredos consists of a series of pointed arches, the central arch housing a statue of the Madonna, and above it a circular window. The corresponding chapel of St Francis has a marble altar and a stone reredos with crenellated turrets. The intervening spaces are panelled with marble and mosaic infill, and within a central niche is a figure of St Francis by Mayer. To the north-west of the church there is the Sacred Heart Altar, of Sicilian marble, with a carved statue. The Chapel of Our Lady of Sorrows houses a sculpted *pietà*, after Michelangelo. The baptistery has an octagonal font, remarkably hewn from a block of Aberdeen granite. It also has a marble altar, and walls extensively faced with marble, in the manner of Westminster Cathedral.

Around the church there are various statues, including carved figures of St Patrick and St Antony; and a carved St Joseph signed DVP.

Bibliography
Kelly, pp. 311-12; Rottmann, pp. 274-78; Centenary booklet 1966; *BN*, 12 October 1966, p. 687; *The Tablet*, 2 July 1859, p. 421; 9 July 1859, p. 438; 22 August 1863, p. 534; 14 January 1865, p. 22; 29 September 1866, p. 611; 13 October 1866, p. 645

Peckham Rye, St James the Great, Elm Grove, SE15

In 1904, Miss Frances Ellis gave two houses and money to build a church. No firm attribution can be made to the design of the church, but it resembles the style of F.W. Tasker. Owing to a proposed major road, rebuilding on another site was considered in the 1960s. Since the prospect of the new road appeared to be some 20 years away, Mgr Edward Mahony added some semi-permanent extensions, which included a new sanctuary, adjacent chapel, sacristy and parish hall. These additions designed by Tomei, Maxwell & Pound of Wallington, Surrey, were completed in 1971.

11. Peckham Rye, St James

The exterior viewed from Elm Grove appears as a typical modest Ellis church built of London stock brick. It consists of a rectangular nave with front gable and large circular window, and a series of rectangular mullioned clerestory windows along the (ritual) north side. Matching additions include a lower north aisle and a gabled porch with a pointed window.

Inside, the nave nucleus derives its character from its structural details, especially its windows and its king-post roof. Above the chancel arch there is a Risen Christ in fibre glass, and to one side a carved figure of Our Lady of Lourdes. To the left of the nave there is an added aisle containing the former high altar, rich with sculpted detail. In its frontal are two roundels with relief renderings of the Agony in the Garden and St Margaret Mary's Vision of Jesus. In the reredos are sculpted figures in pinnacled niches—the Sacred Heart, St Gertrude of Helfta, and St Catherine of Siena. Between these there are groups of angels in extensively detailed gabled niches. Beside the altar there is a statue of St James the Great.

The spacious chancel of 1971 is as broad as the nave. Its altar and other furnishings are all of timber. There is a cast copy of Leonardo's Last Supper set in the frontal of the tabernacle stand, and above the tabernacle is a canvas painting of the Crucifixion. The extension to the right of the chancel is wholly given over to extra congregational space. Here one wall contains a modest fresco depicting Calvary and Jerusalem.

Bibliography
Southwark Diocesan Visitation Reports; *The Tablet*, 8 October 1904, p. 594; *CBR.S*, 1971, pp. 86-87

XI. SOUTHWARK

Rotherhithe, St Peter and the Guardian Angels, Paradise Street, SE16

From 1855, Fr James Lawes came from Bermondsey to say Sunday Mass at Stroud Cottage, Trinity Road. The mission was separated from Bermondsey in 1858. In that year a large house in Rotherhithe Street was purchased, and three rooms were adapted for use as a chapel. An adjacent site for a church was also acquired. The foundation stone was laid on 25 March 1861 and the Church of the Immaculate Conception was opened by Bishop Thomas Grant on 2 July following. The church was built of brick in the Early English style and cost £1,000. Edmund J. Kelly was its architect.

12. *Rotherhithe, St Peter and the Guardian Angels*

When this ceased to be central, a new school chapel was opened in Paradise Street in October 1892. The present church in the Romanesque style was built in 1902–1903 during the rectorate of Fr Joseph Haynes. Ludovica, Lady Renouf erected the church in memory of her husband, Sir Peter le Page Renouf, at a cost of £6,000. The architect was F.W. Tasker.

The exterior is best inspected from the north, where it presents its long side to Paradise Street. Of stock brick, it has six tall round-headed windows, followed by the entrance which is inset, arched and gabled.

The interior is a wide, rectangular room containing internal buttresses to north and south, with arches and windows between them. The timber roof is of the king-post type, supported on hammer-beams springing from the walls, owing to the considerable width of the nave. At the west end there is a choir gallery containing a Positive Organ of 1922. In the gable is a circular window, a regular characteristic of F.W. Tasker the architect.

The sanctuary occupies the easternmost bay, and includes an apse containing a baldacchino (with Egyptian capitals) which houses the tabernacle and remnant of the old altar. This and the forward altar, the ambo and retaining walls are all of Sicilian marble, installed about 1925–30 by Fr David Leahy.

Fr Leahy also built the Lady Altar, and had its surrounding walls panelled with various marbles. Its reredos of stone has a figure of the Madonna within a central niche, flanked by representations of St Joseph and King David, Fr Leahy's patron. Nearby is the stone font raised on five stout columns, with sacred symbols sculpted on its eight panels. The Stations of the Cross are competent canvas paintings. Among the statues there is a carving of St Joseph by Mayer, and a carved *pietà* by La Statue Religieuse.

Bibliography
Kelly, pp. 335-36; *The Tablet*, 20 April 1861, p. 251; 13 July 1861, p. 437; 11 October 1902, p. 591

Surrey Docks, Our Lady of the Immaculate Conception, St Elmo's Road, SE16

This church is a descendant of the Church of the Immaculate Conception that was opened in Rotherhithe in 1861. When the chapel in Paradise Street was opened in 1892, the church and presbytery of the Immaculate Conception became a convent. The church was destroyed by enemy action in 1942, and not rebuilt. Various halls and borrowed churches served then as Mass centres, which were given up with the decline in population. Subsequently, Fr William Maher SJ set up a Mass centre at the Fisher Club, and obtained the site for the present church. The foundation stone was blessed by Bishop Tripp on 18 December 1987, and the church was complete by October 1988. The architect was Gerald Murphy of Burles, Newton & Partners.

Standing within its spacious site, the brick-built church is of square plan, with an L-shaped tower hugging its north-east corner, and two lower projections diagonally opposite. All the roofs are of single slope. Inside there is a squarish vestibule flanked by a small hall and the sacristy, both capable of being opened to the nave by means of folding screens. The priest's quarters lie above these areas.

The space for worship is fan-shaped, with the altar at the angle, opposite the entrance. Its timber roof is raked, and punctuated by rectangular windows descending towards the sanctuary. There are recesses to right and left, for the Blessed Sacrament and the baptistery. All the sanctuary furniture is of matching stone—altar, chair, lectern, font and

13. *Surrey Docks, Our Lady of the Immaculate Conception*

tabernacle. Also here are six stained glass windows with sacred symbols worked in multicoloured blocks, designed by Charles Norris OSB of Buckfast. The small, square, unframed Stations of the Cross are original drawings, especially made for this setting. The statue of Our Lady of the Immaculate Conception is of Ancaster stone.

Bibliography
Kelly, pp. 335-36; *The Universe*, 18 December 1987, p. 5; *CB*, Summer 1989, pp. 61-64

Walworth, English Martyrs, Rodney Road, SE17

A school chapel in Northampton Place designed by L.A. Stokes was opened in 1890. Land was acquired in 1893 for a proposed Church of the English Martyrs. The dedication honours those executed on the North Surrey gallows at St Thomas's Watering at the junction of Albany Road and Old Kent Road. The clergy house designed by F.A. Walters was built in 1894–95. A design for a church by Benedict Williamson was published in 1900, but not carried out. The foundation stone of the present church was blessed on 15 February 1902; the first Mass was said on 19 March 1903; and the church was formally opened on 29 September following. Fr Peter Amigo (later archbishop) was the founder; F.W. Tasker was the architect; and Messrs N. Gough of Hendon were the builders. A daughter church of St George's Cathedral, it became an independent parish in 1929. The old altar was removed in 1961 during redecoration by F.G. Broadbent & Partners, and the crucifix was remounted on a new reredos. The church has been in the charge of the Order of Carmelites since 1980. Following their arrival the sanctuary was reordered under the architects Gerald Murphy, Burles Newton & Partners.

Prominently sited at the corner of Rodney Road and Flint Street, the exterior is reminiscent of some French churches, being tall and compact, with a *flèche* above the chancel arch. There are Gothic lancet windows singly and in groups of three. Above a plinth of blue brick, the main body is of yellow brick, laid in English bond and dotted with occasional blue headers. The clergy house and the (ritual) south-west porch are at an angle to the rest owing to the vagaries of the site.

Inside, all is of red brick. Internal buttresses pierced to form access aisles impart a monumental character. Beyond the west gallery there are five bays of nave and aisles, with triple lancet windows and an arch-braced timber roof. The sanctuary is straight-ended, with trios of clerestory lights.

The sanctuary furnishings, which date from the reordering of the eighties, include the altar and ambo of Portland stone, with a motif of wrought iron introduced as a focal point. Above the tabernacle the large crucifix dating from 1904 is framed by a timber reredos decorated with shields and Instruments of the Passion. The arms are those of Humphrey Middlemore, John Fisher, Thomas More, John Arrowsmith and

Richard Whiting. The reredos and the panelled tester above it were the work of G. Jackson & Sons of Fulham in 1961.

In a polygonal space south of the chancel is the baptistery, with a font of Portland stone, cone-shaped and lightly incised on its 12 sloping sides. On the wall is another symbolic wrought-iron wheel. Adjacent to the baptistery are the shrines of Our Lady and the Sacred Heart, with figures carved by Mayer behind marble balustrades. Off the south aisle is the Lady Chapel, glazed to the nave since 1972. Its marble altar given in 1919 stands within a shallow apse decorated in opus-sectile. Also in the chapel is a figure of St Joseph carved by Mayer.

Around the church are the Stations of the Cross consisting of coloured prints in simple frames, in the pre-1914 modest style of Mayer. Much more striking are eight carved statues of English and Welsh martyrs prominently mounted on corbels raised on the buttresses, the work

14. *Walworth, English Martyrs*

of Anton Dapre. Also in the nave is a carved figure of St Antony; and a large bronze figure of St Peter modelled on that in St Peter's in Rome, of 1904 from Froc-Robert of Paris.

Bibliography

Kelly, pp. 412-13; Little, p. 163; David Waite, *English Martyrs Walworth 1890–1990* (London: Carmelites, 1990); *The Architect*, 23 March 1900, p. 192; *BN*, 21 February 1902, p. 267; 9 October 1903, p. 475; *The Tablet*, 11 October 1902, p. 591; 3 October 1903, p. 550; *CBR.S*, 1961, pp. 144-45

XII
Tower Hamlets

Bethnal Green, Our Lady of the Assumption, Victoria Park Square, E2

THE Augustinians of the Assumption expelled from France came to the district in 1901, in response to the request of Cardinal Vaughan. Mass was first celebrated in a small shop at the corner of Digby Street and Globe Road. Then a temporary chapel was opened in a former warehouse in North Passage, Green Street (now Roman Road). In 1904 another temporary chapel in Cambridge Road was taken over from Polish priests. The foundation stone of the permanent church was blessed on 6 May 1911, and it was opened on 22 June 1912 by Cardinal Bourne. The architect was Edward Goldie; the builders Messrs Goddard & Sons of Farnham and Dorking; and the cost was £8,700. it was financed jointly by the Order and by Mrs Florence Cottrell-Dormer, in memory of Clement, her late husband.

1. *Bethnal Green, Our Lady of the Assumption*

The exterior of London stock brick with Bath stone dressings holds a prominent corner site. A shallow porch projects from the west front, flanked by two small windows. Above it is a seven-light window with Decorated tracery, surmounted by a gable cross. Along the north side the lower wall is sheer, and recessed above it are five clerestory windows between stone-capped buttresses, which surmount the wall by several feet. The lower, unobtrusive chancel has two clerestory windows with tracery based upon trefoil shapes.

Inside, there is a tall wide nave of five bays, the first bay with gallery above it, glazed to the nave in 1971 and designated as a narthex. The aisleless

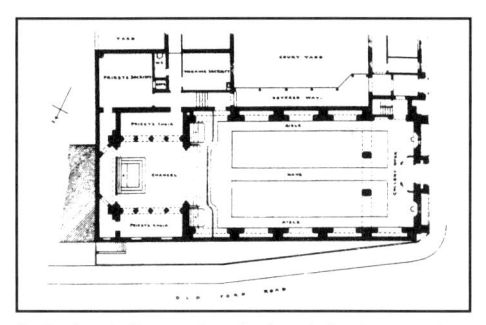

2. Bethnal Green, Our Lady of the Assumption, plan

nave and the raised sanctuary demonstrate the flexibility of the Gothic style, with its potential for planning with clear sight-lines free from obstructive piers. This functional plan is further developed by placing altars, shrines and confessionals within shallow niches between the buttresses. There are three oaken confessionals, carved by Fr Gregory Chedal; on the south side the Altar of St Joseph, of stone with a panelled reredos and a carved statue within a niche. On the north side St Teresa; St Antony's Altar of marble, mostly verde antico; and the pulpit, ingeniously corbelled from the wall, of stone with slender columns framing arched marble panels. In the nave are three traceried clerestory windows of 1913 by Hardman; and the Stations of the Cross, tableaux carved in high relief. In the narthex is the Altar of Our Lady of Lourdes, with a timber reredos in the form of a panelled arch, containing a central statue in a gabled niche, flanked by paintings of Our Lady of Perpetual Help and Our Lady of Good Counsel.

The sanctuary has on either side narrow arcaded spaces, designated originally for the priests to say the office in community. Above a shallow apse there is a lunette with stained glass depicting the Assumption. The original altar (by Earp & Hobbs) has a carved and gilded representation of the Last Supper as its frontal. Its timber reredos has openwork panelling, with a central canopy and niches containing statues of St Augustine and St Clement. Also by Earp & Hobbs are the flanking altars with statues in canopied niches of the Sacred Heart and Our Lady of Bethnal Green (by the Art and Book Company). Each altar is of plain stone with a timber reredos. These and the sanctuary reredos are panelled in the Perpendicular tradition, and are slightly different in detail from each other, with an assortment of Gothic

3. Bethnal Green, Our Lady of the Assumption

decorative forms. They are finished in bright colours, with gold predominating. In front are the daintily curved altar rails, of wrought iron with a brass coping, of 1913 by Hardman.

Bibliography
Kelly, pp. 75-76; Rottmann, pp. 188-91; *BN*, 22 December 1911, p. 871; *The Tablet*, 29 June 1912, p. 1017; *Br*, 18 April 1913, p. 454; *Westminster Cathedral Chronicle*, 1912, p. 79

Bow, Our Lady and St Catherine of Siena, 179A Bow Road, E2

The architect was Gilbert Blount, and though much less impressive than his church of St Anne, Underwood Road, this church is of interest for the light that it throws on the influence of nuns on missionary development. The work of the Dominican sisters for orphans in Walthamstow not proceeding too successfully, Mother Margaret Hallahan approached Archbishop Manning in 1866 and asked for 'the hardest work he could find for her and the Sisters'.[1] As a result, the nuns undertook teaching work in the district of Bow. They obtained possession of Alfred House in Bow Road, which they renamed St Catherine's Convent. Adjacent to the convent they built a chapel for themselves, to which, with considerable altruism, they had a church attached for public worship.

4. *Bow, Our Lady and St Catherine*

1. Rev. Wm. Brown, *A Short History of the Parish of Our Lady and St Catherine* (Bow: The Catholic Church, 1970), p. 2.

Archbishop Manning blessed the foundation stone on 20 July 1869, and opened the church on 9 November 1870. The builder was Mr Perry of Stratford. The north transept and sacristies were added in 1882 by the architect A.E. Purdie, Blount having died in 1876. When the Dominican sisters left Bow for Stone in Staffordshire in 1923, the church was made over completely to the diocese, and part of the convent became the presbytery. The nave of the church was destroyed by enemy action in 1943. After the war it was rebuilt in exactly the same form, of Kentish rag with Portland stone dressings.

The (ritual) west front faces Bow Road with a porch to one side. The major impact comes from the large wheel window, which is flanked by statues and sculpted heads, above a series of lancet windows. The receding view to the right punctuated by buttresses reveals the former choir of the nuns.

The interior consists of an aisleless nave and sanctuary. There is a west gallery raised on three arches, with organ by Norman, Hill & Beard, formerly at Holloway Prison. The nave, six bays long, has lancet windows and an arch-braced timber roof. The altar rails are of marble, mainly Sicilian. Flanking the sanctuary are sculpted statues in niches of the Virgin and Child, and St Joseph.

Beyond a forward altar stands the spectacular altar designed by Blount, executed by Farmer & Brindley and installed in 1874. Its frontal bears in a single panel a bold sculpture of the multiplication of the loaves, populated by no less than 22 figures. Its reredos consists of a central pinnacled monstrance throne behind the alabaster tabernacle; at its sides in gabled niches are statues of Ss Catherine, Rose of Lima, Dominic and Hyacinth. Behind is the east window, with the Madonna and Child in the centre, flanked by Ss Peter, Catherine, Thomas the Apostle and Patrick. In the tracery is the Sacred Heart adored by angels. The chancel ceiling is of timber, fashioned as an octopartite ribbed vault. The sanctuary is still paved with its original Staffordshire tiles.

To the right, beyond a double arch with foliage capitals, is the former convent choir, now designated the Lady Chapel. It is three bays deep, with a gallery, traceried windows and wrought-iron communion rails. Left of the sanctuary, behind a trio of arches raised on columns of Aberdeen granite, there was formerly an altar which faced the nuns' choir. This space now contains two large sculpted angels.

In the north transept there is the Sacred Heart Altar, of timber with a panelled reredos and recessed frontal, bearing floral decorations. Its carved statue is the work of Mayer. Close to it is the polygonal pulpit, of stone with cusped and traceried arches along its sides. The Stations of the Cross, carved in relief, are variously signed TS and HR.

Bibliography
Kelly, pp. 92-93; Rottmann, pp. 193-94; *BN*, 30 July 1869, p. 94; 18 November 1870, p. 374; *Br*, 10 December 1870, p. 994; *The Tablet*, 24 July 1869, p. 249; 12 November 1870, p. 625; 26 September 1874, p. 404; 8 April 1882, p. 554

XII. Tower Hamlets

Bow Common, The Holy Name and Our Lady of the Sacred Heart, 117 Bow Common Lane, E3

The mission was founded by Cardinal Manning to serve Catholics living in this part of Bow. From 1891 a temporary chapel was established at 187–89 Devons Road and served from Our Lady and St Catherine Church. Shortly before his death on 14 January 1892, the cardinal placed Fr Gordon Thompson in charge of the mission. The foundation stone of the permanent church was blessed by Cardinal Vaughan on 26 July 1893. The completed church was consecrated by Cardinal Vaughan on 30 June 1894, and Fr Thompson said the first Mass two days later. F.A. Walters was the architect for the church, presbytery and schools. Messrs Gregory & Co. of Clapham Junction were the contractors.

The presbytery and school buildings were destroyed by enemy action in the early part of the Second World War. The church was also burnt out in 1944, only the walls surviving. It was restored by the architect David Stokes and reopened in July 1957. A low-pitched aluminium roof was substituted for the former steep roof of slate.

The long side to St Paul's Way is all of red brick, with clerestory windows rising above the aisle roof. The entrance is at the foot of the tower. This is of four storeys plus the octagonal bell-stage surmounted by an aluminium spire. Over the door is a niche containing a statue of the Virgin and Child. To Bow Common Lane the chancel wall is slightly canted, and unglazed.

Inside, there is a wide entrance bay containing the baptistery, with gallery above. The font is raised on numerous columns, with busy sculpture on its eight faces. There are arches with wrought-iron gates to the baptistery and the body of the church. This consists of the wide nave of four bays, with flanking passage aisles, plus the sanctuary of two bays and a north chapel. The windows throughout are lancets, single or in pairs, in the austere Early English manner.

Stylistic economy is also observed in the nave piers, of square plan, chamfered at their corners, and lacking capitals; and the arcade arches of simple profile. Walters the architect joined the nave to the narrower chancel with two slender angled arches, a device he developed further at Vauxhall St Anne. Above these arches there are four sculpted statues of saints, thought to be (from left to right) Pope Pius XII, St Peter, St Oliver Plunkett and St Edward the Martyr.

The sanctuary has a forward altar of timber. The post-war altar in white marble remains, with its baldacchino of aluminium decorated with gold leaf. The steps and floor are of white and green marbles. The north chapel has a plain stone altar, above it a statue of the Sacred Heart. Two windows filled with Christian symbolism bear the signature MD. Along the north aisle there are statues of St Joseph, St Patrick and St Francis, the last by Statuaria Sacra of Rome.

To the south-west is a shrine to Our Lady, with a carved statue. Here also are memorial tablets, of marble framed in stone, to William Lyall +1900 and Susan his wife, founders of the church; and to Fr Gordon Thompson +1905, the first priest of this mission. Off the south aisle is a chapel with a marble altar and marble pavement, containing a statue of St Teresa of Lisieux. Spanning these three aisle bays are six lancet windows containing figures of Ss Thomas More, John Fisher and other English martyrs, designed in sombre reds, purples and blues. Nearby there is an imposing figure of St Antony with the Child Jesus carved by Anton Dapre. By the sacristy door is the holy water stoup, rough-hewn of Cornish granite.

Bibliography

Kelly, p. 92; Rottmann, pp. 194-96; *BN*, 4 August 1893, p. 160; *The Tablet*, 29 July 1893, p. 189; 7 July 1894, p. 24; *CBR.S*, 1957, pp. 46-49; 1958, pp. 64-67

Commercial Road, St Mary and St Michael, Lukin Street, E1

The modern parish is descended from the Virginia Street mission. The chapel in Virginia Street was in the eighteenth century part of a hospital for foreign sailors. Catholics among them were permitted, through the interest of the Portuguese ambassador, to receive the services of a priest. Local Catholics also attended regularly, and so the mission flourished. The chapel was destroyed, however, in the Gordon Riots of 1780. With compensation from the Government, a chapel 'in the plainest style, totally devoid of ornament' was subsequently built.[2] Its lease was to expire in 1857, and collections for a new church were begun by Fr Richard Horrabin as early as 1815. A freehold site was acquired in 1842 for £3,000. The drawings of W. Wardell the architect are dated 1852, the year in which Messrs Bird entered into a contract to build. The foundation stone was laid by Cardinal Wiseman on 24 May 1853. But the collections fell off, and the builders stopped work and removed their scaffolding. With dogged persistence, however, Fr William Kelly begged for years for funds to complete the building and subsequently to pay off the outstanding debt. The church, while still unfinished, was opened by the cardinal on 8 December 1856, over 40 years after the collections were begun. The total cost was about £30,000. There were alterations to the chancel in 1898 by F.A. Walters. Following damage by enemy action in 1945, restoration was directed by A.V. Sterrett. Reordering of the church took place in 1992. The architect was Martin Goalen, and the contractors were Messrs Peak of Harlow.

The exterior, of Kentish rag with Caen stone dressings, has a symmetrical emphasis to its (ritual) west front which faces Commercial Road. Here, the intended tower with spire was not completed, and projects from the nave to a height of 60 feet. Above its central entrance is a five-light window, and atop its heavy buttresses are statues of St Mary and St Michael. In a gabled niche is Christ the King.

Inside, the genius of Wardell's design

2. Harting, p. 146.

becomes apparent. With maximum accommodation in view, the arrangements are as open as possible, with 11 continuous bays for nave and aisles, chancel and chapels, 185 feet long by 75 feet wide, and uninterrupted by a chancel arch, transepts or screens. Here, Wardell's inspiration may well have been such large East Anglian mediaeval churches as St Stephen's, Norwich, and St Nicholas, Kings Lynn, whose arcades run without any structural division. The arcade piers with bases of Portland stone are octagonal in plan and have plain moulded capitals. In each bay is a clerestory window of three lights, and over all is a cross-beamed roof of pitch pine with supports resting on stone columns at clerestory level.

5. *Commercial Road, Ss Mary and Michael, Wardell's design*

In the south-west corner is the baptistery, with wrought-iron rails and a mosaic floor. Its font and walls are panelled in marble, in the manner of Westminster Cathedral. Set in the rear wall is the Baptism of Christ executed in mosaic and opus-sectile. The large five-light window in the entrance is modern, with Christ the King and the English Martyrs for its subject. Off the north aisle are confessionals, compactly designed, with a penitent's space on either side of the priest. West of the confessionals, three arches give way to a shallow projection which Wardell designated as organ chamber. It originally housed a Bishop organ, and is now partly occupied by a repository. At window level are the Stations of the Cross, relief carvings in Gothic-derived frames. The varied tracery of the aisle windows is characteristic of Decorated Gothic. The original red and blue Staffordshire floor tiles survive.

In the alterations to the sanctuary of 1898, F.A. Walters added an arcaded reredos, the wrought-iron screens with monogrammed shields, and a pavement of encaustic tiles. Walters also moved the flight of steps from the middle to the entrance of the chancel, and the original galvanized iron communion rails by Hardman from the middle of the sanctuary to the lowest step in front. At the time of writing, there is a neat stone altar with marble-faced supports and matching ambo facing the people, well forward in the fifth bay from the east wall. This is slightly raised on a marble tiled pavement.

Behind are the communion rails which superseded the earlier ones in 1916, of alabaster and white marble,

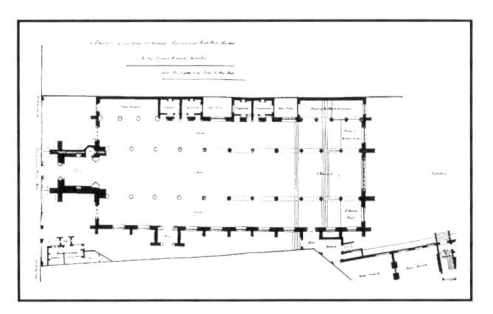

6. Commercial Road, Ss Mary and Michael, Wardell's plan

designed by R.L. Curtis. The high altar, of Caen stone, erected in 1911 as a memorial to Dean Dooley, was also designed by Curtis. Its frontal contains a single relief panel depicting the Last Supper. The east wall is lined with tiles bearing IHS and MM monograms. The great east window depicting the Crucifixion with saints and beati was installed by Hardman in 1957.

To the right is the Sacred Heart Chapel, previously known as the Blessed Sacrament Chapel, and initially designated as St Patrick's Chapel. Its altar is original, executed by Bolton & Swailes. It bears relief panels of the Last Supper and the Multiplication of the Loaves in its reredos; the Crucifixion and the brazen serpent set up by Moses in its frontal. The window above the altar is by Hardman, depicting Our Lady, Ss Thomas Aquinas, Tarcisius, Pascal Baylon and Juliana Falconieri. Two adjacent windows destroyed in the war have not been renewed with stained glass. There are tracery fragments in one, of the glass commemorating Mother de Sales's 30 years' work in the parish, installed in 1934 by Arthur Orr of Harrow. In the chapel is the statue of St Patrick, signed by T. Phyffers, 1855, large, coloured, and meant to be viewed high up and from a distance, along with another in the Lady Chapel. In front of the chapel is the organ by Slater of London, raised on timber arches.

The corresponding Lady Chapel on the north side has a stone altar, marble-faced, with a panelled and columned frontal. In its reredos are the Nativity and the Magi framing a central Madonna and Child. The window by Hardman celebrates Our Lady. Also in the chapel is Our Lady of the Immaculate Conception by T. Phyffers, and a carved figure of St Joseph.

To the left is the Martyrs' Chapel, with an altar of marble and stone. In its reredos are two relief panels of the Stepney Martyrs, and the Barque of Peter entering London. The window by Hardman depicts Our Lady Queen of Martyrs, with the Venerable Henry Webley, St John Fisher and St Thomas More. On the wall there is a stone-framed marble plaque in memory of the Stepney Martyrs.

Bibliography

Kelly, pp. 140-41; Harting, pp. 144-50; Ward, pp. 106-10; Rottmann, pp. 178-82; Little, p. 135; *The Catholic Handbook*, 1857; *The Tablet*, 15 November 1856, p. 724; 13 December 1856, p. 788; 21 February 1857, p. 116; 24 April 1858, p. 260; 25 December 1909, p. 1034; 21 October 1916, p. 548; *BN*, 14 October 1898, p. 533; *CD*, 1934, p. 155; 1939, p. 177; Information of Rev. Francis van Son

German Church, St Boniface, Adler Street, E1

The year 1808 marked the appointment of Fr John Becker as German chaplain at Virginia Street Chapel. He was joined by Fr Franz Muth, and together they opened a chapel in 1809 at 22 Great St Thomas Apostle Street in the City. Between 1849 and 1853 the Redemptorists were in charge of the chapel. For them, the architect William Wardell designed a large Gothic church, but this was never begun. Owing to financial difficulties, the first chapel was abandoned, and a Dissenting Chapel in Friar Street was adapted for Catholic use in 1859. A magnificent design by E.W. Pugin for a new church, school and presbytery was publicised in 1860, but this too was never built. The lease expiring, the clergy acquired in 1862 the former Zion chapel on the present site, and opened it for worship. Unfortunately, the heavy central cupola of this large circular structure collapsed in 1873. Initially, a design in German Gothic by E.W. Pugin was intended as the replacement. Archbishop Manning, however, financed the new church, in the Romanesque style that he personally preferred. Pugin and Gothic intentions were thus dropped, and John Young was the architect of the Romanesque church opened in 1875. A spire was added to it in 1882. The sanctuary was extended, and four bells from the Whitechapel Foundry were installed in 1885. Sadly, this church was badly damaged in an air raid in 1940, and temporary accommodation was then found in the school buildings. The architect of the post-war church and presbytery was D. Plaskett Marshall. Its foundation stone was blessed on 7 November 1959 by Cardinal Godfrey, who officiated at the opening on 2 October 1960. Since 1903, the church has been served by priests of the Society of the Catholic Apostolate, commonly called Pallotines, after their founder St Vincent Pallotti.

Facing Mulberry Street is the entrance with the gallery above it, slightly lower than the nave. Facing Adler Street is the nave south wall, sheer with a high clerestory beneath the copper roof. On the corner is a tall slender tower, with the four bells rescued from the wreck of the previous church exposed high up. The structure is of portal steel frames encased in concrete. Its presentation is enhanced by differing shades of brick and by contrasting panels of patterned mosaic.

7. German Church, St Boniface

Beyond the spacious entrance glazed to the interior, the plan consists of a broad nave and less broad sanctuary. The high altar, Lady Altar, tabernacle plinth and font are all of rich green marble; the chancel floor of Sicilian. To the right of the sanctuary is a raised tribune with a wooden altar and a statue of St Joseph. Above the tabernacle is a large scagliola mural of Christ in Glory with St Boniface preaching to the faithful, by Herbert Reul. On the front of the ambo is the parable of the sower, ingeniously represented in wrought iron. There are similar wrought-iron panels fronting the tribune, and mounted on the sanctuary east wall, worked by Reginald Lloyd of Bideford. Also by him is the stained glass window depicting Pentecost above the gallery. Here too is the organ, of 1965 by Romanus Seifert. Fronting the gallery are the Stations of the Cross, coloured relief carvings from Oberammergau, 11 of them dating from 1912, the remainder being post-war replacements. Below these stands the font, strikingly fashioned in the plan of a spherical triangle. Its bronze cover is inscribed in memory of Fr Josef Simml +1976. This and the tabernacle are the work of H. Reul. The carved Madonna and Child on the Lady Altar is a replica by G. Wehling of a Rhenish statue of about 1600.

Bibliography
Kelly, p. 430; Rottmann, pp. 182-86; *The Tablet*, 11 June 1859, p. 372; 9 July 1859, p. 438; 18 August 1860, p. 517; 4 October 1862, p. 630; 13 May 1865, p. 294; 2 October 1875, p. 435; 22 July 1882, p. 153; *BN*, 4 May 1860, pp. 357, 359 (illustrated); *Br*, 6 June 1874, p. 487; *CBR.S*, 1957, pp. 42-43; 1960, pp. 46-51

Limehouse, Our Lady Immaculate, 636 Commercial Road, E14

The mission was started here in February 1881 for the benefit of the large Irish population. Mass was first said in a room over a chandler's shop and then in a large room in the priest's house, number 9 Turner's Road. Fr F.G. Maples was the first priest.[3]

Soon after the foundation a temporary chapel was erected in Commercial Road and Turner's Place. The architect was Henry John Hansom (1828–1904), a son of the more famous Joseph Aloysius Hansom. The temporary church remained in service until 1934, when it was replaced by the present church designed by A.J. Sparrow. It represents the achievement of Fr Frederick Higley, rector from 1888 to 1934.

The walls are wholly of brick—red on a blue base—the usual stone dressings omitted for reasons of economy. The plan runs north to south, with entrances from Island Row to the church and presbytery. The main front makes its impact by means of an Italianate clock-tower, five storeys high, with an arched bell-stage and a pyramidal roof. Alongside and facing Commercial Road is a niche containing Our Lady's statue. At the opposite end of the church is a smaller tower, with two storeys of blank arches surmounted by a statue of Our Lord.

The inside is reminiscent of the Early Christian basilicas. The nave and aisles have piers of square plan, with moulded capitals supporting round arches. There

---

3. Kelly, p. 249.

are two round-headed aisle windows to each bay, and the curved ceiling is penetrated by lunettes above the arcade arches. The west bay has a gallery with concave front to the nave, wrought-iron rails, and organ by Conacher, Sheffield & Co. Ltd, rebuilt in 1960 by Robert Slater & Son. Beneath the gallery is a massive font of marble, square with chamfered corners.

The sanctuary consists of one bay and an apse. Beyond a forward altar of timber is the original altar, of various marbles, principally Sicilian. Above it is a mural of Our Lady and angels. To right and left are the marble altars of the Sacred Heart and Our Lady, each with a carved statue.

There are stained glass windows in the nave to St Margaret Ward and St Peter; and in the gallery to St John the Evangelist, St Joseph and St Frederick. In the body of the church there are carved figures of St Anne with her daughter St Mary, Blessed John Roche by C.H. Sheill, and St Gabriel Possenti, 1936 by Robert F. Tooley.

8. *Limehouse, Our Lady Immaculate*

Bibliography
Kelly, pp. 249-50; Rottmann, p. 175; *BN*, 22 July 1881, p. 121; Rev. Peter Day, *Our Lady Immaculate with St Frederick* (Island Row: Limehouse Parish, 1981).

Lithuanian Church, St Casimir, The Oval, E2

The mission was founded in 1901, with a church on the corner of Christian Street and Cable Street. Fr Boleslas Szlamas had his quarters at 197 Whitechapel Road. The present church dates from ten years later, during the rectorate of Fr Casimir G. Matulaitis. It was opened by Cardinal Bourne on 10 March 1912, and the Mass on this occasion was said by Fr Benedict Williamson, who was the architect of the church.

The church exterior is not particularly prominent, huddled within a group of parish and domestic buildings, all of them built of London stock brick. The gable cross and a bell-cote, however, guide the visitor to the church entrance.

As so often happens, the inside, bright and inviting, belies the exterior. Beyond a (ritual) north-west porch, the layout of this small church is easily read, with nave, aisles and chancel all within three bays. The capitals of the round-headed arcade are given the Egyptian decoration that Williamson favoured. There are no aisle windows, but circular

9. Lithuanian Church, St Casimir

windows appear in the west wall and throughout the clerestory.

The major focus of the interior, however, is the altar-piece, a large wooden representation of the Coronation of Our Lady, carved in high relief, with figures also of the Trinity and angels in the background. It is of Tyrolese workmanship, and was shown at the 1851 Exhibition. To its right is the shrine of St Casimir, with a wooden altar, and a statue of 1951 by James Dagys.

At the west end of the aisle there is the Shrine of Our Lady of Lourdes, its statue set within an imaginatively devised grotto. Above it is the west gallery, with organ by Baldwin. Around the walls are the Stations of the Cross, canvas paintings in ornate oaken frames. A redecoration of 1980 did much to brighten this interior. It included wall paintings of two angels flanking the altarpiece, and in the north aisle Jesus in the Tree, and the Virgin and Child.

Bibliography
Rottmann, pp. 206-207; *The Tablet*, 16 March 1912, p. 418

Mile End, Guardian Angels, 377 Mile End Road, E3

The mission commenced when an independent chapel was purchased by a Catholic gentleman. After conversion to Catholic use this was opened by Archbishop Manning on 8 December 1868, Fr David Lewis being the priest in charge. Eventually condemned by the LCC as insecure, this was pulled down to make way for the present church. During the rebuilding, a temporary church at 381 Mile End Road served as a chapel. Lady Mary Howard undertook to defray the whole cost of the new church, in memory of her sister the late Lady Margaret Howard. The foundation stone was blessed by Cardinal Vaughan on 5 October 1901, and the church was opened by Bishop Bagshawe on 25 March 1903. F.A. Walters was the architect, and James Smith & Sons of Norwood were the builders. The cost was in the region of £11,000.

Although Early English was originally intended, the Perpendicular style was in fact employed. Thus the (ritual) west front in uncompromising red brick with spare dressings of Ancaster stone establishes its bold presence in Mile End Road. Its seven-light traceried window is balanced by a square tower of two storeys followed by an octagonal bell-stage, crenellated and surmounted by a Hertfordshire spike. The presbytery is part of the overall design, built in matching materials and also crenellated.

The entrance through the base of the tower leads into the narthex, glazed to the interior, and with a gallery overhead. Owing to the restricted site, the sacristies were constructed beneath the chancel, and a large crypt or hall beneath the nave. The church proper consists of a short nave of three bays with a narrow north aisle and a broader south aisle, a deep chancel and north-east Lady Chapel with organ over. Above the nave arcade the clerestory displays two two-light windows in each bay. The nave roof contrives to combine both the hammer-beam and scissor principals, resting on angel corbels. The roof and all the original structural timberwork is of pitch pine.

Prominently central is the font designed for baptism by immersion, octagonal in plan, with two flights of steps, and all of matching stone, with mosaic symbols of the evangelists on four of its sides. Complementing this is the large altar table, also in the nave. The lectern and president's chair are in the sanctuary, and the Blessed Sacrament is reserved here, in the tabernacle of the original altar. The altar is simply panelled, and lightly decorated with foliage groups. The tall reredos executed by Earp & Hobbs makes a strong impact, having openwork panels with cusped arches and numerous foliage motifs picked out in gold. Its tester is also

10. Mile End, Guardian Angels

panelled, and decorated with repeated IHS motifs. The traceried east window of five lights was the work of N.H.J. Westlake, given by the Fifteenth Duke of Norfolk in memory of his sister, Lady Margaret Howard.

To the left is the Lady Chapel with a forward altar of timber. The original altar has a panelled frontal with lilies and MR motifs. Its reredos, also panelled, has a central statue of Our Lady flanked by angels with scrolls that display her titles. The wrought-iron gates to this and the corresponding chapel (converted to a sacristy in 1977) were the work of Bainbridge Reynolds.

The area about the chancel arch is most tastefully furnished. On high is the rood with carved and painted figures. To left and right are statues of St Thomas of

Canterbury and St Dunstan, standing in niches with crocketed gables. Below St Thomas is the pulpit projecting from the wall, with IHS and an eagle bearing a scroll. Corresponding to the pulpit is the entrance to the crypt with wrought-iron gates, above it a carved figure of the Sacred Heart. Also in the church is a carved statue of St Joseph; and the Stations of the Cross, which may be those recorded by Kelly as being installed in the previous church in 1876.

Bibliography
Kelly, p. 278; Rottmann, pp. 186-87; *The Tablet*, 12 December 1868, p. 201; *BN*, 13 April 1900, p. 509; 7 June 1901, p. 760; 11 October 1901, p. 506; 18 October 1901, p. 518; 27 March 1903, p. 443; *Br*, 4 April 1903, p. 368; Information of Miss J.O. Maynard

Millwall, St Edmund, 297 West Ferry Road, E14

A school chapel was opened here in 1846, served from Wade Street Chapel and later from Our Lady and St Joseph's Church in Poplar. It was one of the earliest works of the architect W. Wardell, Gothic in style and consisting of nave (doubling as the schoolroom), chancel and sacristy.

This was replaced in 1874 by a new church, presbytery and schools, designed by F.W. Tasker for the Reverend Joseph Biemans. The foundation stone was laid on 3 June 1872 and the church was opened on 19 August 1874. The builder was Mr Linzell of Tottenham.

Designed in the Early English style, the church is built of Kentish bricks, with dressings of Portland stone outside and Bath stone within. The south side faces West Ferry Road, exhibiting a high nave

11. *Millwall, St Edmund, 1877*

with lancet windows and a flèche towards the chancel. Below is the aisle with lean-to roof, penetrated by the gables of the porch and the south east chapel.

Internally, the plan consists of nave and aisles of six bays, followed by the apsidal sanctuary and two side chapels. The west vestibule was glazed to the nave about 1965. The nave piers are of circular plan, with plain moulded capitals. The sanctuary is one bay deep and terminated by an apse. At clerestory level, the apse bears an arcade of 15 lancets, alternately glazed and blank. To the left is the Lady Chapel, and adjacent to it a built-in confessional. To the right is the Chapel of the Sacred Heart.

At the time of writing in 1996, the continued existence of this building is in question owing to subsidence problems. There have been discussions for an outline design, but no firm decisions have been taken.

Bibliography
Kelly, p. 279; Rottmann, pp. 173-74; *Catholic Handbook*, 1857; *The Tablet*, 8 June 1872, p. 719; *The Architect*, 22 December 1877, p. 344; 9 February 1878, p. 78; Information of Mr C. Fanning

Poplar, Ss Mary and Joseph, Canton Street, E14

The mission at Poplar was founded in 1816 when Fr Benjamin Barber of the Virginia Street mission opened a school in Wade Street for the families of the Irish labourers who worked in the docks. By 1819 there was a chapel 'still in a very rude and unfinished state'.[4] In 1821 Fr Barber bought ground in Wade Street for a new chapel and a burial ground. The new chapel is recorded as opened in 1835. Fr Barber died in 1838, and was succeeded by Fr James Hearsnep, who was instrumental in building the large new church in Wade Street. Designed by the architect William Wardell, it comprised nave, aisles, transepts and chancel with crossing tower, plus two side chapels and an organ chamber. Opened in 1856, this fine church in Decorated Gothic style was destroyed through enemy action on 8 December 1940.

The foundation stone of the present church on a new site was blessed by Cardinal Griffin on 7 October 1951, and the church was first used on 13 June 1954. Adrian Gilbert Scott was the architect, and John Mowlem & Co. were the contractors. The guiding hand was that of Canon John Wright, rector from 1946 to 1970.

The church has a good corner site in the angle of Canton Street and Upper North Street. Built of brick with stone dressings and tiles for the roofs, the progressions and recessions and differing heights of its parts present a well-proportioned exterior. The plan is cruciform, with a large octagonal tower at its centre, carrying a recessed upper stage crowned by a pyramidal roof, all highly reminiscent of the octagon at Ely Cathedral. The vertical windows narrow towards their round-headed tops in the

4. *CD*, 1819.

12. Poplar, Ss Mary and Joseph

manner of those in the great hall at the ancient palace of Ctesiphon, Iraq. This elliptical arch motif is especially prominent in the tall projecting porch. Over its central door there is a crucifix supported by angels sculpted in Hopton Wood stone.

Beyond the main entrance with a gallery above a glazed screen, the interior plan is perceived to be a Greek cross forming a generous central space with broad transeptal arms of equal length and width to the nave. Opposite the entrance is the sanctuary, with its altar of marble and stone, above it a baldacchino with columns of Verona marble. The reredos is patterned in geometrical shapes by variously coloured marbles. The altar rails and chancel floor are also of marble. A forward altar projects into the nave, and to one side is the pulpit, ingeniously built into the chancel arch, its front bearing sculpted symbols of the evangelists.

About the crossing are four tall elliptical arches supporting the tower, whose dimensions recede in its upper storey. On its ceiling is an emblem of the Holy Spirit within a gold star. To the right of the high altar is the Chapel of St Joseph, with an altar of marble and a figure of the saint holding the Child Jesus. A timber reredos with coupled columns frames an arch containing the workshop at Nazareth carved in relief. To the left is the Lady Altar, of marble, with a carved statue.

This church is exceptional for the repose of its interior, which derives not least from the consistency of its artwork. The stained glass windows—about 20 in number—contain single figures set in clear glass. Clearly all by the same hand are the carved statues—the Sacred Heart,

XII. TOWER HAMLETS

Our Lady, St Joseph, St Patrick and St Antony, perhaps the work of Ferdinand Stuflesser of Ortisei. The building materials support this artistic unity—quarry tiles for the floor, Hopton Wood stone for the font, the pulpit and the stylised figures of the Stations of the Cross. The singular success of this church derives from its centralised plan and the uniformity of its furnishings. To those who collaborated in erecting it we should be eternally grateful.

Bibliography
Kelly, p. 318; Rottmann, pp. 175-78; W. McConalogue, *A Tribute To The Canon* (Poplar: Ss Mary and Joseph Church, 1980); *The Tablet*, 31 May 1851, p. 346; 16 February 1856, p. 101; 19 April 1856, p. 243; 27 September 1856, p. 613; 4 October 1856, p. 628; *Illustrated London News*, 4 October 1856, p. 346

Tower Hill, The English Martyrs, Prescot Street, E1

The church has been in the charge of the Oblates of Mary Immaculate since its inception. Fr Robert Cooke rented accommodation in Paston Row, and opened the mission on 25 March 1865. A corrugated-iron building erected to serve as a church and school was blessed by Cardinal Manning on 12 December 1866. The Oblate Fathers moved to 24 Prescot Street, and a school was built in 1870–72, its top floor being used as a chapel. Fr William Ring then initiated the present church towards the end of 1872. The foundation stone was laid by Archbishop Manning on 18 May 1873, and it was opened on 22 June 1876. The architect was Edward Pugin, and, following his death on 5 June 1875, it was completed to his design by his brothers Peter Paul and Cuthbert, practising under the style of Pugin and Pugin. Mr Lascelles of Bunhill Row was the builder, and the contract figure was £10,000.

The front of yellow stock brick with Bath stone dressings presents to Prescot Street a pair of doors, both arched and gabled, and above them a band of eight vertical lights beneath a large traceried circle. There are stair towers to left and right, that on the left being octagonal, with a louvered bell-stage and a dormered spire. To the sides there are narrow aisle windows. Above the doors are mosaics by Arthur Fleischmann of Ss John Fisher and Thomas More.

13. *Tower Hill, English Martyrs*

The overall style is Edward Pugin's concept of the Decorated phase of

Gothic. Limited ground space compelled him to plan his church in an L-shape, with a large transept to the (ritual) north. The chancel and lateral chapels are unusually shallow, allowing the maximum space possible to the nave and aisles. Edward Pugin reduced the aisles to the width of access passages, and, to add sufficient room for a designated congregation of 1,200, he introduced substantial galleries over the aisles, as well as a deeper gallery to the west.

For this unaccustomed innovation he blamed the restricted space, and cited the church of St Germain l'Auxerrois in Paris as a respectable precedent. Here, the gallery tends to dominate the interior. Bases and capitals of Mansfield stone, generously carved with lush foliage frame stout columns of granite—Aberdeen red and Bessborough grey. The columns in turn support the galleries on a series of elliptical arches. The roofs are vaulted, octopartite above the galleries and arched above the nave. The clerestory consists of two-light windows in pairs, to each bay.

The high altar was designed by J.S. Gilbert in 1930 as a shrine to the English Martyrs. The actual altar of stone and marble is decorated with monograms of Our Lord's Passion. Behind it is a curved wall inset with blank arches which hold wrought-iron grilles carrying the arms of English martyrs. To left and right are corbelled niches with 12 statues of martyrs, and further outwards are larger statues within gabled niches of Our Lady Help of Christians and St Joseph. The chancel window of 1930 by William Earley of Dublin depicts 30 English Martyrs surrounding Christ.

To the right is the Chapel of the Holy Ghost, its stone reredos sculpted with Pentecost in three panels. Before the chapel is the circular font, bearing foliage decoration. The alabaster communion rails are preserved in part. To the left is the Sacred Heart Altar with symbolic devices in its frontal. Above is the Sacred Heart Statue in a niche with figures of King David and St Margaret Mary within gabled panels.

The north transept is occupied by the Chapel of Our Lady of Graces. Within a polygonal arched recess there stands the altar of alabaster, its frontal and gradine panelled and decorated with Marian symbols. The wall behind is pierced by a cusped arch, and beyond is the figure of Our Lady of Grace, sculpted by Boulton in Carrara marble, and flanked by angels. To left and right are blank arches fully decorated by Arthur Fleischmann in mosaic work that commemorates King Edward III's founding of the Cistercian monastery of Our Lady of Graces in 1350. The donor of the chapel was Susannah Rachel Walker.

Around the walls are the Stations of the Cross, coloured relief carvings within Gothic frames. Also in the body of the church are a pietà by Mayer, and the Gothic memorial tablet in marble and stone to Fr Robert Cooke +1882.

Bibliography
Kelly, p. 396; Rottmann, pp. 165-69; J. Hartford, *History of the English Martyrs Church Tower Hill* (Prescot House: The Oblates, 1994); *Tower Hill Centenary Souvenir* (1965); *The Tablet*, 24 May 1873, p. 666; *Br*, 6 June 1874, p. 487; 1 July 1876, p. 645; *BN*, 5 February 1875, p. 150; 24 December 1875, p. 696

XII. TOWER HAMLETS

Underwood Road, St Anne, London E1

There was a school here as early as 1825. Before the church was built, Mass was said in the largest classroom. The founder of the parish was Fr Quiblier, a priest of the Sulpician Order, who laboured in the district from 1849 to 1852. He was instrumental in inducing the Marists to undertake the mission, and priests of this order have served the parish to the present time.

The first Marists arrived on 2 September 1850. The presbytery was completed in 1852. The site of the church was purchased in 1853 for £600, Mr Pursell being the donor. Gilbert Blount the architect designed a large church with nave, aisles, transepts, crossing tower, sanctuary and two side chapels. When the nave and aisles were complete they were opened for use on 12 September 1855. The cost of £11,351 12s 2d was met by the generosity of the Marists in France. The incomplete church was renovated in 1877, and the sculpting of heads and angels in the nave and aisles was undertaken by Farmer & Brindley. Building was not completed to Blount's design. When the sanctuary and side chapels were added in 1894, Blount's intended transepts and crossing tower were omitted. In 1904 the church was again renovated, and decorated from designs of Joseph A. Pippet. A day chapel between the monastery and the church was erected in 1972 by the architects Burles Newton. The historic style hovers between Early English and Decorated.

Externally, the materials are Kentish rag with Bath stone dressings; internally, Caen stone was used. The symmetrical (ritual) west front to Underwood Road has a central door bearing four orders of columns. These support moulded arches which are skirted by gables. Above is a large wheel window, and niches for statues within the gable. To the nave and aisles there are substantial buttresses, with chamfered bases and pinnacled turrets.

14. *Underwood Road, St Anne*

Inside there is a large entrance with a projecting polygonal arcade supporting the organ gallery. The organ by Bishop & Starr was blessed on 31 May 1857. The plan consists of nave and aisles of five bays, followed by the sanctuary and side chapels. The piers of the noble arcade are basically octagonal in plan, with attached shafts bearing Early English foliage capitals. Above the capitals, angels face inwards, and more angels playing musical instruments support the arch braces of the king-post roof. Alongside these are the clerestory windows—two lights to a bay, enriched with double arcading. The aisles are similarly adorned, with sculpted heads supporting the roof corbels, and pairs of lancet windows in alternate bays. Off the aisles there are no less than nine built-in confessionals of the triply compartmented type, presenting their doors in several series of arcades.

The chancel is of one bay followed by a polygonal apse. This and the two chapels are rib-vaulted. The marble altar rails installed in 1935 have survived in the chapels. There is a striking forward altar faced with brass, its frontal inset with Gothic panels. The major altar was installed in 1901, by Edmund Sharp of Dublin, from designs of the Rev. M.J. Watters, at a cost of £800. Huge even for this large church, it is all of marble, mainly Carrara. Its panelled frontal has sculpted angels adoring the Sacrament, enclosed by Alpha and Omega. Flanking the tabernacle and pinnacled monstrance throne there are gabled niches with figures of angels bearing symbols of the Passion. At its extremities are taller pinnacled niches containing statues of St Anne and St Joachim. This tour de force is complemented by the window containing St Margaret Mary adoring the Sacred Heart.

To the left is the Chapel of St Anne, with an undistinguished altar of marble installed in modern times, topped by unmatching carved figures of St Anne and the Blessed Virgin. The reredos insensitively penetrates the Pippet decoration.

To the right is the Lady Chapel, also with an altar of marble, its frontal subdivided by columns and panels bearing geometrical and foliage decoration. Above and behind the tabernacle there is a timber reredos with an openwork niche containing the Lady statue. The reredos and walls bear Pippet decoration well restored.

In the Lady Chapel is a window to Mary Potter +1913, foundress of the Little Company of Mary, installed in 1992 by Goddard & Gibbs. Along the south aisle are windows to Fr Stephen Chaurin; and to Fr Stephen Cummings, by Mayer. In the converted south porch is the shrine of the Venerable Jean-Claude Colin, founder of the Society of Mary, with a statue by Verdier-Larme of Lyon. Near to the entrance is the font, its eight sides briskly sculpted with symbols of Our Lord and the Evangelists; the shrine of Our Lady of Lourdes with a carved statue; and the War Memorial 1914–18, incised on Sicilian marble by F. Osborne. The Stations of the Cross, bold coloured casts in Gothic frames, are by Besand.

Bibliography
Kelly, p. 368; Rottmann, pp. 191-93; Little, p. 137; W. Salmon, *St Anne's, Underwood Road* (London: Salesian Press, 1950); *SOL* 27, pp. 270-71; *Catholic Directory*, 1856, p. 231; *The Tablet*, 15 September 1855, p. 582; 22 September 1855, p. 598; 29 September 1855, p. 615; 16 April 1870, p. 496; 4 May 1877, p. 146; 23 March 1901, p. 459; *Br*, 10 April 1858, p. 252; *BN*, 23 September 1904, p. xvi

XII. TOWER HAMLETS

Wapping, St Patrick, Green Bank, E1

The mission was formed from that of St Mary and St Michael, Commercial Road, and opened at Christmas 1871. Fr Angelo Lucas was the first priest of the mission, but Cardinal Manning was firmly in charge of building matters. This explains why the style of the church is the Classical that Manning favoured, rather than the customary Gothic. The site, that of a former workhouse, was acquired for £7,250. The building tenders were £4,000 for the church and £1,000 for the presbytery. The architect was F.W. Tasker, and the builder Mr Nightingale. The unfinished church was opened for use on 15 August 1879. When the nave had been completed and a narthex added, the church was reopened on 9 June 1892.

Viewed from Green Bank, St Patrick's is a stout, rectangular building, mainly of yellow brick, with dressings of Portland stone. Its exterior detailing is spare, but there is an iron-framed bell above the east gable and an apse protruding to Green Bank. At the west end it has an Early Christian narthex with a series of round-headed arches supported by pilasters. Above this in the gable is a circular window, a regular fingerprint of this architect.

15. *Wapping, St Patrick*

Inside, the narthex is fitted as a day chapel, having a timber altar with a panelled and carved frontal. Beyond this, the main interior contains nave and sanctuary in a structural unity of six continuous bays. There is an imposing arcade of Ionic columns of Bath stone which support the entablature and the panelled barrel vault of fir. The aisles and chapels have flat panelled ceilings and high rectangular windows in pairs.

The sanctuary with its timber furnishings occupies the second bay. In the first bay is the marble altar of 1879, panelled in various shades of white, red and grey. Behind it there is a large canvas painting of the Crucifixion flanked by fluted Corinthian pilasters, now bereft of their pediment. This was in place by 1899, having been painted, along with mural decorations, pictures and frescoes by P. Greenwood. There are surviving frescoes of the Annunciation and St Cecilia high on the east wall.

To the right of the sanctuary is the organ (Gray & Davison) and before it the Sacred Heart shrine, with a carved statue and a base of marbles similar to those of the high altar. Then clockwise around the church, there is a carved figure of St Patrick, by Mayer; a large crucifix by Raffl of Paris; and the pietà, in memory of Fr F.C. Beckley +1908, with alabaster rails and wrought-iron panels by Jones & Willis.

Crossing to the north aisle, there is first the apsidal baptistery, with wrought-iron railings and a stone font whose eight faces are sculpted with Christian symbols. This is followed by a figure of St Peter modelled on that in Rome, and carved by Mayer; the shrine of St Joseph with a carved statue standing on a stone plinth; and the shrine of Our Lady of Lourdes. The Stations of the Cross consist of framed coloured relief carvings.

Beyond a timber screen bearing Renaissance detail is the Lady Chapel. Its wooden altar was formerly at the Oratorian Chapel in King William Street. The frontal, behind glass, is painted with Marian symbols. Within a pedimented arch of coupled fluted pilasters, the reredos consists of a canvas of the Madonna and Child, said by Rottmann to be Spanish work.

Bibliography
Kelly, p. 414; Rottmann, pp. 169-71; Little, p. 140; V. Worley, *The Story of Catholic Wapping* (Wapping: St Patrick's Church, 1971); *Br*, 3 August 1878, p. 819; *The Architect*, 27 December 1879, p. 383; *The Tablet*, 18 June 1892, p. 993; 23 December 1899, p. 1031; 1 September, 1900, p. 353

XIII

Wandsworth

Balham, Church of the Holy Ghost, Nightingale Square, SW12

BALHAM mission was formed from Clapham in 1887, when the Sisters of Perpetual Adoration purchased land and built a convent in the square. The convent chapel of the Holy Ghost was dedicated by Bishop Butt on 12 June 1890, and local Catholics were admitted to it. The nuns gave some adjacent land for the building of a church and a school. The foundation stone was laid by Bishop Bourne on 17 June 1896, and the church was first used on 14 February 1897. The builder was J.T. Scott of Blomfield Street, London Wall.

The architect was Leonard Stokes who, like J.F. Bentley, had a genuine feeling for Gothic art. Stokes carefully avoided copying the styles of his teachers, preferring a fresh approach to Gothic. His churches are marked by an absence of buttresses, and the consequent expanses of plain wall, in which he favoured bands of differently coloured bricks or stone.

Bishop Butt objected to the narrowness of Stokes's proposed nave, and insisted that it be widened to 30 feet. This Stokes did, at the expense, however, of the aisles, which he reduced to what were by then conventional access passages. In

1. *Balham, Holy Ghost*

order to avoid the unneccessary duplication of services for the parish and the convent, Stokes planned a permanent chapel for the nuns on the south side of the church. When this was added in 1901, the bays were perforated, enabling the nuns to worship from the privacy of their own quarters. The nuns moved away in 1931 and the convent was made over to secular use. However, the parish subsequently acquired the convent chapel, which in 1963 was converted to the Lady Chapel of the church. The west porch was added by 1915, the north aisle widened in 1931 and the Stations—cast three-dimensional works supported on cast corbels of imitation stone—were installed in the same year. All three altars were reordered (by Bartlett & Purnell) in 1971.

After such piecemeal building history, the exterior fails to match Stokes's original design, looking now unaccented and undistinguished. The interior, however, is most inviting, being light, spacious and uncluttered. The historic style is Perpendicular, conceived by Stokes as a natural development of English late Gothic. Such clarity of expression is rarely found in Gothic Revival work before this time: note particularly the lightness of the nave arcade, its piers reduced to a hexagonal plan and lacking capitals.

The five-light chancel window gleams down upon a profusion of polychrome marbles comprising altar, ambos, retaining wall, floors and steps, that would do credit to Westminster Cathedral. The crucifix is Oberam-mergau work of the eighteenth century, and flanking the chancel are statues in niches of St Anne and St Joachim. The glory of the Lady Chapel is the altar-piece designed by Douglas Purnell (after the white glazed terracotta Visitation attributed to Luca della Robbia in the church of San Giovanni Fuorcivitas, Pistoia) carved by Dorigo Vigilio Prugger and painted by Henry Farmer. North of the chancel the Chapel of St Joseph has an altar and marble surround of verde antico, above the tabernacle a statue of the saint with the boy Jesus, and flanking relief tableaux carved by Prugger in 1964. The altars are tasteful and happily unified in style. A more extensive use of stone, however, would have suited this north European Gothic setting even better.

Bibliography
Kelly, p. 63; M. Bennett, *The Parish Church of the Holy Ghost, Balham* (London: Balham Parish, 1986); *AR* 1 (1896–97), pp. 52-54; 100 (1946), pp. 173-77; *Br*, 1 January 1926, p. 7; *Tooting Gazette*, 11 December 1926, p. 11; *The Architect*, 24 December 1926, pp. 745-47; *Holy Ghost, Balham, Year Book* (1967, 1974)

Battersea (West), The Sacred Heart, Trott Street, SW11

Before his death, Don Bosco arranged for a settlement of the Salesian Congregation in England, and in 1887 the priests were given charge of the Trott Street mission by Bishop John Butt. A small iron church sufficed at first, but the growth of the mission soon demanded a larger building. The first design by the architect F.A. Walters was in Perpendicular Gothic style, with generous sculpted detail inside, and turrets and a tower outside. Its sheer size (100 feet by 80 feet) suggests that the cost would have been prohibitive. More realistic is the executed design, longer and narrower (120 feet by 63 feet) in a simple style of Italian Romanesque, brick-built and uncluttered by expensive detail. The foundation stone was laid on 3 August 1892, and the church was opened on 14 October 1893. The builders were Messrs J. Langley & Co. of Crawley, and the cost was upwards of £9,000.

This design was in fact based upon a study of the Salesian church of St John the Evangelist in Turin, built in 1873–82 by the architect Edoardo Arberio Mella. A close likeness of the order's mother church built for Don Bosco himself would clearly appeal to the community in London for associative reasons. Both churches have a symmetrical west front with a central tower rising to a spire. At Battersea, the central columned entrance decorated with incised crosses is arched and gabled. Above an upper windowed storey, the square tower turns octagonal and ends in a spire. Walters artfully hides the lean-to aisle roofs by means of transverse limbs.

Inside, Walters's revised plan provided all that was required. The first bay is occupied by a west narthex, above it the organ gallery, railed to the nave. Within the atrium is the baptistery, also with wrought-iron rails, a solid Victorian stone font and a triptych by Westlake, formerly in the chancel. There are four bays of nave and aisles, the square piers having chamfered corners, demi-columns at the faces and moulded capitals. There are single round-headed windows to each bay of the aisles and clerestory, and a quadripartite nave vault.

The chancel floor is unusually high, having seven steps to the altar and another seven to the tabernacle in the apse. Also unusual is the triple-arched division between chancel and nave. The altar, ambo, steps and rails are of a

2. Battersea (West), Sacred Heart

sombre marble, all very dignified. The north and south Chapels of Our Lady and St Joseph within the transepts have been reduced in depth, and now amount only to altars of marble and alabaster within shallow apses, lacking any sense of spatial setting. The chancel and chapels were remodelled in 1970, and at the same time the Chapel of St John Bosco off the north aisle was constructed by Greenhalgh & Williams. It has an altar of Sicilian marble, statues of Carrara, and slim windows glazed with abstract coloured lights.

There are remnants of extensive paintings by Fr George Fayers that once covered the arcades and aisles. Above the chancel arch are the Lamb and angels; and above three sacristy doors are the Annunciation, Nativity and Deposition in a style approximating to that of the pre-Raphaelites. The Stations of the Cross—framed plaster relief tableaux—came from the Salesian house at Turin, and among various plaster statues that to St Teresa is signed M. Bernard.

Bibliography
Kelly, pp. 69-70; Rottmann, pp. 291-95; *The Tablet*, 21 October 1893, p. 655; *CBR.S*, 1970, pp. 110-11; Designs of July 1890 and May 1892 at the RIBA Library

Battersea Park, Our Lady of Mount Carmel and St Joseph, Battersea Park Road, SW8

The mission was founded from Clapham by Fr Thomas Drinkwater, to serve the growing population of Irish Catholics. The original small church was opened on 22 November 1869. It was designed by Charles Alban Buckler, and given by Mrs Boschetta Shea; the Duke of Norfolk contributed £500. This was considerably enlarged in 1879 by the addition of a nave and chancel, so that it became a side chapel. The reopening took place on 19 June 1879. The architect of this work was John Adams of Battersea.

The original church, now the Lady Chapel, consists of an apsidal sanctuary and three bays arcaded towards the nave. Adjacent are the sacristy, a built-in confessional and the baptistery, with an octagonal stone font bearing the dove framed by a quatrefoil. Its altar was designed by C.A. Buckler. The sculpted frontal is divided into three cusped panels flanked by shafts of red marble. In the centre Our Lady invests St Simon Stock with the scapular, and attendant angels occupy the lateral panels. Also within the chapel are three stained glass

3. *Battersea Park, Our Lady of Mount Carmel and St Joseph*

windows, and a good carving of the Salvator Mundi, 1961 by L.F. Dapre.

The church proper consists of a six-bay nave with west gallery and apsidal sanctuary. The nave with its wagon roof is punctuated by tall lancet windows throughout, and by pilasters dividing the bays. Within the apse is the large altar (presented by Sir John Stuart Knill) in two shades of red marble, with its domed tabernacle and gradines bearing extensive diaper work. The columned frontal too is decorated with varied geometrical figures. A plainer forward altar, of pink and white marble, blends well in its setting. In the chancel clerestory are two stained glass windows. There are cast Stations of the Cross, and several statues of Our Lady and saints.

Bibliography

Kelly, p. 69; Henry S. Simmonds, *All About Battersea* (Battersea: Ashfield, 1882); *The Tablet*, 17 July 1869, p. 218; *BN*, 23 July 1869, p. 76; 27 June 1879, p. 764

Clapham Common, St Vincent de Paul, Altenburg Gardens, SW11

The mission was founded in 1903 by Bishop Bourne. Fr George Grady purchased a house and some adjacent land in Altenberg Gardens for £3952 12s 5d with the assistance of Miss Frances Ellis. Fr Grady then converted the ground floor to an oratory, opened on 3 October. When sufficient money was in hand, a permanent church was commenced next to the house, at an estimated cost of £3000. The foundation stone was laid by Bishop Amigo on 28 July 1906. The architect was Claude Kelly (in partnership with Archibald Campbell Dickie); the builder F.J. Bradford of Leicester; and the style Early Christian.

A proposed Italian campanile was never erected, but the architect's watercolour in the presbytery shows a tall, triple-arcaded tower with pyramidal tiled roof surmounted by a cross. It was designated to the south-east, where now stands the sacristy. This and the south-west baptistery were erected c. 1962. At the opening on 19 March 1907, Mgr Walter Croke Robinson 'considered it a wise and magnificent idea to place comparatively inexpensive churches among the toiling masses of London'.[1]

Inexpensive it may have been, but the appearance is certainly not cheap. The

4. *Clapham Common, St Vincent de Paul*

1. *The Tablet*, 23 March 1907, p. 475.

tall west front, of red brick with stone dressings, cuts an impressive dash among the otherwise staid houses of Altenburg Gardens. What one sees is an aisleless front, its ground floor projecting westwards with a lean-to roof. A central gabled doorway flanked by circular window openings bears a tympanum with a mosaic of the Virgin and Child, of 1987 by Anna Weiner. The upper floor has in the centre a dominant Diocletian window, above it a statue of St Vincent by Thomas Rudge; and a projecting Tuscan gable which follows the example of the church at Putney.

The interior is even more attractive than the exterior. The traditional Roman plan is followed, with west atrium and nave of five bays succeeded by the choir and apsidal chancel. The roof is steel-framed, with an elliptical surface of lath and plaster, penetrated by the clerestory windows. Aisles are suggested by means of blank arches, punctuated by tall Corinthian pilasters.

The chancel bay is charmingly sub-divided into two lower arches, a wrought-iron screen separating it from the domed Lady Chapel. This is reached via a low two-bay aisle beneath the organ gallery. Over the Lady Altar there is a copy of the Virgin and Child of Fra. Bartolommeo, its surround of highly polished marble, with freestanding columns supporting a triangular pediment.

The altar, tabernacle stand and chancel floor are of marble; the Stations of the Cross, formal stylised figures carved in low relief, are Italian work installed in 1935. The baptismal font is of stone with marble panels; the pulpit north of the chancel is composed of various marbles, including Sicilian, Cork red, verde antico and Algerian onyx.

Bibliography
Kelly, p. 456; G.W. Grady, *The First Decade* (Clapham Common: Church of St Vincent de Paul, 1914); L.P. Seglias, *Our Parish* (Clapham Common: Church of St Vincent de Paul, 1984); *BN*, 3 August 1906, p. 167; *The Tablet*, 4 August 1906, p. 180

Earlsfield St Gregory, 306 Garratt Lane, SW18

A plain church in the Romanesque style was inaugurated quietly on 20 November 1904, the building made possible by the generosity of Miss Frances Ellis, and the work carried out by artisans and young men of the Southwark Rescue Society. This answered the need of local Catholics for a church between Wandsworth and Tooting. Fr Benedict Williamson was priest in charge from 1909 to 1915, and on 29 September 1910 the church was reopened after remodelling and enlargement by John Marsland & Sons of York Street, Walworth. Fr Williamson was his own architect, and reporting on his extensions, The Tablet wrote: 'During his stay in Rome for his ecclesiastical studies, he became saturated with the Roman spirit, and took the Roman basilicas as his model.'[2] The enlarged church was now based upon the original of St Gregory on the Coelian

2. 8 October 1910, p. 581.

Hill, from which St Augustine and his 40 monks set out. It consisted of nave, sanctuary and apse, with two side altars.

This church was completely destroyed in the air raids of 1944. A presbytery was ready by 1952, and the present church was opened by Bishop Cowderoy on 30 September 1957. There were alterations in 1982 including the introduction of a new altar. All of these building works were carried out by Peytons & Sons of Earlsfield. The exterior pays token acknowledgment to the Perpendicular style. It is of stock brick, with spare stone dressings to the windows and parapets. There is no tower as the external symbol of a church, but the eye is drawn to the straight-headed banks of windows containing groups of identical lights with convex arched heads.

Inside, the (ritual) west gallery and four bays of the nave are now partitioned to form a large parish room, which may be used as a church extension at Christmas and Easter. The truncated worshipping space consists, therefore, of a short nave and transepts with the altar at the crossing, that is T-shaped in plan, with the addition of two chapels placed diagonally to the west. On the chancel is a matching ensemble of marble altar, font and ambo; a large mosaic reredos

5. *Earlsfield, St Gregory*

patterned with stars; and robust stylized carvings of the Risen Christ, St Joseph and St Gregory. The furnishings of the Blessed Sacrament Chapel and the Lady Chapel are very similar, each having a marble altar, mosaic reredos and statue. The semi-abstract memorial glass in the Blessed Sacrament Chapel is by Martin Farrelly of Scotland, and that in the Lady Chapel is by Tony Taylor of Birmingham. There are the Stations of the Cross and several statues dotted around the church, but regrettably not one of these works is signed or dated.

Bibliography
Kelly, p. 161; *BN*, 30 September 1910, p. 493; *Wandsworth Borough News*, 30 September 1910; *The Tablet*, 8 October 1910, p. 581; 24 August 1912, p. 298; 31 August 1912, p. 338; *CBR.S*, 1957, pp. 74-76; Information of Mr John Thorpe

Putney, Our Lady of Pity and St Simon Stock, Hazlewell Road, SW15

In this developing suburb of Wandsworth, the mission was opened at Christmas 1902, when Fr Robert Collinson rented the former Primitive Methodist Chapel in Coopers Arms Lane (now Lacy Road). Among the new houses south of Upper Richmond Road, a site in Hazlewell Road was given by Lady Westbury. The original architect was J.C. Radford. When it was opened on 2 September 1906, only half the church was erected, and the rest, which

6. Putney, Our Lady of Pity and St Simon Stock

included the chancel, is attributed to F.A. Walters.

Leaning on Italian sources, the front is of stock brick with red brick dressings. Four giant pilasters enclose two mean doorways and a large central niche which contains a statue of St Simon. To the left is a plain unfinished tower. The pedimented front is absolutely dominated, however, by its projecting eaves, which give the 'Tuscan barn' effect of earlier Catholic churches at Hassop and Glossop in Derbyshire, although lacking the portico of the prototype: Inigo Jones's church of St Paul, Covent Garden.

The clean lines of the interior do credit to the otherwise unknown architect J.C. Radford. There are two (ritual) west entrances with ancillary rooms and an organ gallery; then three bays of nave and narrow passage aisles, with square piers and a straight entablature, and a minimum of moulded decoration. There are no aisle windows, but penetrating the barrel vault are semicircular openings with two mullions—surely derived from similar examples in the thermae of Diocletian at Rome. More recently, however, Bentley had incorporated these shapes into the fenestration of Westminster Cathedral, and they were indeed widely imitated following the cathedral's opening.

The chancel, two bays deep, is separated from the south-east chapel by a wrought-iron grille. Several furnishings blend well with the interior, especially the baldacchino over the original altar of 1936, the large Siena-type crucifix, the statues of St John Fisher and St Thomas More that flank the chancel, and the Stations of the Cross, sculpted with spare, restrained detail.

Bibliography
Kelly, p. 325; *The Tablet*, 3 January 1903, p. 36; 10 March 1906, p. 381; 8 September 1906, p. 380

Putney Polish Church, St John the Evangelist, St John's Avenue, SW15

This former Anglican church was acquired by the Polish community and dedicated to Catholic use by Bishop W. Rubin on 29 May 1977. The church was erected in 1858–59 to the design of Charles Lee. Stone-built and open to view on three sides, it has a strong presence, characteristic of contemporary Anglican churches. In Middle Pointed style its full-blown plan consists of nave, aisles, transepts, north-west tower with broach spire, south porch, a deep chancel and east chapels.

The interior is a joy to experience, spacious, stylistically correct and lovingly maintained. There are five bays of nave and aisles, the last bay doubling as non-projecting transepts. Octagonal piers with generously moulded capitals are punctuated by clusters of sculpted foliage. The aisle and clerestory windows are all of two lights with varied geometrical tracery. There are five stained glass windows in the church and evidence of others destroyed in the war of 1939–45. The roofs are variously structured, though all are panelled in timber.

The altar is placed at the crossing and is wholly of timber, its base bearing relief carvings. Near to it is a pulpit dating from 1902, its faces variously distinguished by figure sculpture and openwork tracery. Across the chancel arch there is a tall openwork screen of wrought iron with brass fittings.

The chancel is three bays long and more elaborately structured, having circular piers with attached shafts of marble, and foliage capitals. Its floor is extensively tiled and mosaiced. The easternmost bay is faced in marble and arcaded. There is a central arched setting for the tabernacle, with the Last Supper depicted in hand-made tiles and mosaic. To the left is the Lady Chapel, with a painting of Our Lady of Czestochowa flanked by votive offerings. Below it is a depiction of Calvary painted on three panels.

7. Putney, Polish Church

Bibliography
Information of Rev. Czeslaw Osika

Roehampton, St Joseph, Roehampton Lane, SW15

The Jesuits bought Manresa in 1861, and from 1865 they opened their private chapel to the public. This arrangement was converted into a regular mission in 1869. In 1876 the Rector Fr George Porter requested Bro. Michael Fearn, who had been a master builder, to prepare plans for a church. The foundation stone was laid on 16 July 1878. Then work was suspended and the services of a professional architect were sought. Frederick Arthur Walters was recommended to the rector by Fr Francis Goldie SJ. Walters had been with the firm of Goldie & Child, and had lately begun to practise on his own account.

8. Roehampton, St Joseph

The Roehampton church was therefore his first important commission, but the plan and stylistic details appear to be those already designated by Fearn. Bro. Fearn was appointed as Clerk of Works; Lucas & Sons were the builders; the church was formally opened on 8 May 1881 and consecrated in July 1883.

St Joseph's Church is of stock brick with Bath stone dressings, cruciform in plan and in the Early English style. The main approach is via a lych gate of English oak, designed by Walters and constructed in 1881 by Parmenter of Braintree. Almost detached from the (ritual) south transept is a substantial sacristy with plate-traceried windows. The focal point of the exterior is a small tower east of the south transept, the belfry in the upper storey being of half timber work, with a saddle-back roof that is surmounted by a *flèche*. A new presbytery, west baptistery and two porches were added in 1963 by Tomei and Maxwell.

Inside, the simple con-ventional plan is perceived as an aisleless nave of five bays with a scissor-beam roof, transepts and chancel. A west gallery stands above an Early English three-bay arcade. The lancet lights of the nave have stained glass of 1885 by Hardman, renewed in 1975 by Goddard & Gibbs; the Stations with their gold backgrounds were painted by Westlake in 1881. In the south transept is the organ by T.C. Lewis. In the north transept is a memorial brass (formerly in the chancel) to Anne Gertrude Garcia +1875, in whose memory the

9. Roehampton, St Joseph, interior

church was erected. Off the transept is the Lady Chapel (the former Fullerton Chantry) with a Carrara marble statue.

With an increased congregation from the new housing estates, the chancel was extended to the east in 1958, and now consists of four bays with triple lancet windows and a wheel window over the tabernacle. Gone, however, are the wrought-iron chancel screen, the altar and the tabernacle all designed by Fr Ignatius Scoles SJ, and the handsome oak stalls by Thomas Earp. Only the rood and the communion rails survive, before a marble arcaded reredos and tabernacle standing on a plinth, and a forward altar.

The building has its significance, as Walters's first church, characteristically individual with such features as its lych gate, the unusual detailing of the tower and the independent siting of the sacristy.

Bibliography

Kelly, p. 334; St Joseph's *Roehampton* (Centenary booklet, 1981); Humphrey House and Graham Sturry (eds.), *Journals and Papers of Gerard Manley Hopkins* (Oxford: Oxford University Press, 1959), p. 407; *BN*, 27 May 1881, p. 623; 3 August 1883, p. 185; *The Architect*, 12 November 1881, p. 319; 24 December 1881, p. 413; *CBR.S*, 1963, p. 102; 1975, pp. 40, 42

Tooting, St Boniface, Mitcham Road, SW17

The Catholics of Tooting were served from Balham in the 1890s, a priest saying Mass at Holly Lodge. About 1899, Fr Rudolf Bullesbach opened a chapel in Hereford Lodge, Mitcham Road. By 1903, when Catholic schools were opened in Undine Street, Catholics in Tooting numbered about 2000. The successor of Fr Bullesbach, Fr George Williams, was responsible for erecting the present church. The foundation stone was laid on 17 November 1906 and the church, still unfinished, was opened for worship on 18 April 1907. Miss Frances Ellis paid for the site and the initial building; Mary Allanson settled the debts on the schools and the presbytery, and paid for the completion and decoration of the church.

The architect, usually known as Benedict Williamson, was born in London in 1868, studied law for a time, then trained in the office of Messrs Newman & Jacques, architects and

10. *Tooting, St Boniface*

surveyors of Stratford. His given names were William Edward, but following his reception into the Catholic church at Farm Street in 1896, he was known as Benedict Williamson. For ten years he practised as an architect, working on Farnborough Abbey and St Ignatius Church at Tottenham. Then in 1906 he entered Beda College in Rome where he studied for the priesthood, being ordained in 1909. The Church of St Boniface was Williamson's last architectural work before he left for Rome.

Williamson initially modelled his design upon the Church of Ss Vincenzo and Anastasio, Tre Fontane. The final church bears little resemblance, however, to its Roman prototype. When opened in 1907, the unfinished church consisted of five bays of nave and aisles with a temporary sanctuary arranged in the nave. The scheme was eventually completed, the last instalment being the west end in 1927, in collaboration with J.H. Beart Foss. Whatever Williamson had intended to build in 1906—probably a simple version of his prototype's nave gable, with a low atrium before it which masked the lean-to aisle roofs—his ideas by 1927 had crystallized into something considerably more complex. In the commentary that accompanies his illustration, Williamson claims that the west front 'has not been built in any of the recognised styles of architecture; rather is it an endeavour directed towards the production of a new style'.[3] In this west front, Williamson incorporates a north-west campanile, the belfry stage ornamented with alternating bands of purple brick and Portland stone; and terminated by a copper-covered spire;

the rose window of the nave is framed beneath a boldly moulded arch and supported by massive columns; the great central doorway, with its lofty arch supported on engaged columns, is flanked by arcading on either side, with smaller entrances to the aisles.

By 1927 Williamson had long been interested in ancient Egyptian architecture, and his preoccupation here with Egyptian capitals together with his overgenerous use of Portland stone result in a confection far removed from the restrained Early Christian revival work characteristic of the turn of the century. The repose of the interior is in pleasing contrast. Above the west narthex and first bay is the gallery, its organ case designed in 1950 by C.S. Kerr Bate. Seven bays of nave and aisles are followed by the apsidal chancel and flanking chapels one bay deep. There are round-headed windows to the aisles and clerestory, and circular piers with cushion capitals bearing bold relief symbolism on their faces. The nave is surmounted by a king-post roof. From the west entrance the overall impression is one of familiar and competent Early Christian revival work.

A major attraction are the aisle walls, panelled to a height of seven feet, and between this and the springing of the lean-to roofs a large continuous iconographical scheme in mosaic of the Stations of the Cross, with stylized figures and generous surrounds in subdued colours, all tastefully designed and executed c. 1930 by L. Oppenheimer. The original high altar, with gradine and tabernacle, is still in situ and there is a new forward altar and ambo in memory of Canon Thomas Clifton,

---

3. *Br*, 10 June 1927, p. 939.

1939–67. The apse is extensively panelled and partially arcaded in Sicilian marble, with its central monstrance throne still extant. Also of Sicilian are the flanking north and south chapels: the Lady Chapel altar with a tall reredos forming an arched frame for a pedimented statue; St Joseph's Altar dominated by a tall reredos with a wild pediment and the Egyptian capitals that Williamson favoured.

Bibliography
Kelly, p. 394; Anson, p. 297; *BN*, 30 November 1906, p. 756; 10 May 1907, p. 650; *Br*, 10 June 1927, pp. 928, 939; *The Tablet*, 24 November 1906, p. 822; 27 April 1907, p. 662; *CD*, 1935, p. 178

Tooting (South-East), Our Lady of the Assumption, Links Road, SW17

The mission was founded from St Boniface, Tooting, by Canon Thomas Clifton in 1963, with a temporary church and hall. The present church designed by Sanders & Michelmore as a permanent parish hall was built in 1975, and consecrated by Archbishop Bowen on 7 December 1990.

The rectangular exterior is wholly of red brick and has a circular window above the main entrance. Beyond a modest west vestibule, the steel-framed interior with its plain rectangular windows consists of a broad aisleless nave with north and south shrines, and a shallow recess for the chancel. Here, the tastefully matching altar, ambo and tabernacle plinth are constructed of stone from the twelfth-century building of Merton Priory.

The Shrines of Our Lady and the Sacred Heart contain panels set with flint, also from Merton Priory; and the use of flint is then continued in the altar frontal and in the consecration crosses. The small carved Stations of the Cross match the scale of the church, as do the carved statues of Our Lady, St Joseph and St Teresa.

Bibliography
CBR.S, 1974, pp. 234-35; 1975, p. 49-51

Tooting Bec, St Anselm, Balham High Road, SW17

In 1905 a former Wesleyan chapel in Balham High Road was acquired for Catholic use, and dedicated to St Anselm. It was served initially from Balham, and became the church of the newly formed mission of Tooting Bec under Fr Charles Donovan, in 1909. The present church designed by John Bernard Mendham dates from 1933. It is reputed to have been modelled on a simplified version of Saragossa Cathedral.

Facing the road is the long, symmetrical north front, of red brick with bands of white stone. St Anselm's statue stands in a central niche, which has a busy Spanish surround; this is flanked by the lancet windows of the north aisle which bear similar decorative elements. Above these is a balustrade, and over the nave a central cupola (of

11. Tooting Bec, St Anselm

London stock brick) surmounted by a shallow dome with a gold cross. A well-proportioned pedimented entrance bears the date 1933.

Inside, the wholly traditional plan consists of a narrow west narthex with organ gallery above, nave, aisles, chancel and side chapels. Its historic style is Romanesque. The austere nave, only two bays long, has massive brick piers and round-headed arches of unequal height, the first bay groin-vaulted and the second bearing pendentives which rise to the inner octagon. From the nave, the psychological drive eastwards to the Holy of Holies is strongly felt in this church, as one views the well-lit sanctuary with its central baldacchino. The broad aisles have a series of tall lancet windows, their arches cusped in the Muslim-derived Spanish manner. The chancel and the chapels are all vaulted, and clerestory windows penetrate the vaults. The old marble-panelled high altar and tabernacle survive beneath the handsome baldacchino which is raised on columns bearing Romanesque capitals. These date from 1952.

In 1979 the sanctuary was reordered by Kendal Building Services, and a new forward altar, ambo and font of Bath stone were installed, inscribed respectively in gold lettering 'Christ is Risen', 'The Good News' and 'New Life'.

There are matching arcades between the chancel and chapels, with complex Romanesque capitals, whose design recurs throughout the church. The (south) Lady Chapel is one bay deep, with its marble altar within a shallow apse. In the chapel there is a good stylised carving of St Bernadette. The (north) Chapel of the Sacred Heart has a stone altar backed by a marble panelled reredos. In the chapel are statues of the Sacred Heart, St Joan of

XIII. WANDSWORTH 257

Arc and St Joseph. Another St Joseph (by Mayer) stands in the nave. The Stations of the Cross present formal figures in low relief.

Saragossa apart, the influence of Westminster Cathedral is also felt in the church, in the massive piers, the baldacchino, the generous use of marble, and the Diocletian windows in the Lady Chapel.

In 1988 a large meeting hall was arranged beneath the church by Paul Michelmore Associates, with new complementary premises at the rear.

Bibliography
Tooting Gazette, 11 December 1926, p. 11; *CBR.S*, 1979, p. 52; *CB*, Autumn 1988, pp. 52-53

Wandsworth, St Thomas a Becket, West Hill, SW18

The mission began in 1841 in a rented room in a cottage in West Hill, with a scattered congregation that consisted mostly of Irish field labourers. Six years later, a school chapel described by *The Tablet* as 'a new and elegant structure' was erected by A.W.N. Pugin for Fr Joseph Bower on a rectangle of land between the Wandle and Wandsworth Plain. Wandsworth having developed from a rural suburb to an extensively populated borough, a larger church on a new site was eventually called for.

The church designed by Edward Goldie for Fr Edward Murnane stands prominently on the corner of West Hill and Santos Road. Of red brick with Bath stone dressings, it has a sturdy north-west tower with octagonal bell stage, a double entrance decorated with Gothic forms beneath a large traceried west window, and statuary in the gable. The view along Santos Road taking in the porch, the south aisle with its transept, and the east chapel, shows a skilful massing of parts in a late Decorated style. This is all the more remarkable since Goldie's scheme was realized by instalments. The foundation stone was laid on 23 September 1893 and the nave and south transept were opened in July 1895. The Lady Chapel (now the Blessed Sacrament Chapel) was built in 1897–98, and the chancel was solemnly opened on 24 September 1899. There followed the south aisle and porch, completed in December 1901. The north aisle and transept were opened on 17 March 1912, built under the direction of Fr Benedict Williamson. Finally, the tower was erected in 1926–27 by Joseph Goldie, the bell-stage being redesigned by J.P. Conlan.

12. *Wandsworth, St Thomas a Becket*

Inside, the overall vista of nave, aisles, transepts and chancel shows a variety of roof constructions mostly of oak—segmental arches with moulded tie-beams to the nave, a rib vault to the chancel, flat panelled ceilings to the aisles, and tunnel vaults to the transepts. Goldie's taste for variety extends also to the nave piers, whose faces are slightly hollowed in a new variation on the familiar octagonal column.

The chancel consists of three bays with more complex piers and foliage capitals, above them a blank arcade in two tiers and a tall clerestory. The chancel was reordered in 1961 by F.G. Broadbent, and is dominated by the reredos, a large oaken panel framing a fine Calvary by Arthur Ayres. The communion rails of Sicilian marble happily still survive, and flanking the chancel are two large statues of St Joseph and St Thomas.

Both the transepts are double-naved, with circular piers bearing attached keeled shafts. In the north transept is the Sacred Heart Altar, designed by Fr Benedict Williamson, with a variety of marble surfaces, the statue by Ferdinand Stuflesser. Off the south transept is the Blessed Sacrament Chapel, three bays deep, with a panelled ceiling supported by four-centred arches, and brass gates at the entrance. Its altar and reredos are extensively panelled and traceried in the Gothic manner, the spaces busily decorated with foliage motifs in gold, red and green. From the south aisle, the narthex is reached by way of an ogee-arched doorway with foliage decoration, the arch ascending to a niche containing a statue of St Michael. There are numerous stained glass windows, all of them post-1945. In the reordering of 1961, the choir and west gallery over the narthex was enlarged, and the pipes of the organ (of 1928 by Willis) were divided, to provide a clear view of the west window.

Beneath the tower is the large baptistery, roofed with a quadripartite vault in brick and stone, with its massive font and cast-iron gates.

The Stations of the Cross, complex sculpted tableaux beneath four-centred arches, date from 1940. Also in the aisles and transepts are St Teresa, St Patrick, a Madonna and Child signed Fredk G. Croke, St Antony and St Elizabeth both signed Marmon.

Bibliography
Kelly, pp. 413-14; R. Milward, *This Most Extraordinary Mission* (Wandsworth: Parish of St Thomas of Canterbury, 1991); *The Tablet*, 8 May 1847, p. 295; 6 November 1847, p. 709; 4 January 1902, p. 38; 16 June 1906, p. 942; *The Architect*, 22 September 1893, pp. 184-85; *BN*, 11 May 1894, p. 633; 9 June 1894, p. 441; 9 August 1895, p. 208; 10 January 1902, p. 57; *Br*, 9 June 1894, p. 440; 9 August 1895, p. 208; 27 December 1929, pp. 1091-92; *Wandsworth Borough News*, 3 January 1902, p. 6; 30 June 1922, p. 9; *Academy Architecture*, 1894, p. 55; *CBR.S*, 1961, pp. 146-47

Wandsworth East Hill, St Mary Magdalen, East Hill, SW18

Bishop Bourne offered the charge of this new mission to the Salesians at Battersea in December 1902. The Fathers took a house and opened a temporary oratory in February 1903. The foundation stone was blessed on 8 September 1905, and the church was opened on 25 October 1906. Its architect was Lawrence Butler;

its round-arched style in the Byzantine manner of Westminster Cathedral rather than that of Italian models.

The rather unprepossessing red brick exterior displays a windowless (ritual) south aisle to the road, with two porches and a clerestoried nave. Inside, however, all is spacious, light and agreeable, with a large, raked west gallery, a short but wide nave with aisles, followed by shallow chancel and side chapels. The round-arched arcade of three bays is raised upon square piers, with pilastered faces to north and south. The aisles are windowless, but there are three clerestory lights to a bay. The sanctuary is the same height as the nave, with a rood beam across the chancel arch. The forward marble altar is panelled in front, with mosaic margins.

The artwork of the church is generous and graceful. There are panelled ceilings throughout, painted with figures of saints and various monograms. All of these, together with the rood and reredos were the work of Fr George Fayers SDB, a pupil of Burne-Jones. The reredos centre panel, of the Crucifixion with Mary Magdalen and a background evocative of Wandsworth, was done in 1960 by Ivan Tomlanovich, Director of Art at the Academy of Zader, Yugoslavia. By him also are the four walls and ceiling of the baptistery, mainly figure work delineated with appropriate linear clarity.

Around the church are other works of varying quality: the Stations of the Cross, painted in oils; the Virgin and Child on the Lady Altar; St Teresa, carved with admirable economy of line; a similar carving of St Joseph and the young Jesus, suspended from the north wall, with no ground, however, beneath their feet; and the Sacred Heart, by Mayer.

Bibliography
Kelly, p. 414; *The Tablet*, 16 September 1905, p. 479; Information of Rev. J.P. McCormack

Wimbledon Common, Our Lady and St Peter, 15 Victoria Drive, SW19

A large private house of the 1930s, number 11 Victoria Drive, was converted into a church-cum-presbytery in 1962 by Messrs Tomei & Maxwell. A scheme of 1965 for a new church in the plan of a Greek cross was not executed. There followed a primary school on the site in 1967–68 by Tomei & Mackley. The first church was then demolished in June 1970 since it was already too small, and work was begun on the present church designed by Tomei, Mackley & Pound, working in close co-operation with Fr Patrick McLoughlin. This was completed in 1971.

From the road the appearance is dominated by the tall, square, lanterned central space surrounded by lower irregular flat-roofed blocks. Once inside the planning becomes clear: that is, a square nucleus with the altar in the east corner, facing the main entrance. Over this, the eight panels of the pyramidal roof are carried on steel lattice beams which ascend to the large glazed lantern. The ancillary spaces noted outside contain various entrances, parish rooms, sacristies, confessionals, altars and shrines. There are some good modern furnishings including the ground-floor glass in well-behaved abstract patterns, and the two windows over the Chancel to Our Lady and St Peter, with symbolic details, by Whitefriars Studios. There are also the Stations of the Cross done in ceramic panels, the stone font, the large crucifix and several carved statues signed with a cross. This well-designed church has the additional advantage of parish rooms placed adjacent to the narthex, so that the worshipping space may be secured while community activities are in progress.

Bibliography
CBR.S, 1962, p. 151; 1965, pp. 80-81; 1967, pp. 260-61; 1970, pp. 290-91; 1971, pp. 86-87; 1972, p. 179; 1973, pp. 86-88

13. *Wimbledon Common, Our Lady and St Peter*

Glossary

Aisle: a lateral space within a church, frequently in parallel with the nave.
Altar-piece: strictly, synonymous with **reredos**, frequently applied, however, to a painting above the altar.
Ambo: a reading-desk in the vicinity of the altar, sometimes installed in pairs.
Ambulatory: an arcaded processional walk behind the altar.
Apse: semicircular or polygonal end of a chapel, chancel or sanctuary.
Arcade: range of arches, freestanding or attached to a wall.
Aumbry: cupboard for the safe-keeping of holy oils.
Baldacchino: canopy supported on columns, usually over an altar.
Baptistery: space reserved for baptisms, containing the font.
Barbican: tower-like outwork to a castle designed to give added protection.
Baroque: a phase of Renaissance architecture somewhat free and wayward in character, seen in the works of Wren and his eighteenth-century successors.
Boss: ornamentally sculpted keystone at the intersection of ribs in a stone vault.
Buttress: vertical mass of masonry projecting from and strengenthing a wall; a widespread characteristic of Gothic architecture.
Campanile: a bell-tower, sometimes detached from its church.
Capital: topmost block of a column, an appropriate place for moulded or carved decoration.
Cartouche: inscribed scroll or tablet carved or painted, with ornate edges resembling paper.

Cathedra: throne of a bishop or archbishop.
Cenotaph: tomb or monument to honour someone whose remains are elsewhere.
Chamfer: surface occurring when the angle of a 90-degree corner has been cut away.
Chancel: east portion of a church wherein the altar is placed, also termed 'sanctuary'.
Cinqfoil: see **cusp**.
Classical Orders: the Classical Orders of architecture are based upon the proportions of three types of column. The fluted Doric column has a plain flat capital. The Ionic Order is a slender column with capitals consisting of spiral volutes. The Corinthian Order is slenderer still, its capital decorated with acanthus leaves.
Clerestory: windowed upper storey of a nave or chancel.
Coffering: species of decoration to a vault or dome by means of deeply sunken panels.
Colonette: a small column.
Column: cylindrical pillar often designated by the type of its capital, e.g. Doric, Ionic, Corinthian.
Confessional: a place designed for a priest to hear a penitent's confession through a grille. Freestanding timber examples were introduced into England in the seventeenth century. Built-in examples developed from c. 1840.
Corbel: bracket of stone or timber projecting from a wall.
Corinthian column: see **Classical Orders**.
Cornice: projecting moulded feature at the junction of a wall and a ceiling.
Credence: table at one side of an altar, for holding requisites for Mass.

Crenellation: term applied to the continuously raised and lowered top of a parapet; a decorative survival derived from military architecture.
Cresting: repeated ornamental topping to a roof or screen, etc.
Crocket: carved, ornamental, repeated leaf shape applied in Gothic architecture to spires and gables.
Crypt: underground room used for worship or interment.
Cupola: curved polygonal roof crowning a building.
Cusp: ornamental pointed member projecting from the underside of an arch. Cusped circles in window tracery may yield leaf shapes designated trefoil, quatrefoil, cinqfoil, sexfoil or octofoil.
Dado: the lower part of an internal wall; also the decorative covering of same.
Decorated: see **Gothic**.
Diaper: Repeated wall covering consisting of decorated quadrilateral shapes.
Diocletan window: name applied to semicircular windows with two symmetrical mullions, occurring in the Baths of Diocletian in Rome.
Doric column: see **Classical Orders**.
Dormer: a vertical window projecting from a sloping roof or spire.
Early English: see **Gothic**.
English bond: brickwork laid in alternate courses of headers and stretchers.
Entablature: the horizontal portion of a Classical building above the columns.
Façade: the face or front of a building.
Fenestration: the arrangement of windows in a façade.
Flemish bond: brickwork consisting of alternate headers and stretchers laid in every course.
Font: the vessel of stone or metal containing the water used in baptism.
Fresco: a wall painting executed on wet plaster.
Frontal: a covering or decoration on the front of an altar.
Gable: vertical portion of a wall, usually triangular, abutting a ridged roof.
Geometrical tracery: tracery consisting of strictly geometrical forms; characteristic of early Decorated architecture c. 1300.

Gothic: Style of architecture flourishing in the Middle Ages. Its innovative characteristics were the pointed arch, the rib vault and the flying buttress. Its long life is subdivided for convenience of study into successive stages: Early English, c. 1200–c. 1300; Decorated, c. 1300–c. 1370; Perpendicular, c. 1370–1540. The Gothic Revival in architecture had tentative eighteenth-century beginnings, and flourished in English church design from c. 1820 to c. 1914. The same stages had their fashions and are customarily distinguished by the same terms. Different judgments, however, may be applied to mediaeval Gothic and Gothic Revival work.
Gradine: a raised shelf behind the mensa of an altar for placing candlesticks.
Hammer-beam roof: roof truss lacking a tie-beam but bearing instead two cantilevers or hammer-beams supported on struts or arched braces; a mediaeval English invention aesthetically most admirable.
Hood mould: continuous projection from an arch; externally to protect against rain, internally as decoration.
Ionic column: see under **Classical Orders**.
Keeled shaft: shaft with moulding which resembles in section the keel of a ship.
King-post roof: roof with a central upright timber ('king-post') between tie-beam and ridge.
Lancet: tall window topped by a pointed arch.
Loggia. recessed space open on one or more sides of a building, which may by colonnaded.
Louvre: wall opening or roof turret with inclined slats to ease ventilation.
Lucarne: small, high window to admit light; a dormer.
Lunette: crescent-shaped opening.
Medallion: a plaque, oval or round.
Moulding: a small ornamental projection, usually in rows, in the cornices of Classical buildings.
Mullions: vertical members dividing a window into 'lights'.
Mensa: the actual slab of stone or other material that constitutes an altar.

Narthex: covered porch or vestibule across the main entrance of a church

Nave: the central space inside a church, leading to the sanctuary.

Niche: wall recess, its top possibly arched, capable of receiving a statue.

Octofoil: see **cusp**.

Ogee arch: a pointed, doubly curved arch, its lower curve convex, its upper curve concave.

Opus-sectile: Latin term applied to two-dimensional artwork consisting of differently coloured materials cut to appropriate shapes.

Patera: a small flat circular ornament in Classical buildings.

Pediment: a gable of low pitch used in Classical-derived styles over altars, shrines, niches and porticos. Its sides may be straight or segmentally curved.

Pendentive: a curved triangle formed between two adjacent piers in the construction of a dome over a square space.

Perpendicular: see Gothic.

Pilaster: a shallow pillar projecting from a wall, frequently carrying one of the Classical orders.

Pinnacle: an ornamental member of pyramidal or conic form, surmounting a spire, tower or buttress.

Piscina: basin with a drain for disposing of blessed water left after Mass, normally set in the wall to the south of an altar.

Plate tracery: earliest form of tracery in which a decorative shape is punched into the stone arch above a pair of pointed windows.

Plinth: projecting base of a wall or column.

Quadripartite vault: term meaning 'in four parts' applied to the earliest type of Gothic rib vault.

Quatrefoil: see cusp.

Quattrecento: Italian for the 1400s, i.e. the fifteenth century.

Queen-post roof: roof with two symmetrically placed upright timbers between a tie-beam and a purlin.

Re-entrant angles: exterior right angles formed by the arms of a Greek cross; the areas thus formed may be developed as part of the building.

Reredos: the ornamental structure behind and above an altar.

Respond: a half-pier supporting one end of an arch.

Reticulated tracery: intercepting ribwork occurring in the upper part of Decorated Gothic windows, consisting of repeated openings that resemble the mesh of a net.

Retro-choir: space beyond the high altar in a large church.

Revetment: decorative facing, e.g. of marble slabs on a structural core of brick or concrete.

Romanesque: name applied to round-arched styles of Western Europe derived from ancient Roman architecture.

Sanctuary: east portion of a church where the altar is placed; also termed 'chancel'.

Sarcophagus: stone coffin which may be elaborately carved.

Scagliola: plaster painted to simulate marble.

Sexfoil: see **cusp**.

Spandrel: quasi-triangular space formed by an arch and its adjacent vertical and horizontal; also the 'V' shape between two arches.

Swag: decorative festoon of carved fruit and flowers suspended by knotted ribbons.

Tester: sounding board over a pulpit or altar.

Tierceron: intermediate rib in a Gothic vault; also applied to a vault containing intermediate as well as principal ribs.

Tracery: pattern of intersecting bars in the heads of Gothic windows.

Transept: transverse portion of a cruciform church, also designated 'north transept' and 'south transept'.

Transom: horizontal member crossing the 'lights' of a window.

Trefoil: see cusp.

Tribune: a gallery or upper storey.

Triforium: arcade either open or blank above the nave arcade and below the clerestory.

Triptych: representation of sacred subjects enclosed by two lateral doors which also bear designs.

Vesica: decorative shape resembling an oval with pointed ends.

Vestibule: ante-room, entrance hall or lobby.

Select Bibliography

I Books

Anson, P.F., *Fashions in Church Furnishings* (London: Studio Vista, 1965).

Bogan, B., *The Great Think* (London: Burns and Oates, 1958).

Colvin, H.M., *Biographical Dictionary of British Architects* (London: John Murray, 2nd edn, 1978).

de l'Hopital, W., *Westminster Cathedral and Its Architect* (2 vols.; London: Hutchinson, 1919).

Eastlake, C., *A History of the Gothic Revival* (London: Longmans, Green, 1872).

Gillow, J., *Bibliographical Dictionary of the English Catholics* (5 vols.; London: Burns and Oates, 1885–1898).

A Guide to Worship in Central London ed. H. Willows (London: Central YMCA, 1988).

Harting, J., *London Catholic Missions* (London: Sand's, 1903).

Kelly, B.W., *Historical Notes on English Catholic Missions* (London: Kegan Paul, Trench, Trubner, 1907).

Kirk, F.J., *Reminiscences of an Oblate* (London: Burns Oates, 1905).

Little, B., *Catholic Churches Since 1623* (London: Robert Hale, 1966).

Rottmann, A., *London Catholic Churches* (London: Sands, 1926).

Watkin, E.I., *Roman Catholicism in England* (London: Oxford University Press, 1957).

Ward, B., *Catholic London A Century Ago* (London: Catholic Truth Society, 1905).

II Periodicals

The Architect, 1869–.
Architectural Review, 1896–.
Building News, 1855–1926.
The Builder, 1843–.
Catholic Annual Register, 1850.
Catholic Building Review, southern edition, 1956–.
Church Building, 1984.
Illustrated London News, 1842–.
The Tablet, 1840–.

Index

INDEX OF PERSONS

Adams, John   246
Adams-Acton, John   38
Aikman, W.   170
Akers, Fr George   113
Allanson, Mary   253
Alleyn, Justin   170
Aloysius, Fr   214
Alphonsus, Brother   136
Amigo, Archbishop   178, 189, 200, 219, 247
Anderson, Michael   53
Annessens, C.   79
Anning Bell, R.   35, 38
Anrep, Boris   28, 37, 39
Anstey   45
Apollini, Fr Antonine   155
Arguello, Kiko   53
Argyll, Duchess of   166
Armitage, Edward   141
Arnaud of Caraglio   78
Ashlin, G.C.   82
Ayres, Arthur   258

Bagshawe, Bishop   232
Bainbridge Reynolds, W.   39
Baker, Fr Arnold   157
Balmes, E.   107
Banks, Alfred   201
Baranowska, Janina   127
Barber, Fr Benjamin   235

Barber, John   192
Barker, Miss   156
Barry, Canon William   61
Bartlett, Mgr Francis   88
Bate, Stanley Kerr   87
Beach, J.   76
Beart Foss, J.H.   254
Becker, Fr John   229
Beckley, Fr F.C.   242
Beecher, Fr Ernest   105
Belton, Dorothy   76
Belton, John   76
Beningfield, G.   90
Bentley, J.F.   22-24, 28, 32, 34-36, 38, 39, 41, 44, 52, 53, 61-63, 65, 66, 70, 148-51, 156, 157, 160-62, 171-75, 243
Bentley, Osmond   35, 38, 162, 172, 175
Bernard, M.   246
Bernin, Fr Claude   206
Beyaert, Charles   142
Biemans, Rev. Joseph   234
Biloschi   76
Binns, W.   172
Birchall, Edward   58
Birchall, T.G.   68
Bird, Edward   136
Bird, John   136
Black, Georgina   77
Blakeman, Charles   27, 55, 70, 158
Blakeman, May   55, 70

Blanchard 162
Blount, Gilbert 22, 23, 73, 223, 224, 239
Blyth, John 133
Boehm, Sir Edgar 166
Boileau, Louis-Auguste 47
Bonomi, Joseph 61, 62, 64
Boone, Fr Augustine 101
Bortrievikz, K. 118
Bosco, Don 244, 245
Bosio, Fr Philip 154
Boulton, R.L. 27, 59, 75-77, 83, 125, 154
Bourne, Cardinal 54, 95, 126, 129, 142, 143, 184, 188, 221, 243, 247, 258
Bowden, Mrs Elizabeth 122, 123, 167
Bowen, Archbishop Michael 76, 211, 255
Bower, Fr Joseph 257
Bradford, F.J. 194, 247
Bradshaw, Laurence 166
Bramston, Bishop 56
Breheny, Jim 81
Bridge, George 28, 36, 37, 41
Bridgeman, Robert 175
Brindley, W. 36
Broad, Clive 48
Broadbent, F.G. 51, 83, 98, 219, 258
Brooks, James 24
Brown, Atri Cecil 203
Brown, Bishop William 184, 192
Brown, Miss 156
Bryson, John Miller 78
Buckler, C.A. 23, 73-75, 77, 113, 246
Buckler, John 199
Buletti, Antonio 155
Bullesbach, Fr Rudolf 253
Bulmer, H.T. 42, 44, 142
Bunsch, Adam 27, 143
Burges, William 23, 166
Burke, Michael 113
Burton, Mary 30
Buss, A.E. 135
Bute, Marquess of 166
Butler, Charles 94

Butler, Fr Peter 202
Butler, James 98
Butler, Lawrence 24, 258
Butt, Bishop John 94, 171, 180, 184, 187, 204, 205, 243, 244
Butt, Fr Joseph 119, 121

Calegari, Santo 167
Canning, Mrs 138
Capello, A. 168
Carden, Andrew 166
Carew, J.E. 27, 64, 66
Carfiato, Hector 26
Carnelys, Teresa 58
Carolin, Fr James 177
Caron, Fr Benedict 95
Carpenter, R.C. 85
Casey, Bishop 147
Cashman, Bishop 134, 139
Cassidy, Wilfred 130
Cauchi, Carmel 81, 111
Chadwick, Fr F.G. 110
Challoner, Bishop 71, 86
Chantral, M. 127
Chaunac-Lanzac, Robert 47
Chaurin, Fr Stephen 240
Chavalliaud, L.J. 164
Chedal, Fr Gregory 27, 96, 188, 222
Chevins, Hugh 195
Clark, H. 27, 98, 200, 201
Clark, Michael Lindsey 28, 48, 57, 116, 158, 182
Clark, Philip Lindsey 28, 36, 38, 55, 183
Clayton, J.R. 41
Clifton, Canon Thomas 254, 255
Clutton, Henry 22, 23, 32, 44, 147, 160, 163
Cock, A.M. 71
Cocteau, Jean 47
Coffey, Fr Desmond 187
Cohen, Fr Herman 159
Cole, Charles 69

Index of Persons

Cole, Fr Alfred   209
Cole, J.K.   106
Coles, Fr Cornelius   106
Collins, Fr Michael   93
Collinson, Fr Robert   249
Collinson, G.F.   71
Comolli, Giovanni Battista   31
Compton, John   200
Con, George   21
Condon, Fr   124
Conlan, J.P.   257
Connelly, J.J.   142
Cooke, Fr Robert   82, 237, 238
Corfiato, Hector   47
Corr, G.M.   154
Cosgreave, J.   166-68
Cottrell-Dormer, Clement   221
Cottrell-Dormer, Florence   221
Covin, E.G.   106
Cowderoy, Archbishop   102, 195, 202, 206, 213, 249
Cowland, John   203
Cox, Bernard   173
Craven, Bishop George   111
Craze, Romilly B.   200, 202
Credi, Lorenzo di   155
Cribb, Joseph   75, 178, 195
Croke, Frederick G.   258
Crossley, Norman   196
Crush, J. Arnold   63
Cummings, Fr Stephen   240
Curley, F.J.   153
Currie, Edward   75
Curtis, Robert L.   68, 124, 228

Dagys, James   232
Danaher, Fr Philip   84
Daniel, Fr Thomas   130
Dannell, Bishop James   94, 101, 206
Dapre, Anton   28, 60, 112, 113, 123, 139, 183, 209, 214, 220, 226
Dapre, L.E.   80
Dapre, L.F.   247
Dapre, Vincent   158
Daymond, J.   30
Delarue, Anthony   132
Denny, Robyn   48
Devas, Fr Francis   44
Devriendt, F.   137
Dickie, Archibald Campbell   247
Dieussart, Francois   26
Donovan, Fr Charles   255
Dooley, Dean   228
Doorne, Fr Hendrick van   170
Douglas, Archibald   48
Douglass, Bishop   58, 86, 99
Dove, Deidre   101, 105
Dove, Myles   101, 105
Downes, Ralph   167
Doyle, Provost Thomas   198-200
Drinkwater, Fr Thomas   246
Dunn, A.M.   32

Earley, William   238
Earp, Thomas   50, 63, 88, 142, 191, 222
Einler, B.   79
Elgar, Edward   35
Ellis, Frances   24, 92, 95, 170, 176, 178, 179, 182, 189, 204, 210-13, 216, 247, 248, 253
Ercoreca, S.   153
Evans, Alan   201
Evelyn, John   69
Eyre, Edward   126, 129

Faber, Fr   163, 166, 167
Farmer, Henry   244
Farrelly, Martin   249
Faure, Fr Charles   47
Fayers, Fr George   245, 259
Fearn, Bro Michael   251, 252
Fehr, H.C.   36
Fergusson, James   61
Ferry, Fr Bernard   80

Filippi, Don Giuseppe de   78
Fish, Mr   78
Fitzgerald, Percy   50
Fleischmann, Arthur   56, 83, 135, 162, 237, 238
Floris, Frans   168
Foran, Fr Edward   125
Formilli, C.T.G.   165, 166
Fortescue, Mrs   75
Foster, Anthony   76
Froc-Robert   27, 139, 220
Fullerton, Lady Georgiana   44

Galli, L.   155
Gallini, Jessie   56, 57
Gallini, Louise   56, 57
Galton, T.H.   53
Gambardella, Miss   44, 45
Garcia, Anne Gertrude   252
Gardiner, Starkie   168
Garner, Thomas   62, 63, 167
Gauthier of Saluzzo   78, 79
Gaze, W.H.   59
Geary, Frank   180
Gervais, Eugène-Jacques   95, 97
Gibberd, Vernon   70
Gibbons, Grinling   26
Gifkins, Fr Martin   204
Gilbert, J.S.   238
Gill, Eric   36, 41, 45, 118, 195
Gimson, Ernest   39
Giovanni, Luca di   168
Goalen, Gerard   147
Goalen, Martin   226
Godfrey, Cardinal   38, 110, 134, 158, 229
Goldie, Charles   44
Goldie, Edward   23, 62, 63, 152, 221, 257, 258
Goldie, Fr Francis   251
Goldie, George   44, 152, 157
Goldie, Joseph   208, 257
Gondomar   69

Goodhart-Rendel, H.S.   51, 62, 202
Gordon, Lord George   199
Gough, N.   219
Gourdon, R.   176
Grace, Mrs   53
Grady, Fr George   247
Grant, Bishop Thomas   214, 217
Gray, Nicolette   35
Greenwood, J.H.   70
Greenwood, P.   242
Gregory, Thomas   206
Grew, Thomas   140
Gribble, Herbert   163-66, 168
Griffin, Cardinal   38, 56, 235
Griffiths, Bishop   41, 122, 133, 140, 199
Griffiths, Rev. John   198
Grimwood, George   154
Grosch, Mgr Henry   142
Groves, Canon George   143, 147
Gualandi, Francesco   78

Hadfield, Fr Edmund   55
Hales, Barbara   209
Hall, John George   48
Hallahan, Mother Margaret   223
Hallett, Tim   183
Hammer, George   154
Hansom, Henry John   101, 230
Hansom, J.A.   120, 154, 156, 163, 230
Hansom, J.S.   154, 155
Hansom, Joseph   140
Hardman, John   27, 44, 76, 77, 83, 116, 120, 121, 123, 140, 148, 150, 162, 177, 201, 222, 223, 227, 228, 252
Hargrave, Mrs Helen   147
Harper, Geoffrey   200, 201
Harrison, Elizabeth   109
Harrison, Robert   109
Harrison, William   109
Hasbury, Robert L.   64
Haslang, Count   64
Hatton, Christopher   68, 69

INDEX OF PERSONS

Hatton, Lady Elizabeth   68
Haynes, Fr Joseph   217
Hearn, Fr John   133
Hearsnep, Fr James   235
Heenan, Cardinal   48, 85, 116, 130, 147
Held, Fr de   172
Hemans, Fr Philip   185
Hendra, Robert   200, 201
Hendrix, J.   142
Henelt, J.Z.   143
Henrietta Maria   21
Herrezuolo, Fr Joseph Fernandez   111
Hicks, James Joseph   68, 142
Hier, Gary   129
Higgins, Stanley G.   143
Higley, Fr Frederick   230
Hinsley, Cardinal   147
Hodgson, Fr Joseph   50
Hoffman, Mr   58
Holbein, Thomas   153
Holdich, G.M.   143, 153
Holland, Mr   139
Hone, Evie   45
Horrabin, Fr Richard   226
Howard, Lady Margaret   232, 233
Howgate, Ian   135
Hughes, J. O'Hanlon   170
Hume, Cardinal   87, 132
Hunter, A.   64, 106, 146, 175
Hutton, Edward   39
Huyssens, Peter   87

Ibbertson, Harry   147
Ivers, Rev. Hardinge   80

Jackson, Clement   25, 182
Jackson, George   39, 220
Jackson, Thomas   42
John, David   192
Jones, Henry   155
Jones, Inigo   21, 250

Kaye, B.D.   110
Kearney, Fr J.M.   50
Keene, Dr   69
Keens, Canon C.J.   48, 52, 125, 138, 152
Kell, W.   113
Kelly, B.W.   25, 176
Kelly, Claude   24, 194, 247
Kelly, Edmund J.   22, 132, 203, 217
Kelly, Fr Michael   114, 115
Kelly, Fr William   119, 122, 125, 226
Kelly, John   58-60
Kelly, Michael   112
Kerr Bate, C.S.   254
Kerr, Fr R.F.   163
Kiddie, Robert   180
Kirby, John   83, 209
Klecki, Alexsander P.   127
Knill, Sir John Stuart   100, 247
Knox, J.E.   53
Kossowski, Adam   90

Laby, M.A.   137
Lamb, Percy   143, 168
Langford, W.G.   146
Langley, J.   245
Langlin, Codina   167
Lawes, Fr James   217
Lawson, John   90, 112
Leahy, Fr David   217
Lecuona, Fr John   111
Ledger, T.   51
Lee, Stirling   39
Lees, Maurizia   53
Leggett, G.   64
Leigh, Caroline   76
Leigh, William   76
Leonori, Cavalier Aristide   41
Leroux, Jacob   89
Lewis, Fr David   232
Lewis, T.C.   38, 70, 162, 181, 252
Linthout, J.   173
Lloyd, Fr William   181

Lloyd, Reginald   230
Lockhart, Fr William   69, 115
Lucas, Fr Angelo   241
Lucy, Richard de   92
Lyall, Peter   158
Lyall, William   226
Lythgoe, Fr Randall   42

Mabley, P.J.   120
Maderna, Stefano   167
Madsen, Michael   159
Maher, Fr William   218
Mahony, Mgr Edward   216
Major, E.H.   54, 78
Maloney, Rev. John Baptist   198
Mander, A.P.   110, 124, 196
Mander, Noel   65, 70, 96
Mangan, Wilfrid C.   116, 191
Manning, Cardinal   32, 38, 61, 62, 64, 69, 70, 101, 113, 138, 147, 154, 156, 223-25, 229, 232, 237, 241
Mansel, John   170
Maples, Fr F.G.   230
Marche, Jean François de la   90
Marinali, Orazio   167
Marshall, D. Plaskett   125, 178, 207, 229
Marshall, George   65
Marshall, J.   35-39, 41, 63
Marshall, William   190
Marsland, John   248
Martin, Miss   38
Martins-Edmunds, W.M.   76
Mascarenhas, Keith   182
Masero, G.   71, 72
Mazzuoli, Giuseppe   165
Mayer of Munich   61, 83, 134, 141, 151-53, 155, 159, 175, 176, 190, 191, 193, 203, 204, 215, 217, 220, 224, 238, 242, 259
McCarthy, Henry   37, 151
McCarthy, J.   53
McDaniel, Fr Simon   204

McGlynn, Thomas   76
McGrath, Canon   180
McLoughlin, Fr Patrick   259
McManus, Canon Owen   202
McManus, John   128
Measures, Robert   180, 181
Melia, Dr Raphael   78, 79
Mella, Edoardo Arberio   245
Mendham, John Bernard   255
Meo, Gaetano   39
Meschini, Arthur   52
Meschini, Linda   52
Meyer, Thomas   22, 147, 148
Mildred, Dame   54
Mitchell, Robert   47
Molitor, Peter   44
Moneta, Girolamo   166
Monk, Canon William   108
Monselle, Fr Vincent   77
Montesquieu, Baroness de   202
Moore, M.   141
Moore, R.   141
Morel, Jean Jacques   71, 72
Morris, Fr John   104
Moss, Bernard F.   92
Mostyn, Canon John   143, 147
Mount, Cyril   79
Mowlem, John   235
Msatulaitis, Casimir G.   231
Mullen, Canon Richard   149
Murillo Bartolomé   60, 62, 153, 198
Murnane, Canon William   205
Murnane, Fr Edward   257
Murphy, Gerald   137, 218
Murphy, John   90
Murray, Mrs L.   210
Muth, Fr Franz   229
Myers, George   27, 122

Newman, Cardinal   164, 165
Newman, John   29
Newman, John Henry   163

Index of Persons

Newton, A.J.   89
Nicholl, S.J.   52, 111
Nolan, Harry   182
Norfolk, Duchess of   166
Norfolk, Duke of   166, 233, 246
Norris, Charles   219
Norris, Dom Charles   211
North, Canon Joseph   100, 191
North, Canon Richard   99, 100, 190
Nuttgens, Edward   70

O'Connel, Daniel   106
O'Connell, Noel   147
O'Donoghue, Fr James   208
O'Halloran, Canon Michael   101
O'Leary, Fr Arthur   58, 59
Oakeley, Canon Frederick   138, 141, 142
Oates, Burns   207
Oppenheimer, L.   254
Orr, Arthur   195
Orr, Thomas   121
Osborne, F.   240
Oti, Sylvester Ijoma   137
Oxborn, Mr   109, 114

Pallotti, Dr Vincent   78
Panario, Francis   192
Parisi, L.G.   135
Parker, Charles   61
Partridge, David   39
Pate, Thomas   45
Payne, Alexander   143
Pearce, J.M.   75
Pearce, J.N.   75
Pecorin, J.S.W.   59
Perry, Emma   76
Perry, Joseph   76
Perry, Lewis Henry   76
Perry, Stephen   76
Petcherine, Fr   172
Petre, Edward   201
Petre, Mrs Charlotte Elizabeth   128

Pevsner, N.   34
Pezzatti, Pietro   168
Phelps, Arthur J.   170
Phillips, D.L.S.   180
Phillips, Derek   178, 182
Phyffers, Theodore   27, 44, 53, 60, 151, 162, 228
Pippet, Joseph A.   239, 240
Plazzotta, Enzo   153
Pluncknett, J.   39
Pollen, Arthur   39, 149, 167
Pollen, John Hungerford   149
Porter, Fr George   251
Porter, George   154, 158
Potter, Mary   240
Powell, John   123, 148, 150
Power, George   148
Pownall, F.H.   50, 138, 139
Pownall, Fr Arthur   128
Pownall, Fr Bernard   128
Pownall, Gilbert   28, 30, 38, 59
Poynter, Bishop   58, 71
Pozzi, B.   166
Pradera, Joe   71
Prugger, Dorigo Vigilio   90, 244
Pugin, A.W.N.   100, 106, 122, 149-51, 199, 257
Pugin, C.   237
Pugin, E.W.   23, 27, 38, 57, 80, 82, 83, 94, 99, 100, 107, 109, 116, 136, 140, 148, 150, 159, 173, 184, 198, 200, 201, 215, 229, 237, 238
Pugin, P.P.   120, 237
Purcell, Canon   71
Purdie, A.E.   24, 44, 45, 94, 180, 224
Purnell, Douglas   65, 66, 244
Pursell, Mr   75, 239
Pycke, Canon Leopold   142
Pye, Patrick   209

Quail, Paul   152
Quiblier, Fr   239

Radford, J.C.   249, 250
Raffl of Paris   242
Randall, J.W.   77
Rawes, Fr Henry   160
Raymond, Geoffrey   97, 128
Reeves, Gordon   144
Reid, D.A.   196
Reid, Elizabeth   197
Reni, Guido   166
Renouf, Lady   217
Renouf, Sir Peter le Page   217
Reul, Herbert   230
Reynolds, Bainbridge   233
Rickards, Edwin   164
Ridge, Sue   201
Ring, Fr William   237
Robbis, Luca della   244
Roberts, C.P.   47
Robertson, Charles   155
Robinson, A.J.   209
Robinson, Fr Gerard   71
Robinson, Mgr Walter Croke   247
Romain, Mr   188
Romaine Walker, W.H.   44, 45, 46, 204
Rooke, Fr Austin   76
Roome, E.H.   54
Rottmann, A.   71
Rubin, Bishop W.   250
Rudge, Thomas   248
Ruer, Thomas   167
Ruggieri, G.   153
Russell, Michael Watts   137
Rust, R.   181
Ryan, Fr Peter   213

Salviati   77
Santanella   50
Santley, Sir Charles   137
Saupique   47
Scholastica, Charlotte   109
Schultz, Robert Weir   39
Scoles, Canon A.J.C.   97, 120, 128

Scoles, Fr Ignatius   44, 253
Scoles, J.J.   22, 23, 42, 57, 120, 121, 140-42, 149, 163, 166, 199, 202
Scott, Adrian Gilbert   26, 42, 72, 158, 235
Scott, J.T.   243
Scott, Sir Giles Gilbert   23, 70, 159, 173
Scott, T.H.B.   84, 117, 126, 129
Scott, Thomas Birchall   126
Searle, C.G.   146
Sears, John   62
Settegast, J.   173
Sharp, Edmund   125, 137
Shattock, L.H.   38, 41
Shaw, Fr Gerard   202
Shea, Mrs Boschetta   246
Sheehy, Fr David   180
Sheen, Canon John   101
Sheill, C.H.   231
Shepherd, B.C.   47
Sherrin, George   30, 31, 164
Shrewsbury, Countess of   138
Sibthorp, Thomas   180
Simml, Fr Josef   230
Simoni, Fr Pyritheus   154, 155
Simpson, G.L.   71
Skinner, Freda   209
Slater, Robert   231
Smail, Henry   212, 213
Smith, Caroline   77
Smith, D.N.   94
Smith, Fr A.   98
Smith, James   87, 205, 232
Smith, W.E.   105
Smith, William Basset   104
Snead-Cox, J.G.   34
Sparrow, A.J.   162, 230
Stacey, John   157
Stafford, A.   160
Stalley, A.J.H.   209
Sterrett, A.V.   226
Sterrett, John E.   110, 113
Stevens, R.F.   205

INDEX OF PERSONS

Stokes, David 167, 225, 243, 244
Stokes, L.A. 219
Stokes, Leonard 155
Stone, W. 178
Street, G.E. 24, 58, 115
Stuflesser, Ferdinand 114, 135, 258
Swift, Rev. Robert 109
Swkowska, A. 117
Swynnerton, J.W. 45, 155
Sykes, Sir Tatton 32
Sykes, Stephen 196
Symes, A.E. 124
Symons, C. 39
Symons, W.C. 36-38
Szlamas, Fr Boleslas 231
Szoldatits, Ferenc 166

Talbot, Bishop James 22, 198, 202
Tarring, John 80
Tasker, Countess 121
Tasker, F.W. 23-25, 80, 125, 141, 148, 170, 178, 179, 186, 189, 204, 213, 216, 217, 219, 234, 241
Tasker, Joseph 121
Tasker, Louis 121
Taunton, Fr Ethelred 117
Taylor, Andrew 183
Taylor, Chevallier 63
Taylor, Emile Watson 79
Taylor, James 99, 198
Taylor, Tony 249
Tennant, Fr Horace 56
Theed, W. 76
Thompson, Fr Gordon 225, 226
Thuburn, William 179
Tiernan, Mr 140
Tipping, W. 154
Todd, Rev. Dr. William 93
Tollemache, Fr Robert 134
Tooley, Elizabeth 137
Tooley, Robert F. 231
Torre Diaz, Count de 50

Trew, Fr Alex 177
Trinick, John 41, 169
Tripp, Bishop 218
Tucker, E.B. 176
Tynan, Canon 141

Vanpoulle 140, 193
Vaughan, Cardinal 32, 34, 35, 86, 124, 152, 180, 185, 221, 225, 232
Vere, Canon Langton 59
Vernon, Russell 208
Vicars, Albert 136
Vignola, Giacomo 140
Vincenzo, Mussner G. 177
Vinck, F. 142
Vulliamy, Justin 39

Wailes (William) 199
Walker, J.W. 57, 79, 135, 141, 151, 167, 187, 203
Walker, Susannah Rachel 238
Wall, A.B. 27, 53, 128, 181
Wallace, Fr Wilfrid 101
Walsh, Rev. John 71
Walsh, Rev. Thomas 198
Walters, F.A. 23, 87, 103, 107, 161, 184, 185, 191, 195, 204-206, 212, 219, 225-27, 232, 244, 245, 250, 251, 253
Wardell, William 22, 23, 72, 80, 99, 111, 115, 119-21, 173, 174, 226, 229, 234, 235
Waterhouse, Alfred 163
Watney, Mrs Claude 66
Watters, Rev. M.J. 240
Watts, G.N. 162
Watts, John 131
Watts, Peter 152
Webb, Geoffrey 63, 76, 166
Wehling, G. 230
Weiner, Anna 248
Welch, Edward 143
Welland, Fr Arthur 89

West, Benjamin 88
Westbury, Lady 249
Westlake, N.H.J. 52, 76, 83, 107, 123, 136, 148, 151, 161, 162, 185, 233
Westlake, Philip 77
Whall, Veronica 129
Wheeler, David 51
Whelan, Fr 91
Whelehan, Fr Thomas 103
Whiffen, Charles 45, 46
Whistler, Rex 167
Whitby, John 162
White, G.P. 44
Whitham, A.M. 75
Widmer, L. 115
Wigley, G.J. 149, 159
Wilberfoss, 121
Wildenburgh, Van den 56
Wilkins, Frank 155
Williams, Fr George 253
Williamson, Fr Benedict 23, 25, 72, 92, 126, 129, 176, 231, 248, 253, 255, 257, 258, 259
Willis, Fr 77
Willis, Henry III 38, 112
Willson, T.J. 52, 111
Winkley, Austin 44, 72, 201, 202
Wiseman, Cardinal 32, 46, 52, 73, 78, 80, 82, 114, 119, 122, 147, 159, 172, 173, 214, 226
Wispelaere, de of Bruges 46
Wolsey, Cardinal 92
Woodthorpe, Edmund 127
Worsley, Fr Joseph 54
Wray, C.G. 64
Wren, Christopher 21, 87
Wright, Canon John 235
Wright, Edward 39

Young, John 115, 229

Zulaski, Marek 58

Index of Churches by Borough

Camden

The Blessed Sacrament, Copenhagen Street 68

Immaculate Heart of Mary, Kilburn West 84

Our Lady Help of Christians, Kentish Town 80, 81

Our Lady of Hal, Camden Town 67

Sacred Heart of Jesus, Kilburn 82

St Anne, Laxton Place 26, 84, 85

Ss Anselm and Cecilia, Lincoln's Inn Fields 27, 85, 86, 88

St Aloysius, Somers Town 22, 26, 88, 89

St Dominic, Haverstock Hill 23, 27, 73, 74

St Ethelreda, Ely Place 23, 27, 68, 69

St Mary, Hampstead 23, 24, 27, 71, 72

St Peter, Italian Church 78

St Thomas More, Swiss Cottage 26, 90, 91

Greenwich

Christ Church, Eltham 23, 27, 97

Holy Cross, Plumstead Common 105

Our Lady Star of the Sea, Crooms Hill 99-101

Our Lady of Grace, Charlton 27, 95, 96

Our Lady Help of Christians, Cresswell Park, Blackheath 24, 93, 94

St Benet, Abbey Wood 92, 93

St Catherine Laboure, Woolwich 26, 108

St David, Abbey Wood 26, 93

St John Fisher, Kidbrooke 26, 102, 103

Ss John Fisher and Thomas More, Eltham Well Hall 98

St Joseph, Greenwich East 23, 101

St Joseph, Shooters Hill 106

St Patrick, Plumstead 103, 104

St Peter, Woolwich 22, 106, 107

Hackney

Immaculate Heart of Mary and St Dominic, Homerton 27, 113, 114

Our Lady and St Joseph, Kingsland 26, 115, 116

Our Lady of Good Counsel, Stoke Newington 25, 117, 118

St John the Baptist 27, 111, 112

St Jude, Clapton Park 110

St Scholastica, Clapton 109, 110

St Monica's Priory, Hoxton 114, 115

Hammersmith and Fulham

Holy Cross, Parsons Green 25, 125, 126

Holy Ghost and St Stephen, Shepherds Buch 27, 128

Holy Trinity, Brook Green 27, 119-21

Our Lady of Fatima, White City 26, 130, 131

St Andrew Bobola, Polish Church 127

St Augustine, Hammersmith 124

St Thomas of Canterbury, Fulham 22, 122, 123

Our Lady of Perpetual Help, Stephendale Road 25, 129

Islington

Our Lady of Czestochowa and St Casimir, Polish Church 143

Sacred Heart, Holloway 27, 139, 140

St Gabriel, Upper Holloway 145

St Joan of Arc, Highbury 26, 27, 135, 136

St John the Evangelist 22, 24, 141, 142

St Joseph, Bunhill Row 132

St Joseph, Highgate 24, 137-39

St Mellitus, Tollington Park 143, 144

Ss Peter and Paul, Clerkenwell 24, 27, 134

Kensington and Chelsea
Holy Redeemer and St Thomas More, Chelsea 24, 27, 152, 153
Immaculate Heart of Mary, Oratory 27, 163-65, 167
Our Lady of Dolours, Fulham Road 153, 154
Our Lady of the Holy Souls, Kensal New Town 156, 157
Our Lady of Mount Carmel and St Simon Stock, Kensington 159, 160
Our Lady of Victories, Kensington 26-28, 32, 157, 158
St Francis of Assisi, Notting Hill 23, 27, 160, 161
St Mary, Chelsea 27, 149-51
St Mary of the Angels, Bayswater 147
St Pius X, St Charles Square 168

Lambeth
Corpus Christi, Brixton Hill 170-72
English Martyrs, Streatham 24, 180
Our Immaculate Lady of Victories, Clapham 172-75
Our Lady of the Rosary, Brixton 170
St Anne, Vauxhall 184
St Bartholomew, Norbury 27, 176, 177
St Bede, Clapham Park 176
St Francis of Sales and St Gertrude, Stockwell 178
St Matthew, Norwood West 25, 177
Ss Simon and Jude, Streatham Hill 182, 183

Lewisham
The Annunciation, Beckenham 187
The Assumption, Deptford 190, 191
Catford, Holy Cross, Catford 189
Our Lady of Lourdes, Lee 25, 192, 193
Our Lady and St Philip Neri, Sydenham 27, 195, 196

The Resurrection of the Lord, Sydenham 196
St Mary Magdalen, Brockley 24, 27, 187, 188
St Saviour 193, 194
St William of York, Forest Hill 27, 191, 192

London, City of
St Mary, Moorfields 22, 27, 29-32, 61

Southwark
English Martyrs, Walworth 23, 27, 219, 220
Holy Trinity, Bermondsey 22
Holy Trinity, Bermondsey Dockhead 202
Our Lady of the Immaculate Conception, Surrey Docks 218
Our Lady of La Salette and St Joseph, Bermondsey 203
Our Lady of Sorrows, Peckham 214
Precious Blood, Bermondsey 205
Sacred Heart, Camberwell 206, 207
St Gertrude, Bermondsey 204
St James the Great, Peckham Rye 216
St Margaret Clitherow, Dulwich Wood Park 26
St Peter and the Guardian Angels, Rotherhithe 217
Ss Philip and James, Herne Hill 210, 211
St Thomas the Apostle, Nunhead 213
St Thomas More, Dulwich East 208-10
St Wilfrid, Kennington Park 212
Southwark Cathedral 22, 23, 27, 198, 200

Tower Hamlets
English Martyrs, Tower Hill 237
Guardian Angels, Mile End 23, 232, 233
The Holy Name and Our Lady of the Sacred Heart, Bow Common 225
Our Lady of the Assumption, Bethnal Green 23, 27, 221, 222

Our Lady Immaculate, Limehouse 230, 231
Our Lady and St Catherine, Bow 23, 223
St Anne, Underwood Road 23, 27, 239
St Boniface, German Church 229
St Casimir, Lithuanian Church 231, 232
St Edmund, Millwall 234
Ss Mary and Joseph, Poplar 26, 235, 236
Ss Mary and Michael, Commercial Road 27, 226-28
St Patrick, Wapping 241

Wandsworth
Holy Ghost, Balham 24, 243
Our Lady of the Assumption, Tooting (South East) 255
Our Lady of Mount Carmel, Battersea Park 246
Our Lady of Pity and St Simon Stock, Putney 249
Our Lady and St Peter, Wimbledon Common 259, 260
Sacred Heart, Battersea (West) 24, 244, 245
St Anselm, Tooting Bec 255, 256
St Boniface, Tooting 253
St Gregory, Earlsfield 26, 248
St John the Evangelist, Putney Polish Church 250, 251
St Joseph, Roehampton 251, 252
St Mary Magdalen, East Hill 258
St Thomas a Becket 257
St Vincent de Paul, Clapham Common 247

Westminster, City of
Corpus Christi, Maiden Lane 48, 49
Holy Apostles, Pimlico 27, 28, 54, 55
The Immaculate Conception, Farm Street 27, 42, 43
Notre Dame de France, French Church 46
Our Lady, St John's Wood 22, 28, 56, 57
Our Lady of the Assumption, Warwick Street 27, 28, 64-66
Our Lady of Lourdes and St Vincent de Paul, Harrow Road 48
Our Lady Queen of Heaven, Queensway 56
Our Lady of the Rosary, Marylebone 26, 50, 51
Our Lady of Sorrows, Paddington 54
St Charles Borromeo, Ogle Street 23, 27, 52, 53
St James, Spanish Place 23, 27, 61-63
St Patrick, Soho Square 24, 27, 52, 58-60
Westminster Cathedral 24, 25, 27, 28, 32-34, 40, 41, 87, 118

INDEX OF CHURCHES BY NAME

The Annunciation, Beckenham, Lewisham 187

The Assumption, Deptford, Lewisham 190, 191

Blessed Sacrament, The, Copenhagen Street, Camden 68

Christ Church, Eltham, Greenwich 23, 27, 97

Corpus Christi, Brixton Hill, Lambeth 170-72

Corpus Christi, Maiden Lane, City of Westminster 48, 49

English Martyrs, Streatham, Lambeth 24, 180

English Martyrs, Tower Hill, Tower Hamlets 237

English Martyrs, Walworth, Southwark 23, 27, 219, 220

Guardian Angels, Mile End, Tower Hamlets 23, 232, 233

Holy Apostles, Pimlico, City of Westminster 27, 28, 54, 55

Holy Cross, Catford, Lewisham 189

Holy Cross, Parsons Green, Hammersmith and Fulham 25, 125, 126

Holy Cross, Plumstead Common, Greenwich 105

Holy Ghost and St Stephen, Shepherds Bush, Hammersmith and Fulham 27, 128

Holy Ghost, Balham, Wandsworth 24, 243

Holy Name and Our Lady of the Sacred Heart, The, Bow Common, Tower Hamlets 225

Holy Redeemer and St Thomas More, Chelsea, Kensington and Chelsea 24, 27, 152, 153

Holy Trinity, Bermondsey Dockhead, Southwark 22, 202

Holy Trinity, Brook Green, Hammersmith and Fulham 27, 119-21

The Immaculate Conception, Farm Street, City of Westminster 27, 42, 43

Immaculate Heart of Mary and St Dominic, Homerton, Hackney 27, 113, 114

Immaculate Heart of Mary, Kilburn West, Camden 84

Immaculate Heart of Mary, Oratory, Kensington and Chelsea 27, 163-65, 167

Notre Dame de France, French Church, City of Westminster 46

Our Immaculate Lady of Victories, Clapham, Lambeth 172-75

Our Lady of the Assumption, Bethnal Green, Tower Hamlets 23, 27, 221, 222

Our Lady of the Assumption, Tooting (South East), Wandsworth 255

Our Lady of the Assumption, Warwick Street, City of Westminster 27, 28, 64-66

Our Lady of Czestochowa and St Casimir, Polish Church, Islington 143

Our Lady of Dolours, Fulham Road, Kensington and Chelsea 153, 154

Our Lady of Fatima, White City, Hammersmith and Fulham 26, 130, 131

Our Lady of Good Counsel, Stoke Newington, Hackney 25, 117, 118

Index of Churches by Name

Our Lady of Grace, Charlton, Greenwich 27, 95, 96

Our Lady of Hal, Camden Town, Camden 67

Our Lady Help of Christians, Cresswell Park, Blackheath, Greenwich 24, 93, 94

Our Lady Help of Christians, Kentish Town, Camden 80, 81

Our Lady of the Holy Souls, Kensal New Town, Kensington and Chelsea 156, 157

Our Lady Immaculate, Limehouse, Tower Hamlets 230, 231

Our Lady of the Immaculate Conception, Surrey Docks, Southwark 218

Our Lady of La Salette and St Joseph, Bermondsey, Southwark 203

Our Lady of Lourdes, Lee, Lewisham 25, 192, 193

Our Lady of Lourdes and St Vincent de Paul, City of Westminster 48

Our Lady of Mount Carmel and St Joseph, Battersea Park, Wandsworth 246

Our Lady of Mount Carmel and St Simon Stock, Kensington, Kensington and Chelsea 159, 160

Our Lady of Perpetual Help, Stephendale Road, Hammersmith and Fulham 25, 129

Our Lady of Pity and St Simon Stock, Putney, Wandsworth 249

Our Lady Queen of Heaven, Queensway, City of Westminster 56

Our Lady of the Rosary, Brixton, Lambeth 170

Our Lady of the Rosary, Marylebone, City of Westminster 26, 50, 51

Our Lady and St Catherine, Bow, Tower Hamlets 23, 223

Our Lady, St John's Wood, City of Westminster 22, 28, 56, 57

Our Lady and St Joseph, Kingsland, Hackney 26, 115, 116

Our Lady and St Peter, Wimbledon Common, Wandsworth 259, 260

Our Lady and St Philip Neri, Sydenham, Lewisham 27, 195, 196

Our Lady of Sorrows, Paddington, City of Westminster 54

Our Lady of Sorrows, Peckham, Southwark 214

Our Lady Star of the Sea, Crooms Hill, Greenwich 99-101

Our Lady of Victories, Kensington, Kensington and Chelsea 26-28, 32, 157, 158

Precious Blood, Bermondsey, Southwark 205

Resurrection of the Lord, The, Sydenham, Lewisham 196

Sacred Heart, Battersea (West), Wandsworth 24, 244, 245

Sacred Heart, Camberwell, Southwark 206, 207

Sacred Heart, Holloway, Islington 27, 139, 140

Sacred Heart of Jesus, Kilburn, Camden 82

St Aloysius, Somers Town, Camden 22, 26, 88, 89

St Andrew Bobola, Polish Church, Hammersmith and Fulham 127

St Anne, Laxton Place, Camden 26, 84, 85

St Anne, Underwood Road, Tower Hamlets 23, 27, 239

St Anne, Vauxhall, Lambeth 184

St Anselm, Tooting Bec, Wandsworth 255, 256

St Augustine, Hammersmith, Hammersmith and Fulham 124

St Bartholomew, Norbury, Lambeth 27, 176, 177
St Bede, Clapham Park, Lambeth 176
St Benet, Abbey Wood, Greenwich 92, 93
St Boniface, German Church, Tower Hamlets 229
St Boniface, Tooting, Wandsworth 253
St Casimir, Lithuanian Church, Tower Hamlets 231, 232
St Catherine Laboure, Woolwich, Greenwich 26, 108
St Charles Borromeo, Ogle Street, City of Westminster 23, 27, 52, 53
St David, Abbey Wood, Greenwich 26, 93
St Dominic, Haverstock Hill, Camden 23, 27, 73, 74
St Edmund, Millwall, Tower Hamlets 234
St Ethelreda, Ely Place, Camden 23, 27, 68, 69
St Francis of Assisi, Notting Hill, Kensington and Chelsea 23, 27, 160, 161
St Francis of Sales and St Gertrude, Stockwell, Lambeth 178
St Gabriel, Upper Holloway, Islington 145
St Gertrude, Bermondsey, Southwark 204
St Gregory, Earlsfield, Wandsworth 26, 248
St James, Spanish Place, City of Westminster 23, 27, 61-63
St James the Great, Peckham Rye, Southwark 216
St Joan of Arc, Highbury, Islington 26, 27, 135, 136
St John Fisher, Kidbrooke, Greenwich 26, 102, 103
St John the Baptist, Hackney 27, 111, 112
St John the Evangelist, Islington 22, 24, 141, 142
St John the Evangelist, Putney Polish Church, Wandsworth 250, 251
St Joseph, Bunhill Row, Islington 132

St Joseph, Greenwich East, Greenwich 23, 101
St Joseph, Highgate, Islington 24, 137-39
St Joseph, Roehampton, Wandsworth 251, 252
St Joseph, Shooters Hill, Greenwich 106
St Jude, Clapton Park, Hackney 110
St Margaret Clitherow, Dulwich Wood Park, Southwark 26, 209, 210
St Mary Magdalen, Brockley, Lewisham 24, 27, 187, 188
St Mary Magdalen, Wandsworth East Hill, Wandsworth 258
St Mary of The Angels, Bayswater, Kensington and Chelsea 147
St Mary, Chelsea, Kensington and Chelsea 27, 149-51
St Mary, Hampstead, Camden 23, 24, 27, 71, 72
St Mary, Moorfields, City of London 22, 27, 29-32, 61
St Matthew, Norwood West, Lambeth 25, 177
St Mellitus, Tollington Park, Islington 143, 144
St Monica's Priory Hoxton, Hackney 114, 115
St Patrick, Plumstead, Greenwich 103, 104
St Patrick, Soho Square, City of Westminster 24, 27, 52, 58-60
St Patrick, Wapping, Tower Hamlets 241
St Peter and the Guardian Angels, Rotherhithe, Southwark 217
St Peter, Italian Church, Camden 78
St Peter, Woolwich, Greenwich 22, 106, 107
St Pius X, St Charles Square, Kensington and Chelsea 168
St Saviour, Lewisham 193, 194
St Scholastica, Clapton, Hackney 109, 110

INDEX OF CHURCHES BY NAME

St Thomas More, Dulwich East, Southwark 208
St Thomas More, Manor House, Hackney 117
St Thomas More, Swiss Cottage, Camden 26, 90, 91
St Thomas a Becket, Wandsworth 257
St Thomas of Canterbury, Fulham, Hammersmith and Fulham 122, 123
St Thomas the Apostle, Nunhead, Southwark 213
St Thomas, Fulham, Hammersmith and Fulham 22
St Vincent de Paul, Clapham Common, Wandsworth 247
St Wilfrid, Kennington Park, Southwark 212
St William of York, Forest Hill, Lewisham 27, 191, 192

Ss Anselm and Cecilia, Lincoln's Inn Fields, Camden 27, 85, 86, 88
Ss John Fisher and Thomas More, Eltham Well Hall, Greenwich 98
Ss Mary and Joseph, Poplar, Tower Hamlets 26, 235, 236
Ss Mary and Michael, Commercial Road, Tower Hamlets 27, 226-28
Ss Peter and Paul, Clerkenwell, Islington 24, 27, 134
Ss Philip and James, Herne Hill, Southwark 210, 211
Ss Simon and Jude, Streatham Hill, Lambeth 182, 183
Southwark Cathedral 22, 23, 27, 198, 200

Westminster Cathedral, City of Westminster 24, 25, 27, 28, 32-34, 40, 41, 87, 118